English Civic Pageantry
1558-1642

MEDIEVAL AND RENAISSANCE
TEXTS AND STUDIES

VOLUME 267

English Civic Pageantry 1558–1642

David M. Bergeron

Revised Edition

Dust jacket image: Elizabeth I's coronation passage through London, 1559. Reproduced from Egerton MS 3320. By permission of the British Library.

Library of Congress Cataloging-in-Publication Data
Bergeron, David Moore.
    English civic pageantry, 1558–1642 / David M. Bergeron. — Rev. ed.
      p. cm. — (Medieval and Renaissance texts and studies ; v. 267)
    Includes bibliographical references and index.
    ISBN 0-86698-310-4 (alk. paper)
    1. Pageants — England — History. 2. Municipal ceremonial — England
— London — History. 3. Rites and ceremonies, Medieval — England —
History. 4. Courts and courtiers — England — History. 5. England —
Social life and customs. I. Title. II. Medieval & Renaissance Texts &
Studies (Series) ; v. 267.

GT4043.B47 2003
394'.5'0942–dc22   2003062754

Printed in the United States of America

CONTENTS

List of Illustrations

Figures

Acknowledgements

REVISION: to look again, to revisit. This revised edition of *English Civic Pageantry 1558–1642* involved a new look at what I had written years ago. Indeed, the research for what became this book began forty years ago, when, as a graduate student, I first examined the materials of English civic pageantry under the guidance of Cyrus Hoy. With years of additional research, this sustained effort culminated in the publication of *English Civic Pageantry* (London: Arnold; Columbia: University of South Carolina Press, 1971). The last phase of that research came in England, thanks to the support of an American Council of Learned Societies Fellowship. I note that the British Museum Library where I spent long hours in the late 1960s and the Guildhall Library and the Corporation of London Records Office have all subsequently gained new buildings and even a new name for the British Library. They have changed, and so have I.

But I have continued to pursue this topic, continuing to believe in its importance and to enjoy its company. This looking back to the first edition of this book did not include wholesale rewriting, except for the Introduction, which is completely new, and updating of the text and Bibliography. I had the opportunity to revisit every sentence, and I have often resorted to rewriting them in some way. I abandoned some conclusions—such as the seemingly well-established but false issue about the antipathy between Thomas Middleton and Anthony Munday—and I added new material—such as the manuscript document from the Folger Library that impinges on Elizabeth's coronation royal entry pageant of 1559. And I have included citation to subsequent scholars who have contributed to the subject of English civic pageantry.

For a long time I have wanted to make this book available again, and I am most grateful to Robert E. Bjork and the Arizona Medieval and Renaissance Texts and Studies for the opportunity. I thank Bob for the alacrity—almost unprecedented in academic publishing—with which he reached a decision about the desire to publish a new edition of *English Civic Pageantry*. And I thank my friend Richard W. Clement, of the Kenneth Spencer Research Library, University of Kansas, for first smoothing the way and assisting in the initial contact with Bob Bjork. And then, fortunately for me, this project became part of Rick's extraordinary energy and expertise as he shepherded it through technical production. I have deferred to Rick's technical knowledge, and I have rejoiced in his interest and support, for which I am profoundly indebted.

In the early phase of trying to ready this book for possible publication, I approached—once again—the exceptional people who make up the Wescoe Word

Processing Center, University of Kansas. I refer to the help and care generously given by Paula Courtney, Pam LeRow, and Lynn Porter. They have succeeded in creating an oasis of technical support for scholars in the humanities at my university. And I benefited from a grant from the General Research Fund of the University of Kansas, which supported time in Summer 2002 to rewrite the Introduction and track down new bibliographical items. My graduate student Kara Northway also kindly entered this collaborative enterprise by doing major proofreading, checking bibliographical entries, and asking serious questions. I acknowledge the kind permission of the Folger Shakespeare Library and the Spencer Research Library to reproduce illustrations.

My revisioning includes a large measure of nostalgia as I recall the many libraries and archives where I have worked. Early in my experience I remember encountering the sentiment of the great E. K. Chambers who referred disparagingly to the "tedium" of English civic pageants. This view I do not share—except on the odd day when things have not gone well. Instead, I have found these pageants to be rich in accomplishment and crucial in understanding English culture of the Tudor and Stuart periods. And my foraging in sacred places of original texts, manuscripts, and archives has informed and enlivened my study and enhanced my life.

David M. Bergeron
Lawrence, Kansas

Introduction

A FIRE, BREAKFAST, CHILDREN, AND A DRAMATIST: preparations for a dramatic performance. Late fourteenth-century York? A dramatist assisting with production matters for the medieval Corpus Christi drama? No. On a late October morning in 1623—the year of publication of the Shakespeare First Folio—Thomas Middleton, by then a well-established dramatist and Chronologer of the City of London, provided a fire and breakfast for the children scheduled to perform in his Lord Mayor's Show, *The Triumphs of Integrity*. Like his medieval predecessors, Middleton participated in the full range of activities required for civic drama, in this case a civic pageant honoring the inauguration of London's new Lord Mayor. This book seeks to recover and analyze this world of English civic pageantry, opening its richness for inspection and wonder. We will take the road less traveled through a myriad array of theatrical experiences in city streets and on great aristocratic estates. We will join the thousands of spectators who never entered the Globe Theatre but who nevertheless encountered theater about them. Dramatic speeches and action, music, colorful costumes, processions, triumphal arches, and professional actors gave civic occasions imaginative life.

This book focuses on the period 1558-1642, from the accession of Queen Elizabeth to the closing of theaters by Act of Parliament. This historical frame encompasses one of England's richest literary epochs and arguably the most successful in the country's theater history. Various forces collide and collude by design and by accident to produce an exceptional theater. For example, the 1570s provide the first permanent theater buildings in London, thanks to the enterprise of the Burbages and others. One cannot overestimate the importance of having established buildings for the regular production of drama, leading to solidifying adult acting companies and their repertory system of performance.[1] Possibly early theater builders derived from pageants ways and means of erecting stages and designing properties, and they may have also sensed the public's enthusiastic delight in civic entertainments and hence sought to capitalize on that in a regular pattern of performance. Despite an ongoing attack on them especially from Puritan forces, actors began to secure social status and a modicum of respectability, no longer treated as vagabonds and riff-raft. Patronage by aristocrats certainly assisted this development, culminating in King James's placing all adult companies under royal patronage in 1603. And, of course, somewhere and somehow we have to acknowledge dramatic geniuses whose artistic talent intersected with new buildings and stable acting companies. If these conditions do not inevitably produce skilled playwrights, they do nevertheless encourage the likelihood and make

---

[1]See Andrew Gurr, *The Shakespearean Stage, 1574-1642*, 3rd ed. (Cambridge, 1992).

1

it possible for the first time in English history to have professional playwrights. I will be arguing that civic pageants partake of this burgeoning theater world, indeed contribute significantly to it.

Such pageants can capture the public imagination in an aesthetic climate that readily embraces symbolic, emblematic, and iconographical art: in a word, a world rich in metaphorical possibilities and understanding. Glynne Wickham has persuasively argued that the Shakespearean stage was emblematic as opposed to photographically real; we may add with him that the pageant theater stands as the quintessence of emblematic theater.[2] One need only look at Renaissance paintings, tapestries, emblem books, or read *The Faerie Queene* to recall how metaphor, symbolism, and allegory governed imaginative creations. Our retrospective and somewhat blurred vision finds difficulty with the idea of Time or Truth or Fame appearing as persons in London's streets or with the Graces strewing flowers along Elizabeth's path in Elvetham. But, given the frequency of such moments in civic pageants, we must conclude that Shakespeare's world welcomed and embraced rich connections between their physical space and a fictional space rich in metaphor.

Civic pageantry refers to consciously planned dramatic entertainments that typically offered access to the public, seen most clearly in London pageants. The involvement of trade and craft guilds and city governments in the preparation, financing, and production of many of these entertainments also accounts for the "civic" nature of the shows. Indeed, one can trace a relatively unbroken line from the fourteenth through the seventeenth centuries of guild and city involvement in public drama. Such pageants always occurred outdoors, enhancing civic possibilities. I restrict the term "pageantry" to planned entertainments with a clear dramatic purpose designed for a specific occasion. This rules out routine displays or processions that have no dramatic content. When the occasion ended, so did the dramatic life of the pageant as it becomes thereby an insubstantial pageant faded. Only records and published texts sustain the memory of the pageant.

Three main types of entertainments constitute civic pageantry. First, outdoor dramatic shows presented for sovereigns while on summer provincial tour or "progress" can be designated progress pageants. Although these took place on the private estates of noblemen being visited by the sovereign, the public frequently had a part in the event either as spectators or as participants. T. S. Eliot's Prufrock underscores his insignificance not only by not being Hamlet but also by merely being able to "swell a progress," start a scene or two. Lavish preparation, hiring poets, and publishing texts suggest that the earlier era thought that progresses had considerable claim on our attention. The "royal entry" constitutes the second major category of civic pageantry. These pageants occurred when the sovereign made an official procession through city streets with dramatic scenes en-

[2]Glynne Wickham, *Early English Stages* (London and New York, 1963), II, 209.

acted along the route; the most elaborate celebrate coronations. They help ratify
the monarch's claim to the throne and define the city's response to such claims
by honoring and celebrating the sovereign. London in particular gave rise to the
third form of civic pageantry, the "Lord Mayor's Show," which took place on 29
October on the occasion of the new mayor's inauguration. Well-established
playwrights increasingly wrote such pageants in collaboration with the guilds to
which the mayor belonged. Rather like the arrangement of royal entries, mayoral
pageants involved a procession through the city with dramatic presentations,
including sometimes entertainment on the Thames also. Obviously, other civic
entertainments do not fit neatly into these categories; they will be discussed if
they share the essential form of the pageants outlined here.

Accepting these categories as useful distinctions, I have organized the book
around them. Part One thus concentrates on royal entries and progresses, the
public entertainments primarily concerned with the monarch or some other
member of the royal family. The discussion moves chronologically, enabling us
to see, for example, how the pageants in the reign of Charles I compare with
those in Elizabeth's. Part Two turns to the remaining major pageant form, the
Lord Mayor's Show, discussed, after an initial chapter on the Elizabethan show,
according to the dramatists who wrote them. One must bear in mind that the
pageants for the sovereign and for the mayor occur in the same historical period;
the division serves only as a convenient way to discuss them. The analysis attempts to observe the common ground that exists among such civic pageants.
Part Three, using a traditional distinction, focuses on the "soul" and "body" of
the pageants, the spirit as opposed to the tangible, physical form, the word as
opposed to the flesh. The thematic, symbolical, allegorical, and emblematic nature of the pageants forms the "soul"; the stage properties, expenses, and the
builders of the devices (the artificers) make up the "body."

One major insistent thread runs through this book: namely, that civic pageants as drama, theater, political and cultural events must be taken seriously. This
would seem self evident; but patterns of neglect, benign and otherwise, have
greeted the study of civic pageantry, it often suffering by comparison to the relative attention given to its cousin the court masque.[3] For example, the editors of *A
New History of Early English Drama* state that the book's "primary aim is to provide the most comprehensive account yet available of early English drama."[4]
They add that "readers can consult individual essays on specific topics in the confidence that what they are reading is reliable and authoritative." But beyond
Gordon Kipling's fine essay on royal entry pageants, which ends with Elizabeth's
pageant of 1559, this "comprehensive account" finds no room for discussion of

---

[3]This subject I have explored in some detail in "Pageants, Masques, and Scholarly Ideology," in my
Practicing Renaissance Scholarship (Pittsburgh, 2000), pp. 164-92.
[4]*A New History of Early English Drama*, eds. David Scott Kastan and John Cox (New York, 1997), p. 1.

Lord Mayors' Shows or of progress pageants nor of royal entry pageants beyond 1559. By contrast, court masques get some notice. This 1997 anthology of essays typifies a kind of disregard for the subject of civic pageantry for reasons that can be hard to fathom. After all, did not most of the major dramatists of the period, excepting Shakespeare, write civic pageants? How can one purport to offer a history of theater or of individual playwrights without including the rich material of pageants? Lucrative financial rewards certainly encouraged these dramatists to try their hand at pageant-writing. Clearly they did not stand on some elevated aesthetic principle and deign not to write pageants. In the rough and tumble world of theatrical writing, surely potential employment that involved writing must have seemed attractive, whether a civic pageant or something else. Therefore, I proceed to take pageants seriously, recognizing that one would never choose a Lord Mayor's Show over, say, *King Lear*. Fortunately, one does not have to make such a choice. We can, however, no longer choose to ignore civic pageants.

This book weaves into the diachronic narrative of civic pageantry at least five recurring topics that constitute the predicates of this study: place, politics, poetics, plays, and publication. By *place* I refer literally to the locations that helped give rise to pageants, responding to the occasion. The writer of the text for Elizabeth's 1559 royal entry likens London to a vast "stage" whereon the spectacle occurred. The urban setting, whether London, Norwich, Bristol, or other cities encouraged a processional form for the pageant. This setting provided the place for spectacle and dramatic action, and writers exploited its possibilities. Thus, royal entries and Lord Mayors' Shows in London frequently used the same locations for the dramatic tableaux. Stephen Harrison, the architect for the 1604 royal entry for James, consciously utilized parts of the city setting as inspiration for the triumphal arches. The great aristocratic estates led to a different type of entertainment for progresses, typically spread out over several days and different locations. Demands of hospitality often governed how the noblemen shaped these estate pageants. Regularly pageants of various kinds made use of the materials at hand, making place serve dramatic purpose. Or, as in the case of the Earl of Hertford at Elvetham in 1591, one might create a new place: here, a specially constructed crescent-shaped pond for the battle between the wood gods and sea gods. In these places audiences gathered, made up of multiple social and economic classes. Certainly in the cities nothing could constrain the shape of the audience, who, while remaining on the margin of the action, nevertheless constituted an essential ingredient for the pageant. Great and small came; foreign ambassadors jockeyed with one another for key places from which to witness the entertainment; members of the guilds resplendent in their livery took their appointed places along the processional route; ordinary citizens peered through windows or took their chances in the streets. The place for civic pageants became a vibrant scene, indeed a vast celebratory theater, constructing community even as this community responded to its construction.

By definition civic pageants are *political* events. They involve the presence of the ruler—either sovereign or mayor—they utilize public monies of city or guilds, they take place in the public arena, and they celebrate national and civic virtues. Such street shows function as part of the political discourse of the realm. The pageants celebrate political power even as they confirm such power. Clifford Geertz notes that the ruling classes "justify their existence and order their actions in terms of stories, ceremonies, insignia, formalities, and appurtenances that they have either inherited or ... invented. It is these ... that mark the center as center and gives what goes on there its aura of being not merely important but in some odd fashion connected with the way the world is built."[5] Civic pageants remind us, however, that more than one center of power existed; this recognition forces us to move away from what I have called the "Whitehall syndrome" that focuses relentlessly and exclusively on monarchical power. Local, guild, and national politics manifest themselves in the political concern of pageants.

The pageants could reflect other kinds of practical political issues. In testimony provided in the Venetian State Papers we learn of the struggle over precedence among the ambassadorial corps in London; that is, which ambassador would occupy some favored position along the pageant route. Such a struggle led, for example, to the ambassadors' absence at James's 1604 royal entry pageant. On such occasions the pageant becomes a battleground on which conflicting political forces play out their quarrel, a place where competing governments stake out their political positions. Under the patronage of guilds, these pageants, particularly the Lord Mayors' Shows, reinforce the position of the Lord Mayor of London as the king's "substitute." In possible reaction to a Stuart court increasingly withdrawn, contentious, insulated, and bankrupt, these civic shows demonstrate the vitality, wealth, and public nature of city life in London. Perhaps they deliberately rival the court masque, that quintessential Stuart entertainment: expensive, indoors, at times self-indulgent, and performed before a select audience. Years ago Glynne Wickham made this argument: "Indeed it is by no means farfetched to regard the swelling splendour of the Lord Mayor's shows in Jacobean and Caroline times as deliberately rivalling the opulent masks of the Court at Westminster."[6] Such a tension reflects shifting political fortunes.

Civic pageants regularly display political content in their subject matter, usually honoring the virtues of national or local life and accomplishment. After all, pageants set out to connect with the honored person and to stake out the community's claims and desire. In a word, the pageant needs the guest, and the

---

[5]Clifford Geertz, "Centers, Kings, and Charisma: Reflections on the Symbolics of Power," in his *Local Knowledge: Further Essays in Interpretive Anthropology* (New York, 1983), p. 124. This essay appears on pp. 121-46.
[6]Glynne Wickham, *Early English Stages 1300 to 1660* (London and New York, 1963), II, 237. For further discussion see my "Pageants, Politics, and Patrons," *Medieval & Renaissance Drama in England* 6 (1993): 139-52.

guest needs the pageant. These entertainments can ratify a sovereign or mayor's claim, and their presence ratifies the political life of the city. Royal entry pageants in particular go to great lengths to underscore the political legitimacy of the monarch. Politically they therefore help secure the ruler's charisma, the interdependent relationship between the governed and their ruler, sustaining an ongoing dialogue.

Poetics remains a largely under-investigated topic about pageants. This concept can range from verse form to music to genre to fundamental concepts of representation. While no one could make a completely compelling case for the poetic accomplishment of the verse of civic pageants, sometimes we encounter effective verse that transcends the usual, rather pedestrian couplets that dominate. One thinks, for example, of Anthony Munday's experimentation with rhyme royal stanzaic form in his 1605 Lord Mayor's Show. Speech gains considerable life and dramatic effect in the hands of Jonson and Dekker in the 1604 royal entry. Songs fill the pageants; a few printed texts actually preserve the musical notation, such as Middleton's 1613 Lord Mayor's Show. Mainly we find the words for songs without much idea of what music accompanied them, and yet we find a number of recognizable names involved in creating music for the pageants. When one thinks about the "resurrection" of Hermione's statue in *The Winter's Tale*, one can also recall similar poetic devices in Munday's 1611 and 1616 shows. At such moments pageants mark the transition and tension between ritual and exhibition. As we shall see, pageants create their own genre, no matter how much they may be indebted and linked to other dramatic and poetic forms.

These pageants place little emphasis on plot or character development, such as one might expect in regular stage plays. The processional form and episodic structure dictate that emphasis fall on visual display and thematic connections. In the best entertainments, a consistent theme envelops the whole production; such themes proceed from an ethical bias not unlike most of the drama and literature of this period: namely, a belief in the teaching purpose of fiction. Pageant writers found their thematic content in essentially three vast areas: history, mythology, and moral allegory. In many ways these entertainments look back to earlier medieval drama. Indeed, the emphasis on moral theme, the presence of allegorical characters, and even some elements of staging (such as processional form) remind us of medieval dramatic productions.

While civic pageants, like the regular theater, appropriate metaphors, symbols, allegory, and historical reality to construct their fictions, they have matters of representation not common with the drama of public theaters. The pageant stands at the intersection of fiction and reality because it occurs in real time (an actual occasion and real place) and yet evokes a fictional world through emblematic techniques and historical allusion.[7] The presence of the sovereign, for example, blurs the boundaries between fiction and reality, the sovereign being a sign moving between the two. An exhilarating tension runs through these civic entertainments and through the texts that describe them: total representation involves the real *presentation* of the sovereign and the *representation* of a dramatic fiction. We will, in a sense, witness in these pageants the "self fashioning" of the sovereign (or mayor) and the City, such a fashioning made possible by the work of dramatists, musicians, actors, architects, and others. As the sovereign stands before a scaffold or arch in the streets of London at which a dramatic episode occurs, he or she exists in a perpendicular relationship to the device—at moments even literally true. The sign of the triumphal arch becomes manifest in its dramatic scene. One can think of the Fenchurch arch in 1604 which depicted the City of London carved in miniature on its top. When James arrived, the silk curtain that shrouded this arch vanished. Jonson explains the "allegory" of this scene as reflecting the erasing of sorrow and the emergence of a new day for the country. Thus within the City citizens can gaze at this arch that represents the City and evokes its symbolic idea. The spectators see multiple signs because their gaze fixes also on the sovereign, seeing in this person the sign and manifestation of power and rule. The fiction of the scaffold stages joins the reality of the streets to create a theatrical scene that presents and re-presents a joyous people honoring their sovereign. An impressive array of spectacular devices assist the pageant dramatist in representing an imaginative world situated in a real one.

In the last act of Shakespeare's *Love's Labour's Lost*, a group of the characters decides to present the "Pageant of the Nine Worthies" in honor of the visiting Princess and her retinue. Despite the serious subject matter—rather like the play itself—this pageant collapses under the weight of the ineptitude of the actors and their inability to sustain necessary dramatic illusion. But such moments have encouraged scholars to link pageants with *plays*, finding parallels or analogues between civic pageants and plays for the regular theater. Shakespeare's Elizabethan comedies, for example, have provided fertile ground for such investigations, made evident in the early work of Alice Venezky Griffin, *Pageantry on the Shakespearean Stage* (1951). Or, one might come at the topic in terms of how civic pageants may have influenced the design of the early theater buildings; this perspective governs George Kernodle's *From Art to Theatre* (1944). One can also find many connections between properties used in the public theaters and in street pageants. A longer historical view sees obvious links between civic pageants and the earlier medieval drama, which shares a civic nature in terms of performance space and financial sponsorship of the guilds. The processional form of allegorical and historical drama, first solidified in the fourteenth century, finds its ongo-

---

[7]For further discussion see my "Representation in Renaissance English Civic Pageants," *Theatre Journal* 40 (1988): 319-31.

ing counterpart in civic pageants of Tudor-Stuart England. Clearly, strands of influence flow between plays and pageants, even if we cannot always be sure how and where they begin.

Because major dramatists wrote the pageants, we have a ready body of material which allows investigation about connections between their pageants and their plays. I have observed, for example, how Thomas Middleton's speech for Zeal in the 1604 royal entry pageant lingers in his artistic consciousness as evident in his *No Wit, No Help like a Woman's* (1611), a curious and neglected play, filled with irony, satire, and unmistakable romance.[8] For Middleton, the year 1613 has particular importance because in this year he wrote his finest comedy, *A Chaste Maid in Cheapside*, and his finest Lord Mayor's Show, *The Triumphs of Truth*, thereby making possible an immediate and obvious comparison of what the same dramatist produced in two radically different genres, one bitingly satiric and the other, relentlessly idealistic.[9] My own analysis found surprising common ground between these dramatic products of 1613, while acknowledging their different purposes and tone. I argue that they represent two sides of the same moral coin in Middleton's imagination, both drawing their inspiration, indeed their reason for existence, from the City of London. Yellowhammer, the Goldsmith of the play, bounces off London's new mayor, a Grocer who negotiates between the allures of Error and the demands of Truth. Certainly discoveries of truth abound amidst the plentiful errors of the play. I cite the example of Middleton to encourage additional investigation into how dramatists' plays intersect their pageants.

Indeed, a large part of the focus of *Pageantry in the Shakespearean Theater* (1985) centers precisely on these interconnections, as, for example, Bruce Smith's essay "Pageants into Play: Shakespeare's Three Perspectives on Idea and Image" (pp. 220-46). Smith argues that pageants within the early plays maintain a separate and subordinate identity. In the second period, however, they fuse with the drama, offering a single perspective view; and in the final period, that of the romances, the pageant elements coordinate the drama, providing a reality more compelling than the fable itself. The spectacle of Shakespeare's last plays has indeed led many to see a pageant influence at work. One can imagine that spectators seeing the apparition of Diana in *Pericles*, the descent of Jupiter in *Cymbeline*, or the restoration of Hermione in *The Winter's Tale* may have concluded that they had seen similar spectacles in London's streets.

---

[8]See my discussion, "Middleton's *No Wit, No Help* and Civic Pageantry," in *Pageantry in the Shakespearean Theater* (Athens, GA, 1985), pp. 65-80.
[9]See my essay, "Middleton's Moral Landscape: *A Chaste Maid in Cheapside* and *The Triumphs of Truth*," in *"Accompaninge the players": Essays Celebrating Thomas Middleton, 1580-1980*, ed. Kenneth Friedenreich (New York, 1981), pp. 133-46.

Playwrights and actors offer another obvious link between regular plays and civic pageants. Seeing Middleton's pageants in the second decade of the seventeenth century or Heywood's in the 1630s may have caused one to think also of their plays. As noted above, established and successful dramatists did not forgo the opportunity to write pageants; in fact, guild records contain ample evidence of active competition among playwrights for employment by the guilds for civic shows. What may at first be less apparent is the appearance of professional actors in these pageants. For the magnificent 1604 entry both William Bourne (Bird) and Edward Alleyn performed, Alleyn in the role of Genius at the first arch at Fenchurch. The best-known actor from the King's Men, Richard Burbage performed in the pageant *London's Love to Royal Prince Henry*, written by Munday for the installation of Henry as Prince of Wales in 1610.[10] A small part for such a powerful actor one might conclude, but Burbage seems to have had no difficulty in accepting such a role. Similarly, John Lowen, also of the King's Men, performed in Munday's *Chruso-thriambos*, the Lord Mayor's Show for 1611. Various child actors from the children's companies also took part in civic pageants. All of this reminds us of the blurred boundaries between the regular stage and the street drama; only later scholars have created categories and limits. Perhaps Burbage thought that acting was acting, no matter the venue.

Publication means that printers, playwrights, and patrons collaborated in creating a printed text and distributing it. By the time of the Jacobean Lord Mayor's Show such publication became fairly standard. This had not always been the pattern. Why should these ephemeral pageants assume printed form? The question presupposes an answer: publication thwarts disappearance. Stephen Harrison, the architect for the 1604 pageant, also created a text complete with magnificent engravings of the seven triumphal arches. He constructed this book, he suggests, to give the pageant "lastingness." He even sells the book from his house. The publishing of pageant texts tracks increased publication of various kinds of dramatic texts. The guilds regularly ordered 300-500 copies of mayoral pageant texts, presumably for their own distribution. Without such texts, we would know relatively little about civic pageants.

But pageant texts have problems not ordinarily encountered in other theatrical texts. Pageant texts should both report and represent an actual event that occurred in city streets or on aristocratic estates, and yet they should also present the fiction which the playwright prepared. Increasingly, playwrights intend pageant texts for readers; these texts become commemorative books that both capture and immortalize the event and add to it. They assume an expository and narrative function that sets them apart from the typical dramatic text. Daryl Palmer writes tellingly about the texts for progresses: "Unlike the playwright who

[10]For further discussion, see my "Actors in English Civic Pageants," *Renaissance Papers 1972* (1973): 17-28.

produces a text for performance, the author of the progress narrative asserts that
his text will do business in the culture, recording the culture's practices of hospitality and the rewards of royal power."[11] He adds: "When an author produces a
pamphlet account of a progress, the textualization of the events nearly always
reinforces the ideological shaping of the various hospitalities" (p. 126). Some of
these texts may therefore move far beyond merely recording what happened and
the speeches given.

    I believe that pageant printed texts exhibit a growing self-consciousness as
books and that these publications do not obliterate theatrical performance or
displace it so much as they complete it.[12] A major problem emerges: how faithfully does the printed text represent the event? Thomas Dekker helps bring this
issue into focus in his address "To the Reader" that comes at the end of his account of the 1604 royal entry. He tells us that a great part of the speeches remained unspoken, so as not to let the event become tedious for the king. This
vexing confession lets us know of the problem but does not enlighten about
which speeches fell prey to the exigencies of time.

    A fundamental paradox arises: as the book seeks to "fix" the event of the
pageant, it apparently liberates the dramatist to create materials not represented
in the street entertainment. The playwright thus constructs a gap between the
printed text and actual performance; and through this gap he moves with digres-
sions, descriptions, and discourses on sometimes arcane topics. We therefore
come to experience the pageant text as an event itself, resembling but differing
from the show. The playwright often intrudes in the text in self-conscious ways,
sometimes revealing personal information or details about his negotiations with
the guild. He might instead decide to discourse learnedly about the history of the
office of London's Lord Mayor, for example. Or about the history of the world,
for that matter. And many of the leading London printers, such as George
Purslowe, William Jaggard, Edward Allde, Nicholas and John Okes, decided to
place into print these pageants, assuring their survival and sustaining a develop-
ing tradition of book publication.

    A few words about where we have come from in pageantry studies and our cur-
rent status. We owe an enormous debt to John Nichols, who in the nineteenth
century brought together in seven volumes the texts and other information for
dozens of pageant events in the reigns of Elizabeth and James (cited frequently in
the pages to come). This gold mine merits repeated trips. Robert Withington's
work constitutes the starting point in the twentieth century. His *English Pag-*

---

[11]Daryl W. Palmer, *Hospitable Performances: Dramatic Genre and Cultural Practices in Early Modern
England* (West Lafayette, Indiana, 1992), p. 123.
[12]For further discussion see my "Stuart Civic Pageants and Textual Performance," *Renaissance Quarterly* 51 (1998): 163-83.

eantry: An Historical Outline (1918-20) touches on tournaments and masques, but primarily it offers a historical survey of folk mummings, royal entries, progress entertainments, and Lord Mayors' Shows. Revealing an evolutionary perspective, Withington writes: "Like all dramatic, or semi-dramatic forms, the pageant is a growth. ... Utilized by the Church, developed by the guilds, this form of entertainment grew with more and more elaboration until the pageant, as we know it, came into existence" (I, 84). Rather bluntly he insists that the "pageant is the lowest form of dramatic expression; but it is a form deeply rooted in the heart of the people" (xx). Such views obviously do little to encourage a serious exploration of pageants. Fortunately, the several volumes of Glynne Wickham's *Early English Stages*, referred to earlier, lift the discussion of pageants to a new level, placing them in an emblematic and iconographical tradition, as well as a dramatic tradition. Wickham observes: "The problem that confronted the devisers of all these occasional entertainments was to achieve a satisfactory balance between static tableaux, set speeches and the combative, processional or choreographic actions, which they adorned and explained."[13] These disparate components, if coherently linked, lead to an emblematic whole.

This artistic perspective gets short shrift in Sydney Anglo's *Spectacle, Pageantry, and Early Tudor Policy* (1969), because Anglo emphasizes the political significance of the entertainments. Indeed, Anglo sees a twofold political purpose: "they were related to a European tradition of the magnificence expected of a potentate"; and "many festivals were political, either through the desire to enhance great diplomatic occasions, or because they actually included specific comment on an international situation" (p. 2). Anglo therefore examines festivals, disguisings, masques, plays, tournaments, and royal entries, beginning with Henry VII and closing with Elizabeth's royal entry pageant of January 1559, which is where the present book begins. Gordon Kipling's *Enter the King: Theatre, Liturgy, and Ritual in the Medieval Civic Triumph* (1998) focuses on the medieval period, basically 1370 to 1550, and ranges across Europe. As Kipling says: the book "attempts to describe for the first time the ritual purposes, symbolic vocabulary, and quasi-dramatic form of one late medieval courtly festival: the royal entry" (p. 2). Kipling argues "that the spectacular pageant emblems invented to interpret and celebrate the meaning of this particular court fête can largely be described as the statement and variation of a single, albeit complex, informing *idea*." Thus for Kipling, unlike Anglo, political considerations play a much less important role.

One can get a reliable overview of pageant traditions throughout western Europe in Roy Strong's *Art and Power: Renaissance Festivals* (1984). "Magnificence" becomes the key word for Strong, the very idea being of central importance "both to the Renaissance and Baroque court," Strong insists (p. 22). Strong

[13] *Early English Stages*, III, xix.

writes: "If I had to define the Renaissance court fête in relation to the prince, I
would say that its fundamental objective was power conceived as art" (p. 40). Art
thus serves the purposes of expressions of regal power. A variation of this can be
found in the art form of the tournament, a subject ably explored by Alan Young
in his *Tudor and Jacobean Tournaments* (1987). The Accession Day tournaments
gained great importance under Elizabeth and continued under James. The spectacle, however, begins to wear a bit thin; and by the reign of Charles, such tournaments have largely disappeared. Young notes: "participants were anxious to
glorify their monarch and thereby add to the general magnificence of the occasion, but they were also invariably anxious to use the impresa as a means of enhancing their own relationship with the monarch" (p. 143).

I also call attention to the six installments of the "Preliminary Checklist of
Tudor and Stuart Entertainments," compiled by C. E. McGee and John C.
Meagher and published in volumes 24, 25, 27, 30, 36, and 38 (1981-1999) of *Research Opportunities in Renaissance Drama*. Broken down by specified historical
periods, these checklists offer an extraordinary resource of information about all
kinds of entertainments, including pageants and masques. Combing through
these instructive lists, one can only conclude that much remains to be done.
McGee and Meagher have unearthed material previously unknown or over-
looked. I note how many items in these lists the compilers designate as "unpublished." Three pages of information in *RORD* 30 cover Middleton's *Civitatis
Amor*, a civic pageant designed to honor the installation of Charles as Prince of
Wales in 1616. These sources range from British Library manuscript materials
(one item as yet unpublished), Public Record Office documents, Inner Temple
and Middle Temple records, and manuscripts in the Bodleian and Guildhall Libraries. Exploring all of these items would greatly expand the understanding of
Middleton's pageant, making it much richer. Similar procedures could be pursued for many other civic pageants, based on the McGee-Meagher checklists.

In 1985, I pointed out that we have no adequate study of the music in civic
pageants. This remains the case. Yet we know that music filled the streets and the
noblemen's estates on the occasions of pageant entertainments. Several of the
songs serve crucial thematic purposes in the entertainments. At least two quarto
texts of Lord Mayors' Shows include musical notations for songs; so far as I
know, neither has been discussed musically. We have guild records that document the participation of well-known musicians, such as William Byrd, John
Bull, Orlando Gibbons, and Nathaniel Giles. But what about the connections—in
words, music, style, or purpose—among the music of the regular theater, the
masques, and civic pageants? Standing in the London's streets in 1604, King
James would have heard many songs. Where did they come from, who wrote
them, and how do they compare in purpose to other dramatic forms? Such important questions await satisfactory attention.

The situation about editions has improved recently. With the edition of Middleton's pageants, which I have edited, forthcoming in *The Complete Works of Thomas Middleton*, a major gap will have been filled. Jean Wilson's *Entertainments for Elizabeth I* (1980) includes an edition of four pageants: "Four Foster Children of Desire" (1581) and two progress pageants from 1591 (Cowdray and Elvetham), and Ditchley (1592). Nevertheless, a number of pageant texts still lack critical editions. But even recent anthologies of Renaissance drama have begun to include the occasional civic pageant text. Richard Dutton has prepared an edition of four pageants, designed for classroom use (*Jacobean Civic Pageants*, 1995). Such efforts will eventually pay off in heightened awareness of this important dramatic form.

Three additional areas require further study: visual, local politics, and language. Like the court masque, the civic pageant relies heavily on visual representation. Unfortunately, we have few pictorial records of the pageants. Thus, we must infer from the texts what these shows looked like. The visual nature of these shows, including iconographical traditions, remains a rich area for study. By "local politics" I have in mind especially guild politics. What can we learn about the internal workings of London's guilds that can illuminate the negotiations that went on between the guild and the playwrights, musicians, carpenters, artificers, and others? What intramural struggles or disagreements find their way into the pageant events? We know that a keen sense of rivalry developed so that each guild tried to outstrip the other to offer a particularly dazzling show. What motivated the guilds to assess their members in order to support the construction and performance of the pageants? The language of the pageant texts has usually been brushed by quickly. But surely it merits study—from verse forms to word choice to prose style. What kind of discourse does the writer use; what rhetorical resources does he adopt? What achievement occurs in the construction of dramatic speech? Thus many questions begin to open new avenues of thinking and to suggest new approaches to studying civic pageantry.

Where we have been and where we might yet go suggest the richness inherent in a study of civic pageantry. These pageants captured the attention of thousands of spectators in London's streets or wherever they took place, they engaged outstanding dramatic talent (playwrights and actors), they displayed extraordinary technical skill (from triumphal arches to fireworks), they utilized large sums of financial support from city governments and guilds, and they participated in the political and symbolic ratification of the sovereign's or mayor's office. This revised book seeks to call renewed and vigorous attention to this sometimes marginalized dramatic form by insisting that civic pageants constituted a major part of cultural and theatrical life in early modern England. Dekker writes near the conclusion of his text of the 1604 royal entry pageant: "upon this day began a new *Creation*, and ... the Citie was the onely Workhouse wherein sundry nations

were made." Diligent, imaginative, and collaborative work creates "sundry nations" of fictional drama set in real locations. New creations renew cities and
estates; such capability civic pageants have.

Part one

Progresses and Royal Entries

LIKE CHAUCER'S PILGRIMS ON THEIR APRIL JOURNEY, the sovereign in the summer longed to go on a progress. And January, March, or June or any month is fit season for a royal entry. Long before the Elizabethan period English monarchs made provincial tours and entries, many containing pageant entertainment. One recalls the elaborate entry of Henry VI into London in 1432 after his coronation in Paris, or the coronation entry of Anne Boleyn in 1533 (part of the action in Shakespeare's *Henry VIII*), or the royal entry of Mary Tudor.[1] The subsequent historical periods ring changes on a type of entertainment already well established.

Various impulses, ranging from practical to ideal, prompted the monarch to go on progress. Reasons of health and sanitation made it advantageous to be away from London during the summer's warmth—a bit of fresh air for the sovereign. Presumably, one could lower the expenses of the court by visiting various noblemen who typically bore the brunt of the cost for the visit; such an economic consideration may have been rather appealing to James, who constantly received sad news about the depleted treasury. Ambivalent must have been the feelings of any nobleman for whom the monarch's visit ranked as high in cost as it did in prestige. Watching the retinue of hundreds of people and animals approach one's door did not offer an unmixed pleasure. The sovereign doubtless had an important political reason for progresses; namely, to see and to be seen. They afforded the opportunity for visits to the neglected provinces and a chance for winning additional loyalty and support, a political impulse very much in Elizabeth's mind at least. Of course, not all progresses contained entertainments that can be classed as civic pageants, as I have defined them. Others offered a variety of entertainment usually spread out over several days with emphasis on figures and scenes out of the pastoral tradition and classical mythology.

[1]See Robert Withington, *English Pageantry: An Historical Outline* (Cambridge, Mass., 1918-20), I, 141-89, *passim*; Glynne Wickham, *Early English Stages* (London and New York, 1959), I, 63f; and Gordon Kipling, *Enter the King: Theatre, Liturgy, and Ritual in the Medieval Civic Triumph* (Oxford, 1998).

Though the most spectacular of the royal entries concern coronations, others also provide pageant entertainment. Typically the honored person was met outside the city, perhaps by the mayor and aldermen, escorted into the city by them, given a purse of money (or some other gift) and a speech by the Recorder; and in the ones that qualify to be designated pageants, dramatic tableaux occurred at various points in the city. Even the places become somewhat institutionalized in London with entertainment for Elizabeth in 1559 and for James in 1604 occurring at virtually the same locations. The guilds and the city bore responsibility for these entertainments, which became quite expensive. To honor the sovereign, to entertain, and to instruct became the basic purposes of such civic pageants.

Other shows which do not fit very precisely into either category of progress entertainment or royal entry have been included if they in some way involve the royal family or the court. As we move from Elizabeth to James to Charles, we can observe an obvious decrease in the number of progress shows and royal entries; indeed, the Elizabethan period establishes a high-water mark never attained in the two immediately subsequent eras. The cause for this change cannot accurately be laid at the feet of the citizenry, who simply transferred much of their attention to the burgeoning Lord Mayor's Show, the subject of Part Two.

1 The Reign of Elizabeth (1558-1603)

ELIZABETH'S REIGN affords the unique opportunity of seeing all the various kinds of civic pageantry, and thus this period becomes especially crucial in helping us understand the nature of the civic entertainments. The theme that binds together all the pageants, whether progress shows or royal entries, focuses on a celebration of Elizabeth's power, her spiritual, mystical, transforming power. She can set men free, still the loud voices of war, and provide a refuge for the distressed. Later pageants document and fulfill the hope implicit in the 1559 coronation royal entry, as the pageant-dramatists offer an apotheosis of Elizabeth.

From the outset, the 1559 royal entry firmly establishes this form of civic pageantry, and the later entries at Bristol and Norwich offer simple variations of the basic pattern of processional drama with allegorical tableaux, set speeches, and limited dramatic action. But when civic entertainments occur outside the narrow confines of city streets, they appear more expansive, more diverse, and usually more dramatic, as if the movement out of the city liberates them. Bristol and Norwich provide especially interesting examples in this respect, as we shall see, for they have both a formal entry on one day and a much different, more dramatically unified, entertainment in subsequent days occurring outside the city. Being quite diverse and episodic, progress pageants lack coherent form; but as we move from the Kenilworth entertainment (1575) to the Elvetham one (1591), we can perceive a development of dramatic unity in these pageants. Throughout the Elizabethan period speech remains of secondary importance in the royal entry form, whereas in the progress shows it occupies a much more crucial place, reflecting no doubt the involvement of such poets as Churchyard, Gascoigne, Sidney, and Lyly in these entertainments who naturally would have an interest in the language of pageantry as well as the visual display. Also, the relative importance of speech corresponds to the attempt at dramatic unity in the progress pageants. One senses a growing consciousness of pageantry as drama. This appears also in the movement from the visual, implicit morality conflict as found in the 1559 entry to the dramatically realized conflict, such as in part of the Norwich show. Such changes serve as precursors of what will be found in later pageantry, as the Jacobean and Caroline pageant-dramatists build on what had been accomplished in the Elizabethan period.

We can logically begin a discussion of the royal entries and progresses in the Elizabethan period with Elizabeth's official passage through London on 14 January 1559, the day before her coronation. One might start with this pageant whether intending chronological order or not, for it epitomizes the chief charac-

teristics to be found in all royal entries and represents a high achievement of this
dramatic form. The following extract from the Corporation records dated 7 December 1558 reveals the preparation by the city of London:

> Itm this day the Worshipfull Commyners hereunder namyd were
> nomyatyd appoyntyd and chardgid by the hole Courte to take the
> chardge Travell and paynes to cause at the Cytyes costes and chardges
> all the places hereafter mentonyd to be very well and semely trymyd and
> deckyd for the honor of the Cyty agaynste the comynge of our Sov-
> rangne Lady the Quenes majesty that nowe is to her Coronacon thor-
> oughe the Cyty with pageantes fyne payntyngte and riche clothes of ar-
> ras sylver and golde in suche and lyke mannr and sorte as they were
> trymyd agaynst the comyng of our late Sovrangne lady Quene Mary to
> her Coronacon and muche better if it conveynyently may be done.... [1]

Then follows a list of men charged with the tasks of the pageants; and a further
list gives the places, such as the Little Conduit in Cheapside, to locate the main
devices. One could read special meaning into the statement that the preparations
should be "muche better" than at Mary's entry; at any rate, the city busily dis-
charges its duty to honour the new sovereign. Additional records show payments
to painters for decorating the Conduit in Cheapside (*Repertory*, XIV, fol. 103b,
109b) and orders to the Bachelors of the Mercers company to stand in Cheapside
for the processional (fol. 104). The Aldermen took extraordinary action two days
after the royal processional: "Itm yt was orderyd and agryed that Mr Chamber-
lyne shoulde cause all the pageantes to be taken downe with spede and to save
asmoche of the stufe of them as may be to serve at an other tyme" (*Rep.*, XIV, fol.
110). A simple matter of the necessity of the movement of carriages might dictate
the speedy dismantling of the devices, but principally economy urges that the
"stufe" be preserved—not the last time that such an order will be made. We may
doubt, in this case at least, that the city benefited from saving some of the devices, but who could have known in 1559 that Elizabeth's reign would be so long?

The pamphlet that describes the festivities of 1559 provides a marvellous
piece of propaganda as well as a record of the events; the text presents Elizabeth
in an extremely favorable light. Whether he actually devised some of the entertainment or not, Richard Mulcaster seems clearly to have been largely responsible for the preparation of the text as shown in the following entry in the Corporation of London records dated 4 March 1559:

> Itm yt was orderyd and agreyd by the Court here this day that the
> Chamberlyn shall geve unto Rychard Mulcaster for his reward for ma-

kyng of the boke conteynynge and declaryng the historyes set furth in and by the Cyties pageantes at the tyme of the Quenes highnes com-myng thorough the Cytye to her coronacon xl^s which boke was gevyen unto the Quenes grace.²

One can imagine the city's eagerness to place the book in the queen's hands; and we see something of the city's concern for the total event, even to the point of having someone commemorate the pageants in printed form in a text, which incidentally became rather popular, or so it seems, with two editions in 1559 and another in 1604, the year of James's royal entry into London.³ This text Heywood knew well when he wrote *Englands Elizabeth* in 1631, and it influenced Dekker in his play, *The Whore of Babylon.*

The chief contemporary account in addition to the specially prepared quarto comes in the dispatch of Il Schifanoya, Venetian Ambassador, to the Castellan of Mantua, dated 23 January 1559.⁴ This Italian ambassador, doubtless familiar with similar pageants in Venice, adds valuable information and offers interpretation of some of the devices, though his report does not cover the whole pageant. He provides something of the color of the setting:

> The houses on the way were all decorated; there being on both sides of the street, from Blackfriars to St. Paul's, wooden barricades, on which the merchants and artisans of every trade leant in long black gowns lined with hoods of red and black cloth, … with all their ensigns, banners, and standards, which were innumerable, and made a very fine show. Owing to the deep mud caused by the foul weather and by the multitude of people and of horses, everyone had made preparation, by placing sand and gravel in front of their houses. (*CSP Ven*, p. 12)

He estimates the number of horses at 1,000 behind which came the queen "in an open litter, trimmed down to the ground with gold brocade...." Continuing his

---

²Ibid., fol. 143.

³The 1559 editions: *The Quenes Majesties Passage through the Citie of London to Westminster the Day before her Coronacion* and *The Passage of our most drad Soveraigne Lady Quene Elyzabeth through the citie of London to Westminster the day before her coronacion.* The 1604 edition is called *The Royall Passage of her Majesty from the Tower of London, to her Palace of White-hall ... ;* another impression of this edition has a different title page. For some reason none of these texts are listed in Greg's *Bibliography of English Printed Drama,* though other pageant texts are included. The 1604 edition is a reprint of the earlier edition. And we may accept as plausible James M. Osborn's suggestion that of the 1559 texts, both printed by Richard Tottel, *The Quenes Majesties Passage* precedes the other one with substantive variants relatively few and minor.

⁴*Calendar of State Papers Venetian 1558-1580* (London, 1890), VII, 12-16. For a fuller discussion of this whole subject see my "Venetian State Papers and English Civic Pageantry, 1558-1642," *Renaissance Quarterly* 23 (1970): 37-47.

emphasis on the "color" of the event, Il Schifanoya describes Elizabeth as "dressed in a royal robe of very rich cloth of gold, with a double-raised stiff pile, and on her head over a coif of cloth of gold, beneath which was her hair, a plain gold crown without lace, as a princess, but covered with jewels, and nothing in her hands but gloves" (p. 12). Lord Robert Dudley, the Lord Chamberlain, and members of the Privy Council followed the queen.

In the papers of Sir Thomas Cawarden, Master of the Revels when Elizabeth came to the throne, two items bear specifically on this pageant. These papers form part of the Loseley Manuscripts, housed at the Folger Shakespeare Library: Folger MS.L.b.33 and MS.L.b.109. In the first, the Queen orders Cawarden to provide apparel and other materials for the coronation pageant; the second provides a list of garments that Cawarden delivered to John Gresham and John Elyot. These documents reveal Elizabeth's keen interest in such festivities, as she readily assists the city in its attempt to honor her. She thus becomes not only recipient of the pageant, spectator of and "actor" in it, but also provider of costume.[5]

The whole report in the pamphlet creates the unmistakable impression that this queen in the golden litter forms very much part of the action, one of the actors in the total pageant, part of the theatrical experience. As the pamphlet states: "For in all her passage she did not only shew her most gracious love toward the people in generall, but also privately if the baser personages had either offred her grace any flowres or such like as a significacion of their good will, ... she most gently, to the common rejoysing of all the lookers on, ... staid her chariot, and heard theyr requestes."[6] Such vital rapport serves theater of course; and thus not surprisingly the writer, presumably Mulcaster, adds: "So that if a man should say well, he could not better tearme the citie of London that time, than a stage wherin was shewed the wonderfull spectacle, of a noble hearted princesse toward her most loving people, and the peoples exceding comfort in beholding so worthy a soveraign ..." (p. 28). Elizabeth makes a histrionic response to the gift of a purse of gold presented by the Recorder:

[5]For discussion of this material see my "Elizabeth's Coronation Entry (1559): New Manuscript Evidence," *English Literary Renaissance* 8 (1978): 3-8, plus 4 plates; revised and reprinted in *Practicing Renaissance Scholarship*, pp. 36-42.

[6]*The Quenes Majesties Passage*, ed. James M. Osborn (New Haven, 1960), p. 28. For its convenience and general availability, I use this facsimile edition for all quotations from the original pamphlet. Accounts of this pageant are reprinted in volume I of John Nichols, *The Progresses and Public Processions of Queen Elizabeth*, new edition (London, 1823); and volume IV of *Holinshed's Chronicles of England, Scotland, and Ireland*, 1586 edition (London, 1807). See also the edition in Arthur F. Kinney's *Elizabethan Backgrounds* (Hamden, Conn., 1975), pp. 7-39. For discussion see Sydney Anglo, *Spectacle, Pageantry, and Early Tudor Policy* (Oxford, 1969), pp. 344-59; Richard DeMolen, "Richard Mulcaster and Elizabethan Pageantry," *Studies in English Literature* 14 (1974): 209-21.

I thanke my lord maior, his brethren, and you all. And wheras your request is that I should continue your good ladie and quene, be ye ensured, that I wil be as good unto you, as ever quene was to her people. No wille in me can lacke, neither doe I trust shall ther lacke any power. And perswade your selves, that for the safetie and quietnes of you all, I will not spare, if nede be to spend my blood, God thanke you all. (p. 46)

This takes the element of the "unscheduled actor" about as far as it can go when the person delivers speeches of her own, of course to the great delight of the audience. Other examples of similar responses occur, whether accepting gifts from citizens along the way or acknowledging their shouts; in fact, the text closes with a section of such examples called "Certain notes of the quenes majesties great mercie, clemencie, and wisdom used in this passage." Part of that wisdom consists in exploiting the dramatic possibilities on this stage of London, which "received [her] merveylous entierly."

Beginning from the Tower about two o'clock in the afternoon of 14 January, Elizabeth and retinue proceeded first to Fenchurch street where "was erected a scaffold richely furnished, wheron stode a noyes of instrumentes, and a child in costly apparel, which was appointed to welcome the quenes majestie in the hole cities behalfe" (p. 29). When Elizabeth approached the location, the child uttered the welcoming oration, pledging that the town offered her two gifts: "blessing tongues" and "true hertes" which praise and serve the queen. "At which wordes of the last line the hole peple gave a great shout, wishing with one assent as the childe had said" (p. 30). Elizabeth thanked them for their gracious welcome. This extremely simple beginning of a show that becomes more elaborate as it unfolds isolates some important ingredients of pageant entertainment. Impressively the elements of actor, audience, and honored guest fuse into a single compound of entertainment with a give-and-take here and an intimacy of reaction, eventually lost with the later proscenium stage. The rapport between actor and audience may remind one of the medieval theater.

Much more complex, the pageant device at Gracious street to which the queen processed offered "A stage ... whiche extended from thone syde of the streate to thother, rychelye vawted with batlementes conteining three portes, and over the middlemost was avaunced iii. severall stages in degrees" (p. 31). The Venetian ambassador adds that the "arch had three fronts and three entrances ... two small, and a great one, with columns, capitals, and bases, etc." (*CSP Ven*, p. 13). On the lowest stage in the middle section of the arch sat personages representing Henry VII and his wife Elizabeth, Henry "proceding out of the house of Lancastre, was enclosed in a read rose, and thother which was Queene Elizabeth being heire to the house of Yorke enclosed with a whyte rose ..." (pp. 31-2).[7] The

---

[7]In his dispatch the Venetian Ambassador identifies the wrong color rose with Henry and Elizabeth.

royal couple, dressed appropriate to their station, sit with joined hands. From the roses on this level "sprang two braunches gathered into one, which wer directed upward to the second stage or degree" (p. 32) whereon sat the figures of Henry VIII and his wife Anne Boleyn—this particular wife chosen because she was the mother of Elizabeth—"apparelled with Sceptours and diademes, and other furniture due to the state of a king and quene ..." (p. 32). And to the top level a branch proceeded to another "seate royall, in the whiche was sette one representynge the Quenes most excellent majestie Elizabeth nowe our most dradde soveraygne Ladie ..." (p. 32). Understandably, the pageant arch, entitled "The uniting of the houses of Lancastre and Yorke," had all the empty places on the arch filled with sentences commending unity, and "the hole pageant garnished with redde roses and white ..." (p. 33).

"Oute of the forepart of thys pageaunt was made a standyng for a chylde, whiche at the quenes ... comyng declared unto her the hole meaning of the said pageaunt" (p. 32). But "the noyse was great by reason of the prease of people, so that she could skace heare the childe ..." (p. 34). Realizing that hearing would continue to be a problem, Elizabeth sent representatives to all the other devices "to require the people to be silent for her majestie was disposed to heare all that shold be said unto her" (p. 37). The implicit theme of the pageant here at Gracious street becomes explicit in the verses spoken by the child who interpreted the arch and admonished the queen:

Therefore as civill warre, and shede of blood did cease
When these two houses were united into one
So now that jarre shall stint, and quietnes encrease,
We trust, O noble Queene, thou wilt be cause alone. (p. 35)

The text views Elizabeth as an important part of a ruling house which brought unity and peace to England, part of the "Tudor myth" of history, a story and theme explored even more fully on the public stage decades later in Shakespeare's history plays. Shakespeare could build on what had been stated in the pageant theater in brief, emblematic terms.

On the way to the second device the queen passed the water conduit in Cornhill "which was curiouslye trimmed against that time with riche banners adourned, and a noyse of loude instrumentes upon the top therof ..." (p. 37). At the lower end of Cornhill an arch stretched across the street with three gates, "and over the middle parte therof was erected one chaire a seate royall with clothe of estate ... wherein was placed a childe representing the Queenes highnesse ..." (p. 37). This "seate of worthie governance" appeared to the audience "to have no staie, and therfore of force was stayed by lively personages" who happened to be four virtues: Pure religion, Love of subjects, Wisdom, and Justice, "which did treade their contrarie vices under their feete"; namely, Pure religion did tread upon Superstition and Ignorance; Love of subjects upon Rebellion and Insolence; Wisdom upon Folly and Vainglory; and Justice upon Adulation and Bribery (p. 38). This mute struggle between vices and virtues, a conflict often found in morality drama, displays itself here in a symbolic way. The pamphlet makes clear that each of these figures "was aptelie and properlie apparelled, so that his apparell and name did agre ..." (p. 38); this visual appeal relies on iconographical traditions, which suggest the costume of many such allegorical characters.

Before the seat of the figure personating Elizabeth, a child addressed the actual queen when she drew near the pageant and interpreted the scene:

While that religion true, shall ignorance suppresse
And with her weightie foote, breake superstitions heade
While love of subjectes, shall rebellion distresse
And with zeale to the prince, insolencie down treade.

While justice, can flattering tonges and briberie deface
While follie and vaine glory to wisedome yelde their handes
So long shall government, not swarve from her right race
But wrong decayeth still, and rightwisenes up standes. (p. 39)

The child closes by hoping that the virtues shall maintain Elizabeth's throne and that vices will be suppressed. The pamphlet writer clarifies the message and adds: "The grounde of this pageant, was that like as by vertues ... the Queenes majestie was established in the seate of government: so she should syt fast in the same so long as she embraced vertue and helde vice under foote" (p. 40). This gets a different emphasis from the Venetian ambassador, who, besides including six virtues and giving the virtues and vices slightly different names, concludes this meaning: "that hitherto religion had been misunderstood and misdirected, and that now it will proceed on a better footing ..." (*CSP Ven*, p. 13). Of the vices whom he names as Ignorance, Superstition, Hypocrisy, Vain Glory, Simulation, Rebellion, and Idolatry, he says that they hint of the past. He seems to seize upon one part of the pageant and see it all in terms of recent history, which probably occurred to other spectators as well. Perhaps the ambassador simply makes explicit what he thought the device implied. Heywood adds the queen's supposed verbal response to the scene: "*I have taken notice of your good meaning toward mee, and will endeavour to Answere your severall expectations.*"[8]

Passing the great Conduit in Cheapside "which was bewtifyed with pictures and sentences accordingly agaynst her graces coming thither," the queen processed to Soper lane where another pageant stretched across the street, again with three

[8]Thomas Heywood, *Englands Elizabeth Her Life and Troubles* (London, 1631), p. 229.

gates. Over the middle one, three stages had a child seated on the top stage, three on the middle one, and four on the bottom stage; they represented the Eight Beatitudes as found in St. Matthew's gospel "applyed to our soveraigne Ladie Quene Elizabeth" (p. 41). "Everie of these children wer appointed and apparelled according unto the blessing which he did represent," and all the "voide places" in the pageant contained sentences concerning the promises and blessings of God. Musicians also found room atop the arch as did another child who spoke. This child, who associates each of the Beatitudes with Elizabeth, reminds her: "Therfore trust thou in god, since he hath helpt thy smart / That as his promis is, so he will make thee strong" (p. 42). This dramatic presentation shows clearly a religious influence in civic pageantry which, however, becomes increasingly rare as we move forward into the Elizabethan era. One assumes that the audience understood such patently religious or moral instruction as not aimed exclusively at the sovereign; perhaps that realization Heywood acknowledges by adding that at the close of the speech the multitude cried out "*Amen, Amen.*"

The Venetian ambassador adds details about the Standard and Cross in Cheap which the queen passed on her way to the next presentation. Il Schifanoya says that on the Standard "there were painted to the life all the kings and queens chronologically in their royal robes down to her present Majesty" (*CSP Ven*, p. 14). Of the Cross he reports that it was "like a pyramid, completely gilt and somewhat renovated, with all the saints in relief, they being neither altered nor diminished...." Moving past representatives of guilds who lined the way, the sovereign came to the upper end of Cheapside where Ranulph Cholmley, Recorder of the city, presented her with a purse containing 1,000 marks in gold and offered greetings on behalf of the Mayor and the Aldermen. At this point Elizabeth made her speech, cited above in the discussion of her role as actor, and readied herself to witness one of the most elaborate devices of the whole entertainment.

Differing from the arch constructions of the previous devices, the pageant located at the Little Conduit in Cheap had "square proporcion" containing two hills or mountains. The one on the north side "was made cragged, barreyn, and stonye, in the whiche was erected one tree, artificiallye made, all withered and deadde, with braunches accordinglye" (p. 46). At the foot of this tree sat "one in homely and rude apparell crokedlye, and in mournyng maner" with the title of the pageant, *Ruinosa Respublica* (a decayed commonwealth), hanging above his head. Dangling from this same tree, tablets contained mottoes or sentences which specified the causes for a decaying republic. Contrastingly, on the south side the other hill was "fayre, freshe, grene, and beawtifull, the grounde thereof full of flowres and beawtie" (p. 47); likewise, a fresh and flourishing tree had a youthful person who stood under the tree. This device, *Respublica bene instituta*, and its tree carried in its boughs the causes for a flourishing state: "Fear of God, A wise prince, Learned rulers, Obedience to officers, Obedient subjects, Lovers of the commonweal, Virtue rewarded, Vice chastened." Thus every part of the northern hill counters its opposite and prospering number in the south hill to the point of having the youth sitting in the first one and standing in the second. The pageant-dramatist makes concrete and visual here the metaphor in much Elizabethan literature, especially Shakespeare's *Richard II*, of the state being analogous to a garden, the relationship of microcosm and macrocosm, microcosm and body politic. One can almost hear (several years before Shakespeare, of course) the admonition to "go, bind thou up yon dangling apricocks."

This symbolically contrasting landscape contains also another element; namely, a small cave located in the middle between the two hills. Out of which issued at the queen's arrival "one personage whose name was *Tyme*, apparaylled as an olde man with a Sythe in his hande, havynge wynges artificiallye made" (p. 47); he led another person "fynely and well apparaylled, all cladde in whyte silke" representing Time's daughter, Truth, who carried the word of Truth—the English Bible. A child standing on the flourishing hill addressed the queen, interpreted the pageant, and added:

Now since that Time again his daughter truth hath brought,
We trust O worthy quene, thou wilt this truth embrace.
And since thou understandst the good estate and nought
We trust welth thou wilt plant, and barrennes displace. (p. 48)

This obviously implies that the propitious moment has been reached in which Truth can reappear. No doubt the Venetian ambassador rightly understood when he wrote: "The whole implied in their tongue that the withered mount was the past state, and the green one the present, and that the time for gathering the fruits of truth was come …" (*CSP Ven*, p. 15). The dramatist studiously avoids any overt criticism of the previous reign while making his points nevertheless; direct attack seldom forms part of the scheme of things in pageantry.

The drama here in Cheapside closes with the speaker handing toward the queen the book "which a little before, Trueth had let downe unto him from the hill" (p. 48); Sir John Parrat received it and delivered it to Elizabeth, who "as soone as she had received the booke, kyssed it, and with both her handes held up the same, and so laid it upon her brest, with great thankes to the citie therfore" (pp. 48-9). Again the queen rises triumphantly to the dramatic occasion, not letting the opportunity pass to underscore the new regime's reliance on Truth and her Word. Not only does the queen strike a dramatic pose here, but also she makes a political point by emphasizing the place of the *English* Bible in her government. The Venetian ambassador takes note of this response as do other writers more removed in time. Heywood, for example, cites the whole scene in his *Englands Elizabeth* (1631), but much earlier he had included a modified version of it at the closing of the first part of his two-part play about Elizabeth, *If You Know Not Me* (1605-6), in which the queen receives a Bible from the mayor. In the dumb show that precedes Act I of his *The Whore of Babylon* (1607), Dekker presents Time, Truth, and Titania (i.e., Elizabeth), who receives a book (presumably the Bible) which she accepts and kisses.

Clearly the entertainment here at the Little Conduit in Cheapside represents something of a "dramatic climax," if one may use such a term in plotless drama, at least the thematic culmination of all that has preceded it. The pamphlet writer senses this, for he suggests that the meaning of this pageant depends on the previous ones, the queen having already been instructed about unity, the virtues which support the seat of government, and the blessings which accompany her. This fourth device proposes "to put her grace in remembrance of the state of the common weale, which Time with Truth his doughter doth revele, which Truth also her grace hath received, and therfore cannot but be merciful and careful for the good government therof" (p. 50). How striking and meaningful it must have been to the spectators to see Truth in visible union with their new sovereign; such drama of course flatters the queen, but also it derives from a world view sympathetic and attuned to metaphor and that lets abstractions take on concrete reality. And morally Truth has chosen between good—the flourishing hill, the future, Elizabeth—and evil—the sterile mount, the past, false religion and a false queen. Such defines the path to salvation.

After hearing a Latin oration delivered in St. Paul's Churchyard by a child of Paul's school and passing by Ludgate where a "noyse of instrumentes" greeted her, Elizabeth moved onward to the conduit on Fleet street where the last pageant entertainment appeared. On the north side of the street "was erected a stage embattelled with foure towres and in the same a square platte rising with degrees, and upon the uppermost degree was placed a chaire, or seate roiall, and behinde the same seate in curious, artificiall maner was erected a tre of reasonable height"—a palm tree (p. 53). The occupant of the chair, "apparelled in parliament robes, with a sceptre in her hand," was "Debora the judge and restorer of the house of Israel" (p. 54). Six persons surrounded her, two each representing the nobility, the clergy, and the commonalty—Deborah's advisers. Near the bottom of the device stood the child who opened the meaning, reminding the queen and the audience of Deborah's achievements:

> In war she, through gods aide, did put her foes to flight,
> And with the dint of sworde the bande of bondage brast.
> In peace she, through gods aide, did alway mainteine right
> And judged Israell till fourty yeres were past. (p. 54)

This figure taken from Biblical history appears to Elizabeth as "a worthie president," "a worthie woman judge." And the use of historical figures as worthy examples to be imitated becomes a mainstay of the instructional techniques of pageantry. Important too, the ruler must seek wise counsel from a range of people, including commoners. This makes the previous instructions about government more concrete. Virtues suppress vices, and Truth presents her Word, but on a more practical level speakers bid the sovereign to seek good advisers. The entertainment which began at the first arch with the historical examples of the Tudor house now closes in the final device with another concrete example. Allegory and symbolic abstraction flow within simple, historical realities. The dramatist does not let us lose our way; one foot remains firmly planted on earth.

One of the children of Christ's Hospital made an oration as the queen passed St. Dunstan's church. Finally Elizabeth reached Temple Bar "whiche was dressed finely with the two ymages of Gotmagot the Albione, and Corineus the Briton, two gyantes bigge in stature furnished accordingly, which held in their handes even above the gate, a table, wherin was writen in laten verses, theffect of al the pageantes which the citie before had erected ..." (p. 57). The tablet held by the giants of British mythical history accompanies another one which offered the English translation of the Latin; the verses review each device and its meaning and offer a final wish for the sovereign: "Live long, and as long raigne, adourning thy countrie, / With vertues, and maintain thy peoples hope of thee ..." (p. 58). The dramatist gains unity by this recapitulation, as he drives home one last time the teaching presented by the shows. From the group of singing children nearby, "one child richely attyred as a Poet" gave the farewell to the queen. Part of the speech reminds her of the burden placed on her:

> For all men hope in thee, that all vertues shall reygne,
> For all men hope that thou, none errour wilt support,
> For all men hope that thou wilt trueth restore agayne,
> And mend that is amisse, to all good mennes comfort. (p. 59)

Elizabeth, to the end part of the drama, responded: "While these wordes were in saieng, and certeine wishes therein repeted for maintenaunce of truthe and rooting out of errour she now and then helde up her handes to heavenwarde and willed the people to say. Amen" (p. 59).

From Fenchurch to Temple Bar the sovereign has moved through the city amid the shouts and acclamations of London's citizens; it has indeed been a theatrical experience of the highest sort with actors, stage properties, music, audience, and honored guest joining for one great entertainment. The dramatist has sounded the theme of unity, warned about the need for virtue to drive out vice and error, called for the Word of Truth to be the guiding presence for a fruitful kingdom, and given a concrete example of a sterile and arid kingdom. And Deborah who judged Israel for over forty years becomes something of a prototype of Elizabeth. In addition to theme, we observe an excellent example of the form of

the royal entry pageant—the processional, allegorical tableaux, speeches; later
entries will not differ strikingly from this pattern, though by 1604 dramatic
speech appears, unlike the verses delivered by the children here. The somewhat
rigid, static form and structural simplicity in 1559 give way to more complex and
ornate architecture, dramatic action, and dramatic speech in the 1604 royal entry.

The scene shifts to Edinburgh and to the woman who became one of Elizabeth's problems; namely, Mary Queen of Scots, who in September 1561 made a
royal entry into Edinburgh, returning to Scotland after many years' absence in
France. In a few short years through pressure she abdicated in favor of her one-
year old son, James, who became James VI of Scotland, and, of course, James I of
England in 1603. Information about Mary's pageant entertainment comes from
local records of Edinburgh; no printed text exists. Throughout the summer the
city made preparations for the entertainment; for example, on 27 August, authorities bid the treasurer "with all diligence possible, to mak preparatioun for
the banquet and triumphe."[9] Purchased canvas and other materials helped decorate various places in the city. An entry of 3 September 1561 sets forth the esti-
mate of potential cost and the method of collecting it from "bayth merchant and
craftisman," "with all deligence to be collectit and debursit for the releif of the
creditouris, furnissaris of the necessaris of the said banquet triumphe and propyne" (p. 189). As in London a few years earlier, so in Edinburgh the guildsmen
of the city constitute the center of the preparations for a civic pageant, assuming
the financial burden.

Although Withington remains uncertain about whether a pageant took
place,[10] the burgh records give the particulars of Mary's entry into the city. At
Castle hill her highness encountered a delegation of young men from the city
dressed in yellow taffeta, wearing black visors and several gold chains; sixteen of
the leading citizens dressed in velvet gowns also attended. Purple velvet and red
taffeta lined her coach after which "wes ane cart with certane bairnes, togidder
with ane coffer quhairin wes the copburd and propyne quhilk suld be propynit to
hir hienes ..." (p. 189). The group made its way to Butter Trone where the first
device appeared: "ane port made of tymber, in maist honourable maner, cullorit
with fyne cullouris, hungin with syndrie armes" upon which a group of children
sang "in the maist hevinlie wyis" (p. 189). A mechanical device in the form of a
cloud opened as the queen came under the port, and a child "discendit doun as it
had bene ane angell, and deliverit to hir hienes the keyis of the toun, togidder
with ane bybill and ane psalme buik, coverit with fyne purpourit velvot ..." (p.
190). We do not know the content of the speeches. One can imagine that Mary's

[9]All quotations from records for the 1561 entry are taken from Anna Jean Mill, *Mediaeval Plays in Scotland*, St. Andrews University Publication, no. XXIV (Edinburgh & London, 1927), p. 188.
[10]Robert Withington, *English Pageantry*, I, 203.

reception of the Bible and psalm book, signs of a reformed faith, may have been something less than enthusiastic.

At Tolbooth a construction consisting of two scaffolds one atop the other contained on the top a figure personating Fortune, and underneath "thrie fair virgynnis, all cled in maist precious attyrement, callit [Love] Justice and Policie" (p. 190).[11] After a speech, the queen moved on to the Cross where "thair was standand four fair virgynnis, cled in the maist hevenlie clething, and fra the quhilk croce the wyne ran out at the spouttis in greit abundance ..." (p. 190). Exactly what took place at the Salt Trone seems difficult to determine; the burgh records refer to speakers and the burning upon "the skaffet maid at the said trone, the maner of ane sacrifice ..." (pp. 190-91). Other sources refer to the effigy of a priest being burnt and a condemnation of the mass (p. 191n). If true, then pageantry here loses some of its tact; we recall the political and propagandistic nature of many of the entertainments.

The final device, stationed at the Nether Bow, had a scaffold containing a dragon, also burned. After, the queen heard "ane psalme song, hir hienes past to hir abbay of Halyrudhous with the said convoy and nobilities ..." (p. 191). The cupboard, which had been carried throughout the processional, the authorities presented to her, and she received it graciously. From the events of this civic pageant several points, rather unrelated, emerge. First, having to depend on scanty burgh records reminds us how difficult a study of pageantry would be without printed texts, such as the one used as the basis for discussion of Elizabeth's 1559 entry. Again we see considerable reliance on the use of scaffolds, here relatively simple ones, on which the "dramatic action" can take place. Most of the show here in Edinburgh relies on allegorical figures and depends on a religious background as well. But the overt confronting of Mary with signs of a religion which she did not embrace is unusual; yet we see that something as innocent as a civic pageant can be a two-edged sword in serving nationalistic purposes. The use of the cloud that opened to reveal the young boy illustrates a sophistication of machinery not found in the earlier London pageant; such machines will play increasingly important roles in the pageants to come. Obviously, we find a recognizable dramatic form for the royal entry, whether in London or in Edinburgh.

While on progress in 1565, Elizabeth paid a visit to Warwickshire, partly to visit the Earl of Leicester, and while in the area made an entry into Coventry in the middle of August. Leaders of the city met her outside the city and escorted her in, and citizens lined the streets to welcome her. The Recorder made a speech and presented the queen with a purse of gold. The records of the city are unfortunately very brief and not full of detail. For example, the Annals indicate: "The Queen came to this City the Tanners Pageant stood at St. Johns Church the Drapers Pageant at the Cross the Smiths pageant at Littlepark Street end and the

---

[11]There is a blank in the MS. of the records; other sources name Love.

Weavers Pageant at Much Park street"; and "she came on Saturday night and stayed untill Monday and on Tuesday the Mayor and Aldermen went to Dine with the Court at Kenelworth...."[12] The precise nature of these "pageants" remains uncertain, and no more detail appears. One could guess that they somehow correspond to the "pageants" established by the medieval guilds in Coventry.

Similarly, a few years later Elizabeth again came to Warwickshire, this time to Warwick itself in August 1572. A manuscript preserved in the Records Office in Warwick provides full details of the visit in which the queen got a traditional welcome with a speech by the Recorder. The only feature worth much of our attention here was the mock-battle which took place one evening, and sham battles occur with some frequency throughout Elizabeth's reign. A fort contained "slender tymber coverid with canvais in this fort were apointid divers persons to serve as soldiers, ... Some others apointid to cast out fire woorks as squibbes and balles of fyre."[13] Across from this fort stood another one commanded by the Earl of Oxford with a "lusty band of Gentlemen." Mortar pieces brought up from London provided much of the noise between the forts; assaults and charges occurred. The author notes a strange quality about some of the materials: "For the wild fyre falling into the Ryver Aven wold for a tyme lye still, and than agayn rise and flye abrode casting furth many flasshes and flambes whereat the quene Majesty tok great pleasure ..." (fol. 69b-70a). When the time came for the overthrow of the fort, "A Dragon flieing casting out huge flames and squibes lighted upon the fort and so set fyere thereon, to the subversion therof ..." (fol. 70a). This delight with fireworks diminished somewhat because some of the fireworks went astray and set fire to a couple of houses and burned them completely. Dramatic purpose is admittedly minimal in the entertainment here at Warwick, but other writers will take this basic situation of battle and make a dramatic occasion out of it.

A trip westward in the summer of 1574 encouraged another civic pageant in the form of a royal entry; this time the city of Bristol entertained Elizabeth in mid-August. Having a text of the events, we know many of the details of the show, which essentially had two parts: first day an entry into the city where allegorical characters welcomed the queen, and on subsequent days a battle raged at specially prepared forts. Thomas Churchyard was the primary author of the show, evinced by his text and by an entry in the city records; thus for the first

---

[12]Coventry Records Office, *City Annals*, F7, fol. 27[b]; information also given in Nichols, *Progresses of Elizabeth*, I, 192. See also Thomas Sharp, *A Dissertation on the Pageants or Dramatic Mysteries Anciently Performed at Coventry* (Coventry, 1825) in which Sharp discusses the various guilds' pageants; unfortunately there is not enough information about this 1565 visit to know for certain if the companies merely mounted their traditional pageants.

[13]Warwick County Records Office, *Black Book MS.*, fol. 69[b]. A transcription of this MS. is found in Thomas Kemp, *The Black Book of Warwick* (Warwick, 1898). See also Nichols, *Progresses*, I, 319-20.

time in this historical period we can be certain about the identity of the deviser of entertainment.

Records preserved in the Bristol Archives provide information about receipts and expenditures, revealing, for example, that money collected from different wards of the city yielded over £535.[14] Interesting too is the receipt of money for the sale of the canvas which had covered the High Cross and which had been used at the forts; one recalls the city fathers of London back in 1559 wanting to preserve some of the "stuff" of the pageants for possible future use. In Bristol citizens plan to market some of the materials. One whole page in the Audits lists the expenditures which approached £1,000 and ranged from cleaning and repairing the streets, refurbishing the Guildhall, and providing ordnance for the forts to making beer available for the workers. Painting and gilding the High Cross and the gates of the city cost over £93 (Audits, p. 313). In addition there appears an item "for setting up a Scaffold at the highe crosse for the Oracion viij^s iij^d," and an expenditure "for setting up a gallery in the marsh for the Quenes majestie to se the tryumphes xij^{li} iiij^s iiij^d," and to "lxxxv pyoners who wrought at the fortes iiij^{li} v^s." And to Churchyard "for his travayle bothe in the ffortes and concernyng oracions" the sum of £6 13s. 4d. One may take the categories of expenses here at Bristol as typical while wishing for fuller records from other cities.

Standing at the High Cross in Bristol a young boy personating Fame welcomed the queen to the city:

And knowyng of thy commyng heer,
my duetty bad me goe:
Before unto this present place,
the nues therof to shoe.[15]

And when the citizens got word of the sovereign's intended visit—
The youth, the age, the ritch, the poer,
cam runnyng all on heap.
And clappyng hands, cried maynly out,
O blessed be the owre:
Our queen is comming to the town,
with princely trayn and powre.

Fame's speech closes by informing the queen of the pastimes planned for her, "a shoe on land and seas ..." (p. 101). "Than Faem flang up a great Garland, to the rejoysyng of the beholders."

[14]Bristol Archives, *Audits 1570-74*, p. 290.
[15]Thomas Churchyard, *The Firste Parte of Churchyardes Chippes* (London, 1575), p. 100^v-101. All quotations are from this original edition. Also available in Nichols, I, 396f.

At the next gate in the city three boys represented the allegorical figures of Salutation, Gratulation, and Obedient Good Will; two of them spoke, "and all they three drue theyr swords whan it was named, the hoel staet is reddie to defend (against all dissencions) a pesable Prynce ..." (p. 101ᵛ). Salutation gives rather traditional words of welcome, adding: "And wee poer silly boyes, / that cam from skoell of laet: / Rejoyce and clap our hands withall, / as members of thy staet. / Our dueties heer to shoe, / and further moer in deed ..." (p. 101ᵛ). He then specifies some of the entertainment alluded to by Fame:

> Heer is O mightie Queen,
> in way of myrth and sport:
> A matter movd tween Peace and warre,
> and therfore buylt a Fort.
> Dissenshon breeds the brawll,
> and that is Pomp, and Pried:
> The Fort on law and order stands,
> and still in peace would bied....
> The Fortres representith peace,
> and takes thy part O Queen. (pp. 101ᵛ-102)

And Gratulation adds information also about the coming day's events, casting on the entertainment an allegorical coloring through which it should be viewed. This brief royal entry preserves the basic form of earlier ones with no dramatic interaction among the allegorical characters; instead, speeches delivered to the queen have the unique function here of preparing for the next days' events. The entry thus functions as a "prologue" to the fuller drama that takes place outside the streets of the city.

A small fort called Feeble Policy and a much larger one both stood near the water where on a special scaffold sat the sovereign. The speeches spoken on that first day could not be heard by Elizabeth; but Churchyard includes them anyway, "so you must heer the speeches or els shal you be ignorant of the hoel matter" (p. 104). Basically Dissension passed between War and Peace and set about stirring up trouble, including the forces of War; and soldiers moved against the little fort and "wan it with great fury, and so rased it and overthrue hit down to the earth" (p. 106). Help dispatched from the main fort did not avail; in fact, it too suffered siege until the day ended, and the queen went by torchlight back to her lodging.

Several members of the court added to the drama of the next day as they joined in the battle as unscheduled actors, apparently recognizing a good show when they saw one. The assault on the main fort continued, and up the water came three ships chasing another one bringing supplies to the fort. In desperation the fort sent a man to the sovereign to plead for aid; he brought a book cov-

THE REIGN OF ELIZABETH

ered in green velvet which explained the device, and, having swum to where the queen sat, spoke to her begging—

> ... your curtyes ayd,
> in their defence that peace desiers:
> Whose staet is maed afrayd,
> by fals dissenshons kindled fiers.
> As your poer people have,
> throw peace possest great gayn and good:
> So still sutch peace they crave,
> as may avoyd the losse of blood. (p. 106ᵛ)

But the battle continued "*till the very night approtched, at which time the Prince partted and stoed marvelously well contented with that she had seen*" (p. 107). Slowly the dramatist builds toward the total involvement of the queen in the action as she must act out her part in this struggle between War and Peace.

By the final day War had "waxt a weery" as had the Fort, and so Persuasion went forth to try for mediation of the quarrel. Persuasion argues about the destructive nature of war, while also allowing that wars when used well keep the world in fear and awe (a thought of much currency in the Elizabethan court no doubt). In responding to Persuasion, City speaks unreservedly in praise of the queen "by whom our peace is kept: / And under whom this Citie long, / and land hath safely slept"; and he grows more expansive:

> O England joy with us:
> And kis the steps whear she doth tread,
> that keeps her countrey thus.
> In peace and rest, and perfait stay,
> whearfore the god of peace:
> In peace by peace our peace presarve,
> and her long lief encrease. (pp. 109-109ᵛ)

But such sentiments could not stay the battle, and on it raged until the enemy saw new forces from the court joining in; then peace came with the Fort insisting that its strength derived from the "corrage of good people, and the force of a mighty prince (who saet and beheld all these doyngs) ..." (p. 109ᵛ). And so with the shouting of "God save the Queen," "these triumphes and warlik pastimes finished...." While forts of feeble policy might indeed fall, no fort supported by "good people" and their sovereign shall be overcome. Heady praise for Elizabeth, who becomes through this roughly allegorical battle the virtual embodiment of Peace, sending to the just cause sufficient aid. Perhaps Churchyard is relying on the traditional three-day battles of the epics in the length of his production; at any rate, each day leads to the final commitment of the queen to the action and the triumph of peace. Thus the mock-battles of earlier years gain lengthy extension at Bristol and have a dramatic purpose with speeches, actors, participating audience, and even a semblance of plot. The lack of the procession and the contained nature of the location help make possible dramatic unity as well as the expected thematic unity. The conflict between opposing forces gets dramatic life, thus abandoning the more static form of the royal entry entertainment.

The busy summer days of 1575 found Elizabeth on progress, receiving entertainment at several places, such as the Earl of Leicester's Kenilworth Castle, located in the Warwickshire which the queen had visited several times before. Accordingly, we have the first civic pageant taking place on the estate of a nobleman who was primarily responsible for the planned dramatic entertainment as well as the many days spent in Elizabeth's favorite recreation—hunting. The days at Kenilworth achieve singular importance, for, among other things, we see the pageant form taking a different shape as location and time dictate new techniques. The processional pattern does not occur except for the sovereign's initial arrival; the entertainment has diverse scope. The primarily mythological and pastoral subject matter reflects the Arcadian world of such estate entertainments. While the shows took place on the Earl's land, the public also participated, as citizens from Coventry came on a Sunday afternoon to provide some dramatic episodes. An established poet-dramatist, George Gascoigne, has links with the pageant. One could indeed designate this as the beginning of the crucially important relationship of dramatists writing not only for the regular theater but also for the pageant theater, a relationship that begins here in the Elizabethan era and continues even more extensively in the Stuart period. Though one can only guess the total costs of the Kenilworth days for the queen's visit which lasted over two weeks, the details of the festivities survive in two sources: Laneham's contemporary letter to Master Martin which appeared as a printed text and Gascoigne's *Princely Pleasures at Kenelworth Castle*.[16] Laneham asserts of these magnificent shows that in all his travels he "saw none any where so memorabl, I tell you plain."[17]

On Satuday, 9 July, about eight o'clock in the evening the queen arrived and gained welcome in the park from one of the ten Sybils clad in white silk who wished for the queen "long prosperitee health and felicitee ..." (p. 8). At the

---

[16]Both texts are reprinted in Nichols, I, 420f. Traditionally Laneham's first name has been "Robert," but Muriel C. Bradbrook in *The Rise of the Common Player* (London, 1962), p. 143f, argues that Laneham was "John" Laneham, an actor in Leicester's Men. In fact Nichols had originally made this suggestion in I, 422n. Obviously "Robert" is wrong, since there seems to have been no such person, but the evidence for John Laneham is not entirely convincing.

[17]*A Letter: Whearin, part of the entertainment untoo the Queenz Majesty, at Killingworth Castl, ... iz signified* ([London, 1575]), p. 2. All quotations for this pageant are from this text except the ones from Gascoigne.

main gate a Porter, dressed somewhat like Hercules with a club and keys, first displayed impatience and annoyance at all the clamor; but he then recognized the queen (in fact, he was "pearced" at her presence), proclaimed free passage to all, yielded his keys and club, and on his knees humbly prayed pardon for his ignorance and impatience—a request readily granted by Elizabeth. Trumpeters each standing eight feet tall sounded "up a tune of welcum ..." (p. 9). At the inner gate the sovereign received greetings from the Lady of the Lake "(famous in king Arthurz book) with too Nymphes waiting uppon her, arrayed all in sylks ..." (p. 10). The Lady used fascinating locomotion: "from the midst of the Pool, whear, upon a moovabl Iland, bright blazing with torches, she [Lady of Lake] floting to land, met her Majesty with a well penned meter ..." (p. 10). She explained something of the ancient history of the castle and then offered Elizabeth the lake and her power therein. Laneham adds: "This Pageaunt was clozd up with a delectable harmony of Hautboiz, Shalmz, Cornets, and such oother looud muzik, that held on while her Majestie, pleazauntly so passed from thence toward the Castl gate ..." (p. 11). Passing across the castle bridge, the queen found on its seven pairs of posts gifts left by seven mythological gods: Sylvanus (birds), Pomona (fruit), Ceres (grain), Bacchus (wine), Neptune (fish), Mars (instruments of war), and Phoebus (musical instruments). Because of darkness, the Latin poem written on a tablet over the castle gate could not be read by the queen; therefore, a boy dressed like a Poet explained the gifts of the gods and read the poem.[18] Laneham's account for that day closes with a farewell to Master Martin and a reminder—"Be yee not wery, for I am skant in the midst of my matter" (p. 15). The world of romance and mythology permeates this opening show, as does the theme of Elizabeth's power.

Sunday passed in a curious conjuction of activities with the day spent in rest, meditation, and divine services, but the night in explosive fireworks. Returning from the hunt on Monday evening, 11 July, Elizabeth encountered in the woods *Hombre Salvagio*, "with an Oken plant pluct up by the roots in hiz hande, himselfe forgrone all in moss and Ivy ..." (p. 18). This Savage Man, in a role written and played by Gascoigne, perplexed by all the goings-on about him, eventually calls out to his friend Echo to help him. Echo assures him of a sovereign's presence to which the Savage responds: "Pauzing and wisely viewing a while, noow full certeynlie seemez thy tale to be true" (p. 19). The occasion dissolves into elaborate praise of the queen with the Savage saying to her:

Could I but touch the strings which you so heavenly handle,
I woulde confesse that Fortune then full freendly dyd me dandle.
O Queene without compare, you must not think it strange,

---

[18]Gascoigne says that the verses were devised by Master Muncaster, probably the same Richard Mulcaster who was connected with Elizabeth's 1559 royal entry.

That here amid this wildernesse, your glorie so doth raunge;
The windes resound your worth, the rockes record your name,
These hills, these dales, these woods, these waves, these fields pronounce
    your fame ... [19]

In such a world of the progress pageant, seemingly spontaneous events occur (planned of course) all with the intent of heaping praises on the honored guest. We often find in the Elizabethan literature the savage animal or man being calmed and charmed by the obvious presence of genuine nobility, such as in Spenser's *The Faerie Queene.*

After some bad weather on Friday and Saturday, Sunday, 17 July, was pleasant enough for several events of entertainment, most of them heavily indebted to folk tradition. "All the lustie lads and bolld bachelarz of the parish" gathered for the burlesque marriage or "brydeale," presented in the tiltyard, including the selection of a mock bride and groom. Of the groom's appearance Laneham writes: "a fayr strawn hat with a capitall crooun steepl wyze on hiz hed: a payr of harvest glovez on hiz hands, az a sign of good husbandry: a pen and inkorn at his bak. For he woold be known to be bookish ..." (p. 27). The uncomplimentary portrait of the "bride" describes her as "ugly fooul ill favord"; but she takes her role seriously, "because shee hard say shee shoold dauns before the Queen, in which feat shee thought shee woold foote it az finely az the best ..." (p. 29). Running at quintain followed this "wedding," becoming a fairly riotous affair. Indeed, Laneham says: "By my trooth Master Martyn twaz a lively pastime, I beleeve it woold have mooved sum man too a right meery mood, thoogh had it be toold him hiz wife lay a dying" (p. 32). The spirit of the Lord of Misrule broods over the events.

The Coventry men also presented another device, their ancient "storial shew," their "Hok Tuesday" play about the historical fight between the English and Danes which occurred in November of A.D. 1002. The redoubtable Captain Cox, "cleen trust and gartered above the knee, all fresh in a velvet cap" (p. 36), led the English forces, and from the first "the meeting waxt sumwhat warm ..." (p. 37). The battle raged on: "Twise the Danes had the better, but at the last conflict, beaten doun, overcom and many led captive for triumph by our English weemen" (p. 37). Failing to see all of this display, the queen asked the Coventry people to return on Tuesday and present the show again which they did to her great pleasure, and she rewarded them with two bucks and some money. An interesting sidelight on this Coventry play emerges: apparently the drama, a regular presentation, had recently been repressed—an apparent victim of the Reforma-

---

[19]Gascoigne, *The Princelye Pleasures at the Courte at Kenelwoorth,* reprint (London, 1821), p. 7. All quotations from Gascoigne are from this reprint. Also found in *The Complete Works of George Gascoigne.* ed. John W. Cunliffe (Cambridge, 1910), vol. II.

tion, or at least Puritanism. As Laneham says: "they knu no cauz why [it was suppressed] on less it wear by the zeal of certain theyr Preacherz," men "sum what too sour in preaching awey theyr pastime ..." (p. 33). Therefore they sent a petition to the queen "that they might have theyr playz up agayn" (p. 34). Similar types of suppression during this same period led of course to the demise of the cycle plays whose origin came in the medieval period.[20]

Swimming upon a Mermaid, Triton, "Neptunes blaster," appeared to Elizabeth on the evening of Monday, 18 July, and sounded his trumpet as her majesty came in sight upon the bridge. He tells her "how a cruel Knight, one syr Bruse sauns pitee, a mortall enmy untoo Ladiez of estate, had long lyen about the banks of this pooll in wayt with his bands heer to distress the Lady of the lake ..." (p. 41); he bids the sovereign to turn her presence toward the pool "whearby yoor only prezens shallbe matter sufficient of abandoning this uncurtess knight, and putting all his bands too flight" and of delivering the Lady (p. 41). Feeling the new deliverance, by and by the Lady "with her too Nymphs, floting upon her moovable Ilands (*Triton* on hiz mermaid skimming by) approched toward her highnes on the bridge ..." (p. 42). She thanks the queen for the freedom in words recorded by Gascoigne:

> Untyll this day, the lake was never free
> From his assaults, and other of his knights,
> Untill such tyme as he dyd playnely see
> Thy presence dread, and feared of all wyghts;
> Which made him yeeld, and all his bragging bands:
> Resigning all into thy princely hands. (Gascoigne, p. 9)

Shortly Arion, "that excellent and famouz Muzicien," came floating up on a twenty-four feet long Dolphin and soon began his song "compoounded of six severall instruments al coovert, casting soound from the Dolphins belly within ..." (p. 43). While Gascoigne, who records the verses and the song of Arion (whom he calls *Protheus*), and Laneham express enchantment with the whole affair, another report indicates that the person playing Arion being hoarse, boldly tore off his disguise and swore "he was none of Arion not he, but eene honest Harry Goldingham," come to bid her Majesty welcome to Kenilworth. Such boldness pleased the queen, "better, then if it had gone thorough in the right way."[21] Mechanical dolphins, music, mythological figures, and praise to the liberating power of the queen all conspire to produce a pageant scene worthy its name. Actually, as Gascoigne reports, this forms an abbreviated version of what had been planned, which would have included two days earlier a battle with the

---

[20]See Glynne Wickham, *Early English Stages* (London, 1963), II, "Book One," chapters I-IV.
[21]British Library, Harleian MS. 6395, item #221, fol. 36[b].

malicious "Bruse sauns pitee." Gascoigne himself had prepared an elaborate play about *Zabeta* and had the actors all in readiness, but they never performed the play.

Laneham writes of Wednesday, 20 July; "A this day allso waz thear such earnest tallk and appointment of remooving that I gave over my noting, and harkened after my hors" (p. 46), though he does include some details of the minstrel who sang of King Arthur. Actually Elizabeth stayed until the following Wednesday when she took her leave of the pleasantries of Kenilworth. At the bidding of the Earl of Leicester, Gascoigne prepared the farewell, and he himself appeared to the queen as Sylvanus while Elizabeth was out on the final hunt. In a long speech which he delivered running alongside her horse, Sylvanus describes the dismay of the gods at her departure and tells her also of the cruelties of a nymph called Zabeta who had turned all lovers into trees. Eventually "her Majestie came by a close arbor made all of hollie; and whiles Silvanus pointed to the same, the principall bush shaked. For therein were placed, both straunge musicke, and one who was there appointed to represent *Deepedesire*" (Gascoigne, p. 26). He speaks and shares the dismay at the queen's intended departure and pleads with her "yet longer to remayne, / Or still to dwell amongst us here!" (p. 27). Finally the musicians sound; and Deep Desire sings his song:

> Come, Muses, come, and helpe me to lament;
> Come woods, come waves, come hils, come doleful dales;
> Since life and death are both against me bent,
> Come gods, come men, beare witnesse of my bales!
> O heavenly Nimphs, come helpe my heavy heart,
> With sighes to see Dame Pleasure thus depart! (p. 28)

And with Sylvanus' closing remarks of farewell, the entertainment at Kenilworth ends. Leicester had every reason to be pleased with the pageant which successfully created an imaginative world of mythological gods and goddesses and of Arthurian romance, not to mention the ingenious mechanical devices. The progress pageants help introduce mythological figures into the whole stream of civic entertainments, and such characters eventually populate all forms of pageantry; clearly the Kenilworth experience offers a vital impetus in this new direction. Besides the obvious unstinted praise of Elizabeth both implicit and explicit, a basic theme recurs: Elizabeth brings in her person power to charm and to free—gods bring her gifts, wild men experience taming, the fearful gain freedom. She appears as a regenerating and liberating force, just as the Coventry "brydeale" might remind us of the renewing power of nature seen here in these "rites of spring." These Kenilworth festivities illustrate the episodic and diffuse dramatic nature of progress pageants—entertainment supersedes dramatic coherence.

At the end of August, Elizabeth arrived at Sir Henry Lee's house at Woodstock for entertainment by this follower of the Earl of Leicester. The atmosphere,
not surprisingly, recalls that at Kenilworth with a mythical world in evidence.
Gascoigne shares in the entertainment because he translated the long story told
by Hemetes here at Woodstock. Unfortunately, the printed text which survives
remains imperfect; and we pick up the action at the point where Hemetes the
Hermit sets the scene for his long tale about two knights and a damsel who accompanied one of them. Hemetes himself had been blind but miraculously recovered his sight in the presence of the queen, a theme familiar in the Kenilworth
shows. A special place, "a fine Bower made of purpose covered with greene
Ivie,"[22] provided seats for Elizabeth and others while they listened to Hemetes.
When the story ended, "the poore Hermit loden as it were with beades and other
such ornaments of his profession" led the way before the queen who fell into
discourse with the hermit (sig. B4). Finally they reached a "most simple Hermit-
age" where Hemetes took his leave of Elizabeth: "I must leave your majestie,
promising to pray, as for my selfe, that whosoever wish you best, may never wish
in vayne" (sig. B4ᵛ). Eventually a Faery Queen with six children in a "waggon of
state" appeared before Elizabeth; and as she made her way home in her coach
"closelie in an Oke she hearde the sound both of voice and instrument ..." (sig.
C2ᵛ), again reminiscent of Kenilworth. This time, however, we hear the tragical
song of Despair:

> But what availes with Tragical complaint,
> not hoping helpe, the furies to awake?
> Or why should I the happie mindes acquaint
> with dolefull tunes, their setled peace to shake?
> O yee that here behold infortunes fare,
> there is no griefe that may with mine compare. (sig. C3)

And thus temporarily, for this summer at least, the revels end.

Sharing some common ground with the pageants at Kenilworth and Woodstock, the entertainment at Wanstead took place in May 1578 at the manor house
near Greenwich which belonged to the Earl of Leicester. This show, generally
known as *The Lady of May*, Sir Philip Sidney wrote, who had been present at
Kenilworth a few summers before. Like the other progress pageants, this one also
relies heavily on a type of pastoral romance. It begins very simply as a "spontaneous" reaction in Elizabeth's walking in the garden at Wanstead: "... as she passed

---

[22]*The Quenes Majesties Entertainment at Woodstock* (London, 1585), sig. B1. All quotations are from
this text of which sheet A in the British Library copy is missing. There is an edition of the entertainment by A. W. Pollard (Oxford, 1903, 1910). See brief discussion in Bradbrook, *Rise of Common
Player*, pp. 251-2.

owne into the grove there came sodenly amonge the trayne one apparelled Like an honeste mans wyf of the Countrie where crienge oute for Justice...."[23] This woman's daughter who has been chosen "May Lady" is "oppressed with tooe [men] both lovinge her, both equally liked of her, both strivinge to deserve her ..." (p. 108); Elizabeth, asked to help, thus becomes involved in the action, much as she had at Bristol and at Kenilworth. From the woods emerged six shepherds who supported the cause of Espilus and six foresters who rallied around the cause of Therion, each side believing its man worthy of the Lady of May. A schoolmaster Rombus from a village nearby accompanied them; his pedantry reminds one of Holofernes in Shakespeare's *Love's Labour's Lost*. When the queen comes in their midst, they do not recognize her, "yet some thinge ther was which made them startle aside and gaze uppon her ..." (p. 109). Lalus, an old shepherd, presents the problem, and then Rombus with his pseudo-Latinity delivers an oration which the May Lady cuts off and says: "Awaie away you tedious foole, your eyes are not worthie to looke to yonder princely sighte, muche Lesse your foolish tongue to troble her wyse eares ..." (p. 110). And the May Lady sets forth her plight, not before saying of Elizabeth whom, of course, she does not recognize as being the queen: "the troth is you excell me in all thinges wherin I desier most to excell, and that makes me geve this homage unto you as to the beautifullest Ladie theis woodes have ever receaved ..." (p. 111). She tries to articulate the differences between the wealthy and stable shepherd Espilus and the "Livelier" forester Therion. They ask the queen to help decide simply "whether the manie Desertes and manie faultes of *Therion* or the smale Desertes and no faultes *Espilus* be to be preferred" (p. 112).

To sharpen the contrast between the two men, Sidney has Therion and Espilus engage in a sort of singing contest; "the sheppherdes and foresters grewe to a greate contention whether of theire fellowes had songe beste, or whether the estate of shepheardes or Fosters were the more worshipfull ..." (p. 113). The "debate" takes another turn as Dorcas the shepherd and Rixus a forester, with occasional interruption by Rombus, discuss the relative merits of each calling and in a sense debate the virtues of the contemplative (shepherd) versus the active (forester) life. Finally, "yt pleased her Majestie to Judge yt *Espilus* did the better deserve her [Lady of May]" and "uppon the Judgemente geven the sheppheardes and fosters made a full consorte of theire Cornettes and Recorders, and then did *Espilus* singe this songe tendinge to the greatnes of his Joyes ..." (p. 117). The transcribers of the manuscript rightly conclude that Elizabeth's choice must have been something of a disappointment to the earl and to Sidney, for Therion appears as a Leicester figure (p. 105). The speeches and songs of this

---

[23]All quotations are from the transcript of the Helmingham MS. found in Robert Kimbrough and Philip Murphy, "The Helmingham Hall Manuscript of Sidney's *The Lady of May*: A Commentary and Transcription," *Renaissance Drama* ns 1 (1968): 107.

entertainment help forge dramatic unity as the queen herself, as in the Bristol pageant, becomes part of the dramatic action.

Later in that summer of 1578 Elizabeth made a progress throughout Suffolk and Norfolk, which included the civic pageant presented in her honor in Norwich where she arrived on 16 August. Thomas Churchyard, who four years earlier had busied himself in the pageant at Bristol, has moved his shop over toward the eastern coast and gets involved with the planning and devising of several parts of the Norwich festivities. He, in fact, prepared a pamphlet which describes most, though not all, the events. Like the Bristol entertainment, this one also contains a royal entry on the first day and different events outside the city on subsequent days. Unfortunately, the Chamberlains' Accounts of Norwich for this historical period do not survive, and we can know little about the city's preparation or expenses.

Upon the sovereign's arrival, Sir Robert Wood, mayor of Norwich, and three score of "the most comelie yoong men of the citie" attired in black and yellow greeted her as did one personating Gurgunt, "sometime king of England, which builded the castell of Norwich...."[24] In response to the mayor's oration, Elizabeth allegedly replied: "... we come not therefore, but for that which in right is our owne, the hearts and true allegiance of our subjects, which are the greatest riches of a kingdome; whereof as we assure our selves in you, so do you assure your selves in us of a loving and gratious soveraigne" (p. 378). The mythical king Gurgunt was to have spoken, but a sudden rain shower interrupted the proceedings—not the last time the weather interferes at Norwich. Nevertheless, the mere presence of Gurgunt lends a historical sanction to the events as he rouses himself out of the past to pay homage to the present queen.

Undeterred by weather, as the English must be, Elizabeth and her entourage moved into the city proper where St. Stephen's gate had been freshly decorated with the queen's arms, the shield of St. George, and the arms of the city. The inner side of the gate carried a historical reminder: "On the right side was gorgeouslie set foorth the red rose, signifieng the house of Yorke [sic]; on the left side the white rose, representing the house of Lancaster [sic]; in the midst was the white and red rose united, expressing the union ..." (p. 380). Verses underscoring the meaning appeared on the gate: "Division kindled strife, / Blist union quencht the flame: / Thense sprang our noble Phenix deare, / The pearelesse prince of fame." Giving mute testimony to the triumph of the Tudors, this gate finds its symbolic prototype back at Gracious street in Elizabeth's 1559 entry into London where a genealogical tree epitomized the union achieved by the Tudors

---

[24]Holinshed, *Chronicles*, IV, 376. All quotations are from this source with the exception of the citations from Churchyard's tract. See also Nichols, II, 136-213 and the original pamphlet, *The Joyfull Receyving of the Queenes most excellent Majestie into hir Highnesse Citie of Norwich* (London, [1578]). Holinshed seems to be largely indebted to this tract.

and carried forth in the person of the present monarch. A song celebrating the citizens' joy at the queen's arrival in Norwich closes this episode.

As the retinue passed farther on, they found a scaffold containing "an excellent boy, well and gallantlie decked, in a long white robe of taffata ..." (p. 381). He appeared to the queen as the music on this scaffold subsided and spoke on behalf of the citizens:

> ... Great is the joy that Norwich feeles this daie:
> If well we waid the greatnesse of your mind,
> Few words would serve, we had but small to saie.
> But knowing that your goodnesse takes things well
> That well are meant, we boldlie did proceed:
> And so good queene, both welcome and farewell,
> Thine owne we are in heart, in word, and deed. (p. 381)

"The boy thereupon flang up his garland," and the queen enjoyed the device.

The first tableau pageant, located on St. Stephen's street, had a scaffold "builded somewhat in maner like a stage of forty foot long and in breadth eight foot. From the standing place upward was a bank framed in maner of a free stone wall ..." (p. 381). Sentences extolling the causes of this commonwealth include: "God truelie preached, Justice dulie executed, The people obedient, Idlenesse expelled, Labour cherished, Universall concord preserved." Singling out such virtues for praise had of course been the function of at least two of the devices in the 1559 entry which enumerated the causes for a flourishing and stable kingdom. Part of the scaffold here in Norwich contained paintings that depicted several looms and weavers busily at them. Live actors join these still figures on the stage area: "at the one end eight small women children spining worsted yarne, and at the other end as manie knitting of worsted yarne hose ..." (pp. 381-2). A "pretie boy richlie apparelled, which represented the common wealth of the citie" stood in the middle of the stage and upon the queen's arrival spoke to her explaining the industry of Norwich.

The final part of the first day's entry came in the form of a device in the market place where a second scaffold, "thwarting the street," had been built some fifty-two feet wide and divided into three gates. Over each gate "was as it were a chamber, which chambers were replenished with musike" (p. 382). Across the top of all the gates stretched a stage, "rich and delitefull. The whole worke ... seemed to be jasper and marble" (p. 382). Five women, representing the city of Norwich, Deborah, Judith, Hester, and Martia "sometime queene of England," occupy the stage; and each in turn speaks to Elizabeth. Norwich confesses: "... Thou art my joy next God, I have none other, / My princesse and my peerlesse queene, my loving nursse and mother" (p. 383). Deborah, not unlike the Deborah of the 1559 entry, reviews her accomplishments and bids Elizabeth—

Continue as thou hast begun, weed out the wicked rout,
Uphold the simple, meeke and good, pull downe the proud and stout.
Thus shalt thou live and reigne in rest, and mightie God shalt please,
Thy state be sure, thy subjects safe, thy commonwealth at ease.
Thy God shall grant thee length of life, to glorifie his name,
Thy deeds shall be recorded in the booke of lasting fame. (p. 383)

Judith cites her own valour and asks the queen to "hold for aie a noble victors part," while Hester urges Elizabeth: "Be still (good queene) their refuge and their rocke ..." (p. 384). And Martia, who has links with Gurgunt, offers the ancient homage to the sovereign—

Which homage mightie queene accept: the realme and right is thine,
The crowne, the scepter, and the sword to thee we do resigne,
And wish to God, that thou maist reigne twise Nestors yeares in peace,
Triumphing over all thy foes, to all our joyes increase, Amen. (p. 385)

After a song of praise, the entertainment closed for the day. Voices of the past whether Biblical or national have bestowed a blessing on the queen, complimenting her while offering instruction about the virtues to be pursued. The royal entry form continues its basic pattern as seen in the 1559 pageant—processional, tableaux, set speeches; dramatic action remains minimal.

Churchyard informs us that he devised the scene on Monday, 18 August, which included the visit of Mercury in a stunning coach that took its place in an open green "before a window at the whyche the Queene stoode, and mighte be playnely seene, and openly viewed."[25] Vast crowds gathered about to see the chariot and Mercury, who in a lengthy speech depicts himself as sent from the gods to greet the queen and to tell her how the citizens busy themselves to prepare entertainment:

... And since I have espyde that Princesse there, ...
I kisse hir steppes, and shew my maisters will,
And leave with hir such graces from above,
As alwayes shall commaund hir peoples love,
(Uphold hir reigne, maynteyne hir regall state,
Find out false harts, and make of subjects true,
Plant perfite peace, and roote up all debate)
So with this grace, good Queene now heere adue,

---

[25]Thomas Churchyard, *A Discourse of the Queenes Majesties Entertainment in Suffolk and Norfolk* (London, [1578]), sig. C2.

For I may now on earth no longer stey…. (sig. C3ᵛ)

Churchyard describes the coach, such "as few men have seene," "the whole …
was covered with Birdes, and naked Sprites hanging by the heeles in the aire and
cloudes, cunningly painted out…. And on the middle of that Coatch stoode a
high compassed Tower, bedeckt with golden and gay jewels, in the top whereof
was placed a faire plume of whyte feathers …" (sig. C4). Mercury himself added
to this display of color, for he came dressed in blue satin lined with gold cloth,
wearing a "peaked hatte" which had on it a pair of wings, "and wings on his heeles likewise." The golden rod which he carried contained wings also, as well as
"two wriggling or scrawling Serpentes, whiche seemed to have life when the
rodde was moved or shaken" (sig. C4). In full iconographical splendor Mercury
has brought sanction from the gods to these entertainments, suggesting the importance of this earthly queen.

Rushed and somewhat inconvenienced, Churchyard hurriedly got his actors
ready for the pageant on Tuesday; the root of the problem seems to have been the
city leaders, as Churchyard puts it: "… I was not well provided of thinges neces-
sarye for a Shewe (by meane of some crossing causes in the Citie) …" (sig. C4ᵛ).
Undaunted, he gathered his forces into an open field where many citizens had
also come, and they awaited the arrival of the queen for the dramatic presentation. A brief morality play unfolds with the forces of Venus and Cupid pitted
against Chastity and her followers; unlike the usual sort of tableau representation, this entertainment contains a discernible, if unconnected, plot. At the beginning Cupid appears riding in a coach and encounters the queen; again she, at
the center of attention, becomes part of the dramatic action. He explains in his
speech how he and his mother Venus had been cast out of heaven and have been
wandering about the earth where they encountered a Philosopher who portrayed
them as "the drosse, the scumme of earth and Skyes" (sig. D2). Venus fell into a
kind of madness because of the harsh treatment, and Cupid has come seeking
succour from the Court. But instead of help, he gets attacked by Chastity who
"suddainely in the view of the Queene, settes upon Cupid, and spoyles hym of his
Coatch, Bowe and all, and sets him a foote, and so rides in his Coatche to the
Queene" whom she addresses (sig. D2). Chastity clearly views herself in the role
of a virtue opposed to vice:

> … that proude ladde [Cupid], that makes so many slaves,
> Must needes find one, to daunt his Peacocks pride.
> Dame *Chastitie* is she that winnes the field,
> Whose breast is armd with thoughtes of vertues rare,
> Who to the fight doth bring no glittering shield,
> But cleane conceytes, which pure and blessed are,
> That strikes downe lust, and tames the wilfull mind,

Maynteynes the just, and holds up learning both. (sigs. D2-D2ᵛ)

Because Elizabeth has herself chosen the chaste life (and thus virtue), Chastity offers her Cupid's bow: "learne to shoote / At whome thou wilt, thy heart is so cleane, / Blind *Cupids* boltes therein can take no roote" (sig. D2ᵛ). While some might view this exaltation of Chastity as simply making a virtue out of necessity, Churchyard likely had a different attitude (at least in the presence of Elizabeth) as did Spenser where the theme of chastity governs Book III of *The Faerie Queene.*

Meanwhile Cupid has been off seeking aid from Wantonness and Riot, but eventually he flees from them so total had been the misery. (Cupid shares the technique of Mankind in *The Castle of Perseverance* wandering about from scaffold to scaffold following Covetousness or the World.) Now Cupid again meets the Philosopher "whose habitation was in a Rocke." He points to Cupid's errors, chiefly the presumption of being a god; and the Philosopher claims that Cupid is only—

> ... a kind of shade, as can no substance shoe,
> Begot by braynelesse blind delight, and nurst with natures foe.
> Fed up with faithlesse foode, and traynd in triflng toyes,
> Awakt with vice, and luld asleepe agayne with yrkesome joyes. (sig. D4)

The Philosopher fulfills something of the traditional role in morality drama of the one who tries to set the "child of sin" on the road to salvation by inducing remorse and abandonment of pride. But seduced again by Wantonness and Riot, Cupid leaves the Philosopher to go dwell with these rogues. The Philosopher then speaks, drawing the moral implications of what has been shown: "Through trifles light, sad things are sene, through vice is vertue found ..." (sig. E1). Modesty, Temperance, Good Exercise, and Shamefastness, "the wayting Maydes of Chastitie returne, come in and Sing" (sig. E1ᵛ). The song, not surprisingly, sharpens the contrast between the chaste life and the "leawd life" with the chaste life alone offering "immortall prayse." Modesty closes the pageant show with a speech addressed to the queen which in effect offers the assistance of her companions and herself:

> That still the feare of God, be burning in hir brest,
> Ther is the only house O Queene, wher we four maids wil rest,
> There we will service shew, there shall our vertues budde.... (sig. E2ᵛ)

This allegorical show thus lavishes indirect and direct praise on Elizabeth, herself a follower of Chastity, and offers instruction about this particular manifestation of the never-ceasing struggle between virtue and vice—a conflict which other pageant-dramatists will embody. Unlike the royal entry, this outdoor pageant abandons the processional form and focuses instead on dramatic action and speech—constant interchange among the characters who speak to one another, not simply to the queen.

Rain forced cancellation of an elaborate device, including water nymphs and the allegorical figures of Beauty, Manhood, Favour, Desert, Fortune, planned for Tuesday, 21 August; and Churchyard's many efforts, such as digging a special place for the nymphs, came to nought. He says somewhat philosophically: "Thus you see, a Shew in the open fielde is alwaies subject to the suddayne change of weather, and a number of more inconveniences than I expresse. But what shoulde I say of that whiche the Citie lost by this cause, Velvets, Silkes, Tinsels, and some cloth of gold, being cutte out for these purposes, and could not serve to any great effect after" (sig. E4ᵛ). Mythological gods and goddesses did appear that evening in "an excellent princelie maske," devised by Goldingham and presented before the queen.

Departure day came on Friday, 22 August; and "the streets towards saint Benets gate were hanged, from the one side to the other, with cords made of hearbs and floures, with garlands, coronets, pictures, rich cloths, and a thousand devises" (Holinshed, p. 401). A stage had also been prepared on which, in addition to musicians, stood the speaker Goldingham who said:

> ... Thou art our queene, our rocke and onelie staie,
> We are thine to serve by night and daie.
> Farewell oh queene, farewell oh mother deare, ...
> For thy great grace, God length thy life like Noy,
> To governe us, and eke thy realme in joy. Amen. (p. 402)

Which was followed by a song lamenting the queen's leaving:

> What have we doone, she will no longer staie?
> What may we doo to hold hir with us still?
> Shee is our queene, we subjects must obaie,
> Grant, though with greefe, to hir departing will.
> Conclude we then, and sing with sobbing breath,
> God length thy life (oh queene Elisabeth.) (p. 402)

Further out of the city Churchyard, himself dressed like a "water Sprite," and twelve boys dressed like water nymphs appeared before the queen out of the corner of a field in order, Churchyard says, "to do somewhat might make the Queene laugh ..." (sig. G2ᵛ). The boys, assuming the role of fairies, danced, as did Churchyard, and seven of them spoke to the queen recounting briefly some of the events of her Norwich visit and also bidding her farewell. Holinshed records ostensibly Elizabeth's parting words from the city: "I have laid up in my breast such good will, as I shall never forget Norwich; and proceeding onward did shake hir riding rod and said: Farewell Norwich, with the water standing in hir eies" (p. 403). The pageant-filled days at Norwich thus end, having contained a royal entry and several devices resembling the progress pageants (the appearance of Mercury, for example), as well as a show by Churchyard which celebrates the virtue of Chastity in morality play fashion. Such diversity of entertainment offers a good example of the wide range of pageantry in the Elizabethan period from the formal entry, through the episodic appearance of Mercury, to the dramatically coherent outdoor entertainment where moral debate manifests itself in dramatic conflict. A corresponding, increased reliance on dramatic speech and dialogue occur as one moves through these events at Norwich, culminating in Churchyard's outdoor drama. Elizabeth remains the magnetic center of the triumphs with the persons of history (national and Biblical), of mythology, and of moral allegory revolving around her and attracted to her, their lodestone, proclaiming her virtues and offering their unified support of her reign.

In the tiltyard at Whitehall in May 1581, Philip Sidney along with Fulke Greville, the Earl of Arundel, and Lord Windsor, calling themselves the Foster Children of Desire, laid siege to the Castle or Fortress of Beauty—the residence of Elizabeth.[26] On the opening day of this mock-battle, reminiscent of scenes earlier at Warwick and Bristol, the challengers had with them a machine called a "Rowling trench," which carried cannons of wood, gunners clothed in crimson, "and within the saide trench was cunningly conveyed, divers kinde of most excellent musicke against the castle of *Beauty*."[27] As the warriors approached in the tiltyard, a young boy presented their speech of challenge, of course praising Elizabeth as the embodiment of beauty and virtue. When the trench neared the queen, a song urged:

Yeelde yeelde O yeelde, trust not on beauties pride,
fayrenesse though fayer, is but a feeble shielde,
When strong Desire, which vertues love doth guide,
claymes but to gaine his due. O yeelde O yeelde. (sig. A8ᵛ)

---

[26]Two events in Edinburgh, James VI's royal entry in 1579 and his wife, Anne's passage through the city in 1590 chronologically belong in this discussion of the Elizabethan period. However, these two pageants will be discussed in the next chapter on the Jacobean period since they concern the principal figures of that era.

[27]Henry Goldwell, *A briefe declaration of the shews, devices, speeches, and inventions, done and performed before the Queenes Majestie, and the French Ambassadours* (London, 1581), sig. A5ᵛ. All quotations will be from this text. Reprinted in Holinshed, IV, 435f; Nichols, II, 312f; and Jean Wilson, pp. 61-85.

Finally, the two cannons fire, "the one with sweet poulder, and the other with sweete water, very odoriferous and pleasaunt ...   And after that, was store of prettie scaling ladders, and the footmen threwe Flowers and such fancies against the walles ..." (sig. B1)—the weapons of love.

Of course the queen does not remain defenseless; one of the defendant's pages, arrayed like an Angel, spoke pledging a resolve to defend her, having been sent from above with assurances of aid. Two of the defenders, Parrat and Cooke, "were both in like armour beset, with apples and fruite, the one signifying Adam, and the other Eve, who had haire hung all down his Helmet" (B2ᵛ). Thus these original parents lend their support to the cause of Elizabeth, as do others, such as the one who appears, dressed like Mercury, and pronounces the fortress invincible. After running at the tilt, each side retires for the day with the children of Desire pledging to renew the conflict on the following day, which they do in grand style, if slightly less vigorous than before, for they "entered in a brave Charriot, (very finely and curiously decked) as men fore-wearied and half overcome ..." (sig. B8). On top of this chariot the knights sat with "a beautiful Lady, representing *Desire* about them, Wherunto their eyes were turned, in token what they desired...." This space also contained a full consort of musicians "who plaied still very doleful musicke as the Charriot moved...." The horses which drew the coach appeared decorated in white and red silk, "beeing the colloures of *Desire*...." The determination and resolution of the challengers got a severe testing in the battle that ensued, "as the shivering of the swordes might very well testefie ..." (sig. C1). As the day draws to a close, so does the battle; and finally the children of Desire dispatch their boy "being clothed in Ash colored garments in token of humble submission," who carries an olive branch and falls prostrate before the queen (sig. C1-C1ᵛ). In the speech of submission, "They acknowledge the blindness of their error"; and, "They acknowledge Noble Desire shoulde have desired nothing so much, as the flourishing of that Fortresse ..." (sig. C1ᵛ). The Fortress of Perfect Beauty (i.e., Elizabeth) thus remains inviolate, a mighty bulwark never failing. This allegorical pageant, performed in the presence of the French ambassadors, shares much with the civic show at Bristol which identified Elizabeth with a fort and the cause of Peace, and members of the court took part in the entertainment.[28] Obviously the technique of the mock-battle becomes a favorite with pageant-dramatists, and one cannot doubt its inherent theatrical appeal even with an assured outcome. We witness a fusion between the medieval tournament and the pageant theater with its allegorical characters and purpose.

---

[28]Perhaps this pageant holds another level of meaning since it was performed in the presence of the French mission which was in England on behalf of the Duke of Anjou's marriage suit, all of which is tied in with the problems of the Low Countries (discussed below). It is not far-fetched to see a prophetic quality to the entertainment which suggests that Elizabeth will not be subject to Desire—i.e., to the duke's suit. At least, historical events work out that way.

The focus shifts now to the Continent, particularly to the Low Countries where in 1582 and again in 1586 civic pageants occurred of great magnitude that directly concern the English and therefore find a place in this discussion of English civic pageantry. Furthermore, they illustrate quite tellingly that pageantry in England is no isolated event, but rather it has many precursors and parallels in the major cities on the European continent. England's involvement with the politics of the Low Countries especially in the 1570s and 1580s forms a long and complex subject as she tried to stave off the threat of Spanish intervention there.[29] Both in 1582 and 1586 the Earl of Leicester attended the pageants, and in the latter year became the honored subject of the entertainments. The struggle in the Netherlands, long and often futile, tested Elizabeth's diplomatic skill and involved in addition to Leicester, Ben Jonson who fought there, and Philip Sidney who received his mortal wound in battle. Some would even speculate, without much evidence, that perhaps Shakespeare saw service in that place; at any rate, many of England's great and would-be-great sons had close connections with those tragic events.

Having failed to win Elizabeth's hand in marriage, though he came rather close, Francis, Duke of Anjou, sailed to the Netherlands in early 1582 to be received as Duke of Brabant in an attempt to bring stability to the provinces. Suffice it to say, the Duke failed spectacularly as a ruler. But his entry into Antwerp in February 1582 gave every reason for hope, as the city put forth magnificent effort in order to present a worthy civic pageant, despite having had but six days to prepare. Holinshed reports that the city could not "in so short time make anie meane apparell new, nor anie rare costlinesse of imageries, pillers, triumphall arces, or other pageants: but were constreined to make a shift with such things as they had in a readinesse aforehand of their owne store."[30] This storehouse of ready materials certainly testifies to a long tradition of pageantry in Antwerp and to the wisdom of the planners who preserved the properties, much as the city fathers in London in 1559 had determined to salvage some of the "stuff" used in Elizabeth's royal entry for future use.

With the Earl of Leicester riding before him and other English lords accompanying him, Anjou entered the outskirts of Antwerp where a "theater was set up towards a corner of the castell ..." (p. 469). Many speeches, principally pledging support of the duke, occupied the time at the "theater." A magnificent chariot, called the Chariot of Alliance and carrying the Maiden of Antwerp, greeted the duke and his party just before they entered the city proper. This device, like most

[29]For background material see Chapter IX, "Elizabeth and the Netherlands," in J. B. Black, *The Reign of Elizabeth 1558-1603*, 2nd edition (Oxford, 1959), and the "Introduction" in R. C. Strong and J. A. Van Dorsten, *Leicester's Triumph* (Leiden & London, 1964).
[30]Holinshed, *Chronicles*, IV, 467; all quotations are from this text. Also found in Nichols, II, 354-385. See also for text and magnificent drawings *La joyeuse et magnique Entree de Monsigneur Francoys* (Antwerp, 1582).

of the others here, depends on visual symbolism. Thus the Maiden, dressed in red and white—the colors of Antwerp—carries in her "left hand a branch of baietree, and on hir head a garland of laurell, in token of victorie against the tyrannies of the king of Spaine, and in token of the deliverance which the people hoped for by means of their new prince ..." (p. 475), to whom she presented the keys of the city. Religion, "holding in hir hand an open booke, named the Law and the Gospell: and in hir other hand a sword; named Gods word," and Justice, "holding a balance and a sword in hir hand and over the balance was written, Yea and Naie," sat on either side of Antwerp in the chariot. Meaningful figures sat in front of the Maiden; for they suggest allegorically what Antwerp needs for unity and stability: namely, Concord, "clothed in white, yellow, and orange tawnie," carrying a shield with emblems on it "betokening commendable governement with providence," and wearing a helmet which signified wisdom. "At Concordes right hand sat Wisedome, and at hir left hand Force"—obviously the two qualities necessary to help achieve the concord of the provinces (p. 475). Rising up in the middle of this chariot, a Corinthian pillar or column elaborately decorated with other symbols pointed to union and discreet government. Upon the corners of the chariot two armed images represented Faithfulness and Watchfulness.

Proceeding through the city beneath a canopy of gold cloth, Anjou first saw two devices that depended on Biblical history for their material. On Easthouse street "was a shew made in the likenesse of a table, verie great and high, which was made by one of the companies of their tragicall and comicall poets" with the title, "Growing up in vertue" (p. 476). Apparently the three compartments of the structure contained painted scenes rather than live actors; at any rate, the first shows Samuel charging Saul with disobedience with "a piece of his garment rent off by him, in token that the kingdom shoulde be plucked from Saules house and given to a better. Whereby was meant, that the sovereigntie of those low countries was taken from the king of Spaine for his abhominable perjuries, tyrannies, and extortions" (476). The other two Biblical scenes obviously also refer to contemporary affairs. The second compartment shows Jesse the father of David bringing forth his sons of whom God would make one prince of his people, and the third depicts how David, being anointed, fought Goliath, and defeated him. Verses written on the device elucidate the meaning. Further on, another device, this one definitely painted, showed the friendship of David and Jonathan, "to betoken the firmenesse of the oth mutuallie made by his highnes and the states of Brabant ..." (p. 477).

At Meerebridge stood an elephant with a castle on its back and carrying the arms of the city and of Anjou. On Clare street a stage had been erected upon which sat "a damsell named Antwerpe, bearing in hir bosome a pretie daughter called the knowledge of God: who held a coffer wherin were privileges, laws, franchises, and truth ..." (p. 477). Thus for the second time in the entertainment the Duke has witnessed the personification of the city. And in the market place stood "the great giant the founder of the citie of Antwerpe ..." (p. 478). This giant had interesting and ingenious movements, "made by cunning to turne his face towards the duke as he passed by, and to let fall the armes of Spaine which he held in his hand, and to put up the armes of Anjou" (p. 479). Carrying further this "civic" theme, the mythological god of the sea, Neptune, appeared on Cornmarket street, on top of a whale, "naked with his threeforked mace in his hand, which betokened the great commodities which the citie of Antwerpe received by the sea and by the river Schelt. Before this monster was an other naked man, and by him two other portraitures, the one of navigation, and the other of merchandize ..." (p. 479). This celebration of the community's industry recalls something already observed in the Norwich pageants.

A triumphal arch of "Ionian worke," located where St. John's gate formerly stood, contained a painting of the sun and under it the sea with ships "and the earth clad with hir verdue" (p. 479). The goddesses, Ceres, Flora, and Pomona, adorned the arch in a painting. And the scene of the earth "clad with greene trees, fruits and fields, replenished with all fruitfulnesse" contrasts with the scene of "drierie and barren fields, the aire everie where lowring and cloudie, and the trees and plants withered" (479-80)—all strikingly reminiscent of the contrasting hills at the Little Conduit at Cheapside in Elizabeth's 1559 royal entry. The sun, linked with Anjou, produces a flourishing commonweath, while the barren soil has been nurtured by "three hellhounds, Discord, Violence, and Tyrannie, who fled awaie at the sight of his highnes ..." (480). As Holinshed records: "... by the beames of that sun, the countrie should receive all peace, prosperitie, and abundance...." The darkness and aridity of the past diminish because of the brightness and hope of the future residing in the person of Anjou.

Representing something of the expectations and hopes of the people, an animal stood at a place near the mint, "a huge and monstrous sea-horsse of twentie foot high, upon whom sat a nymph called Concord, bearing a shield wherein was painted a booke and a rod, which was named the Rule of truth" (p. 480). This monster personified Tyranny, "and he had a bridle in his mouth with double reines of iron chained called Law and Reason." Clearly this applies to Anjou. An arch of Corinthian pillars stood nearby, and indeed from this arch all the way to the palace stood some seventy pillars decorated with the arms of Brabant, Anjou, Antwerp and other devices. Making use of painted animals and allegorical figures, the pageant situated near the palace had on the top a crane and a cock implying the need for watchfulness. Other painted animals included a spaniel "betokening faithfulnesse, and a little lambe betokening peace," which accompanied the Sybils representing wisdom, love, faithfulness, obedience, virtue, and honor. "And all these were guided by the light of the holie ghost, which was resembled by a certeine brightnesse" which uncovered the chief agents of discord— Envy "gnawing hir owne heart, and Slander having double heart, double toong, and double face, howbeit with small effect" (p. 481). This representation adheres to the traditional iconographical method of presenting these two vices. The images of David and Hercules also appear on the device; and underneath, Concord held Discord in chains and drove him "into the dungeon of sorrow," "betokening the same thing which the countrie looketh for at his highnesse hand ..." (p. 481). Finally at the palace another arch some twenty feet high rested "upon three pillars of Phrygian worke" and contained three Graces, here Virtue, Glory, and Honour, "who offered unto his highnesse an olife branch, in token of peace, a laurell bough in token of victorie, and a crowne which was sent him from heaven" (p. 481).

A few days later the city presented the tableaux again because the Duke had not had a complete view because of darkness. In addition two new pageants appeared, the first Mount Parnassus "wheron sat Apollo apparelled like the sun, and accompanied with the nine muses plaieng upon diverse kinds of instruments, and with sweet voice singing a certeine ditie togither written in commendation of his highnesse ..." (p. 482). Across the way was a "mossie rocke" overgrown with decayed trees and containing a cave "verie hideous, darke, and drierie to behold" wherein Discord, Tyranny, and Violence hid from the warmth of Apollo's beams and the sweetness of the Muses' harmony. Light and harmony (or unity) thus serve as adequate deterrents to these vices as had been illustrated previously in this royal entry. The scaffold that the Duke ascended in order to take the oath of the city contained images of several animals: a lion holding a sword to signify the authority of the magistrate; an eagle feeding her young, "and turning hir selfe towards the shining of the sunne, as taking hir force of the prince"; an ox with a yoke, a hen brooding her chickens, and by her a cock—"the ox ... signified obedience: and the cocke and the hen betokened the watchfulnesse, care, and defense of the superior" (p. 483).

The similarities of the qualities and techniques of this royal entry into Antwerp and the ones already studied in England suggest that civic pageantry, especially the royal entry form, achieved its own dramatic form which defied parochial boundaries and nationalities, containing parallels that do not necessarily imply indebtedness. Mythological, allegorical, and historical characters dominate the pageant scene in Antwerp as they do elsewhere, and the theme of nationalism shapes this whole entertainment—the repetition of the figure of Antwerp and the quality of Concord underscore the desperate desire for unity and peace. Many of the scenes set forth the clear disdain of the Spanish and the hope for a new and brighter day. While the festivities here in Antwerp and the civic pageants in England share many things in common, a few rather significant differences occur, such as the absence of speeches at the various pageants, something one has come to expect in English pageantry. Partly this derives from the heavy reliance on painted figures or "images" and painted scenes as opposed to live actors; thus the entry in Antwerp relies almost exclusively on the visual quality. In this sense, it seems less "dramatic" than its comparable number in England, more pictorial than theatrical. It has much more extensive use of animals as "natural" symbols, something almost totally lacking in the civic pageantry of England up to this historical moment, but a quality which becomes later, especially in the Lord Mayors' Shows, an integral part of the devices. Possibly the shortness of time determined the "un-dramatic" nature of the event. One stands in respectful awe of what the city accomplished in the space of six days; to imagine a much more elaborate show would be difficult. Thus the Duke of Anjou has been royally welcomed, doubtless impressing the English lords, too. If only the pageant had had a kind of saving efficacy to bestow on the duke and thus ensure his success, the history of the Low Countries might have been quite different.

Leaving England in mid-December 1585, the Earl of Leicester as the newly created Governor-General of the Low Countries, sailed to meet his responsibilities. This event and the attendant commitment to the cause of the Netherlands heralded a new increase in the political and military efforts on the part of England. And upon his entry Leicester took something of a "progress" throughout the countryside, making what amount to "royal entries" into several cities. Perhaps such spectacular display encouraged Leicester to think of his position as Governor-General as more exalted than Elizabeth had intended; the queen eventually made certain that the earl understood the limitations of his power and position. Considering the nature and number of civic pageants presented in Leicester's honor, one can understand the inclination on his part to suffer from certain visions of grandeur.

Arriving first at Flushing, the English group eventually made its way to The Hague which received the new Governor-General triumphantly on 27 December 1585. The first show, presented on the water, offered a fascinating enactment of a Biblical scene with allegorical overtones for that contemporary moment. The earl encountered certain fishermen representing Peter, James, and John; "by them Christ walking on the water, who commanded them to cast out their nets the second time (according to that of saint Matthew) they drew in abundance...."[31] This striking tableau, without any analogous parallel in English pageantry, doubtless alludes to the "casting of the nets to France, from whence they had returned empty-handed, and the second casting towards England which had brought forth this 'miraculous draught' of Leicester and his mighty army."[32] Such an interpretation corresponds with the religious fervor that made out of the whole expedition a type of holy war. Figures representing Mars and Bellona appeared on the water, underscoring the war-like posture to be assumed with the arrival of the new forces.

[31]Holinshed, IV, 644. All quotations for this Leicester progress are from Holinshed.
[32]Strong and Van Dorsten, *Leicester's Triumph*, p. 46. Some of the engravings made of this entertainment are preserved in this book, p. 38f.

As he entered the city itself, fifteen "virgins all clad in white, with branches of palme or box ... did reverence unto the earle ..." (p. 644). The streets throughout the city had elaborate decorations: "All the waie as the earle passed through, were artificiallie made gates raised of ragged staves, and upon everie snag stood a small wax candle burning, by which hoong the armes of diverse craftsmen of the towne" (p. 644). A high scaffold represented a battle fought between the English and the Spanish, "the English men still prevailing ..." (p. 644). Another arch yielded Minerva, "armed, incompassed about the bodie with the armes of England," surrounded by seven virgins "representing the seaven provinces, everie virgin holding a speare" and the arms of the province which she portrayed. The Seven Liberal Sciences also greeted the earl on another scaffold. Finally, as the procession entered the courtyard of the palace, they could see "placed aloft upon a scaffold, as if it had beene in a cloud or skie, Arthur of Britaine, whome they compared to the earle; within were hoboies, cornets, and divers kinds of musike" (p. 645). Elaborate fireworks closed the festivities for the night. The people of The Hague must have understood the flattering comparison of Leicester to Arthur as the cumulative voices of myth—Biblical and national—speak to the occasion in striking ways.

In what amounts virtually to a "cycle play" of secular events, the citizens of Leiden presented their pageant when the English entourage entered the city on 3 January 1586, involving two "poets" who directed the show on the special stage. First, a woman who represents the town experiences assault "by Spaniards, with false fiers of great and small shot a long time in order of battell ..." (p. 645). Famine and Sickness, with scenes of their ravages, now attack the town, complete with the burial of a captain "who was borne over the stage with dead matches, howling trumpets, wrapt up ancients, trailed pikes, drawne peeces ..." (p. 645). Trying to win her with different tactics, the Spaniards dispatched letters to the town, "all which she read and refused, without returne of answer...." Eventually Hope possessed the town, and it set up light as a plea to the prince of Orange for succour; in turn, "by devise of a dove, [he] sent them promise of aid ..." (p. 646). Finally, God's Providence helped scatter the enemy, "and so with the woman, as it were now at libertie that presented the towne, they marched awaie merilie with great triumph" (p. 646). Another woman came on stage, "besieged with a Spaniard, intised with a Frenchman, and flattered with an Italian twise"; she responded by leaping off the stage and hiding "hir selfe under the earls cloke, whom he shadowed, and the Spaniard threatning marched awaie" (p. 646). Leicester becomes part of the action as the illusion separating audience and actor disappears. The verses written on the scaffold underscore the meaning of this mimetic action:

We Flemings being banished, now wailing here,
We are as they in Babilon, by the water clere

Bicause we would not worship idols, but Gods word, ...
But our deliverance is now verie neare,
For God hath looked upon our miserablenesse,
And sent us a prince whom he will blesse ... (p. 646).

At Haarlem in early March the earl saw several pageant-scenes, the first a maiden, probably representing the city, "apparelled all in white, holding a scutchion in hir hand, wherein were painted the armes of England, and all about were painted red roses ..." (p. 650). Another scaffold contained the Maiden of Belgia bearing in one hand a scutcheon with England's arms and in the other a sword, "and diverse persons lieng dead before hir ..." (p. 651). Further in the town on a high scaffold a person portrayed "the queene of England with hir sword in her hand, under whome laie envie, tyrannie, and diverse other the like, all whom she had brought under ..." (p. 651). Elizabeth as a Justice figure has thus conquered vice and offers her hand in support of the oppressed Dutch. Other decorations throughout the city reminded the public of England's in-volvement in their affairs and Leicester's leadership. Even the fireworks that night showed Envy being burnt. The cost of the entertainment here at Haarlem "ran through well over £1,000.... No one watching this hectic revelling would have believed that complete financial collapse was practically upon them."[33] Festive pageantry thus again belies the harsh reality, but its function to cheer and to compliment necessitates an optimistic view.

Two boats, one in the shape of a fish and the other in the likeness of a sea-horse, each contained a figure personating Neptune, as the English party made its entry by water into Amsterdam on 10 March 1586. In the market place a scaffold had on one level showed armed men fighting, one group overcoming and the other fleeing. Above on another "stage" an old man kneeled in prayer "holding up his hands towards heaven" and other persons supported his hands: "Which signified that Josua and the Israelits prevailed, and overthrew the Philistines, so long as Moses did praie for them ... ; and so now through the praier of good men, God had at length sent them succour and releefe" (p. 652). Two more tab-leaux located on other scaffolds illustrated the direct intervention of Elizabeth in behalf of the oppressed peoples of the Low Countries. In one scene the aid of the queen rescued a man in great distress, "a tyrant being readie to kill him"; thus he "was sheilded, defended and delivered, and the enimie repelled and driven awaie ..." (p. 652). Elsewhere the other scaffold presented a person in the likeness of the queen "most sumptuouslie apparelled, and on both sides of hir was hanged all sorts of armour and munition for the wars ..." (p. 652). The dominant theme of the aid and assistance of the English exemplified in the person of the queen unifies this civic pageant.

---

[33]Ibid., p. 65.

For the entry into Utrecht on 22 March, three scaffolds had been especially built; the first located in the market place contained Faith who offered Leicester a gold ring. Seven young men representing the seven united provinces stood on the second arch, and occupying the last stage a figure personated Elizabeth before whom was a likeness of a lion with a sore foot. The "queen" caused her handmaiden to bind up the wound of the Belgic lion. That night like many succeeding ones "was spent in fier works, bonfiers, and shewes of marvellous joie" (p. 654). Leicester made another processional through Utrecht on St. George's day when a colorful display guided the earl's way to the sumptous feast designed for the celebration. This entertainment confirms a pattern observable in the various pageants since the one at Leiden; namely, a playing down of the role of the Governor-General and an increase of attention on Elizabeth—all corresponding to activity in the world of diplomacy no doubt. Nationalism understandably forms a large part of the pageants as they seek to rally people around a cause. While a number of religious or Biblical scenes occur throughout the several entertainments, they have no emphasis "on the materialization of some European pan-Protestant union. It represents the continuance of the Orangist policy of sinking religious differences and concentrating on a potential national image around which all could rally regardless of creed."[34] As in the Antwerp entertainment in 1582, the technical burden throughout these shows falls on the visual and mimetic resources. The tableau or scene must present its allegorical content largely through pictorial devices and the techniques of the "dumb show," familiar in Renaissance drama. Thus pageant-drama in the Low Countries, at least in these examples, remains primarily a mimetic drama sometimes with a remnant of a plot, as in the Leiden pageant; and the interplay of the verbal and visual diminishes, which makes of these pageants a theater experience different from the English ones.

In pageants similar in form and thematic content to the Kenilworth shows, Elizabeth received entertainment in the summer of 1591 as she went on progress. On Saturday, 14 August, she arrived in the evening at the estate of Lord Montague at Cowdray in Sussex. As she entered the estate, loud music sounded until she reached the bridge; "Then was a speech delivered by a personage in armour, standing betweene two Porters, carved out of wood, he resembling the third: holding his club in one hand, and a key of golde in the other...."[35] Resembling the Hercules figure who welcomed the queen at Kenilworth, the porter here presents her with the key: "*Enter, possesse all, to whom the heavens have vouchsafed all. As for the owner of this house, mine honourable Lord, his tongue is the keie of his*

---

[34]Ibid., p. 68.

[35]*The Speeches and Honorable Entertainment given to the Queenes Majestie in Progresse at Cowdray in Sussex, by the Right Honorable the Lord Montacute* (London, 1591), sig. A3-A3ᵛ. All quotations are from this text. See also Nichols, III, 90f; Jean Wilson, pp. 88-95.

heart: and his heart the locke of his soule" (sig. A3ᵛ-A4). Thus the Lord through the porter's speech greets "*Natures glorie, Fortunes Empresse,*" offering his duty and service. While hunting on Monday, Elizabeth came to a special bower in which musicians performed a song of elaborate praise of her.

Strolling in the gardens at Cowdray on Tuesday evening, the queen confronted a Pilgrim who, among other things, spoke a short prayer in her behalf: "God graunt the worlde maie ende with your life, and your life more happie then anie in the world ..." (sig. B1). The Pilgrim then brought her to an oak whereon hung her arms and the arms of the noblemen of the shire. Here also a Wild Man clad in ivy addressed the queen, making symbolic application of the scene:

> *This Oke ... resembles in parte your strength and happinesse. Strength, in the number and the honour: happinesse, in the trueth and consent.... your majesty they account the Oke, the tree of Jupiter, whose root is so deeplie fastened, that Treacherie, though she undermine to the centre, cannot finde the windinges, and whose toppe is so highlie reared, that envie, though she shoote on copheight, cannot reach her, under whose armes they have both shade and shelter....* (sig. B1ᵛ-B2)

This "wild man" also complains about the distorted nature of the world, a world which takes refuge in disguise: "*Everie one seeming to be that which they are not, onely do practise what they should not*" (sig. B2ᵛ). This enunciates of course a familiar theme in much of Renaissance drama—the gap which too frequently separates appearance and reality. A song praising true love "which springs, though Fortune on it tread" closes the show.

Again on Wednesday evening "her Majestie comming to take the pleasure of the walks, was delighted with most delicate musicke, and brought to a goodly Fish-pond" where she met an Angler who took no notice of her but instead spoke to the Netter nearby. Finally the Netter turned to Elizabeth and spoke:

> *Madame, it is an olde saying, There is no fishing to the sea, nor service to the King: but it holdes when the sea is calme, and the king vertuous. Your vertue doth make Envie blush, and Envie stands amazed at your happines. I come not to tell the art of fishing ... but with a poore Fishermans wishe, that all the hollowe heartes to your Majestie were in my net, and if there bee more then it will holde, I woulde they were in the sea till I went thether a fishing....* (sig. B3ᵛ-B4)

A witty play on the metaphor of love and fishing contained in the song of a Fisherman ends the festivities at Cowdray. As in earlier progress pageants the theme of Elizabeth's power over vice looms large in these pleasantries because she possesses an oak-like strength and an honesty that does not disguise the truth. Such is her appeal, expressed in these quasi-dramatic terms, that even humble anglers and netters seek to serve her, part of the response of nature to her charm.

A month later on the estate of the Earl of Hertford at Elvetham (*see* figure 1) a pageant took place which surpasses in its unexcelled charm anything performed as a progress entertainment since the days at Kenilworth in 1575. The central part of the show takes its dramatic form from the several mock-battles witnessed before, especially the one at Bristol. And again the world of pastoral romance and of mythology comes alive on the grounds at Elvetham as elaborate preparations and meticulous attention to costume forge an entertainment worthy of its honored guest. At her arrival on Monday evening, 20 September, the queen met a Poet "clad in greene, to signify the joy of his thoughts," wearing a laurel garland on his head, carrying an olive branch and "booted" to demonstrate his authenticity as a poet.[36] With typical praise the Poet welcomes her:

> *O sweete* Elisa, *grace me with a looke,*
> *Or from my browes this Laurell wreath will fall,*
> *And I unhappy die amidst my song....*
> *To whom all things are joyes, while thou art present,*
> *To whom nothing is pleasing, in thine absence....*
> *Thy presence frees each thing that liv'd in doubt....* (*sig.* B3-B3ᵛ)

Initially the Poet has sounded a theme which recurs in many of the progress pageants and which Elvetham develops at least implicitly: the liberating force of Elizabeth's presence. As the Poet spoke, "six Virgins were behind him, busily remooving blockes out of her majesties way; which blocks were supposed to be layde there by the person of *Envie*, whose condition is, to envie at every good thing, but especially to malice the proceedings of *Vertue*, and the glory of true *Majestie*" (sig. B3ᵛ). Just as the Netter at Cowdray had spoken of the queen's virtuous power over Envy, so here the women remove the tangible reminders of a malicious vice. These virgins represent the mythological Graces and Hours "which by the Poets are fained to be the guardians of heaven gates" (sig. B4). They wear striking costume: "They were all attired in gowns of taffata sarcenet of divers colours, with flowrie garlands on their heads, and baskets full of sweet hearbs and flowers uppon their armes" (sig. B4)—a scene worthy of a Botticelli.

---

[36] *The Honorable Entertainment gieven to the Queenes Majestie in Progresse, at Elvetham in Hampshire, by the right Honorable the Earle of Hertford* (London, 1591), sig. A4ᵛ. All quotations are from this edition. Also found in Nichols, III, 103f., who claims to have seen a different text, and indeed his edition varies somewhat from the 1591 edition. The textual problems are discussed by Greg, *Bibliography*, I, 98. Another reprint, *Elvetham: An Account of Queen Elizabeth's Visit there in 1591* (London, n.d.). See also, Jean Wilson, pp. 99-118. For an illuminating discussion of the songs in this entertainment see Ernest Brennecke, "The Entertainment at Elvetham, 1591," in *Music in English Renaissance Drama*, ed. John H. Long (Lexington, Ky., 1968), pp. 32-56.

When the Poet finishes his speech and hands Elizabeth a scroll containing his words, the Graces and Hours walk before the queen "strewing the way with flowers, and singing a sweete song of six parts":

> Now birds record new harmonie,
> And trees doe whistle melodie:
> Now everie thing that nature breeds,
> Doth clad it selfe in pleasant weeds.
> O beauteous Queene of second Troy,
> Accent of our unfained joy. (sig. B4ᵛ)

With such dulcet melodies extolling the harmony of all nature permeating the air, Elizabeth comes to the Earl's house where a feast and more music filled the first night at Elvetham.

For Tuesday's entertainment a special crescent-shaped pond had been created as the center for the dramatic action between the sea gods and the wood gods—the mock-battle. The text gives some of the details, even the dimensions, of the three constructions placed in this artificial pond: a *Ship Ile*, a *Fort*, and a *Snail Mount*—places for some of the action. At the head of the pond in a special place the queen sat under an elegant canopy of green satin, fringed with green silk and silver; she arrived about four o'clock for the afternoon's pageant. From a special bower at the opposite end of the pond emerged "a pompous array of seapersons, which waded bresthigh, or swam til they approched neare the seat of her majestie" (sig. C1ᵛ). Nereus led the group "attired in redde silk, and having a cornered-cappe on his curlde heade ..." (sig. C2). Following him five Tritons sounded their trumpets, and Neptune and Oceanus came with the sea retinue also. A highly decorated boat carried three virgins who "with their Cornets, played Scottish Gigs ..." (sig. C2). Neaera, another nymph of the sea and "the old supposed love of *Sylvanus*, a God of the Woodes" came also, and together the entourage in proper costume made its way toward the queen, each sea figure "armed with a huge woodden squirt in his hand ..." (sig. C2). Before Nereus delivers his speech to the one at the center of attention, Elizabeth, he gives a signal to a member of his train who promptly casts himself down from the *Ship Ile*, doing a flip into the water. Nereus presents a jewel to the queen as from the earl, informing her also that the Fort has been raised by Neptune in her defense and that the elements of nature receive life from the "Verdue" of her looks. The virgins in the boat sing to the accompaniment of the lute, "and the end of every verse was replied by Lutes and voices in the other boate somwhat a farre off, as if they had beene Ecchoes" (sig. C3ᵛ).

With the sounding of the Tritons' trumpets, Sylvanus and his attendants came forth from the woods, he being appropriately attired "from the middle downewards to the knee, in Kiddes skinnes, with the haire on, ... his head

hooded with a goates skin, and two little hornes over his forehead, bearing in his
right hand an Olive tree, and in his left a scutchion ..." (sig. C4). His comrades,
all covered with ivy leaves, "bare in their handes bowes made like darts." Sylvanus greets this fair Cinthia—

> ... *whom no sooner Nature fram'd,*
> *And deckt with Fortunes, and with Vertues dower,*
> *But straight admiring what her skill had wrought,*
> *She broake the mould: that never Sunne might see*
> *The like to* Albions *Queene for excellence.* (sig. C4ᵛ)

Nereus then points out to Sylvanus that his former love, Neaera, sits nearby, and
Sylvanus hopes that she "*may relent in sight of beauties Queene*" (sig. D1). She will
come on shore, Nereus says, if Sylvanus "*plight a solemne vow, / Not to prophane
her undefiled state.*" This Sylvanus agrees to do and proffers his hand as a sign of
his vow, which hand Nereus takes and uses to pluck Sylvanus head over heels
into the water, asserting "*that water will extinguish wanton fire*" (sig. D1). All of
which causes great merriment among the sea figures who duck Sylvanus and "in-
sult over him"; finally, they allow him to creep to land "where he no sooner set
footing, but crying *Revenge, Revenge,*" rallies his forces into a skirmish with the
sea troops, "the one side throwing their dartes, and the other using their squirtes,
and the *Tritons* sounding a pointe of warre" (sig. D1-D1ᵛ). Nothing stills the battle until Nereus "parted the fray with a line or two, grounded on the excellence of
her Majestyes presence, as being alwaies friend to peace, and ennemy to Warre"
(sig. D1ᵛ).

As with the earlier sham battles presented as pageant entertainment, this one
also dissolves into the recognition and indeed exaltation of Elizabeth as the veritable incarnation of Peace. Her energizing, liberating presence engenders harmony among men as it does among nature; and she therefore represents not only
personification of Peace, but also she brings in her person dramatic force which
can alter events, change or modify them. Her "dramatic" presence all pageant-
dramatists sense and grant to her directly or indirectly a significant role in the
action. As Sylvanus and his fellows steal away into the woods, Neaera addresses
Elizabeth recalling that she has been told that her eyes—

> ... *shall in time behold*
> *A sea-borne Queene, worthy to governe Kings,*
> *On her depends the Fortune of thy boate,*
> *If shee but name it with a blisful word.*
> *And view it with her life inspiring beames.*
> *Her beames yeeld gentle influence, like fayre starres,*
> *Her silver sounding word is prophesie.* (sig. D1ᵛ)

Elizabeth obliges and names the boat *Bonadventure,* and Neaera closes by wishing for her "endlesse joy, with glorious fame." With the sounding of the trumpets in the queen's honor, Nereus and his band withdrew to their bower, and thus closes this theatrical experience shared not only by the sovereign but also by many of the local people gathered around the pond. Costume, properties, speeches, action, setting, combine to sing the praise of the queen whose role as peacemaker the pageant dramatizes. Direct dramatic conflict and speeches revealing the interaction among the characters contrast with the more static presentations of the earlier royal entries.

Music began the final day (Thursday) as the "Fayery Queene" came into the garden, "dauncing with her maides about her" (sig. D4ᵛ). She informs Elizabeth that she is "Aureola, *the Queene of* Fairy *land*" who comes to welcome "*your* Imperiall Grace"; "*And humbly to salute you with this Chaplet, / Given me by* Auberon, *the* Fairy *King. / Bright shining* Phoebe, *that in humaine shape, / Hid'st heavens perfection, vouchsafe t' accept it*" (sig. E1). This greeting closes with a "song of sixe parts, with the musicke of an exquisite consort, wherein was the Lute, Bandora, Base-violl, Citterne, Treble-violl, and Flute":

Elisa *is the fairest Queene,*
That ever trod upon this greene.
Elisaes *eyes are blessed starres,*
Inducing peace, subduing warres.
Elisaes *hand is christall bright,*
Her words are balme, her lookes are light.
Elisaes *brest is that faire hill,*
Where Vertue dwels, and sacred skill,
O blessed bee each day and houre,
Where sweet Elisa *builds her bowre.* (sig. E1ᵛ)

This anatomy of Elizabeth's virtue epitomizes the complimentary nature of the whole pageant entertainment.

An hour later as she took her leave of Elvetham, she found Nereus and the sea gods and Sylvanus and his company sitting about the pond and in her path the Graces and Hours, "all of them on everie side wringing their hands, and shewing signe of sorrow for her departure" (sig. E1ᵛ-E2). The Poet who bids the queen farewell asks simply, "how can Sommer stay when Sunne departs? / ... Leaves fal, grasse dies, beasts of the wood hang head, / Birds cease to sing, and everie creature wailes, / To see the season alter with his change ..." (sig. E2). The songs of joy and triumph have been transmuted into tears of sadness as all nature responds to the effect of their sovereign's departure. Just as the Poet bids the queen either to stay or to come again, so the song which greets her from a hidden bower pleads:

O Come again faire Natures treasure,
Whose lookes yeeld joyes exceeding measure.
O come againe heav'ns chiefe delight,
Thine absence makes eternall night.... (sig. E2ᵛ)

The sadness lessens only with the joy of remembrance of what has passed during the festive days at Elvetham. Appropriately the figures who greeted Elizabeth upon her arrival with such charm and those who performed the main action on Tuesday should come together for the farewell; this union reveals continuity and design in the Elvetham pageant-drama. Throughout this progress entertainment moods of joy and exaltation have been tempered by harsher realities—battle and departure—an interweaving of dramatic theme. One recalls the songs of Summer and Winter which close *Love's Labour's Lost.* Even at Elvetham in a vast world of romance the song of experience sounds with its plaintive melody. While the entertainment at Elvetham evokes memories of Kenilworth, one also notes an important difference: a central dramatic action exploring the conflict between the wood gods and sea gods. In the sixteen years since Kenilworth the progress pageant form has moved in the direction of dramatic unity, plot, character conflict, and increasing dependence on speech that helps carry the dramatic burden.

The busy summer of 1592 likewise produced several progress entertainments, the first being the one in August at Quarrendon, the estate of Sir Henry Lee. The speeches in this pageant as well as in the two previous ones at Cowdray and Elvetham and the ones at Bisham, Sudeley, and Rycote (later in September 1592) and the ones at Harefield Place in 1602 have all been attributed to John Lyly.[37] And later scholarship has also assigned to him the brief show at Mitcham in 1598.[38] Each of these final entertainments celebrates the power of Elizabeth. At Quarrendon, for example, an old knight appears who has been enchanted by the Fairy Queen in her bower and has been imprisoned in a sleep, but this day he has been set free through the mystical power of the queen. Indeed the song after dinner notes this efficacy: "To that Grace that sett us free, / Ladies let us thankfull be; / All enchaunted cares are ceast, / Knightes restored, we releast ..." (I, 458). The following day at Quarrendon a Chaplain brings word of the miraculous recovery of his master, Loricus.

Later at Bisham (Lady Russell's estate) Elizabeth's power over evil forces gets referred to as the queen encounters on a hill Pan and "two Virgins keeping

---

[37]R. Warwick Bond, ed., *The Complete Works of John Lyly* (Oxford, 1902), I, 404. All quotations for the Quarrendon entertainment are from this edition.
[38]Leslie Hotson, ed., *Queen Elizabeth's Entertainment at Mitcham* (New Haven, 1953).

sheepe, and sowing in their Samplers ...."[39] All praise Elizabeth, and one in particular notes:

> One hande she stretcheth to *Fraunce*, to weaken Rebels; the other to
> *Flaunders*, to strengthen Religion; her heart to both Countries, her vertues to all. This is shee at whom *Envie* hath shott all her arrowes and
> now for anger broke her bow ... Daunger looketh pale to beholde her
> Majesty: and Tyranny blusheth to heare of her mercy.... (sig. A3ᵛ)

Waiting at the bottom of the hill, Ceres appears in a harvest cart; she surrenders her crown: "I lay downe my feined deity, which Poets have honoured, truth contemned. To your Majesty, whome the heavens have crowned with happines, the world with wonder, birth with dignitie, nature with perfection, we doe all Homage, accounting nothing ours but what comes from you" (sig. A4ᵛ). Even a mythological goddess recognizes this higher, compelling power of Elizabeth. At Sudeley Castle the conflict between Daphne and Apollo subsides when Daphne flees to Elizabeth explaining: "I stay, for whither should chastety fly for succour, but to the Queene of chastety" (sig. B2ᵛ).

The last progress pageant of Elizabeth's reign, the entertainment at Harefield Place in 1602, celebrates the cosmic power of the queen. Before she entered the Countess's home, she saw two figures, Place "in a partie-colored roobe, like the brick house," and Time "with yeollow haire, and in a green roabe, with a hower glasse, stopped, not runninge."[40] These appropriately costumed characters engage in a discussion, with Time referring to Elizabeth as the "Wonder of this time," and Place observing that "noe *place* is great ynough to receive her" (p. 589). Time points out that "the Guest that wee are to entertaine doth fill all places with her divine vertues, as the Sunn fills the World with the light of his beames." Responding to Place's observation about his clipped wings and stopped hour glass, Time explains: "My wings are clipt indeed, and it is her hands hath clipt them: and, tis true, my glasse runnes not: indeed it hath bine stopt a long time, it can never rune as long as I waite upon this Mistress. I [am] her *Time* ..." (p. 589). Indeed, from our perspective of many years removed from the event, Time's appearance here at Harefield conveys an ominous prophecy with the hour glass no longer running—an unknowing hint of things to come. A note of appropriateness occurs, too, that on one of the last progresses and the last one offering pageant entertainment Elizabeth should again encounter Time, having been greeted

---

[39] *Speeches Delivered to Her Majestie this Last Progresse, at the Right Honorable the Lady Russels, at Bissam, the Right Honorable the Lorde Chandos at Sudley, at the Right Honorable the Lord Norris, at Ricorte* (Oxford, 1592), sig. A2ᵛ. Quotations for these pageants will be from this text. See Nichols, III, 131f.

[40] Nichols, III, 588.

by him and his daughter Truth on the streets of London in 1559 at the beginning of her reign. The wheel has come full circle.

Throughout these progress entertainments and royal entries in the Elizabethan period one constant feature dominates: the rather complete apotheosis of Elizabeth, variously regarded as Deborah, Phoebe, the Fairy Queen, Chastity, Peace, or the Fortress of Perfect Beauty. Mythological gods and goddesses surrender their claims on deity in her presence, the one who seemingly embodies all virtue. She brings in her person unmistakable religious or mystical powers sufficient to release men from their bondage; indeed, she seems to be the Truth that sets men free. Her charming power tames nature as well as men; even wild men recognize her innate nobility. All of which constitutes a grand compliment to the sovereign, no matter its overstatement. In such a milieu Spenser's *The Faerie Queene* appears a natural outgrowth.

Clearly the queen serves as the focus of attention in this drama, which has accurately been referred to by Muriel Bradbrook as "drama as offering." It comes as a gift and hence much of its exaggeration. Elizabeth, or whoever the honored person, not only occupies the thematic center but also the dramatic center of the pageant entertainment. On many occasions she actively participates in the outcome of the dramatic presentation. She functions as an "unscheduled actor" in the sense that she has no explicitly written part; on the other hand, the playwright intends that she will be an "actor" in the whole dramatic scene. As the examples have shown, this role could take several forms whether the queen is touring a city and acknowledging its gift to her or actively mediating quarrels or deciding issues in estate entertainments.

This drama, being prepared by such people as Sidney, Gascoigne, and Lyly, makes no claim to be realistic; rather, it forms part of the emblematic and symbolic tradition of theater. Whereas the Shakespearean drama may be regarded as drama of eloquence, the pageant theater relies less on words than on visual impact—therefore the dependence on allegory and symbolic properties and costumes. Where the processional element does not occur, as in most progress pageants, then an increased demand or burden on language exists, much of it made manifest in song. This drama remains largely episodic without many examples of dramatic unity, and this episodic nature the tableau technique serves well.

The differences between royal entries and progress entertainments probably derive as much from location as anything else. The processional movement through the city governs the form of the entry; thus tableaux, stationed at various parts of that city, present scenes largely grounded on history or moral allegory. The progress entertainments, frequently spread over several days, rely heavily on mythology, while using other areas of subject matter as well. The appearance of wood gods, or sea gods, or Ceres, or Pan, or shepherds seems a natural response to the setting for these dramatic shows. Occasionally, such as at Bristol and again at Norwich, we seem to get a combination, with first a royal entry followed on subsequent days by entertainment similar to the progress pageants. The theatrical experience of mock-battles becomes a favorite with a number of pageant-dramatists who succeed in making these events praise Elizabeth. Generally, we may conclude that in the Elizabethan era mythology and romance dominate in the progress entertainments while historical subjects and moral allegory abound in the royal entries. Both forms share, of course, many of the same thematic concerns.

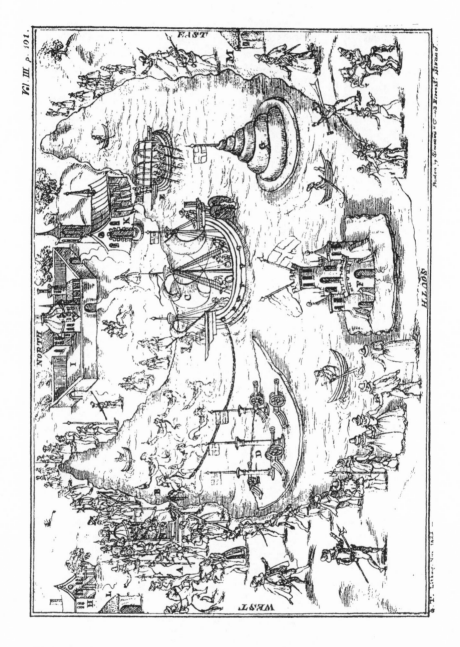

Figure 1. The crescent-shaped pond at the pageant at Elvetham in 1591, from John Nichols, *Progresses of Elizabeth*, vol. II. Courtesy of the Kenneth Spencer Research Library, University of Kansas.

2 The Reign of James I (1603-25)

FEWER PROGRESS PAGEANTS IN THE JACOBEAN ERA fully compare to, say, the Kenilworth or Elvetham entertainments of Elizabeth's reign. Partly this decline may be tied in with the temperament of James, who, on the basis of several accounts, simply did not care much for the "public" shows; thus he could not be as gracious as an Elizabeth who used the entertainments to enhance her position. Lack of response does not beget more pageants; it saps the strength from them. Economic problems weigh heavily in consideration also, especially in the provinces where the progresses occurred. The Venetian Ambassador, Zorzi Giustinian, offers a report in the summer of 1607 virtually repeated by him in the following summer as well; in his dispatch dated 29 August 1607, he writes: "These Progresses, which were started with the object of studying and alleviating the needs of the subjects, have now become a great burden to them."[1] Toward the end of James's reign another Venetian ambassador, Alvise Valaresso, reports in the summer of 1624: "His Majesty begins his progress tomorrow; it will be the most extensive he has made for a great while, involving journeying of almost 200 miles. It will cost about 30,000 *l.* and impose a burden upon the country of about as much again, about 600 carts being required for the baggage, and it will prove very inconvenient for all other business."[2] In such a world of financial strain progress entertainments understandably suffer; and when the received view says that progresses have become a burden, then the Arcadian world of romance evaporates, and the "spontaneous" songs and "wild men" no longer appear along the roadside or in the great parks of the noblemen's estates.

Two important developments in drama influence the shift away from progress shows. Under the active sponsorship of the crown, the court masque received encouragement, and the great collaboration of Ben Jonson and Inigo Jones began in the early years of James's reign, which helped the masque gain new sophistication and new prestige. This retreat into the court circle and away from the public shows connects with the personality of the king, though it does not create the exclusive cause for the popularity of the masque. Another strand of civic pageantry, the Lord Mayor's Show, which had its origin in the Elizabethan period, truly begins to flourish in the same Jacobean age and aids the movement of attention away from progress pageants with the pageant-dramatists focusing their efforts on London. We cannot be precise when trying to sort out causes and

[1] *Calendar of State Papers Venetian 1607-1610*, XI, 27.
[2] *Calendar of State Papers Venetian 1623-25*, XVIII, 400.

effects in this kind of situation; nevertheless, the masque and the Lord Mayor's Show do reach a new level of achievement during the reign of James and help make London the dominant location for all dramatic forms, including of course the active public and private theaters.

The royal entry pageant as epitomized in the 1604 London entertainment develops more dramatic form than the Elizabethan royal entry, providing a further breakdown of static tableau by dramatic action with dramatic links, as well as thematic ones, existing between pageant scenes in the 1604 show. Unlike the Elizabethan counterpart, the Jacobean entry has dramatic dialogue among the characters—another sign of a more mature dramatic form. These developments result, at least in part, from having major dramatists preparing the pageant—planning the action, writing the speeches, as well as devising the visual splendor. Before discussing the 1604 royal entry, the highest achievement in this form of pageantry in the late Tudor and early Stuart eras, we should look at entertainments in Edinburgh during James's tenure as King of Scotland and a show that took place in England in the summer of 1603.

Because James was a mere infant when his mother, Mary, abdicated the Scottish throne in his behalf, understandably no coronation royal entry took place in Edinburgh. In 1579, however, the adolescent king did make such an entry in late October, and records in Edinburgh reveal some of the preparations that took place in anticipation of the event, preparations similar to those of other entries of the Elizabethan period. For example, on 2 October a committee determined "to tak ordour with the wrychtis for upsetting of daillis and uther tymmer on the Nether Bow and uther places neidfull, for the decoring of the toune agane the triumphe to be maid to the Kingis entres."[3] An official proclamation of 14 October commanded the inhabitants of Edinburgh to clean and decorate the city, and a report after the event requires that William Adamsoun "delyver to the violeris and sangsteris at the Kingis entrie above the Over Bow, the soume of thre pundis for thair dayes wages, quhairof thretty s. to the violeris and thretty s. to the sangsteris" (p. 193). The pageant itself, providing few details, contains scenes from religion, mythology, and allegory. At the West Port, for example, the king witnessed a tableau portraying the "Wisdom of Solomon," and "thair the haill honest men of edinburgh wer cled in blak gownes and bure ane vaill of fyne purpour velvet under the quhilk his grace raid to the abay ..." (p. 193). Coming out of a globe, "ane bony boy" at the Over Bow delivered the keys of the city to James and "thair was melodious singing." Four ladies, Justice, Peace, Plenty, and Policy, greeted the king at the old Tolbooth and each spoke to the sovereign. After a brief service at the church, "his majestie beheld the storie of bachus at the croce quhairat the spoutis The wyne ran aboundantlie ..." (p. 194). Bacchus obviously distributed the fruits of these spouts. The Nether Bow displayed a scene of the

---

[3]In A. J. Mill, *Mediaeval Plays in Scotland*, p. 192. All quotations for this entry are from this source.

seven planets how "they rang the tyme of the kingis birth," and King Ptolomeus interpreted the tableau. Before James processed on to the abbey, he saw at "the cannon croce ane breiff fabill for abbolisching of the paip and of the mess with the authoritie and asisteris thairof for evir." All sorts of echoes of Mary's 1561 entry thus reappear in this royal entry even to the point of the call for the abolition of the pope and the mass. Again pageantry in Edinburgh utilizes its propaganda possibilities, but perceiving any thematic unity in this show becomes difficult partly because we have to be content with so few details of the festivity.

The entry of Anne of Denmark, James's new bride, into Edinburgh in May 1590, prompted elaborate preparations, and detailed accounts of disbursements for material and labor appear in the burgh records. The usual sort of painting and repairing took place, and specific projects receive much attention in the Treasurer's Accounts. For example, "Johnne werkman painter for the gilting of the tua armeis at the nether bow and for painting of the glob" received over £33.[4] Another item includes payment "for tua pair of Irne bandis to put at the west port to the place of the glob to suddenlie discend" (p. 197). The device of a globe, already twice before used in Edinburgh in both 1561 and 1579, figures prominently also in this royal entry. "For making of all the scaffaldis with drink gevin thairto," "Nicoll gilmour wrycht" received £5, and other workmen on the scaffolds got 36s. (p. 198). Gilmour also got an additional £6 "for taking doune of all the scaffaldis and for four dayis wark of himself and tua warkmen ..." (p. 200). Other payments illustrate the diversity of the preparations: "Item gevin to the menstrelis that playit the day of hir majesties entres iij^{li}"; "Item to him [John Werkman] for painting of foure stoupis of ane bed at the salt trone with painting of bachus xx^s"; "Item payit to Johne cuninghame goldsmyth for the tua silver keyis quhilk was gevin to hir majestie ... xviij^{li}" (p. 199). Many other expenditures, ranging from nails to special cloth, exist in the accounts, the fullness of which offers much insight into the typical expenses of such a royal entry.

The eventful day was 19 May 1590, and the new queen, Anne, rode in a chariot with both Danish and Scottish lords on horseback accompanying her. After a Latin oration given by John Russell at the West Port, a boy, Russell's son in fact, "was let downe by a devise made in a globe, which being come somewhat over her Majesties heade, opened at the toppe into foure quarters, where the childe, appearing in the resemblance of an angell, delivered her the keyes of the towne in silver; which done, the quarters closed, and the globe was taken uppe agayne, so as the childe was no more seene there."[5] Mechanical devices thus come to the aid of "supernatural" beings here in Edinburgh as the angel descends to welcome

[4]Ibid., p. 196. All records are from this source.

[5]J. T. Gibson Craig, *Papers Relative to the Marriage of King James the Sixth of Scotland, with the Princess Anne of Denmark.* Bannatyne Club publication (Edinburgh, 1828), p. 40. All quotations are from this source.

Anne. In fact, farther on, in Bow street stood another globe, this one resting on a scaffold with a boy "sitting thereby, who represented the person of a King, and made an oration ..." (p. 40). On a scaffold at the Butter Trone appeared the Nine Muses, "bravely arraied in cloth of silver and gold, ... who sung verie sweete musicke, where a brave youth played upon the organs ..." (p. 40). Carrying emblematic properties, the Four Virtues greeted Anne at Tolbooth: "first Justice, with the Balance in one hand, and the Sword of Justice in the other; then Temperance, having in one hand a cup of wine, and in the other hand a cup of water; Prudence, holding in her hand a Serpent and a Dove, declaring, that men ought to bee as wise as the serpent, ... but as simple as the dove ...; the last is Fortitude, who held a broken pillar in her hand, representing the strength of a kindgome" (p. 41). Such iconographical detail has largely been missing from the other Edinburgh entries.

After the service at the church, Anne came to the Cross upon the top of which a table "whereupon stood cups of gold and silver full of wine, with the Goddesse of Corne and Wine sitting thereat, ... who, in Latin, cried that there should be plentie thereof in her time; and on the side of the crosse sate the god Bacchus upon a punchion of wine, winking, and casting it by cups full upon the people ..." (p. 41). Obviously the pageant-dramatist senses no particular conflict between this scene and the previous tableau which included Temperance; or perhaps he merely presents the best of both worlds. Historical figures personating all the previous kings of Scotland sat at the Salt Trone, "one of them lying along at their feete, as if he had been sick, whom certain souldiers seemed to awake at her Majesties comming, whereupon he arose, and made her an oration in Latine ..." (p. 42). Thus characters from history join the Virtues and the mythological gods in greeting the new queen. The Nether Bow contained a tableau depicting the marriage of James and Anne, and a child spoke explaining the device. From this scaffold a box descended on a silk string, a box covered with purple velvet and precious jewels "esteemed at twentie thousand crownes, which the township gave for a present to her Highnes ..." (p. 42). Singing of psalms closed the ceremony. This royal entry strikingly resembles in so many details the earlier ones made by Mary and James into Edinburgh, as if each event largely repeats that presented on a previous occasion. Perhaps if we had fuller texts of these civic pageants, they would not appear quite so disjointed as they do; one expects them to be episodic of course, but some type of theme ought to envelop them, corresponding with the apparent visual spectacle. The burgh records testify to the immense preparation which preceded these events designed to honor Scottish sovereigns. In planning and execution they parallel in many ways their counterpart of English royal entries, underscoring the existence of a recognizable dramatic form which shapes such pageants no matter the location.

Upon the news of the death of Elizabeth and his subsequent proclamation as King of England, James VI of Scotland made his way from Edinburgh to London where he might assume his new role as James I and thus establish the Stuart line on the English throne. The lengthy journey to the capital on the Thames gave James a chance to see much of this "new" country and to be seen by his new subjects, being enthusiastically received along the way in village and town—the cheers lusty, the ceremonies fitting, and the bonfires gargantuan. But nothing could accurately be called a civic pageant. When, however, his queen and their son, Prince Henry, made the trip somewhat later, they received entertainment at the home of Sir Robert Spencer at Althorp in late June 1603, in a show which resembles the Elizabethan progress pageant. Ben Jonson, the author of the entertainment, had already become a leading figure among dramatists.

Jonson created a world of romance populated with satyrs and fairies; doubtless because of his skill as a dramatist he succeeds in granting to some of his characters personality, especially to the Satyr—a rare commodity in such entertainments. This Satyr first greets the royal pair and concludes that surely "they are of heavenly race."[6] Following his brief appearance, Queen Mab arrives with fairies who dance, and Mab speaks words of welcome to Anne. But the Satyr who is hiding in a bush, warns the queen about this fairy—"Trust her not ..." (122). Which of course provokes a verbal contest between the Fairy and the Satyr who successfully eludes the fairies as they try to catch him. Finally they get him and heed Mab's bidding to "pinch him black and blue ..." (p. 124). Again he escapes, and Mab explains to Queen Anne: "Pardon lady this wild strayne, / Common with the SYLVAN trayne, / That doe skip about this plaine ..." (124). A song follows in praise of Anne: "Long live ORIANA / To exceed (whom shee succeeds) our late DIANA" (p. 125). Then the fairies present Anne with a jewel urging her not to tell the source of this gift. But the Satyr returns and challenges them verbally and defends his own approach to life, which he deems neither rude nor savage:

Here doth no such humour flow.
He can neither bribe a grace,
Nor encounter my lords face
With a plyant smile, and flatter,
Though this lately were some matter
To the making of a courtier....
O that now a wish could bring
The god-like person of a king;
Then should even Envy find
Cause of wonder at the mind
Of our wood-man .... (pp. 126-7)

[6]*Ben Jonson*, ed. C. H. Herford and Percy and Evelyn Simpson (Oxford, 1941), VII, 121. All quotations from Jonson will be from this edition.

The "wisdom" of this "wild man" recalls the type found in several Elizabethan pageants, though Jonson has invested his savage "with some traits of the native Puck, without impairing the *naiveté* of the shaggy woodgod" (II, 261). The Saturday afternoon at Althorp has offered a dramatic presentation of song, romance, humor, and of course praise to the honored visitors.

The long-awaited day of 15 March 1604 finally arrived, and the city of London turned out in full splendor for the royal passage of James I through their streets with seven opulent triumphal arches stationed throughout the city in his honor. For this civic pageant which had been delayed from July 1603 to the following March because of the plague, the city engaged some of the finest talent available to prepare the entertainment. Ben Jonson, who had already written the Althorp entertainment and who was to become the leading exponent of the masque, devised the drama which took place at the first and last arches and the brief scene in the Strand. Making his first excursion into civic pageantry, Thomas Dekker wrote the remainder of the entertainment, excepting the two arches erected by the Italian and Dutch merchants of London. Dekker continued his pageant career by later writing several Lord Mayors' Shows. Both dramatists had texts printed which describe at least their part of the royal entry pageant;[7] not much evidence exists of active collaboration between them.

For the first time a royal entry pageant involves the work of two leading dramatists (actually three since Thomas Middleton wrote one speech): and it also has another claim to distinction: Stephen Harrison served as artificer and joined with the dramatists in the construction of the arches. As Dekker points out in his account: "Over whom [other workers], *Stephen Harrison* Joyner was appoynted chiefe; who was the sole Inventor of the Architecture, and from whom all directions, for so much as belonged to Carving, Joyning, Molding, and all other worke in those five Pageants of the Citie (Paynting excepted) were set downe" (II, 303). For the first time in the pageants we learn the identity of the artificer whom a dramatist singles out for recognition.[8] But Harrison went beyond his assigned function by preparing a folio which includes drawings of the seven arches and some text (much of it lifted from Dekker and Jonson); he called the pamphlet

---

[7]The complete textual problems and relationships are ably discussed by Fredson Bowers, *The Dramatic Works of Thomas Dekker* (Cambridge, 1955), II, 231-52. All quotations from Dekker will be from the Bowers' edition and those from Jonson from the edition cited in footnote #6. See also John Nichols, *The Progresses, Processions, and Magnificent Festivities, of King James the First* (London, 1828), I, 329-401. For discussion see Glynne Wickham, "Contributions de Ben Jonson et de Dekker aux Fêtes du Couronmement de Jacques Ier," in *Fêtes de la Renaissance*, ed. Jean Jacquot (Paris, 1956), I, 279-83. See also Graham Parry's analysis in *The Golden Age Restor'd: The Culture of the Stuart Court, 1603-42* (Manchester, 1981), pp. 1-21. See also my "King James's Civic Pageant and Parliamentary Speech in March 1604," *Albion* 34 (2002): 213-31.
[8]The role of the artificers is more fully discussed in Part Three, Chapter Ten.

The Arches of Triumph, which provides us with the first full set of drawings for an English civic pageant. These beautiful engravings help elucidate a dramatic form which places so much emphasis on visual content[9] (*see* figures 2-8). We also learn about actors who performed in this pageant, including children from the Queen's Revels and from the Children of St. Paul's. Two adult actors from Prince Henry's Men performed: Edward Alleyn and William Bourne (Bird). Alleyn, well-known from his roles in Marlowe's plays, took the role of the Genius Urbis at the Fenchurch arch. These actors' presence adds another dimension of the professional quality of this pageant.[10]

Extensive preparations had begun in the year previous in anticipation of the entry being made in July. Giovanni Carlo Scaramelli writes in July 1603 to the Venetian Senate: "There have been frequent discussions as to anticipating or postponing the date [of the entry] on account of the plague; the dread of plague need not delay the arrival of the Ambassadors, for the Court always lies at an uninfected place. For the Coronation six superb arches have been erected."[11] While the coronation took place as scheduled, the city delayed the processional, necessitating the taking down of the arches which became seven in number rather than six as Scaramelli says. In his text Dekker also refers to preparations:

> As touching those five [arches] which the Citie builded, the *Arbor* in Cheap-side, and the Temple of *Janus*, at Temple-bar, were both of them begun and finisht in sixe weekes. The rest were taken in hande, first in March last, after his Majestie was proclaymed, upon which, at that time, they wrought till a Moneth after Saint *James* his day following, and then gave over by reason of the sicknes: At this second setting upon them, six weekes more were spent. (II, 302)

Dekker mentions the committees established by the city for the planning and executing of the pageant, and he provides the number of laborers involved with the building of the arches under the supervision of Harrison. He also reveals something of the methods used:

> The Streets are surveyed; heigthes, breadths, and distances taken, as it were to make *Fortifications*, for the *Solemnities*. Seaven pieces of ground, (like so many fieldes for a battaile) are plotted foorth, uppon which

---

[9]For a discussion of the discrepancies which occur between Harrison's drawings and the texts of Jonson and Dekker, see my "Harrison, Jonson, and Dekker: The Magnificent Entertainment for King James (1604)," *Journal of the Warburg and Courtauld Institutes* 31 (1968): 445-8. See my additional discussion of Harrison, "Pageants, Masques, and Scholarly Ideology," *Practicing Renaissance Scholarship*, pp. 164-92.

[10]For further discussion of actors see my "Actors in English Civic Pageants."

[11]*Calendar of State Papers Venetian 1603-07*, X 63-64.

these Arches of Tryumph must shew themselves in their glorie: aloft, in the ende doe they advance their proude foreheads. (II, 258)

The Corporation of London records illustrate something of the planning procedure and the expense involved. As early as March 1603 the Common Council established a committee which may call "unto them all suche persons and men of learninge quallitie and experience and for suche auncient precedentes and recordes as they shall thinke fitt" in order to determine "the beste and fyttest meanes to be performed by this citie" in receiving the new king into the city at the time of his coronation.[12] After the initial decision to assess the guilds for £2,500 (*Journal*, XXVI, fol. 78), later assessments in July 1603, February 1604, and May 1604, brought the total sum to £4,100, a generous amount even if all of it did not go specifically to the construction of pageant devices. Small wonder that the Aldermen dispatched a group of Painter-stainers to view the pageants "and all the painters work uppon the same and consider what they shall think and esteeem them worthy to have for their workmanship and whether the said Painters have honestly and trulye done and performed their workes according to their promises and agremt with this Cittye."[13] Though the records contain a payment of unspecified amount to Harrison for his work (*Repertory*, XXVI, pt. 2, fol. 370[b]), no disbursements of money to Jonson and Dekker appear; for such indications of what a dramatist might earn for his labor, we shall have to wait for the records of the companies producing the Lord Mayors' Shows. Perhaps wishing to salvage some of their expenditure, the city council formed a committee in May to "take order aswell for the taking downe of all the said Pageantes carrying them into some fitt and Convenient place of saftye as for the sale of them and of the rayles postes and other thinges used in that service at the best and highest rates they can for the most benefitt and advauntage of all such of the severall Companyes as contributed towardes the charge of them."[14] As in 1559 when the city tried to preserve some of the materials for possible future use, so here in 1604 the city hopes to recoup some of its investment by selling what it can, a procedure first noted in connection with the royal entry into Bristol in 1574. Again the city and guilds collaborate to bring to life the pageant theater of the streets.

The Venetian Ambassador, Nicolo Molin, gives a synopsis of the entertainment in his dispatch; he wrongly claims eight arches, and he notes especially the one erected by the Italian merchants: "which certainly came first, both for the excellence of its design and for the painting which adorned it." And he provides an interesting footnote to the occasion: "None of the Ambassadors were present at any of these festivities, owing to the quarrel for precedence between France

---

[12]Corporation of London Records, *City Journal*, XXVI, fol. 74.
[13]Corporation of London Records, *Repertory*, XXVI, pt. 2, fol. 313.
[14]Corporation of London Records, *Journal*, XXVI, fol. 186.

and Spain,"[15] which reminds us of the political and social significance of these events. The quarrel for precedence which several times affected the make-up of the audience at a court masque here permeates the outdoor pageant theater as well. In order to help re-create the scene Harrison includes several facts about the presentation, observing, for example that James left the Tower between eleven and noon and had completed the trip to Westminster by five o'clock. Harrison notes the various companies lining the streets in their colors; and he adds the following about the conduits: "The Conduits of *Cornehill*, of *Cheape*, and of *Fleetestreete*, that day ran Claret wine very plenteously: which (by reason of so much excellent Musicke, that sounded foorth not onely from each severall *Pegme*, but also from diverse other places) ran the faster and more merrily downe into some bodies bellies."[16] Dekker also assists in presenting the scene on the day of the entertainment:

> The day (for whose sake, these wonders of Wood, clymde thus into the clowdes) is now come; ... The Streets seemde to bee paved with men: Stalles in stead of rich wares were set out with children, open Casements fild up with women.

> All Glasse windowes taken downe, but in their places, sparkeled so many eyes, that had it not bene the day, the light which reflected from them, was sufficient to have made one .... (II, 258)

Dekker underscores the fullness of this scene in contrast to the emptiness of a few months earlier when the plague stalked the streets of London.

The theater scene awaits the person who will complete it and add to the drama. As with Elizabeth's 1559 entry, so here it became difficult to hear many of the speeches, some of which Dekker says remained unspoken. Such continues to be one of the nagging problems of the street theater. James, his wife, and son (Henry) passed through London to universal acclaim; but even though the dramatic center of the festivity, James did not exploit the dramatic possibilities as Elizabeth had done. No references exist to any impromptu speeches which he might have given along the way; James's role seems much more passive. Arthur Wilson subjectively captures the mood:

> ... the City and Suburbs being one great *Pageant*, wherein he must give his ears leave to suck in their gilded *Oratory*, though never so *nauseous* to the *stomach*. He was not like his *Predecessor*, the late *Queen* of famous *memory*, that with a well-pleased affection met her peoples Acclama-

[15]*Calendar of State Papers Venetian*, X, 139. See my discussion in "Venetian State Papers and English Civic Pageantry, 1558-1642," *Renaissance Quarterly* 23 (1970): 37-47.
[16]Stephen Harrison, *Arches of Triumph* (London, 1604), sig. K1.

tions .... He endured the days brunt with *patience*, being assured he
should never have such another .... But afterwards in his *publick* ap-
pearances ... the accesses of the people made him so impatient, that he
often dispersed them with *frowns*, that we may not say with *curses*. So
various are the *natures* of *Princes*. ....[17]

This lack of responsiveness on James's part makes of the total theatrical experience something different from Elizabeth's coronation entry in which she engaged
in a type of continuous dialogue with actors and audience. In London in 1604 the
spectators had to settle for the mute presence of their sovereign.

No English pageant previously studied so depends on triumphal arches as
this one, and they embody highly embellished architectural achievements, the
details fortunately preserved in Harrison's drawings. One might refer to these
arches as good examples of a baroque style, contrasting strikingly in their ornate-
ness with the much simpler arches or scaffolds situated in London for Elizabeth's
coronation entry. The first arch (*see* figure 2) and dramatic presentation was at
Fenchurch, devised by Jonson. This arch, like all the others, functions as the
"stage" for the action, fantastically decorated with the city of London carved in
miniature on the top, with two chambers for musicians, and niches for the live
actors. These actors presenting various characters have costumes rich in full emblematic detail. In writing of his technique, Jonson observes that in these "more
magnificent Inventions," "the garments and ensignes deliver the nature of the
person, and the word the present office" (VII, 91). This awareness of method or
artistic self-consciousness Dekker shares in his text in comments on the function
of symbolism and allegory. Both dramatists clearly depend on an iconographical
tradition which helps make their characters viable, recognizable personifications.

The arch at Fenchurch had a cover of a curtain of silk, "painted like a thicke
cloud," which at the approach of the king vanished. The allegory suggests, Jonson
says, "that those clouds were gathered upon the face of the Citie, through their
long want of his most wished sight: but now, as at the rising of the Sunne, all
mists were dispersed and fled" (VII, 90). Something as simple as a curtain can
thus further the drama and the allegory, assisting also in complimenting the king.
Its removal reveals important allegorical figures, such as the one occupying the
most exalted position on the arch, Monarchia Britannica, a woman "richly at-
tyr'd, in cloth of gold and tissue"; in her hand she holds a sceptre and in her lap a
small globe, while "on her head [was] a fillet of gold, interwoven with palme and
lawrell ..." (VII, 84). Beneath her sat Theosophia, or Divine Wisdom, clothed in
white, "a blue mantle seeded with starres, a crowne of starres on her head. Her
garments figur'd truth, innocence, and cleerenesse" (84-5). In her hands she held

---

[17]Arthur Wilson, *The History of Great Britain, being the Life and Reign of King James the First* (London,
1653), pp. 12-13.

a dove and a serpent, emblems of her simplicity and subtlety; and she had a motto, *Per me reges regnant.*

On another section of the arch stood Genius Urbis, the part played by Alleyn, dressed in a mantle of purple, holding in one hand a goblet and in the other a "branch full of little twigs, to signifie increase and indulgence." Two figures surround him, one representing the counsel of the city and the other the war-like force of the city—"Expressing by those severall mots, connexed, that with those armes of councel and strength, the *Genius* was able to extinguish the kings enemies, and preserve his citizens ..." (86). On the lowest "stage" of the arch rested the personification of Tamesis, "his mantle of sea-greene or water colour, thin, and bolne out like a sayle; bracelets about his wrests, of willow and sedge, a crowne of sedge and reede upon his head, mixt with water-lillies ..." (86). Jonson suggests that such inanimate creatures as Tamesis may have feelings; in fact, "hee, now, no less pertooke the joy of his majesties gratefull approch to this citie ..." (87). The six daughters of Genius appear on the arch in two groupings of three located in descent from Monarchia Britannica. Harrison's drawing shows three of them on the right: Gladness, Loving Affection, and Unanimity; and three on the left: Veneration, Promptitude, and Vigilance. But Jonson lists them in a different order, and thus his descriptions and Harrison's drawing do not coincide.[18] At any rate, Jonson provides detailed costume and emblems assigned to each: Gladness appears in green, "in her right hand a crystall cruze fill'd with wine, in her left a cup of gold: at her feet a tymbrell, harpe, and other instruments, all ensignes of gladnesse ..." (87); Veneration, in "ash-colour'd sute," her hands crossed and her eyes half closed; Promptitude, in a garment of flame-color, "wings at her backe," "crowned with a chaplet of *trifoly*, to expresse readinesse, and opennesse every way ..." (88); Vigilance, in yellow, "a sable mantle, seeded with waking eyes, and silver fringe," "in her one hand a lampe, or cresset, in her other a bell. The lampe signified search and sight, the bell warning" (88); Loving Affection, in crimson fringed with gold, "her chaplet of red and white roses; in her hand a flaming heart: The flame expressed zeale, the red and white roses, a mixture of simplicity with love ..." (88-9); Unanimity, in blue, a chaplet of "blew lillies, shewing one trueth and intirenesse of minde. In her lappe lies a sheafe of arrowes bound together ... her selfe personating the unanimity, or consent of soule, in all inhabitants of the city to his service" (89). All of these figures, quite literally, demonstrate the virtues which support a city, and thus thematically we recall tableaux in the 1559 royal entry. As Jonson says, the arch illustrated "the very site, fabricke, strength, policie, dignitie, and affections of the Citie ..." (90).

This extravagant setting adds the speeches of Genius and Tamesis who welcome James to the city. Genius urges London to "reare / Thy forehead high, and on it strive to weare / Thy choisest gems ... / ... and in every street, / Let throng-

[18]See my essay cited in footnote #9, pp. 445-6.

ing joy, love, and amazement meet" (91). Finally he calls for Tamesis to rouse himself from his sleep, who first puzzled about why he should appear finally claims that he no less than others may "Boast our delights, albe't we silent lie" (93). The scene closes with a lengthy speech of Genius, who speaks directly to James bidding him welcome on behalf of the "councell, commoners, and multitude": "I tender thee the heartiest welcome, yet / That ever king had to his empires seate: / Never came man, more long'd for, more desir'd: / And being come, more reverenc'd, lov'd, admir'd ..." (93). Similar direct praise goes to Prince Henry and Queen Anne. Such an auspicious first pageant bodes well for the rest of the entertainment as Jonson succeeds in fusing action, speech, visual spectacle, and theme.

In Gracious street the arch erected by the Italian merchants in London and described in Dekker's text has paintings and carved figures rather than live actors (*see* figure 3). As Harrison's drawings show, in a large square near the top of the arch a scene depicted Henry VII seated "in his Imperiall Robes, to whome King *James* (mounted on horsebacke) approches, and receyves a Scepter ..." (II, 262)—clearly this picture means to illustrate the continuity between the Tudor and Stuart lines and to link James with another unifier, Henry, who united the warring houses. The arch underscores James's claim to the throne as well. On the top of the arch "stood a Person carved out to the life, (a woman) her left hand leaning on a sword, with the poynt downeward, and her right hand reaching foorth a Diadem," all suggesting the submission of the king's subjects (II, 263). Other figures include Peace bearing an olive branch as the emblem of peace, and sea figures, and another woman "holding in her hand a Shield, beneath whom was inscribed in golden *Caracters,—Spes ô fidissima rerum*" (263). The back side had pictures of a woman, "crown'd with beautifull and fresh flowres, a *Caducaeus* in her hand," probably representing Plenty, of a Triton with trumpet, and figures representing England, Scotland, France, and Ireland, "holding hands together ..." (265). The main square on the back contained a picture of Apollo, "with all his Ensignes and properties belonging unto him, as a *Sphere*, *Bookes*, a *Caducaeus*, an *Octoedron*, with other *Geometricall* Bodies, and a Harpe in his left hand: his right hand with a golden Wand in it, poynting to the battel of *Lepanto* fought by the *Turks*, (of which his Majestie hath written a *Poem*) ..." (265). These various figures and painted scenes constitute, Dekker says, "the Mutes and properties that helpt to furnish out this great *Italian Theater* ...." This mute stage gains life by the speech of conventional welcome spoken to James when he arrived at the arch by one waiting within the arch of the gate: "... All haile, thou Royallest of Kings: live, thou mightiest of Princes, in all happinesse: Reigne, thou wisest of Monarchs, in all prosperity: These are the wishes of us *Italians*: the hearty wishes of us all ..." (266). The Venetian Ambassador's conclusion that this was the most excellent arch must be laid to zealous nationalism.

Near the Royal Exchange the Dutch merchants erected an arch (*see* figure 4), on the top of which stood a woman "holding in one hand, a golden Warder, and poynting with the forefinger of the other hand up to heaven"; she personifies Divine Providence (II, 269). Beneath this "over-arching" presence of Providence a picture portrayed King James in his regal splendour, and "upon his left side stood a woman, her face fixed upon his, a burning hart in her right hand, her left hanging by, a *Heron* standing close unto her: upon his other side stood upright … another woman, winged …" (268). A little higher and on either side of the arch Fortitude (on the right) and Justice (on the left) stood between pyramids which emitted light; both figures have their traditional properties, obvious in Harrison's drawing. In vertical descent, and probably thematic as well, from Providence and James appears the main square on the front part of the arch containing seventeen women who, "(all of them sumptuously adorned, after their countrey fashion,) sate as it were in so many Chaires of State, and figuring in their persons, the 17 *Provinces of Belgia*, of which every one caried in a Scutchion … the Armes and Coate of one" (268). Painted on the front of the arch, scenes illustrate conditions of serenity and of strife, all alluding to the familiar problems of the Low Countries and recalling the pageants of 1582 in Antwerp and of 1586 in Leicester's tour of the Netherlands. The sovereign of England still has an intimate connection to the welfare of the Dutch people.

Dekker's description and Harrison's drawing basically agree except for four figures who appear in the engraving but not in Dekker's text; they range across the middle of the arch, two on each side of the seventeen Belgian women. On the far left a woman holds a cup and a cross, probably personifying Faith, especially religious faith; next, a woman has a bird (perhaps a dove) on her right hand and her left rests on an anchor (Hope); the third has two children clinging to her, probably representing Love; and the last carries a branch (perhaps olive or palm) in her right hand and a wreath in her left, personifying Peace (cf. the figure of Peace in Harrison's last drawing). Why these figures should appear in the drawing and not in the text remains puzzling: perhaps Harrison has simply added them on his own accord, or perhaps Dekker forgot to describe them since he did not design this arch. At any rate, they correspond with the allegory of the arch.

On the backside scenes portray the industry of the Dutch—spinning and weaving and fishing and shipping. Time and his daughter Truth found a place also as did personifications of Art, Sedulity, and Labour; and on top stood another "peace" figure, a woman carrying olive branches with the motto, *Sine caede et Sanguine* (II, 272). The boy who spoke helped bring together the meaning of the pageant and placed great emphasis on the role of Providence who, eminent in the arch, exhibits the controlling power in our lives and determines who shall be king: "God therefore (that guides the Chariot of the world) holds the Raynes of thy Kingdome in his owne hand …" (273). Emphasizing the relationship between the English and the Dutch, the child recalls the devotion of Elizabeth to their cause and pledges:

> The *Love*, which wee once dedicated to her (as a Mother) doubly doe wee vow it to you, our Soveraigne, and Father; intreating wee may be sheltred under your winges now, as then under hers: our Prayers being, that hee who through the loynes of so many Grand-fathers, hath brought thee to so many Kingdomes, may likewise multiply thy yeeres, and lengthen them out to the age of a *Phoenix* .... (II, 274)

Through its visual detail, as well as through verbal, this arch contains a thematic unity lacking in the Italian arch; here all elements point eventually to the role of Providence in men's lives, and kings who rule by divine sanction can be the human agents of this providence helping determine with Justice and Fortitude, as well as other virtues, the destiny of another people (i.e., Belgians) in war and peace.

The first arch designed by Dekker, located in Cheapside at Soper-lane End (*see* figure 5), stirs dramatic interest. Dekker provides the dimensions of the arch, which he titled *Nova Faelix Arabia*, and other details of "this Mechanicke Body," including the chief figure Arabia Brittannica, a woman, "attyred all in White, a rich Mantle of Greene cast about her, an imperiall Crowne on her head, and a Scepter in one hand, a Mound in the other ..." (II, 275). Under her stood the representation of Fame "in a Watchet Roabe, thickly set with open Eyes, and Tongues, a payre of large golden Winges at her backe, a Trumpet in her hand ... all these Ensignes desplaying but the propertie of her swiftnesse, and aptnesse to disperse Rumors" (276). But Harrison does not depict Arabia Britannica at all; instead, he grants the most eminent place to Fame.[19] Around the Fount of Virtue in the main middle section of the arch sat the Five Senses, clothed "in Roabes of distinct cullours, proper to their natures; and holding Scutchions in their handes: upon which were drawne Herogliphicall bodyes, to expresse their qualities" (276). At the bottom of the Fount slept Detraction and Oblivion, each holding a cup representing his poisonous and envious nature. Hand in hand, "attyred like three Sisters," the Graces stood on the right side of the arch—

> ... their countenaunces laboring to smother an innated sweetnes and chearefulnes, that appareled their cheekes; ... their Garmentes were long Roabes of sundry coloures, hanging loose: the one had a Chaplet of sundry Flowers on her head, clusterd heere and there with the Fruites of the earth. The seconde, a Garland of eares of Corne. The third, a wreath of Vine-branches, mixt with Grapes and Olives. (II, 277)

---

[19]Ibid., pp. 446-7.

THE REIGN OF JAMES I

Across from Aglaia, Thalia, and Euphrosyne stood the Hours in loose robes, wings at their feet, holding goblets full of flowers and figs. But these Graces and Hours, lavishly described by Dekker and perhaps reminiscent of the Elvetham pageant of 1591, Harrison conspicuously omits in his sketch. In their stead Harrison includes on the right the Four Cardinal Virtues though only two and part of a third are visible in the drawing—Wisdom, Justice, and Fortitude, obvious with their symbolic properties. On the left only two figures remain visible, both appearing like kings. The absence of the Graces and Hours seems all the more strange, given the action which takes place at the arch.

When James arrived at the device, Fame spoke in amazement that "*Vertues* Fount, which late ran deepe and cleare, / Dries, and melts all her body to a teare" (II, 278). The Graces and Hours, when asked about the cause of this strange event, must reply, "Wee cannot tell." Euphrosyne bids Fame to summon the drooping Senses "To tell the cause of this strange accidence." At the sound of Fame's trumpet, "*Arabia Britannica*, lookes cheerefully up, the *Sences* are startled," while Detraction and Oblivion begin to busy themselves at maliciously trying to suck dry the Fount; "But a strange and heavenly musicke suddainly striking through their eares, which causing a wildnes and quicke motion in their lookes, drew them to light upon the glorious presence of the *King*, they were suddainly thereby daunted and sunke downe ..." (278). Immediately the Fount began to flow "with Milke, Wine, and Balme." A young boy, a chorister of St. Paul's Dekker says, representing Circumspection stepped forward on a special stage and spoke to the king, bringing into perspective the visual scene and dramatic action. He flatters James by linking him to the Brutus mythical history of Britain and refers to the death of Elizabeth which has left the country desperate, with the result that the Fount of Virtue began to freeze and enemies such as Detraction and Oblivion sought to exploit the situation for their own evil ends. But finally—

> ... at thy glorious presence, both are gone,
> Thou being that sacred *Phoenix*, that doest rise,
> From th'ashes of the first: Beames from thine eyes
> So vertually shining, that they bring,
> To *Englands* new *Arabia*, a new Spring:
> For joy whereof, *Nimphes*, *Sences*, *Houres*, and *Fame*,
> Eccho loud Hymnes to his imperiall name. (II, 279)

The allegory of this miniature "morality play," by now obvious, links directly to the many pageants which celebrated the power of Elizabeth to bring beneficial change, to thwart vice and encourage virtue. So James becomes an actor in this drama, bringing light where there had been darkness, quickening Virtue when slumber left her prey to vice.[20] James stayed long enough to hear two boys sing "in sweete and ravishing voyces" that "*Troynovant* is now no more a Citie" because metaphorically she has become a summer arbor "or the nest wherein doth harbour, / The Eagle" (the sovereign), and a bridal chamber, "whose roofe is gold, floore is of Amber." "*Brittaine* till now nere kept a Holiday: / for *Jove* dwels heere: And tis no pittie, / If *Troynovant* be now no more a Cittie" (281). The city surrenders its normal functions in the desire to entertain the king with these substantial pageants, and the song anticipates the next pageant device—a summer arbor.

At the Cross in Cheap various officials of the city awaited the king's arrival, and Sir Henry Montague, Recorder of the City, presented his speech of welcome and a cup of gold to the three members of the royal family on behalf of the city. Then James experienced interruption by one representing Sylvanus, "drest up in greene Ivie, a Cornet in his hand, being attended on by foure other *Sylvans* in Ivie likewise, their bowes and quivers hanging on their shoulders, and winde Instruments in their hands" (282). Sylvanus serves for Dekker as a dramatic link with the next arch located at the Little Conduit in Cheap, for he assumes the role of a messenger dispatched by Peace, one of the chief occupants of the arch, providing at least a semblance of dramatic unity. In his speech Sylvanus in effect describes the arch, welcomes the king, and observes that Peace and Plenty "have languished many heavie moneths" for his presence. Sylvanus says to James: "By mee … shee [Peace] entreates, and with a knee sinking lower than the ground on which you tread, doo I humbly execute her pleasure, that ere you passe further, you would deigne to walke into yonder Garden: the *Hesperides* live not there but the *Muses*, and the *Muses* no longer than under your protection" (284). Thus this wood god, familiar from Kenilworth and Elvetham days, fulfills his role and brings James to the arch at which upon his arrival the nine boys, all choristers of Paul's Dekker tells us, representing the Muses sang a ditty accompanied by "their Viols and other Instruments."

This arch, garnished with all kinds of fruit and flowers "most artificially molded to the life," Dekker appropriately calls *Hortus Euporiae*, as Harrison's drawing illustrates well (*see* figure 6). On top of the arch stands Fortune, but the principal "persons advancde in this Bower, were, *Eirene* (*Peace*) and *Euporia* (*Plenty*) who sate together" (285), both symbolically costumed. Peace wears an upper garment of carnation and a white robe "powdred with Starres," a wreath of olive and laurel on her head; in one hand she holds a caducaeus, in the other ears of corn; on her lap sat a dove. Her daughter Plenty seated on her left wears a "rich mantle of Gold traversing her bodie," on her head a "crowne of Poppy and

---

[20]Cf. the action in Peele's 1591 Lord Mayor's Show, *Descensus Astraeae*, discussed in Chapter Four, in which Superstition and Ignorance try to poison the Fount of Justice, an incident which may have influenced Dekker here.

Mustard seede," in her right hand she holds a cornucopia. Beneath, Chrusos and Argurion, appropriately dressed, support a globe between them, "in token that they commaunded over the world" (286). At either side of these two stand Pomona, "attirde in greene, a wreath of frutages circling her temples," and Ceres, "crowned with ripened ears of Wheate, in a loose straw-coloured roabe." Stretched across the arch on one side sit the Muses, "With musicall instrumentes in their hands, to which they sung all the day," and on the other the Seven Liberal Arts, "Holding shieldes in their hands, expressing their severall offices" (286-7).

Vertumnus appears, "the maister Gardner, and husband to *Pomona*," whose brows "were bound about with flowers"; in one hand "he held a weeding hooke, in the other a grafting knife ..." (288). Dekker does not record his speech, but suggests "the tenor" of the speech; namely, that the arbor and trees growing in the Cynthian [i.e., Elizabethan] garden had begun to droop and despair of the "sharpenesse of the Autumnian malice" until now when they flourish "on the sudden by the divine influence apparelled with a fresh and more lively verdure than ever they were before." The Muses and Arts fearing banishment have new cause for hope. Vertumnus indulges in the garden metaphor by likening the officials of the city to gardeners "who carefully pruine this garden, (weeding-out al hurtful and idle branches that hinder the growth of the good,) and who are indeede, ... faithful Laborers in this peice of ground ..." (288). Those on the arch offer the king this bower "with the loving and loyall harts of all those the Sons of peace, standing about him ..." (289). A song celebrating the new brightness of James closes the scene; one stanza in particular underlines his regenerating power:

O this is Hee!
Whose new beames make our Spring,
Men glad and birdes to Sing,
Hymnes of praise, joy, and glee.
Chor. Sing, Sing, O this is hee! (II, 290)

Thus Dekker pursues the dramatic theme of the previous arch by assigning to the king the power to stir all nature, and this "garden" belongs to the kingdom's chief Gardener. Understandably, the king who can cause the Fount of Virtue to flow again and banish the evil forces, can now in a different setting quicken the pulse of nature, giving hope where there had been despair. In the words of the song: "how far soever, / Hee bides, no cloudes can sever, / His glorie from our eyes" (290).

The last arch designed by Dekker and located in Fleet street he called the *New World* (*see* figure 7), a title derived from the open globe situated in the middle of the arch, a globe which "was there seene to moove, being fild with all the degrees, and states that are in the land ..." (II, 295). Occupying the most promi-

nent place sat *Astraea* or Justice, "as being newly descended from heaven, gloriously attirde; all her garments beeing thickely strewed with starres"; but Dekker
adds: "Having tolde you that her name was *Justice*, I hope you will not put mee to
describe what properties she held in her hands, sithence every painted cloath can
informe you" (295)—a clear recognition of indebtedness to an iconographical
tradition. Directly beneath her sat *Arete* (Virtue), "her garments white, her head
crowned," and Fortune descended from Virtue, "her foote treading on the Globe,
that movde beneath her: Intimating, that his Majesties fortune, was above the
world, but his vertues above his fortune" (295). Again for Dekker the visual arrangement implies the thematic conclusion as we find here a vertical hierarchy.
Close by Virtue stood Envy, "unhandsomely attirde all in blacke, her haire of the
same colour, filletted about with snakes, … in a darke and obscure place by her
selfe …" (295). Harrison depicts two figures seated on either side of Virtue
which, while somewhat gruesome, do not readily fit Dekker's graphic description
of Envy. The tableau arrangement indicates a moral conflict between Virtue and
Envy who glances fearfully at Virtue and then at some of the other occupants of
the arch; namely, the Cardinal Virtues located on the right and the four kingdoms—England, Scotland, France, Ireland—on the left, all appropriately costumed. Surrounding the globe, the Four Elements "in their proper shapes …
upon the approch of his Majestie, went round in a proportionable and even circle, touching that cantle of the Globe, (which was open) to the full view of his
Majestie …" (296). The globe represented the "States of the land, from the Nobleman to the Ploughman …." In a speech written by Middleton, Zeal addressed
James at the arch, observing that the globe had seemed to move backward at the
death of Elizabeth, but it has been set in proper motion again by the presence of
the new king, "And now appeare new faces, and new men." The Elements enjoy
harmony, and the power of Envy wanes partly because James embodies the Cardinal Virtues. Further, the kingdom "By *Brute* divided, but by you alone, / All are
againe united and made *One* …" (298). Astraea has descended to earth again,
"Who with our last Queenes Spirit, fled up thither, / Fore-knowing on the earth,
she could not rest, / Till you had lockt her in your rightfull brest" (298). As in his
two previous arches, Dekker here explores the dramatic theme of the regenerating power of the new king, a power born of virtue, of course. Thematic unity
helps link Dekker's three tableaux.

The final triumphal arch Jonson located at Temple Bar (*see* figure 8), being
responsible for its design and the scene which took place there; and as with his
previous one, this tableau grows out of Jonson's classicism evinced by his elaborate notes. This arch constitutes a Temple of Janus, complete with a Janus head
and the title *Quadrifons*, because as Jonson explains, "he respecteth all climates,
and fills all parts of the world with his majestie …" (VII, 95). Though Janus had
four faces, he could not completely "behold the greatnesse and glorie of that day
…" (96). The chief figure *Irene* or Peace had an olive wreath on her head, on her

shoulder a silver dove; in one hand she held an olive branch, in the other a laurel crown, "as notes of victorie and plentie ..." (97). By her side stood Plutus, figured as a young boy carrying in his arms "a heape of gold Ingots to expresse riches, whereof hee is the god." Under the feet of Peace lay Mars "groveling, his armour scattered upon him in severall pieces"; thus for each of the virtuous allegorical figures Jonson places a vice underfoot, implying visually the typical sort of morality conflict. On the left side of the arch beneath Peace stood *Esychia* or Quiet, "the first hand-maid of peace," dressed in black with a nest on her head "out of which appeared storkes heads to manifest a sweet repose"; she holds in her hand a level as emblem of eveness and rest "on the top of it sate a *Halcion* or kings-fisher" (98). Appropriately, Tumult lay under her feet, "in a garment of divers, but darke colours, her haire wilde, and disordered" as signs of turmoil about her. Across the arch stood Liberty in a white, loose robe, her hair flowing down her back; "In her right hand shee bare a club, on her left a hat, the *Characters* of freedome, and power: At her feet a cat was placed, the creature most affecting, and expressing libertie" (98). She trod on Servitude, "a woman in old and worne garments, leane and meager, bearing fetters on her feet, and hands, about her necke a yoake to insinuate bondage ...." The third hand-maid of Peace was Safety dressed in red, wearing a helmet, carrying a spear in one hand for defense and in the other a cup for medicine; at her feet lay Danger with "a torch out, and a sword broken (the instruments of her furie) with a net and wolves skinne (the ensignes of her malice) rent in pieces" (99). The final virtue Felicity, "apparelled richly," bore in her right hand a "*Caduceus*, the note of peacefull wisedome: in her left, a *Cornucopia* fill'd onely with flowers, as a signe of florishing blessednesse ..." (99). At her feet Unhappiness lay with her cornucopia "turned downward with all the flowers falne out and scattered; upon her sits a raven, as the augury of ill fortune ..." (99-100). The "dumbe argument of the frame," as Jonson puts it, signified a return of golden times "wherein *Peace* was with us so advanced, *Rest* received, *Libertie* restored, *Safetie* assured, and all *Blessednesse* appearing in every of these vertues her particular triumph over her opposite evill" (100).

The speakers emerged from the two figures in the center of the arch, the Flamen Martialis and the Genius Urbis, who stand about an "altar" erected as within the temple. Because Jonson had presented the Genius at the first arch, he does not describe him now, but the Flamen wore a "long crimson robe to witnesse his nobilitie, his typpet and sleeves white, as reflecting on purity in his religion, a rich mantle of golde with a traine to express the dignitie of his function" (100). In his hand "he bore a golden censor with perfume, and censing about the altar (having first kindled his fire on the toppe) is interrupted by the *Genius*" (101). The interesting conversation which follows between the two demonstrates how in the hands of a skilled dramatist and poet the verbal feature of civic pageantry can rival the obvious visual splendor. The characters become viable dramatic characters in Jonson's hands. Essentially the Genius wants to know why the Flamen kindles an "unhallowed fire / Upon this altar." He explains that he has been roused from sleep by the "noise, and present tumult of this day," and recognizing the day as the Ides of March, he has come to celebrate the feast of *Anna Perenna*. But the Genius forcefully argues that—

> ... these dead rites
> Are long since buryed, and new power excites
> More high and heartie flames. Loe, there is hee,
> Who brings with him a greater ANNE then shee:
> Whose strong and potent vertues have defac'd
> Sterne MARS his statues, and upon them plac'd
> His, and the worlds b[l]est blessings: This hath brought
> Sweet peace to sit in that bright state shee ought,
> Unbloudie, or untroubled; hath forc'd hence
> All tumults, feares, or other darke portents
> That might invade weake minds; hath made men see
> Once more the face of welcome libertie:
> And doth (in all his present acts) restore
> That first pure world, made of the better ore. (VII, 102)

Therefore, the Genius bids the Flamen to leave "with thy superstitious fumes, / And cense not here ..." (103). Instead the Genius shall maintain the fire as the flame of Peace, and he closes by wishing for the king highest achievements and blessed fortune. Skilfully Jonson has linked the speeches of conflict of the mythological figures with the "dumbe argument of the frame": the personified allegorical figures, all elements pointing to a new day ushered in by the new sovereign with virtue triumphant over evil.

The final device of this civic pageant Jonson designed and placed in the Strand; not exactly a triumphal arch, it consisted of a rainbow, moon, sun, and seven stars "which antiquitie hath styl'd the *Pleiades* ... advanced betweene two magnificent Pyramid's, of 70 foot in height ..." (106). Electra serves as the speaker, offering an amalgam of learning and instruction. In addition to referring to the previous tableau, Electra pledges that no mist or cloud "may mixe with splendor of thy golden raigne ..." (108). With imperative certainty, Electra articulates the cause of virtue:

> The dam of other evils, avarice,
> Shall here locke downe her jawes, and that rude vice
> Of ignorant, and pittied greatnesse, pride,
> Decline with shame; ambition now shall hide
> Her face in dust, as dedicate to sleepe,

That in great portalls wont her watch to keepe.
All ills shall flie the light: Thy court be free
No lesse from envie, then from flatterie;
All tumult, faction, and harsh discord cease,
That might perturbe the musique of thy peace .... (108)

This hopeful speech grounded in the moral pursuit of virtue makes a fitting con-clusion to a lavish entertainment; and it underscores the seriousness of the pag-eant dramatic form which in the midst of song, elaborate costume, architectural wonders, and endless praise seeks to convey a moral theme.

Thus closes this civic pageant with what one contemporary called its "Tro-phies of glory, Pageants of that magnificence the like was never ...."[21] Elaborate arches with their mute visual arguments, live actors, speeches, all conspire to offer both instruction and entertainment to sovereign and audience alike. The dominance of the figure of Peace implies a hope for the country; the role of Jus-tice, Divine Providence, and Virtue in the affairs of men also gets celebrated. James emerges as one who brings unity and a stable transition, offering hope where there had been despair. Reminiscent of the portraits of Elizabeth, he ap-pears as one with a mystical, transforming power, a theme which dominates the final arches. All about him he can witness the virtues needed for a peaceful king-dom, a kingdom which must be administered with the loving care of a gardener tending his garden.

A brief comparison of the 1604 royal entry with Elizabeth's coronation pro-cessional through London in 1559 suggests something of the development of pageantry within that forty-five year period. One notices, for example, that the triumphal arches appear at almost precisely the same places where the pageant devices had been previously; the involvement of the city and guilds becomes similar in both cases, as also, of course, the processional nature of the entry. Alle-gorical, mythological, and historical figures occur in both to varying degrees; thus the basic subject areas have not altered measurably. Both Elizabeth and James witnessed the representation of virtues that support a kingdom; at the Cornhill pageant in 1559 Elizabeth saw these qualities treading underfoot their opposite vice, a technique duplicated in Jonson's final arch at Temple Bar. The visual motif of the flourishing green hill in the earlier entry Dekker continues in the summer arbor at the Little Conduit in Cheap; interestingly both devices with the fertile hill or arbor locate at the same spot, though separated by some four

---

[21]Gilbert Dugdale, *The Time Triumphant* (London, 1604), sig. B1. Apparently this is an eyewitness account, though somewhat inaccurate. Dudgale mentions most of the arches and recognizes various figures on them. His pamphlet corroborates many of the details found in the printed texts of the entertainment. See my discussion of Dugdale, "Gilbert Dugdale and the Royal Entry of James I (1604)," *Journal of Medieval and Renaissance Studies* 13 (1983): 111-25; and reprinted in *Practicing Renaissance Scholarship*, pp. 147-63.

decades of time. All of these resemblances testify to a basic continuity in pageantry both in form and content.

Instructive differences exist also, the most apparent being the change from the relatively simple scaffolds of 1559 to the highly ornate triumphal arches of 1604, a change which reflects innovations taking place in other dramatic forms, such as the masque which begins to come of age. The 1604 pageant makes sophisticated use of machinery, such as the fount and the mechanical globe and the curtains which disappeared as James approached an arch. Dramatic dialogue becomes more significant in the 1604 pageant than in the earlier one, an ingredient largely missing from Elizabeth's entry where set speeches by children on the scaffolds become the norm. Such dialogue, found also in other Elizabethan pageants and in the emerging Lord Mayor's Show, and its effective use here, at the hands of Jonson and Dekker, illustrate the change of the form from the mid-sixteenth century to the beginning of the seventeenth, opening the way for at least minimal character development and contributing to the "dramatic" nature of the pageants. The dynamic action at the Fount of Virtue and the dramatic function of Sylvanus suggest a mature form beyond merely allegorical tableaux and set speeches. In this Jacobean pageant mythology gets increased use, reflecting again a pattern in all Elizabethan drama and certainly the pageants. The overtly religious presentation loses ground in the period 1559-1604. Elizabeth might receive a Bible from Truth, see the allegorical representation of the Beatitudes, and hear the words of one personating Deborah of Biblical history, but no such events greet James. Most English drama thus moves away from its explicitly Biblical heritage, although the influence of the medieval morality play remains as strong as ever. In a sense, then, this London entertainment for James constitutes a pivotal moment in civic pageantry, for it embodies most of the changes which have occurred in its own form since Elizabeth's accession, and no major developments will take place in the future—slight variations and modifications of course, but no fundamental innovation. Other pageants, particularly the Lord Mayor's Show which becomes annual, will build on methods and content contained in the 1604 royal entry. And with the involvement of such dramatists as Jonson, Dekker, and Middleton, pageantry achieves a new status; certainly the pageants which follow in the Jacobean and Caroline period do not lack for the active participation of well-known dramatists. The simpler, somewhat amateurish drama of Elizabethan civic pageantry gives way to a more sophisticated form. The 1604 royal entry becomes in many respects a turning point, the culmination of what has preceded it and the prototype of what follows.

Jonson's entertainment for James and Anne at the house of Sir William Cornwallis at Highgate in May 1604 in a sense looks backward to the Arcadian world of Elizabethan progress pageants, but with a difference: understandably, Jonson's polished effort brims with classical learning, but the sort of "planned spontaneity" of the Elizabethan shows does not occur here. It shares some char-

acteristics with Sidney's 1578 entertainment at Wanstead, though Jonson provides a much more formal structure, with no native English figures. The royal
couple first encounters two *Penates*, household gods "attir'd after the antique
manner," in a speech which alternates between the two but has a single content
of praise. Being led through the house by the Penates, the king and queen come
to the garden where Mercury, traditionally costumed, greets them and says: "To
tell you, who I am, and weare all these notable, and speaking ensignes about me,
were to challenge you of most impossible ignorance, and accuse my selfe of as
palpable glorie ..." (VII, 138). He refers to the place as the bower of Maia, his
mother, and metaphorically likens it to the Arcadian hill where he was born.
Gathered around his mother, "in the pride of her plentie," sit Aurora, Zephyrus,
and Flora; here May holds state, and "Hither the *Dryads* of the valley, and
Nymphs of the great river come every morning, to taste of her favors ..." (138).
All nature, Mercury suggests, seems to be struck dumb by the presence of "two
such marvailes ..." (139). Then begins the three part song of Aurora, Zephyrus,
and Flora, the opening of which captures the content of this song of praise:

> See, see, o see, who here is come a Maying!
> The master of the Ocean;
> And his beautious ORIAN:
> Why left we off our playing?
> To gaze, to gaze,
> On them, that gods no lesse then men amaze. (139)

When the song ends, May herself speaks, unable to think of a gift adequate "for
the grace, / And honor, you vouchsafe the place," but she vows many gifts of nature if "*you will oft come here a Maying*" (140-41). That evening after dinner Mercury appeared again, this time with his son Pan who with his companions dances
around the "fountain of laughter" or "Bacchian spring," and the conflict between
father and son soon emerges in their dialogue. Pan tries to entice all to drink of
the lusty glass—"A little of this, / Tane downe here in private, were not amisse"
(143). Finally Mercury asks pardon for Pan's indecorous behavior and closes
with this hope for the royal couple—

> That your loves be ever flourishing as May, and your house as fruitfull:
> That your acts exceed the best, and your yeares the longest of your
> predecessors: That no bad fortune touch you, nor good change you. But
> still, that you triumph, in this facilitie, over the ridiculous pride of other
> Princes; and for ever live safe in the love, rather then the feare of your
> subjects. (144)

Mythological figures who offer praise and also instruction again serve the purposes of compliment and welcome.

The city of London participated in the reception of the king of Denmark, Christian IV, Anne's brother, in 1606. He arrived in mid-July and received various entertainment until 31 July when he and James and the royal family made an official entry into London. With short preparation time, in early July the Common Council and Aldermen established committees to arrange entertainment for the event. The order goes out that the streets "bee prepared in the best and most beautiful manner for the honor of this Cytie that in so short a tyme may bee performed As also that our Pageant should bee prepared and placed in some such meet and convenient place within this Cytie as should bee thought meete ...."[22] Another entry in the Corporation records indicates a sum of £1000 levied on the companies for the expenses of the event. The Venetian Ambassador observes the inability of the city to make "such preparations as it desired"; he adds: "All the Ambassadors were invited, but were accommodated in private houses far apart from one another. The ceremony was a magnificent and noble one, both on account of the great gathering of personages, the richness of their robes, and the trappings of their horses ...."[23]

As in the other entries, the companies lined the streets of the processional "in Satten, Velvet, and other Silke Doublets, and Hose, Gold Chaynes about their neckes ...."[24] The route, similar to the one taken by James in 1604, began at the Tower and moved westward to the Royal Exchange where the conduit ran with wine and the city trumpeters sat atop the Exchange sounding their trumpets at the appropriate moment. The Conduit in Cheapside had the form of a garden, adorned with fruit of all kinds; here the Recorder presented a gift and his speech on behalf of the city. Also in Cheapside stood a triumphal arch covered with sea scenes. Over the right hand arch Neptune appeared dressed in blue and mounted on a seahorse; over the left in another sea cave sat Mulciber mounted on a dragon. Rising above these two areas another one surrounded by pyramids contained the personification of Concord "who uppon the neere approach of the Kings, was by a quaint devise let downe in her throne, to the lower and middle concave" where she addressed the kings and "discovered to their Majesties the modell of a faire citie" where sat the Genius of the City of London (sig. D1). The speeches of Concord, London, and Neptune, all in Latin, and conventional speeches of praise, John Marston apparently prepared; at least he gets credit for them in the British Library Royal MS. 18A where the speeches occur. After a song

---

[22]Corporation of London Records, *Journal*, XXVII, fol. 73.

[23]*Calendar of State Papers Venetian*, X, 384.

[24]*The King of Denmarkes Welcome* (London, 1606), sig. C3ᵛ. All quotations are from this source unless cited otherwise. See also the pamphlet by Henry Robarts, *The Most royall and Honourable entertainement, of the famous and renowned King, Christiern the fourth* (London, 1606). Also Nichols, II, 64f., and IV, 1074f.

by sea nymphs, the entourage moved on to Fleet street where another "fine artificiall sommer bower" had inside a shepherd courting a coy shepherdess who will
not love him until she "could behold two Sunnes at one time of equall brightnesse: when there were two Majesties of like splendor, or two Kings in one state
..." (sig. D2). Obviously, the condition has now been met with the arrival of
James and Christian IV at the arbor, a point made by the shepherd. After the
speeches and a song of farewell, the kings departed on to Temple Bar where the
Lord Mayor took leave of them. This brief entry places its emphasis on welcome
to the visiting sovereign but also suggests through the metaphorical (and literal)
descent of Concord the unity which binds their separated kingdoms. Obviously
the 1604 entertainment remains fresh in the memories of the planners for the
civic pageant.

On St. George's Day in 1610 the city of Chester presented an entertainment
in honor of Prince Henry, who apparently was not present; nevertheless the
praise and enthusiasm for him proceeded.[25] A pamphlet containing the description of the pageant by Richard Davies survives; in fact, he may have been the author of the show along with Robert Amerie whose claim of authorship occurs at
the end of the quarto text.[26] The pageant took the form of a processional on
horseback through the city punctuated by occasional speeches. Allegorical figures
dominate the scene, though others appeared, such as the "green-men" dressed in
ivy and bearing Herculean clubs—the element of the savage or wild-man still
retains a certain vitality in pageantry. Many persons on horseback simply carry
properties suggesting Saint George. But Fame with a trumpet in her hand speaks
in praise of the day; a song follows urging the descent of Mercury who obliges by
"descending from heaven in a cloud, artificially Winged, a Wheele of fire burning
very cunningly, with other Fire-workes ..." (sig. A3ᵛ). Mercury says that he has
descended from the throne of the immortal gods, "commanded by them all / To
visite Him whose rare report hath rung / Within their eares, and scal'd the lofty
clouds: / His erned fame on earth hath pierc'd the skie, / Ascending up unto the
highest Heavn's ..." (sig. B2ᵛ-B3). Other characters representing the city Chester,
Britain, and Cambria also speak in unrestrained praise of Henry. An oration by
Rumour, mounted on horseback, alludes to the "matchlesse Magnanimity" of
Saint George, in a sense offering a justification for his position as patron saint of
the country. Peace offers promises: "I'le rend the close-mouth'd rage of emulous
strife, / And wound Distraction, with Connexions knife. / And when damn'd
Malice comes but once in sight / I, with a vengeance, will suppresse her straight. /

---

[25]See my "Prince Henry and English Civic Pageantry," *Tennessee Studies in Literature* 13 (1968): 109-
16.
[26]*Chesters Triumph in Honor of Her Prince. As it was performed upon S. Georges Day 1610 in theforesaid
Citie* (London, 1610). All quotations will be from this text. Text also in Nichols, II, 291f., and reprint
by Cheatham Society.

I'le send pale Envie downe to hell with speed, / Where she upon her Snakes shall onley feed" (sig. C2-C2ᵛ). This forceful Peace has accompanying her Plenty, wearing a garland of wheat and casting and strewing wheat as she rides along; she also speaks, promising bounty for the land in cooperation with Peace. (This joining of Peace and Plenty takes us back to one of Dekker's arches in 1604.)

This somewhat static presentation gains new dramatic energy by the arrival of Envy, "with a Wreath of Snakes about her head; another in her hand, her face and armes besmeard with blood" (sig. A4ᵛ), and Love, who immediately engage in conflict with one another, a conflict shown in their exchange of dialogue. Envy enumerates many of the things which give her pleasure, such as seeing Virtue overwhelmed by Care; to this catalogue of malice Love responds, seeing no sign of grace in Envy, and bids her from this time forth, "ne're frequent this Iland of the North. / Dive to the depth of deepest Stigian flood; / There sucke thou Snakes, and Snakes there suck thy blood. / Or sinke thou quite to the infernall deepe, / Where crawling Scorpions may about thee creepe" (sig. C4). But Envy retorts: "O I could grind and grate thee with my teeth ...." So the conversation continues until Envy, "ugly Monster, Loves Misanthropos," departs after the scathing words of Joy who joins battle against Envy. In a speech which draws together the various persons of the pageant, Joy says to Envy:

> ... thy everlasting shame
> Shall be still blasted by the Trumpe of *Fame*:
> The powrefull tongue of facund *Mercury*,
> Shall to the world display thy Infamy.
> *Chester* abhors thy presence; *Britaine* hates thee;
> And for a damned fury, *Camber* takes thee.
> *Peace*, as a Herrald, shall proclaime to All,
> That thou art damn'd by Justice-Generall.
> *Plenty* detests thy base Society .... (sig. C4ᵛ)

With all the forces of virtue arrayed against her, Envy finds it expedient to exit, and the drama resolves. The dramatic center of this civic pageant in a provincial town focuses again on the ageless struggle between vice and virtue, and great zeal helps expunge vice. This Chester entertainment continues the development we have noted in the Elizabethan period, such as in the Norwich pageant, of granting dramatic substance to the conflict, not settling simply for tableau presentation.

The following month, May 1610, saw the investiture of Prince Henry as Prince of Wales, and festivity abounded, only one small part of which might be called a civic pageant. The show of welcome that took place on the Thames again involved the active participation of the trade companies and the city. Corporation records indicate that the dramatist Anthony Munday, already the deviser of several Lord Mayors' Shows, wrote the pageant; the city orders the Chamberlain to pay Munday "who was ymployed for the devising of two speeches to be delivered to the Prince ... the some of seaven and Fortie shillinges by him disbursed for divers necessaries concerning the same preparation and Foure pounde six shillinge and Four pence for his paines and labour taken ...."[27] Munday's commemorative pamphlet, *Londons Love to the Royal Prince Henrie* contains a description of the entertainment and the two speeches.[28] In terms of theater history this pageant involves one of the most prominent actors of the day, Richard Burbage, offering conclusive evidence of eminent players' participation in pageant drama. The evidence comes in the Corporation records:

> Itm it is ordered that Mr Chamberlen shall pay unto Mr Burbage and John Rice the players that rode upon the two fishes and made the speeches ... Seaventeene poundes tenn shillinges six pence by them disbursed for robes and other furniture for adorning themselves at the same meeting, And that they shall reteyne to their owne uses in lieu of their paynes therein taken all such Taffety silke and other necessaries as were provided for that purpose without any further allowance. (*Repertory*, XXIX, fol. 232b)

With John Rice also involved small wonder that Munday refers to the "two absolute Actors, even the verie best our instant time can yeeld ..." (p. 11).

The companies and the Lord Mayor lined the Thames in their barges for Henry's arrival from Richmond, but the entertainment itself remains rather slight and consists of the two speeches given by Corinea and Amphion mounted on dolphins. Near Chelsea the prince receives greetings from Corinea, "*a very fayre and beautifull Nimphe, representing the Genius of olde Corineus Queene, and the Province of Cornewall, suited in her watrie habit yet riche and costly, with a Coronet of Pearles and Cockle shelles on her head ...*" (p. 14). She bids the Prince to accept the city's boundless love, "which is like to *Jaacobs Ladder*, reaching from Earth to Heaven. Whereon, their hourelie, holie and devoute desires (like to so many blessed Angelles) are continually ascending and descending ... That unpolluted soules may be ever about yee, false harts or foule hands never to come neere yee ..." (p. 16). Further along the river toward Whitehall, Henry encountered Amphion, played by Burbage, on a dolphin, "*a grave and judicious Prophetlike personage, attyred in his apte habits, ... with his wreathe of Sea-shelles on his head, and his harpe hanging in fayre twine before him: personating the Genius of*

[27]Corporation of London Records, *Repertory*, XXIX, fol. 233.
[28](London, 1610), all quotations from this Munday text. See Nichols, II, 315f. See also for additional description *The Order and Solemnitie of the Creation of the High and mightie Prince Henrie* (London, 1610).

Wales ..." (p. 19). Amphion, saddened by the prospect of the prince's departure to land, realizes its necessity; thus he offers the farewell: "Home againe then fayre Fleete, you have brought a Royall freight to landing, such a burden as hath made the River not meanely proude to beare. And since we must needs parte, in our lowdest voyce of Drommes, Trompets and Ordenaunce, be this our last accent: Long live our Prince of Wales, the Royall Henrie" (p. 21). Accordingly, the drums, trumpets, and ordnance respond vigorously. Spectacle and compliment inform this brief theatrical experience. Interestingly, the mock sea battle which took place a few days later lacks the sort of allegorical meaning associated with such battles in Elizabethan pageantry.

The year 1613 seems to have been one of the busiest for entertainments during James's reign; perhaps the festivity attempted to overcome the shocking grief at Prince Henry's death in early November 1612, the death of one already splendidly entertained on two occasions in 1610 and universally acclaimed for his winning personality and abilities. At any rate, the social event which triggered much of the entertainment in 1613 was the wedding of Elizabeth, daughter of James and Anne, to Prince Frederick, Elector Palatine, on 14 February 1613. Several sumptuous masques fill out the days of the wedding; but nothing, however, truly qualifies to be called a civic pageant. The two principal public events included an elaborate fireworks display on 11 February and a mock sea battle on the 13th.[29] The fireworks, ranging from a depiction of St. George slaying the dragon to a battle at the Castle of Envy, truly strain description; but the sea battle, supposedly a re-enactment of the battle of Lepanto between the Turks and Christians, seems rather disappointing with no dramatic meaning emerging from it. For a civic pageant honoring this new royal couple we must shift the scene to the continent.

The circuitous journey to Germany included a tour through part of the Low Countries, with entertainment in Amsterdam, Haarlem, and Utrecht. Similarly many German towns received the couple before they finally reached Heidelberg in June 1613. For example, in Oppenham four elaborate triumphal arches lined the streets, presenting such allegorical figures as Fortitude, Virtue, Fortune, Hope, Concord, and Faith, recognizable by their emblematic properties.[30] One arch even celebrates the union of the Lancaster and York houses, being appropriately garnished with red and white roses. Further along the tour, the citizens of Franckendal offered two arches, one presenting several German kings and the virtues that each represented, and the second depicting Fame at the top of the arch with the virtues Constancy, Justice, Widsom, and Magnanimity located

[29]For descriptions of these events see John Taylor, *Heavens Blessing and Earths Joy* (London, 1613) and *The Marriage of the two great Princes* (London, 1613). Also in Nichols, II, 527f.
[30]For a full description of the whole tour including many excellent illustrations, see *Beschreibung Der Reiss: Emphfahung des Ritterlichen Ordens* ... (Heidelberg, 1613).

across the scaffold—all strongly reminiscent of the elaborate arches prepared for James's 1604 London entry. Elizabeth and Frederick also witnessed in Francken-dal in early June a dramatic rendition of the siege of Troy complete with a battle between the Trojans and Greeks and the presence of a "Horse of extreame pro-portion and greatnesse" left before the walls.[31] A few days later the royal couple entered Heidelberg where "the Streets [were] covered with throngs of people, drawne thither by the fame of such Showes and Pageants as were builded to adde honour to this Entertainment, but especially to behold *Her*, upon whom all their eyes were fixed with love and admiration" (sig. C1-C1ʳ). This city erected several arches, each containing its mute argument of visual meaning. Near the university the faculties of medicine, philosophy, theology, and law, each prepared a scaffold saluting its particular art and the royal couple.

But, for some reason, English sources describing the entertainment primarily focus on the festivities in the tiltyard at Heidelberg shortly after the entry. The entertainment includes a procession of allegorical and mythological figures with slight dramatic value, though a few speeches and songs exist in the German text, but the visual splendor must have been quite rewarding. The first day offered Jupiter and Juno, each in a chariot, Jupiter's drawn by griffins and Juno's by pea-cocks. Attended by appropriate companions, the God of Husbandry and Nep-tune, god of the sea, entered, and on a rock three mermaids sat singing and play-ing their instruments. Arion, playing his lute and sitting on a sea-horse (though the German text and drawing indicate Orpheus instead), soon followed; and be-hind him came the Seven Deadly Sins, chained and driven forward by a dragon, spitting fire all the way—(the German text and illustration include nine rather than seven). Frederick himself got into the scene by personating Jason in a mag-nificent ship containing the golden fleece and having at the stern Envy "eating her owne heart." Mars, Hercules, Venus, and Cupid all preceded the imperial chariot bearing Victory, and "Next unto *Victory* entered *Diana*, in a Chariot made like a Forrest, set out and adorned with living Birds and Beasts" with satyrs and nymphs following. The next day's entertainment continued with Frederick still in the person of Jason, this time on horseback. Two of the chief figures, each accompanied by a number of appropriate attendants, represented Bacchus and Apollo. Mydas with his ass's ears entered as did Marsyas "and a *Saytre* fleaing off his skinne, because hee durst contend with *Apollo*, in Musicke" (sig. C3ᵛ). On a movable Mount of Parnassus sat the Muses, after whom entered the Graces, ac-companied by Hercules and Mercury. No particular theme rises out of this color-ful spectacle, though the mythological gods and goddesses and allegorical virtues by their very presence lend a sanction to the occasion as having deemed the fes-

---

[31]*The Magnificent, Princely. and most Royall Entertainments given to the High and Mightie Prince ... Frederick ... and Elizabeth* (London, 1613), sig. B4ᵛ. Quotations will be from this source. See Nichols, II, 617f.; and John Stow, Annales (London, 1615), pp. 922f.

tivity worthy of their attendance. The pageant imagination in Heidelberg depends greatly on allegory and symbolism, even to the point of Frederick's becoming the enchanting Jason of mythology.

Touring several places and being entertained during 1613, Queen Anne also went on progress where in late April she received welcome by Lord Knowles at Cawsome House near Reading with a show devised by Thomas Campion. Out of a bower upon the arrival of the queen appeared a *Cynick*, "drest in a skin-coate ... set thicke with leaves and boughes ...."[32] After his speech praised a solitary life, a "fantastick Traveller" discovered himself wearing a "silken sute ... made up after the Italian cut, with an Italian hat, ... with a Courtly feather, long guilt spurres, and all things answerable" (p. 79). Soon both men engage in conversation until the Traveller convinces the Cynic to become part of society; they then mount their horses and go to the park gate "where they are received by two Keepers," and around them stood "two *Robin-Hood* men in sutes of greene striped with blacke ... they wore broad flat caps with greene feathers crosse quite over them, carrying grene Bowes in their hands, and greene Arrowes by their sides" (80). Speeches and songs follow. Similar entertainment occurs in the lower garden where with song and effusive praise a Gardener, his man, and boy greet Anne, all dressed in costume representing their trade. In some respects this brief pageant resembles many of the Elizabethan progress entertainments, although less fully developed and rather devoid of dramatic theme.

Anne went to Bristol in early June 1613, where the mayor and others welcomed her into the city. The main entertainment focused on a battle on the water, which may remind us of a similar kind of show provided for Elizabeth's visit to Bristol in 1574. Records of the city contain a number of entries concerning the festivities, especially the building of a bower from which the queen could witness the sport; in fact, Henry Goodman received seventeen shillings "to make the Bower," five shillings disbursed for nails, two shillings for "Rosewater sweete Water to sprinkle the bower," and a couple of maids got one shilling "for dressinge the bower."[33] John Chamberlain writing to Sir Dudley Carleton observes: "there was a Shew made on the river at high-water against the mouth of the river at the Gibb; and there was built a scaffold in Canons' Marsh finely decorated with ivy-leaves and flowers for her Majestie to sit in and see the fight."[34] He estimates the crowd at 30,000 persons, which certainly makes a "public" or "civic" occasion out of the entertainment. Like the mock-battle presented to entertain the new royal couple Frederick and Elizabeth earlier in the year, the one at Bristol presents also a skirmish between Turkish and Christian forces. Robert Naile describes the beginning of the battle in his lengthy poem: "Formost of all an English

---

[32]*Campion's Works*, ed. Percival Vivian (Oxford, 1909), p. 78.
[33]Bristol Archives, *Audits 1610, 1611, 1613*, fol. 29, p. 158.
[34]In Nichols, II, 646.

Ship came stemming with the tyde, / And right before her *Graces* Tent at Anchor did she ride, / ... / But whiles at Anchor there they lay, they gan discry from farre / Two Turkish Gallies well prepar'd, most mighty men of warre ...."[35] Finally the fierce battle begins to abate with the Christian forces victorious. The Turks even leave some of their troops behind, "Which captives brought before her *Grace*, on bended knees did crave / For mercy, which her *Majestie* with pardon freely gave" (sig. D1). Anne becomes part of the drama much as Elizabeth had in many pageants, including the one in Bristol where she decided the issue between war and peace. Interpreting the scene, Naile writes:

> Loe here behold by this triumph, as in a mirror plaine,
> How mighty *Jove* against all foes our quarrell doth maintaine,
> Confounding all their privie plots, and close Conspiracies,
> Who for to undermine our state, against us doe arise.
> Their vaine attempts and boundles thoughts, he turnes to their decay
> Entrapped in the self-same snare, they did for others lay .... (sig. D1)

While Naile may make this interpretation, the dramatic scene itself does not lead one inevitably to that conclusion; again the mock-battle of Jacobean pageantry generally lacks inherent dramatic theme—it lacks an allegorical mold which could give shape and bestow meaning.

The pageant at Wells a few months later fully involved the trade guilds and the city, the evidence of which fortunately survives in records preserved in Wells. By 19 July the city had received word of Anne's planned visit, so they determine to present a gift of a silver bowl, to decorate the streets, and rid the town "of beggars and Rogues ...." [36] Further orders indicate what the mayor and other dignitaries should wear for Anne's entry; a committee formed "to give allowance for the matters of the Shewes whether they bee fit or not And every companie to bee Contributorie as they have binne in tymes past to the shewes aforesaid" (fol. 376). A later entry in the records specifies "that every Companie and every severall man within the Companie shall Contribute such somme and sommes of money towardes the said shewes as shalbee agreed uppon amongst themselves or in defalt of such agreement by them then by the greatest parte of the xxiiij^tie uppon paine of imprisonment and there to lie till such severall rate bee payde and satisfied" (fol. 377). These preparations and the sharing of the financial burden

---

[35]Robert Naile, *A Relation of the Royall ... Entertainment, given to the High, and Mighty Princesse, Queene Anne, at the renowned Citie of Bristoll ...* (London, 1613), sig. C3^v. Quotations are from this text.
[36]Wells, Town Clerk's Office, *Wells Acts of the Corporation 1553-1623*, fol. 374. All quotations are from this manuscript source. See Nichols, II, 673f.

by the companies follow closely the pattern found in other pageant entertainments where extant records give sufficient evidence for the procedures.

The presentation by the various companies in Wells on 20 August may remind us of some qualities of medieval drama, especially the cycle plays in which
the appropriate guild would be matched to a corresponding scene. Thus the first
company group, comprising Hammermen, Carpenters, Joiners, Coopers, Ma-
sons, Tilers, and Blacksmiths, presented a streamer with their arms and "Noath
buildinge the arke. Vulcan workinge at the Forge. Venus carried in a Charriott
and Cupid sittinge in her lapp with his bowe bent. A morrice Daunce. The
Dragon which devoured the virgins" (fol. 376). The Shearmen and Tuckers offered a streamer with their arms. But the third group of Tanners, Chandlers, and
Butchers showed a "Carte of old virgins the carte covered with hides and hornes
and the virgins with their attires made of Cowtayles and bracelettes for their
neckes of Hornes .... Their charriott was drawne by men and boys ... St Clement their saint rode allsoe with his booke And his Frier rode allsoe who dealt his
almes out of his masters Bagge which hee carried verie full of graynes ..." (fol.
376). The fourth company of Cordwainers presented "St Crispian and [blank in
MS.] both of them sonnes to a kinge and the youngest a shoemaker who married
his Masters daughter they allsoe presented a morrice daunce and a Streamer with
their armes." In addition to their streamer the Taylors showed "Herod and
Herodias and the daughter of Herodias who daunced for St John Baptiste hedd.
St John Baptiste beheaded." The final company, the Weavers, offered a morris
dance, a giant and giantess, and "kinge Ptolomeus with his Queene and daughter
which was to bee devoured of the dragon. St George with his knightes who slew
the dragon and rescued the virgin. Diana and her nymphes carried in a Charriott
...." No obvious thematic unity emerges here; instead, each company presents a
tableau scene relevant to its occupation. We cannot know about speeches because
the the records indicate none. Thus we have a civic pageant in its simplest form,
reminiscent of the dramatic offering of the guilds of Coventry in 1565 when
Elizabeth entered that city. This provincial pageant seems far removed from the
sophistication of the London pageants of the earlier years of James's reign.

For the investiture of Prince Charles as Prince of Wales in November 1616,
the city engaged the dramatic talents of Thomas Middleton, and the resulting
civic pageant, which he called *Civitatis Amor*, parallels rather closely the show
presented to Henry in 1610. Because the date of this pageant and the time for the
annual Lord Mayor's Show, 29 October, nearly coincide, the city sought some
way of utilizing the effort for both pageants; thus quite literally the royal entry
and the Lord Mayor's pageant begin to merge. The evidence for this unique cooperation occurs in Corporation of London records where the Aldermen determine to greet the new Prince of Wales with entertainment, requesting the mayor
and others to—

... call before them the Mr Wardens and Comittees of the Company of
Fishmongers appointed for devising and ordering of the shewes prepared against the Lord Maiors day, and conferre with them how their
pageante and other devises may be altered and used for shewe at the
meeting of the prince as aforesaid, and for Chambers to be provided,
and placed against that day and to take consideracion of some
speechees to bee made and then acted to the Prince, and of other
shewes and devises as they shall think fitting for the tryumphe and
honor to be yeelded by the Citty to his highness ....[37]

Apparently the two events shared at least a boat between them, for an entry in
records of the Fishmongers shows a payment "for barg hier at the Lord Maiors
presentment and at the metyng of the prynce on the day of his instalment."[38] The
events of 1616 underscore the active participation of the guilds in pageant drama.
For their part the city spent over £323 for this pageant devised by Middleton.[39]

When Charles arrived by the river at Chelsea, he saw a "personage figuring
London, sitting upon a sea-unicorn, with six Tritons sounding before her, accompanied thither with Neptune, and the two rivers Thamesis and Dee ...."[40]
Charles, the "treasure of hope, and jewel of mankind," receives welcome from
both Neptune and London. The figure London says:

As we on earth measure heaven's works by truth,
And things which natural reason cannot climb,
So when we look into the virtuous aim
Of thy divine addiction, we may deem,
By rules of grace and principles of fame,
What worth will be, now in so high esteem,
And so betimes pursu'd .... (VII, 274)

With London and Neptune and entourage leading the way, Charles arrived at
Whitehall where he found Hope, "leaning her breast upon a silver anchor, attended with four virgins all in white, having silver oars in their hands," and
Peace, "sitting on a dolphin, with her sacred quire ..." (275-6). With words of
compliment Hope says:

Now has my anchor her firm hold agen,

[37]Corporation of London, *Repertory*, XXXII, fol. 372.
[38]Malone Society, *Collections III* (Oxford, 1954), p. 91. For discussion of the 1616 Lord Mayor's Show,
see the chapter on Anthony Munday.
[39]Corporation of London, *Repertory*, XXXIII, fol. 18.
[40]*The Works of Thomas Middleton*, ed. A. H. Bullen (London, 1886), VII, 272-3. All quotations from
Middleton will be from this edition.

And in my blest and calm security
The expectations of all faithful men
Have their full fruits, being satisfied in me.
This is the place that I'll cast anchor in,
This, honour's haven, the king's royal court;
Here will I fasten all my joys agen .... (VII, 276)

In her song Peace welcomes this "spring of joy and peace" whom the city loves, "Whose expectation's sacred thirst / Nothing truly could allay / But such a prince and such a day" (276). The dramatic center of the pageant, Charles, receives both welcome and instruction by the allegorical characters. Whether referring specifically to this pageant or not, the Venetian Ambassador, Giovanni Lionello, writes concerning the celebration of the Prince's investiture: "... the festivities did not attain to the splendour of those which were celebrated for the dead prince."[41] Perhaps the Italian diplomat senses a difference in the response of the people to Henry and to Charles.

After a fourteen-year absence, James in 1617 returned to his native Scotland and there made an official entry into Edinburgh on 16 May. Records of the city reveal plans for the event, for example, on 19 March a committee established to determine what kind of entertainment should be presented to the king; later the city chose John Hay to give a speech for the entry; and the city determines in early May to present a gift of a gold basin and 1,000 marks.[42] But the entry itself appeared almost devoid of splendor, with austerity its chief claim, a far cry from the earlier pageants in Edinburgh, the discussion of which opened this chapter. Quite simply, James entered the city at the West Port, where the city officials received him, heard two speeches including the one by Hay, got the gift from the city, heard a sermon at the church, and then proceeded to the castle.[43] In its baldest terms this describes what took place, the event obviously missing the qualities which could make it a dramatic event—it does not meet the minimum requirements of a civic pageant. Perhaps Anthony Weldon has captured at least part of the truth surrounding this "non-event":

For his Majesties entertainement I must needes confesse ingeniously hee was received into the parish of Edenborough (for a Cittie I cannot call it) with greate shootes and cryes, but noo shews of Charge; For Pageantes they hold Idolatrous thinges and not fitt to be used in soo reformed a place, From the Castle they gave him some peices of ord-

---

[41]*Calendar of State Papers Venetian 1615-17*, XIV, 350.
[42]*Extracts from the Records of the Burgh of Edinburgh 1604 to 1626*, ed. Marguerite Wood (Edinburgh, 1931), pp. 156-9.
[43]Patrick Walker, *Documents Relative to the Reception at Edinburgh of the Kings and Queens of Scotland 1561-1650* (Edinburgh, 1822), p. 68. Nichols, III, 317f.

niance which surely he had given them—since hee was King of England
... They protested, if Christ came from heaven hee could not have bene
better welcome and I beleive it, for, his majestie came but to summon
them to a Parliament, and Christ would have summoned them to a
Judgment, which they love not.[44]

This bland affair disappoints indeed; no triumphal arches, little color, no dramatic speeches, no allegorical or mythological characters to compliment or instruct the king. In short, no pageantry. Perhaps appropriately for a sovereign who
mainly disliked public shows and preferred court entertainment his royal entry
into Edinburgh should be such a poor piece of theater. The heady days of the
1604 pageant clearly belong in the past.

The Jacobean era closes with several progress tours, but with no pageants.
Progresses have become weak imitations of those splendidly indulged in in the
Elizabethan period. The Jacobean progress entertainment comes, seemingly,
simply trailing clouds of former glory. The unrivalled splendor of London in
March 1604 when the royal family processed through the city and saw several
allegorical tableaux staged on opulent arches, contrasts starkly with the failure of
James to make royal entries into provincial towns and have pageants presented
for him. Even Edinburgh of the late sixteenth century emerges as more splendid
than the Edinburgh of 1617 which James visited.

Positive achievements occur nevertheless. If we had only the 1604 royal entry
entertainment, we should have to judge the pageantry of the Jacobean period a
success. Earlier in this chapter I suggested how this civic pageant epitomizes
much of what had preceded it and points the way for future pageants; the dramatic form has become thoroughly conventionalized. Though few, the progress
pageants show, at least in the entertainments of Ben Jonson, a new sophistication
and a new element of quasi-character development. Dramatic dialogue, some of
it quite respectable dramatic speech, surely becomes one of the Jacobean age's
finest contributions to pageantry. Some of the static nature of the pageant breaks
down by effective dialogue and action. Many of these accomplishments become
possible not only because a sound tradition exists upon which the Stuart pageant
could build, but because some of the best dramatists now write the shows. We
may accurately claim that civic pageantry achieves its maturity as a dramatic
form in the Jacobean period.

Whether in progress or royal entry form, civic pageants remain in the early
Stuart era basically non-realistic drama, relying heavily on visual allegory and
symbolism. Dramatic theme offers still the main possibility for unity of the pageant; and when the theme does not, whatever the reason, get effective expression,
then the dramatic form suffers. If diminished in quantity, the civic pageant re-

---

[44]British Library Sloane MS. 3213, fol. 4ᵃ-4ᵇ.

mains nevertheless in the reign of James a viable kind of drama, especially when one adds the Lord Mayor's Show (the subject of later chapters). The appetite for such shows and entertainments continues to be well-nigh insatiable, and city and guild and dramatist together seek to fulfill that need in the midst of an era burgeoning with diverse forms of drama.

Figure 2. Londinium arch at Fenchurch, 1604 royal entry in London. Figures 2-8 are from Stephen Harrison's *Arches of Triumph* (London, 1604) and include all the arches built for the royal entry. Permission of the Folger Shakespeare Library, Washington, DC.

Figure 3. Italian pageant at Gracechurch Street. Permission of the Folger Shakespeare Library, Washington, DC.

Figure 4. Dutch pageant at the Royal Exchange. Permission of the Folger Shakespeare Library, Washington, DC.

Figure 5. *Nova Fælix Arabia* (New Arabia Felix) arch at Soper-lane End. Permission of the Folger Shakespeare Library, Washington, DC.

Figure 6. *Hortus Euporiæ* (The Garden of Plenty) in Cheapside. Permission of the
Folger Shakespeare Library, Washington, DC.

Figure 7. The New World arch in Fleet Street. Permission of the Folger Shakespeare Library, Washington, DC.

Figure 8. The Temple of Janus at Temple Bar. Permission of the Folger Shakespeare Library, Washington, DC.

3 The Reign of Charles I to the Closing of the Theaters (1625-42)

As CHARLES FOLLOWED HIS FATHER, James, to the English throne, so the pattern of civic pageantry evident in the Jacobean period continues in the Caroline era with the eventual closing of the theaters by act of Parliament in 1642. By such legislative order the pageant theater along with other theater forms fades away, and the pageants indeed become insubstantial. Parliamentary decree sped the end of royal entries and progress pageants, but the decline in such entertainments noted in the reign of the first Stuart persists and indeed increases in Charles's reign. The years 1625-42 have a striking paucity of civic pageantry with the notable exception of the Lord Mayors' Shows being written by the dramatists Middleton, Dekker, and Heywood. The masque continues to dominate courtly attention while the citizenry, in London at least, lavishes its attention on its chief citizen, the mayor. The somewhat insulated attitude of James toward public shows prevails in his son as well; and while Charles made several progress tours, again no entertainment truly compares with the estate pageants of the Elizabethan period. Furthermore, but one royal entry—in Edinburgh in 1633—actually qualifies as a civic pageant; prominent dramatists who had designed entertainments in the Jacobean era have largely vanished. Early in Charles's rule events (discussed below) connected with his coronation all but seal the doom to pageants connected with the sovereign and confirm the prominence of the Lord Mayors' Shows—an inverse proportional relationship develops between the decline of one form and the rise of another type of civic entertainment.

For Charles's return to London in 1623 from his Spanish venture vast crowds turned out to greet him with many expressions of joy (doubtless relieved that the marriage negotiations with the Infanta of Spain had not succeeded), loud ringing of bells, and enormous bonfires "so costly, and so high flaming, that had they all beene seene burning in the night-time, that weeke might have boasted, it had gotten one day more than any other weeke in the yeere, so universall was the light."[1] Shouts and fires notwithstanding, no dramatic presentations occurred. The entertainment presented to Prince Charles at Kenilworth in August 1624, written by Ben Jonson and called *The Masque of Owles*, offers an excellent point of contrast to the pageant entertainment presented to Elizabeth at Kenilworth in 1575. Jonson's drama, really an outdoor masque, consists of a series of speeches by one personating Captain Cox, the historical character who figured promi-

---

[1] *The Joyfull Returne of the Most Illustrious Prince, Charles ... from the Court of Spaine* (London, 1623), p. 38.

nently in Coventry's "ancient historical shew" presented to Elizabeth at Kenilworth, thus establishing a link between the entertainments. And Jonson's Captain Cox alludes at several points to the earlier pageant, even to the suppression of the Coventry play. Each of the six "owls" which he introduces represents a stereotype of a character, appearing as rustic actors. Altogether an undistinguished piece of work, it suffers considerably by comparison to the festive-filled days of 1575 at Kenilworth. It epitomizes the demise of the progress pageant from Elizabeth's time to the early decades of the seventeenth century. We shall look in vain for the Lady of the Lake floating about on a movable island, or Arion on a dolphin filled inside with a consort of musicians, or the Savage Man, or the mock bride and groom. The pattern of diminishing progress entertainments observed in the Jacobean reign seems to have become an irreversible process, not merely a tendency.

When Charles came to the throne upon the death of his father and received the crown, one might logically expect to find a civic pageant of considerable splendor associated with the coronation, such as had taken place in London in 1559 and again in 1604 when the new sovereigns received royal entertainment with dramatic tableaux stationed about the city. But Charles dashed this expectation, choosing not to make the anticipated royal entry into London. Such a decision indicates this king's attitude toward public shows and perhaps offers a sign of insensitivity to the demands of the public.

Fully anticipating the King's royal entry, the Aldermen of the City of London decide in April 1625—

> that the Cittizens of this Cittie maye shewe and performe theire loialties, and bounden duties towardes his most excellent Majesty at his passage through the same in preparing of Pagentes and other shewes and thinges necessarie toward the solempnizacon of that his Royall Coronacion in as stately and sompteous manner as hath bin heretofore performed by this Cittie unto any his noble progenitors....[2]

Accordingly, a committee begins to make the necessary preparations and to report from time to time to the Court of Aldermen. The Chamberlain gets authorization to make payments for the workmen employed for the "intended shewes."[3] Obviously everyone assumes that the king will make an entry, and he should be received in a manner and form reminiscent of that which greeted his predecessors. Just as the plague had caused the postponement of James's official passage through the city, so it appeared again in the initial part of Charles's reign and caused delay of the entertainment. But in January 1626 the Common Council set

[2]Corporation of London, *Repertory*, XXXIX, fol. 172.
[3]Ibid., fol. 183ᵇ.

up a committee "for the preparinge appoyntinge and orderinge of such Showes pageantes and tryumphes as againste his Majesties said passage through this Citty should be thought fitt"; further, this group should meet with a similar group of Aldermen to "take care alsoe for the dysbursinge of such moneys and charges ... touchinge the preparinge orderinge and fittinge of the said triumphes and Showes, ... And likewise to consider what course and meanes they conceave most fittest to be taken for the levyinge and raysinge of moneys already disbursed or to be disbursed in and aboute the same...."[4] The procedures and methods of planning recall of course those utilized by the city when readying the pageants for the coronation of Elizabeth and James.

But the best laid plans go for nought when a royal whim comes into play. This royal caprice appears in the directive sent on the king's behalf by the Earl of Pembroke to the Lord Mayor on 25 May 1626:

> My Lord
> Whereas your Lordship and the rest of that Court nowe formerly directed by letters from the right hounorable the Earle Marshall, to prepare and erect in severall places within the Cittie, sondrie Pageantes for the fuller and More significant expression of your joyes uppon his Majesties and his Royall Consortes intended entrance throughe your faire Cittie: His Majesty haveinge now allowed his said purpose, and given mee Comand to signify so Much unto you, it may please your Lordship to take notice therof by these, As also to remove the said Pageantes, which besides the particular charge they cause in the Cittie, do choke and hinder the passages of suche as in Coaches, or with theire Carriages, have occasion to passe up and downe.[5]

Such an order accelerates the fading of the pageants immeasurably. But more seriously, the two arguments advanced here for tearing down the devices, expense and inconvenience, seem at best tenuous, for the money had already been disbursed since the pageants had been readied for the intended entry, and whatever the inconvenience to the flow of traffic had surely been anticipated and apparently accepted as a temporary but necessary nuisance. The two Venetian representatives in England capture something of the reaction to the king's order: "Owing to this scarcity of money the king has given up his procession through London which was arranged for his coronation. Accordingly five most superb arches in the streets, two erected by the citizens and three by divers other nations, at an expense of many thousands of ducats, will prove useless and they have already begun to dismantle them amid the murmurs of the people and the disgust

---

[4]Corporation of London, *Journal*, XXXIII, fol. 182.
[5]Corporation of London, *Remembrancia*, VI, 86.

of those who spent the money."[6] One can readily imagine the murmurs aggra-
vated by the loss of money and effort, all designed to honor the sovereign who
without much evidence of wisdom and little political sagacity decided to with-
hold his person from the drama prepared for him and to destroy the "stages"
where the dramatic action would have been centered. Theater does not easily
survive such trying circumstances. Like the banished Bolingbroke in Shakespeare's *Richard II*, we too can be impressed with the life-giving and life-denying
power of the king. Anthony Weldon observes that the king did not ride through
the city in state "although the same Triumphs were provided for him, as sumptuous as for any others; this, some have taken as an ill omen...."[7]

While the king might carry on his royal duties as blissfully as he chose, the
city had no place of refuge from the expenses which it had incurred for Charles's
"non-entry." In June 1626 the Aldermen negotiate with the artificer Gerard
Christmas over payment for his services,[8] and as late as September 1627 the
Council establishes a committee to—

> take consideracon of such moneys as have byn disbursed and paid out
> of the Chamber aswell for and touchinge the makinge of the Pageante
> and other solempinities and Showes, and worke, for the bewtifinnge of
> this Citty against the late intended tyme of his Majesties passage thor-
> ough the same....[9]

In addition this committee will determine both what remains unpaid of the debts
and how money might be raised to cover them. The investigation revealed that
£4,300 had been spent and it remained unpaid; the committee recommended
levying this sum against the companies.[10] Admittedly not all of this handsome
sum went exclusively for the pageants, but nevertheless, it can hardly be argued
that the city got good value for its investment—a rather dear price for a recalci-
trant king and dismantled pageants. Perhaps a perverse drama emerges in these
events; but the pageant theater of the streets has no life on this occasion, for its
"body" has no "soul."

As early as 1628 the city of Edinburgh busily made preparations for the
king's anticipated entry into that city; but given the event's delay, the city again
made its plans in December 1631 by establishing a committee to devise appropriate entertainment for the scheduled arrival of Charles in either spring or summer

---

[6] *Calendar of State Papers Venetian, 1625-1626*, XIX, 464.
[7] *The Court and Character of King James Whereunto is now added the Court of King Charles* (London, 1651), p. 177.
[8] Corporation of London, *Repertory*, XL, fol. 243 and 268. For a fuller discussion of Christmas's involvement with numerous civic pageants see Chapter Ten.
[9] Corporation of London, *Journal*, XXXIV, fol. 159[b].
[10] Ibid., fol. 163.

1632.[11] But the 1632 visit did not happen; thus in January 1633 the Council of the city meets and, having learned of the king's renewal of his determination to come to Edinburgh, "all in ane voice resolved concludit and ordaint that his Majesty salbe ressavit within this burgh in the most magnificent maner that can be devysit...."[12] Uncertain where the money will come from for the entertainment, the city nevertheless instructed the treasurer to borrow the necessary money. Indeed, with no expense spared, the total sum exceeded £41,000, including coronation, parliament, banquet, and pageant costs. Unusually full details of expenditures exist in the records of the city and particularly in the account of the Treasurer, James Locke, whose record indicates disbursements for everything from nails to actors. Considerable mention in the accounts refers to the "stages"; in fact, something over £1,600 went "for the staiges and acting of thame."[13] Much went for various kinds of cloth and building materials with particular attention given to the device of Mount Parnassus. One section of the expenditures records disbursements made to the artist George Jamesone whose singular achievement for this entertainment included painting portraits of all the Scottish kings, a work consuming many months and considerable money. After the royal entry in June, the city government instructed Locke to pay Jamesone "for his extraordiner paynes taiken be him in the tounes effaires at his Majesty entrie...."[14] Seldom have civic pageants involved the work of such a distinguished artist. Stephen Tilliedaff, musician, received payment "for setting and acting of the musick at Parnassus hill and at his Majesty banquett...."[15] From the various sets of records emerges a pattern of thorough preparation, involvement of skilled craftsmen and artists, vast expense, and participation of the guilds and city government, all comparable to the procedures surrounding the earlier coronation royal entries.

This civic pageant which took place on 15 June 1633 in Edinburgh shares many qualities and features of the royal entries in London in 1559 and 1604, and becomes the chief such entertainment in the Caroline period. It makes much use of the triumphal arch, a form which dominated the 1604 royal entry of James I, and its subject content comes from the usual areas of history, mythology, and moral allegory, with mythology dominant—a continuation of an emphasis observed in the 1604 pageant and a contrast to the Elizabethan royal entry. A printed text which describes the Edinburgh pageant and some manuscript mate-

[11]*Extracts from the Records of the Burgh of Edinburgh 1626 to 1641*, ed. Marguerite Wood (Edinburgh, 1936), p. 46 and p. 100.
[12]Ibid., p. 117.
[13]British Library Add. MS. 40885, "the compt of James Locke Theasurer," fol. 16[b].
[14]Wood, *Extracts*, pp. 129-30.
[15]Ibid., p. 129.

rial provide the essential information regarding the nature of the entertainment.[16]

The manuscript source records that when Charles entered "at the Westporte he saw the Situatioun of the whole Citie Castle Towne Cannogate and palice Togider with all the Stipells and ornaments weill drawin on ane Large Conves be ane called Jamesone ane worthie paintter."[17] This refers to a scene depicting the city of Edinburgh painted on the first arch; doubts about Jamesone as the painter arise because city records credit a John Smith with the achievement. At any rate, the visual representation of the city may remind us of the arch at Fenchurch in 1604 which contained the city of London carved in miniature. Upon one side of the painting of Edinburgh a picture portrayed "the flood *Lithus*, in a Mantle of sea-greene or water colour, a Crowne of sedges and reeds on his head with long locks; his arme leaned upon an earthen pot, out of which water and fishes seemed to runne forth...."[18] How strikingly similar had been the presentation of Tamesis on Jonson's arch at Fenchurch: "His mantle of sea-greene or water colour ... a crowne of sedge and reede upon his head.... His beard, and hayre long, and over-growne. He leanes his arme upon an earthen pot, out of which, water, with live fishes, are seene to runne forth, and play about him" (*Jonson*, VII, 86). Though one figure is live and the other painted, they correspond in the essential details, and perhaps the anonymous deviser of the Edinburgh pageant checked earlier ones for inspiration. Neptune also appears here on the arch at West Port. As Jonson had included *Genius Urbis* in his tableau, so the Edinburgh pageant included *Genius* of the city, located on a mountain which comprised the "theater" under the arch. This Genius "represented by a Nimph ... was attired in a sea-greene velvet Mantle, her sleeves and under roabe of blew tissue, with blew Buskins on her feete, about her necke shee wore a chaine of Diamonds, the dressing of her head represented a Castle with turrets, her locks dangled about her shoulders ..." (sig. A3ᵛ). Allegorical figures support the Genius on either hand: Religion, "all in white taffeta, with a blew Mantle seeded with starres, a Crowne of starres on her head," and Justice, "a woman in a red damaske Mantle, her under garments Cloth of silver, on her head a Crowne of Gold, on a Scutcheon she had Ballances and a Sword drawn" (sig. A3ᵛ-A4). Recapturing a technique used in both the 1559 and 1604 entries in London, this pageant has the virtue Religion suppressing Superstition, who lay beneath her feet trampled, "a woman blind, in

---

[16]For additional discussion see my "Charles I's Edinburgh Pageant (1633)," *Renaissance Studies* 6 (1992): 173-84. I deal with the speculation that William Drummond may have been the author of the pageant text.

[17]British Library Harleian MS. 4707, "A brief not of rare things hapned in Scotland since the taking of King James the first prisoner taken be Englishmen," fol. 59ᵇ.

[18]*The Entertainment of the High and Mighty Monarch Charles ... Into his auncient and royall City of Edinburgh* (Edinburgh, 1633), sig. A3ᵛ. All quotations will be from this printed text except for those from the manuscript source cited in note #16.

old and worne garments," and Justice treading on Oppression, "a person of a fierce aspect, in armes but broken all and scattered" (sig. A4)—a visual statement of the allegorical conflict between virtue and vice.

In addition to presenting Charles with the keys of the city in a basin of silver, the nymph representing the Genius of Edinburgh delivered a speech urging the king "to looke downe on their lownesse, and embrace it, accept the homage of their humble minds, accept their gratefull zeale, and for deeds, accept that great good-will which they have ever carried to the high deserts of your Ancestors ..." (sig. B1). He should use the keys to unlock the hearts of the people. Because of the arrival of Charles "the old forget their age, and looke fresh and young at the sight of so gracious a Prince, the young bear a part in your welcome, desiring many yeares of life, that they may serve you long ..." (sig. A4^v). This dramatic tableau focuses its allegorical theme on a welcome to the sovereign but, more important, on a depiction of the qualities which support a peaceful city, Religion and Justice, while Superstition and Oppression receive defeat. Each major royal entry has somewhere in its presentation such a scene of virtues which lead to a healthy commonwealth.

The second arch located "towards the Gate of the old Towne" contained a painting of a landscape depicting "a countrey wild, full of Trees, Bushes, Bores, white Kine; along the which appeared one great Mountaine" and also a sea-scape. Roman soldiers and "a number of naked persons flying and enchayned, with the figures of the Sunne, Moone, and Starres, drawne on their skins, and shapes of flowers, which represented the Picts" appear in the drawing as well. When the curtain fell from the arch, "the Theater discovered a Lady attired in tissue, her haire was dressed like a *Coruncopia*, two chaynes, one of gold, another of pearle baudricke wayes, hung downe her shoulders, a Crowne of gold hung from the Arch before her, shee represented the *Genius of Caledonia* ..." (sig. B1^v). A woman portraying "new *Scotland*" accompanied her. As the king drew near the arch, the Genius of Caledonia delivered her lengthy speech, a speech filled with praise of Charles, who "The golden age and vertues brings againe; / Prince so much longed for, how thou becalm'st / Mindes easelesse anguish, every care em-balm'st / With the sweet odours of thy presence!" (sig. B2). The country has become a place where Faith, Truth, and Simplicity dwell. And the Genius adds:

> Vouchsafe blest people, ravisht here with me,
> To thinke my thoughts, and see what I doe see,
> A Prince all gracious, affable, divine,
> Meeke, wise, just, valiant, whose radiant shine
> Of vertues ... enlightneth every soule
> Your Scepter swayes, a *Prince* borne in this age
> To guard the innocents from Tyrants rage,
> To make *Peace* prosper, *Justice* to reflowre.... (sig. B3)

In the midst of praise, Charles gains implicit instruction and a challenge to see that virtue achieves a victory.

Concerning the next arch, the manuscript records that "at the west end of the tolbuithe there his Majestie did see the haill number of the Kingis that ever rang in Scotland fra fergis the first to his awin Majestie whiche will exceid to the number of ane hundreth and sevin. And from that place was directed ane Speeche concerning the purpose of the foirseid Kingis to his Majestie in Latein."[19] The representation of the kings would be the work of Jamesone. The printed text adds that among signs and instruments of war stood Mars, while among the emblems of peace stood Minerva. When Charles arrived at the arch, a drawn curtain revealed Mercury, "with his feathered hat, and his *Caduceus*, with an hundred and seven Scottish Kings, which hee had brought from the Elisian fields ..." (sig. C1). No speech exists in the records. Clearly, however, the presentation of all the Scottish kings serves both as a compliment to Charles and as a sanction for the festivities; here the voice of history sounds loudest.

A brief scene at the Cross displayed "*Bacchus* crowned with Ivie, and naked from the shoulders up, bestroad a Hogshead, by him stood *Silenus, Silvanus, Pomona, Venus, Ceres* in a straw coloured mantle, embrodered with eares of Corne, and a dressing of the same on her head ..." (sig. C1). But Satyres interrupted the scheduled speech. The King then moved on to the device showing Mount Parnassus.

In the middle of the street this mountain stood populated by Apollo, the Muses, and "ancient Worthies of Scotland," the Muses appropriately costumed "in varying taffetas, cloath of silver and purle; ... they were distinguished by the Scutcheons they bare ...; every one had a word" (sig. C1ᵛ). Clio bore the word of Charles as prince; Melpomene had the word of King James; Thalia, the word of Queen Anne; Euterpe, the word of Prince Henry: *Fax gloria mentis honestae*. Apollo, who sat in their midst, "was clad in Crimon taffeta, covered with some purle of gold, with a bowdricke like the Raine-bow, a Mantle of tissue knit together above his left shoulder ..." (sig. C2). The manuscript refers to the musicians and to the trees which decorated Mount Parnassus; and it points out that he (i.e., Apollo) "that was in the mides arose at his Majesties hither cuming with ane gilded booke in his hand directed ane larg spech to his Majestie ... and after the speich being endit delyverit the booke to ane Lord whiche Lord delyverit it presentlie to his Majestie" (fol. 61ᵃ). The Muses had also been present on the arch devised by Dekker in the 1604 pageant which stood at the Little Conduit in Cheapside, the arch called *Hortus Euporiae*, thus underscoring again the continuity of pageantry. Doubtless here in Edinburgh Apollo and the Muses intend to suggest the harmony possible in such a kingdom; they have not fled nor been banished, for the king remains sympathetic to the functions of the Muses.

---

[19]BL Harleian MS. 4707, fol. 60ᵃ-60ᵇ.

Near the eastern gate stood an arch the front of which "represented a Heaven, into the which appeared his Majesties ascendant *Virgo*, shee was beautified with sixe and twenty starres, after that order that they are in their constellatioune" (sig. C2ᵛ). Beneath, a scene depicted the "*Titanes* prostrate" on the earth "with Mountaines over them, as when they attempted to bandy against the gods...." "The Chapter shew the three *Parcae*, where was written, *Thy life was kept till these three Sisters spunne / Their threads of gold, and then thy life begunne.*" The chief occupants of the arch were Endymion and the "seven Planets sitting on a Throne," each appropriately costumed: "*Saturne* in a sad blew Mantle embrodered with golden flames, his Girdle was like a Snake byting his tayle"; "*Jupiter* was in a Mantle of silver, embroidered with Lillies and Violets"; "*Mars*, his haire and beard red, a Sword at his side, had his robe of deepe Crimson Taffeta, embroidered with Wolves and Horses, his head bare a Helmet"; "The *Sunne* had a Crowne of flowers on his head, as Marigolds, and Panses, and a Tissue Mantle"; "*Venus* had the attire of her head rising like parts in a Coronet, and roses, shee was in a mantle of greene Damaske embroidered with Doves"; "*Mercury* had a Dressing on his head of parti-coloured flowers, his Mantle parti-coloured"; and the Moon "had the attyre of her head, like an halfe Moone or Cressant of pearle; her Mantle was sad Damasse Frenzend with silver, embroidered with Chamelions and Gourdes ..." (sigs. C2ᵛ-C3ᵛ). From out a verdant grove came Endymion "apparelled like a Shepheard in a long Coat of crimson velvet comming over his knee; hee had a wreath of flowers upon his head, his haire was curled, and long; in his hand he bare a Sheep hooke, on his legs were Buskins of gilt Leather ..." (sig. C3ᵛ).

This tableau of splendid color gets dramatic life by the speeches of these figures, beginning and ending with Endymion, initially dazzled by the spectacle: "Sure this is heaven, for every wandering starre, / Forsaking those great orbes where whirl'd they are, / All dismall sad aspects abandoning, / Are here assembled to greet some darling" (sig. C4); Charles's presence has provoked this gathering, and the figures have come to prophesy the future. Saturn asserts that "His age of gold he shall restore againe, / *Love, Justice, Honour, Innocence* renew, / Mens spirits with white simplicity indue, / Make all to live in plenties ceaselesse store ..." (sig. C4ᵛ-D1). Jupiter observes that at the birth of Charles he proclaimed him a king, and he foresees that "Thou shalt make passion yield to reasons doome" (sig. D1). And in words which rebound with an ironic twist from our historical vantage point, Jupiter says:

New and vast taxes thou shalt not extort,
Load heavy those thy bounty should support,
By harmelesse *Justice* graciously reforme,
Delighting more in calme then roaring storme,
Thou shalt governe in *peace* as did thy *Sire*.... (sig. D1ᵛ)

Mars, of course, assures the king of victory over dismayed armies as he attempts to "free the earth." Believing that Charles "shalt *Parnassus* Cristall gates" open, the Sun also asserts: "*Wealth, Wisedome, Glory, Pleasure,* stoutest hearts, / *Religion, Lawes, Hyperion* imparts / To thy just Raigne ..." (sig. D2ᵛ). Venus offers "pleasant dayes," while Mercury views the sovereign as increasing the "workes of peace" and restoring the arts "to cheere *Perfection*" with Wisdom, Wealth, Honour, Arms, and Arts gracing the kingdom. The Moon predicts that Discord, pale Envy, Malice, Deceit, Rebellion, and Impudence shall be expelled from the island. Endymion closes the scene by urging:

> Let this bee knowne to all *Apollo's* Quire,
> And people let it not be hid from you,
> What Mountaines noyse and Floods proclaime as true:
> Where ever fame abroad his prayse shall ring,
> All shall observe, and serve this blessed King. (sig. D4)

On the back of this arch a painting depicted the Graces "drawn upon it, which were naked and in others hands; they were crowned with eares of Corne, Flowers and Grapes to signifie fecunditie" (sig. D4ᵛ); the presence of the Graces here in Edinburgh in 1633 reminds us again of various links between pageants as we recall their representation at Dekker's first arch in the 1604 royal entry in London or their active participation in welcoming Elizabeth to Elvetham in 1591.

The final device of the pageant comes at the East Gate where on the battlements "in a Coat all full of eyes and tongues, with a Trumpet in her hand (as if shee would sound) stood Fame, the wings of the Bat at her feete, a Wreath of gold on her head ..." (sig. D4ᵛ). Next to her stood Honour, "a person of reverend countenance"; the two stood "above the statue of King *James*, under which was written *Placida populos in pace regebat*" (sig. E1). Verses appear in the text, perhaps the speech of either Fame or Honour; at any rate, they point out that Charles's presence makes every month summer, requiring neither stars nor sun, and add:

> Now Majestie and Love
>   combin'd are from above,
> Prince never Scepter swayd
>   lov'd subjects more, of subjects more obey'd,
>   which may indure whilst heavens great orbs do move. (sig. E1)

With full compliment this civic pageant thus closes as Fame figuratively sounds forth the achievement of this entertainment but more especially celebrates the renown of the king.

From the opening greeting of the Genius of Edinburgh the pageant seems to enlarge its sphere moving next to the Genius of Caledonia, to Mount Parnassus, finally to the planets themselves, providing a sure way of suggesting the universality of praise for the king. While mythological figures clearly dominate the entertainment, they, in addition to complimenting the sovereign, add their voices to the moral challenge confronting the king; therefore, they speak of vices being driven from the kingdom and refer to the positive virtues which ought to be embraced. Thus the instructional and allegorical themes provide the basis for the pageant writer whether illustrated explicitly, as at the first arch where Religion and Justice suppress their contrary vices, or stated more indirectly by various mythological characters. The voices of prophecy carry implicit challenge to Charles to make these words become a reality.

The description of this show confirms the observation made in Chapter Two that after the 1604 royal entry no innovations occur in this form of pageantry. In Edinburgh, as then, triumphal arches provide the essential structure on which the drama takes place. With mythological figures prevailing, the absence of the overtly religious or Biblical scene does not surprise; such had also been the case in the Jacobean entry in London. One may be impressed that this pageant lacks the sort of cohesion of thematic unity which had been especially evident in Elizabeth's 1559 pageant and even in the 1604 one, though written by two different dramatists. Instead, we find episodic scenes or tableaux with little interconnection. Dramatically this Edinburgh entry also seems less satisfying partly because of the slight thematic unity, and also because of the relative lack of "dramatic action"—even the speeches seem not to spark much life into the presentation; thus it retains by and large its tableau form. Nothing here compares favorably with the several types of action found in the earlier coronation entries. Even the series of speeches given by Endymion and the figures representing the planets at the arch near the East Gate remain somewhat isolated from one another, more declamatory than dramatic. Though this civic pageant fulfills its basic role of praise and instruction quite adequately with vast expense, considerable preparation, and much visual splendor, its dramatic nature may seem less than wholly satisfying, especially when measured against earlier achievements. Even so, it retains its basic theatricality with vast crowds responding to sight and sound and to the presence of the sovereign who passes through their midst as the dramatic cause and center of festivity.

Understandably, the city of London anticipated that Charles would make an official entry into London after the events in Edinburgh, an expectation reflected in the dispatch of the Venetian Ambassador, Vicenzo Gussoni, who writes on 5 August 1633: "His Majesty's entry into this city will be delayed for some months still. An idea is current that as the crowned king of Scotland he will have to make a public state entry here also, to be celebrated by arrangements and functions which the people here are devising."[20] But a few months later in October this same Venetian ambassador must record that the king remains far from London, and "They are not going on with the preparations which they had apparently begun for the state entry which it was announced his Majesty would make into this city. There are some who believe that this delay will put an end to the ceremony, which is considered at once superfluous and costly" (p. 153). "Superfluous and costly" sounds like perhaps Charles's official attitude toward public shows, for he certainly did not hesitate to engage in many activities which surely earn the designation "superfluous and costly." Clearly the citizens of London did not refrain from spending effort and money to entertain the new Lord Mayor annually with pageants, which in the most utilitarian sense could be regarded as irrelevant or gratuitous. The absence of the king did indeed put an "end to the ceremony," but at least in 1633 no pageant devices already stood in the streets which the king ordered to be dismembered.

Some entertainments in 1637 and 1639 deserve at least passing notice though they lack the "dramatic" element. The Moroccan Ambassador, Alkaid Jaurar Ben Abdella, received welome from the city of London on an official entry in early November 1637; he and his party began the processional at the Tower "where they were attended by Thousands, and ten Thousands of Spectators, and welcomed and conveyed with his Majesties Coach, and at the least 100. Coaches more, and the chiefest of the Cittizens...."[21] Members of the trade guilds in full color lined the streets of the processional; great ceremony did not lead to pageants. A similar case occurred two years later when Marie de Medici made a trip to England to visit her daughter and son-in-law, the queen and king of England. Anticipating her entry into London, the Aldermen busily made preparations, especially plans to attend the Queen Mother of France as she passed through the city and to present her with a gift.[22] The French text, complete with a number of illustrations, captures well the excitement of the vast spectacle of trumpets sounding and bright colors cheering the scene. The writer of the descriptive text puts it well:

> Si je contemplois encore ce monde de peuple de differantes nations, qui remplissoit egalement et les fenestres, et les rues, je me persuadois a même temps, que tous les Dieux ensemble s'estoient assemblez dans Londre, pour estre spectateurs des magnificences de cette superbe entree.[23]

---

[20]*Calendar of State Papers Venetian*, XXIII, 132.
[21]*The Arrivall and Intertainements of the Embassador, Alkaid Jaurar Ben Abdella, with his Associate, Mr. Robert Blake* (London, 1637), sig. C1.
[22]Corporation of London, *Repertory*, LIII, fol. 1-1ᵇ; fol. 26.
[23]de la Serre, *Histoire de l'Entree de la Reyne Mere du Roy Tres-Chrestien, dans la Grande-Bretaigne* (London, 1639), sig. H2.

But such enthusiastic praise and the numerous bonfires will not compensate for the absence of pageant drama. We strain to imagine that such opportunities would have been by-passed in the Elizabethan era, a period so occupied with giving life to the pageant theater of the streets.

In 1641, the year before the closing of the theaters, Charles journeyed again to Scotland on political business and received a joyous welcome there as he passed through Edinburgh. But the pageant entertainment of 1633 remains but a memory, not duplicated or imitated in 1641. After this pageant-less visit in late summer, the city of London again began to expect an official royal entry. Indeed the Common Council received word from the queen in November "that our most gratious Soveraigne Lord King Charles doth intende (God willinge) in his happy returne from his Kingdom of Scotland to passe through this Citty beinge his Majesties Royall Chamber on Thursday next."[24] A committee had the task "to advise the orderinge and ranckinge of the Companeyes and Cleeringe of the Streetes throughout his majesties whole passage. And to Consider of all other thinges that may best conduce to the Contente of his majesty and the manifestacion of the Citties hearty affeccion towardes him and the Queene and their Royall Issue...." The group should also study what had been done in former times (probably not the earlier efforts in behalf of Charles) to welcome the sovereign and to be in charge of disbursing the necessary money. Thomas Wiseman in writing to Sir John Penington on 18 November 1641 indicates that Charles is beginning his journey from Edinburgh to London where the city makes preparations for his entry. Wiseman adds: "I am glad we are thus dutiful; it makes the Sectaries look about them, and the consideration of his Majesty's having the love of the able citizens will certainly conduce much to settle his affairs."[25] Such remains a futile hope, for the king's battle with Parliament will be drawn out to extremity in the months ahead. This reminds us that civic entertainments could serve as political weapons; most assuredly they had been for Elizabeth. Unfortunately for Charles, color and spectacle in the streets in his honor could not compensate for his own deficiencies. The insubstantial pageant fades; reality remains.

The Venetian Ambassador, Giustinian, expresses hope: "The pomp and circumstance in this connection give rise to hopes that the aspect of affairs here may yet change...."[26] Therefore, he records in some detail how the Lord Mayor and Aldermen and six hundred horsemen of "the most substantial citizens" greeted the king four miles outside London and brought him into the city and its decorated streets. Citizens and members of the guild lined the streets. When Charles entered the city, "he was received everywhere with universal acclamations, while he was careful to thank the people by gesture and speech, thus causing a renewal

[24]Corporation of London, *Journal*, XL, fol. 8.
[25]*Calendar of State Papers Domestic 1641-1643*, p. 168.
[26]*Calendar of State Papers Venetian*, XXV, 254.

of the shouts of welcome." Giustinian notes further that the king and family feasted at the Guildhall; finally, "his Majesty was escorted with the same company and order to his royal palace by torchlight, always amid the same shouts and acclamations." Such form the basic rudiments of the entertainment.

The ambassador's brief description gets augmentation and embellishment by two pamphlets printed shortly after the event: *Ovatio Carolina. The Triumph of King Charles* and *Englands Comfort, and Londons Joy*, the latter generally credited to John Taylor. The author of *Ovatio Carolina* refers to the whole occasion as a "mutuall act of *Love* between his *Majesty* and the *City*...."[27] He also describes the movement of the processional and notes that "As their *Majesties* passed along, the Trumpets and Citie *Musique* were placed in severall parts, sounding and playing, which together with the severall, continuall, and joyfull acclamations of the people, gave great content to both their *Majesties*; the little Conduit in Cheapside, and the Conduit in Fleetstreet running with wine, as the other two Conduits had done in the Morning" (p. 21). The choir from St. Paul's greeted the sovereign with an anthem of praise to God and prayers for their Majesties' long lives. The writer also refers to the festivities at the Guildhall.

John Taylor adds that at eight o'clock in the morning the Aldermen and members of the City Council went to the Lord Mayor's house until ready to go to Moorfield to greet the king. The author adds with some hyperbole: "The banks, hedges, highwayes streets, stalls, and windowes were all embroydered with millions of people, of all sorts and fashions."[28] All along London Wall as far as Bishopsgate "some of the Companies stood in their Liverie, within places conveniently railed with timber, their standings being adorned with Flags, Banners, Pendants, and Escouchions ..." (p. 4). For the journey at night from the Guildhall to the palace of Whitehall the full forces again accompanied the king and his retinue with fourteen trumpeters and "all instruments of musick usuall, with Bells ringing at 121. parish Churches, where there was no failings in expressions of love and loyalty by the people as appear'd by their shouts and acclamations ..." (p. 5). The verses presented to Charles correspond with the euphoric atmosphere; for example:

When He, (our SUNNE of joy) from us set forth
His Raies illustrious, lighted all the North:
Whilst sighes like Clouds, and showers of Teares and Cares,
Was *Londons* and faire *Englands* Southerne shares.
But this returne our sadnesse doth destroy,
Our Teares of griefe are turn'd to Teares of joy....
Hee's come to salve this Kingdomes discontents,

---

[27] *Ovatio Carolina* (London, 1641), p. 4.
[28] John Taylor, *Englands Comfort* (London, 1641), p. 3.

To cure all wrenches, fractures, spraines and rents…. (p. 7)

But not all the expense (the entertainment at the Guildhall alone cost over £1,786),[29] nor all the noise, nor the hopeful and sentimental verses can eradicate what subsequently followed in Charles's increasingly bitter fight with Parliament. Captain Robert Slingesby in writing to Sir John Penington states it succinctly: "Since the King's coming all things have not happened so much to his contentment as by his magnificent entertainment was expected."[30]

No doubt the king enjoyed the entertainment, a relief to the city at last to have the honor of the sovereign's presence after several previously futile efforts. But still one significant difference remains between this 1641 entry of Charles and the earlier ones of Elizabeth and James: here in the Caroline entry we find no dramatic presentations, no pageants. Perhaps the city simply did not have time to construct such things, or perhaps they had grown wary, considering the experiences of 1626 and 1633 in London.

In a few months the death-knell for the theater will be sounded by Parliament, and the pageant stage with other theaters will close its doors. Though, as suggested at the beginning of this chapter and confirmed in subsequent pages, the progress pageant as a viable form had already for all practical purposes died and the royal entry scarcely alive. The decline in the number and quality of pageants associated with the sovereign corresponds with a perceived demise apparent in the regular theater. The seeds of this decline in pageantry sown in the Jacobean era bear their fateful fruit here in the reign of Charles I. A reluctant king and changing political and economic conditions had much to do with this negative evolution; certainly political instability plays havoc with any serious attempt at pageantry or else the entertainments become overblown with complimentary hypocrisy.

When the light of life does flicker in the pageant theater, as in 1633, then the basic dramatic ingredients again appear. We continue to be in the presence of non-realistic drama, a drama populated by historical, mythological, and allegorical characters emblematically presented, a drama which makes its first claim on visual attention. Unfortunately, the Caroline royal entry makes no significant new contribution to the pageant stage; we would not be cynical to conclude that we have seen or heard it all before. The spontaneity which surrounded so much Elizabethan pageantry has long since vanished; the well-structured pageant drama of the Jacobean age remains largely a memory.

Before we wrongly conclude that all became bleak in the reign of Charles, we must give a hearing to what became the dominant pageant form in the Stuart

[29]Corporation of London MS. 86.5, "Extraordinary Disbursements of the Chamber for the Civil War. &c. 1637-1667."
[30]*Calendar of State Papers Domestic 1641-1643*, p. 188.

period: the Lord Mayor's Show. Part Two focuses on this other side of the pageant coin minted in Renaissance England.

Part two

The Lord Mayors' Shows

FOR QUITE SOME TIME there had been processionals at the annual installation of the new Lord Mayor of London, but not until the mid-sixteenth century does a show or civic pageant emerge as a permanent part of the festivities. These new pageants supplant the "Midsummer Shows" which the trade guilds presented in the early part of the Tudor reign; but even before Elizabeth's accession, these summer entertainments had begun to pass from the scene. When the attention shifted to the inauguration of the mayor each 29th of October and the guilds began to compete with one another to see which company could produce the most elaborate pageant, then the end of the Midsummer Shows clearly had come.[1]

Like the royal entry, the Lord Mayor's Show included a procession through London as the new mayor made his way to Westminster to take his oath of office. On his return to the city and to the Guildhall the company to which he belonged would present its dramatic show, consisting generally of various dramatic tableaux stationed along the route. In the simplest form the show would have but one device—generally true of the Elizabethan mayoralty pageant—but elaboration set in, and thus the number of devices increased, with entertainment on the Thames also.

The chapters which follow will demonstrate some of the ways in which the several forms of civic pageantry correspond, the Lord Mayor's Show bearing the closest kinship to the royal entry pageants in terms of preparation, involvement of the guilds, form, and content. Something of the pattern of development sketched in the preceding three chapters will be evident here as well. Well-known dramatists become involved with the mayoralty shows as they had with the pro-

[1] For a history of the development of the Lord Mayors' Shows see Robert Withington, *English Pageantry* (Cambridge, Mass., 1920), vol. II; F. W. Fairholt, *Lord Mayors' Pageants*, Percy Society, vol. I (London, 1843 `11); R. T. D. Sayle, *Lord Mayors' Pageants of the Merchant Taylors' Company in the 15th, 16th, and 17th Centuries* (London, 1931); and Malone Society, *Collections III: A Calendar of Dramatic Records in the Books of the Livery Companies of London 1485-1640*, ed. Jean Robertson and D. J. Gordon (Oxford, 1954). Glynne Wickham's *Early English Stages*, 2 vols. (London, 1959-63) should be included, though he does not make a systematic, historical study of the development of the Lord Mayors' Shows. But his valuable discussions of various kinds of pageantry contain many references to the mayoralty pageants, especially Chapter VI of volume II, "The Emblematic Tradition."

gress and royal entry entertainments. Moral allegory, mythology, and history will provide the basic content for these shows as they did for the other forms of pageantry.

Like the royal entry, the Lord Mayor's Show also reaches its highest dramatic achievement in the Jacobean period; the skilful dramatists involved with the pageants assure this accomplishment. The Elizabethan show retains a basically simple, somewhat static form corresponding to the nature of royal entries in the comparable period, though Peele's 1591 pageant illustrates the beginning of the shift to dramatic action. By the time of Munday's 1611 and 1616 entertainments, Dekker's 1612 show, and Middleton's 1613 pageant, dramatic action becomes paramount and coherently sustained. And when Error in the 1613 show tempts the mayor with verbal arguments, we get a measure of how the form in its development embraces dramatic speech, which now accompanies the visual display in expressing dramatic conflict. By this second decade of the 1600s, the period of the best Lord Mayors' Shows, speech has become the handmaid of the visual, not just a step-child.

4 The Elizabethan Lord Mayor's Show

As THE ACCESSION OF ELIZABETH seemed to spur various dramatic forms, civic pageantry thrived in this new atmosphere, the subject of Chapter One. This present chapter seeks to complete that picture of Elizabethan pageantry by offering a discussion of the Lord Mayors' Shows occurring concurrently with the other forms. A pattern emerges in the mayoral pageants of the period paralleling in many respects the development of royal entry and progress pageants of the same era—the religious milieu eventually fades, well-known dramatists become associated with the shows, a sophistication occurs in the dramatic action and speech. Especially conducive to the rise of the mayoralty entertainments to new heights of splendor and achievement was the increasing wealth of the merchant class, including the guildsmen directly and exclusively responsible for the presentation of these annual pageants. This arrangement implies a healthy competitive rivalry among the companies, each determined to do justice to its member who has been elevated to the office of Lord Mayor; such rivalry bears good fruit in this case. Thus the Lord Mayors' Shows join the other pageant forms to offer a kaleidoscopic view of civic drama, rich in spectacle and sense of occasion.

Henry Machyn's *Diary* provides much information about the early Lord Mayors' Shows, covering the period 1550-63 in the city of London; in fact, he comments on some eight different mayoralty entertainments. One of the fullest accounts and one which sums up the typical show of the pre-Elizabethan era is Machyn's description of the 1553 pageant which stimulated his visual and aural senses by the color and display of the occasion. He notes, for example, the decoration on the boat which carried the mayor down the Thames to Westminster, and "all the craftes bargers with stremars and banars...."[1] As the mayor, Sir Thomas White, Merchant Taylor, returned and landed at Baynard's Castle and moved on to the churchyard of St. Paul's, every craft appeared in full array— "furst wher ij tallmen bayreng ij gret stremars [of] the Merchand-tayllers armes ..." (p. 47). Other figures included one man with a drum and playing a flute and another with a great fife and two giant savage men with great clubs dressed all in green, "and then cam xvj trumpeters blohyng" and seventy men dressed in blue gowns. After a devil "cam the pagant of sant John Baptyst gorgyusly, with goodly speches; and then cam all the kynges trumpeters blowhyng, and evere trumpeter havyng skarlet capes ..." (p. 48). The large retinue made its way to dinner and

---

[1]*The Diary of Henry Machyn*, ed. J. G. Nichols (London, 1848), p. 47. All quotations will be from this Camden Society edition.

after the feast back to St. Paul's "with all the trumpets and wettes blowhyng through Powlles, through rondabowt the qwer and the body of the chyrche blowhyng, and so home to my lord mere['s] howsse" (p. 48).

This description by Machyn indicates several typical features of the Lord Mayor's Show. For one thing, his account clearly establishes the idea of a procession and its general pattern. Colorful costume and plentiful music abound as they will throughout the history of the mayoral pageants. Allusions within the pageant to the sponsoring trade guild whether visual or verbal or both become the *sine qua non* of such entertainments. Machyn also refers to the "pageant" of St. John the Baptist, though he does not describe it, but the reference to historical personages becomes a permanent part of the pageant-dramatist's craft; this particular saint has links with the guild, and we find ourselves in the medieval dramatic tradition of linking guilds with certain presentations or "pageants." The diarist mentions "goodly speeches," though, unfortunately, they do not exist nor do we know who may have spoken them. Speeches thus occur in some of the earliest shows, but not until they clearly become dramatic speeches do we move further in the direction of dramatic form. But the potential ingredients inhere in this pageant form: live actors, speeches, a type of stage. We can witness through the Elizabethan era a refinement and sophistication of these native components of the incipient dramatic form.

The first Lord Mayor's Show for which the speeches exist comes early in Elizabeth's reign in 1561, when Sir William Harper, Merchant Taylor, came into office. The speeches can be found in the guild records which also reveal other valuable information regarding the planning of the pageant. For example, the guild chose John Shutte to construct a device "accordyng to suche a patterne as shalbe Devised to answer the speches...."[2] An artistic consciousness begins to manifest itself here. Payments made by the company include expenditures for a crown for a figure of David in the pageant, remuneration for the children who played and sang in the entertainment, expenses for several painters who assisted with the necessary construction, and the total cost for the entertainment came to £151 14s. 9d. (*MSC*, p. 44).

Mythological characters and one Biblical character constitute the figures presented on the pageant device, apparently some type of scaffold arrangement which could be carried through the city. Each personage, David, Orpheus, Amphion, Arion, and Topas, has his "story" painted about him. In addition, Arion sits on a dolphin in a sea playing a harp, his traditional presentation, and Topas appears before a table of princes. The painting included also on the device the verses of Psalm 150, a psalm of praise that bids us praise the Lord "with the sound of the trumpet: praise him with the psaltery and harp" (verse 3). And, of

---

[2]Malone Society, *Collections III*, p. 41. All quotations from company records will be from this source and are cited in the text as *MSC*. Some of the entries have been slightly modernized.

course, each of the characters represented here has associations with music and
especially the harp. As the figure David says in the opening speech:

> The heavie hand of god, to m'cie wilt thou turne,
> And mollifie mans harte, when it with rage doth burne;
> Then fall to psalme and harpe, for so I David wanne,
> The favor bothe of god, and Saule that furious man / (*MSC*, p. 42)

Orpheus speaks and notes the power of the harp, while Amphion observes that
the stones relent to the sound of music. Arion and Topas echo these sentiments
in their brief speeches; Arion notes, for instance, "The harpe then pearceth
heaven, the harpe the earth can move and that it Ruleth the sea, Arion can well
prove." David, Orpheus, Amphion, speak, again elaborating further the soothing
power of the harp, and Amphion points out that ancient rulers used the harp "to
open them ther highe affaires / when they did sitt at meate" (p. 43). David gives
the closing speech:

> ffor why yor gentle harper may
> with myldenes bringe aboute
> asmoche touchinge good gou'nement
>   as they that be right stoute.
> Wherefore rejoyce ye londoners
>   and hope well of yor mayre
> ffor neu' did a mylder man
>   sitt in yor chiefest chaire / (p. 43)

The virtue of gentleness sounds through all the speeches, thus assisting thematic
unity. An inherent didacticism exists here also, as we should expect—a characteristic of all such civic entertainments. Interestingly, many of the characters imper-
sonated here in the 1561 Lord Mayor's Show appear several times in future pageants, especially Arion and Orpheus. The Biblical influence, apparent here, loses
its force later; its strength in these early shows probably reflects the continuing
influence of the medieval dramatic form, especially the cycle plays, all of which
conforms to a pattern observed in the royal entries of the Elizabethan period.

The pageant of 1566, devised by James Peele, father of the playwright and
pageant-dramatist George Peele, captures our interest. The entertainment honored Sir Christopher Draper, Ironmonger. An entry in the company records illustrates the remuneration given Peele: "Also it is agreed that Mr Pele shall have
xxxˢ paid him for the devising of the pagent besides the mony which he hath dis-
burside" (*MSC*, p. 46). The schoolmaster of Westminster agreed for six of his
children to serve in the pageant for speeches and songs. Additional expenditures
included money paid to Peele for seven pairs of gloves for the children in the

pageant, 13s. 8d. for the children's breakfast and the room in which they got apparelled, and several sums for painting. Interestingly, the guild paid 5s. to the
printer for "printing of posies, speeches, and songs that were spoken and sung by
the children in the pageant" (p. 46). Unfortunately, no printed texts survive, but
the interest in having a text printed becomes a constant concern in these entertainments. Obviously, production demands abounded, witness the matter of
breakfast for the children, and the expenses significant—a total cost of £210 8s.
10d. for this show. The preparations and expenditures remind us again of such
procedures in the royal entries, as in the ones in London, Bristol, and Norwich in
the Elizabethan era.

When in 1568 the Merchant Taylors sought to honor Sir Thomas Roe, the
company called upon Richard Mulcaster, already familiar to us for his involvement with the 1559 coronation royal entry of Elizabeth, to write the speeches and
a man named Keble to oversee the construction of the pageant. At the total cost
of over £317, this represents a considerable increase over the show of just two
years previous. Hired men carried the pageant device; children again participated
in the presentation (and also received breakfast). A Richard Tysdale received
payment for four dozen birds and four rabbits for the pageant (*MSC*, p. 47). In
addition the guild appointed Tysdale, John Holt, and Robert Pavy "to give their
attendance for the oversight of the pageant whilst it is a-painting and a-making"
(p. 50). The famous historian John Stow served as one of thirty whifflers appointed for the procession.

Fortunately, the guild records preserve Mulcaster's speeches, though again
we cannot determine when the speeches might have been presented during the
entertainment. The records identify only one character by name: the person representing St. John the Baptist, thus giving the show a decided religious overtone
(cf. the 1553 pageant). St. John begins by identifying himself as the voice in the
wilderness and suggests that he has been sent by god "To preache unto you all":

> Repent and make the Lordes waye streighte
>   Let workes your will bewraye
> The tyme of your Accompte, is come
>   Amende your Lyves I saye.
>
> The Axe alreadie is in hande,
>   To hew downe ev'y Tree,
> Which dothe not beare so pleasant frute,
>   As god woulde it shoulde be. (p. 48)

The clear didactic intent of this speech joins with the purpose of the three boys
who respond by talking about the swiftness and attentiveness of the roe (pun on
the mayor's name) that hearkens to the voice of the prophet. The third boy notes,

for example: "Our Roe by sighte in governement / Wee truste shall Rule so well / That by his doinges suche may Learne as covet to excell" (p. 49). A fourth boy concludes the speeches by noting that the queen has provided a place for John to preach that "Roe maye heare / The gyftes of heavenly grace":

> The Courte nowe biddes John Baptist preache,
>   under our mayden Quene.
>
> God sende her lyf and honor longe,
>   Her Royall crowne to weare,
> God sende us suche as John to preache,
>   And suche as Roe to heare. (p. 49)

The deviser of the pageant has succeeded not only in complimenting the mayor, as expected, but also in flattering and honoring the sovereign, a technique repeated years later in Anthony Munday's 1605 show in which James I received great praise. Interestingly, certain precepts, such as "ffeare god, be wyse, be true, accepte no bribes," would be written "aboute the Pageant if it shalbe thoughte good." But a later statement reveals: "These verses above recited were not written aboute the pageant ..." (p. 50). Apparently St. John's admonition of repentance adequately conveyed the religious instruction of the show. This overt preaching remains uncommon in the Lord Mayors' Shows even in the Elizabethan era, but moral suasion continues throughout the history of these civic pageants a common, and indeed, necessary ingredient.

References to the shows of 1575 and 1584 appear in historical documents of the period. Fairholt reprints the lengthy account of the 1575 entertainment preserved in the manuscript of a Wyllyam Smythe, citizen and haberdasher of London.[3] It refers to no specifically dramatic presentation; instead, it provides a full description of the procession through the city. In many respects it parallels the report found in Machyn. A certain von Wedel toured England and Scotland and prepared a journal of his travels, including his presence at the Lord Mayor's Show of 1584.[4] He describes in detail the ceremonies when the new mayor took the oath of office, and he portrays vividly the color and total scene of the processional, being particular about the dress of the participants and the decorations on the barges. Apparently attending the mayor's feast, von Wedel also paid a visit to the kitchen. One curious part of the street pageant which he describes occurs in the following statement: "After the trumpets some men were carrying a representation in the shape of a house with a pointed roof painted in blue and golden colours and ornamented with garlands, on which sat some young girls in fine

---

[3]Fairholt, Lord Mayors' Pageants, pt. I, pp. 20-4.
[4]Transactions of the Royal Historical Society (London, 1895), IV (new series), 252-5.

apparel, one holding a book, another a pair of scales, the third a sceptre. What the others had I forget" (p. 255). Unfortunately, he offers no more. One can guess on the basis of the emblematic detail that these girls may be allegorical figures representing perhaps Learning, Justice, and Majesty. Using such allegorical characters in symbolic garb becomes of course in later shows a well-established practice, familiar to us already in the progress pageants and royal entries of the same period as the various pageant-dramatists reveal their indebtedness to iconographical traditions.

In 1585 the Lord Mayor's Show made a significant step in the process of development: for the first time a well-known dramatist, George Peele, writes the entertainment, and for the first time the printed pamphlet has survived and come down to us. This prepares the way for the full-scale involvement of major dramatists, such as Munday, Dekker, Middleton, Webster, and Heywood, in the Jacobean and Caroline Lord Mayors' pageants. Also the practice of preparing printed texts becomes a well established procedure, consistently adhered to in the early decades of the seventeenth century. The availability of these texts grants the mayoralty shows, as it does other civic pageants, a permanence otherwise denied to them by scanty records of the trade guilds.

Peele calls his entertainment simply, *The Device of the Pageant Borne before Wolstan Dixi*, and the pamphlet contains only the speeches, no type of description as became common in the Stuart era. The pageant includes characters impersonating London, frequently portrayed in later pageants as in Middleton's *Triumphs of Truth* (1613), the Country, and the Thames, to be seen in Munday's *Triumphs of Re-United Britannia* (1605). The allegorical qualities of Magnanimity and Loyalty appear also, continuing traditions of medieval morality drama. Four nymphs, a Soldier, Sailor, and a figure representing Science constitute the other characters, with the exception of the initial speaker.

The opening speech, given by the figure riding on the back of a lynx, sign of the Skinners' company, interprets and describes. He comes, the speaker says, to offer to the mayor "This Emblem thus in showe significant,"[5] a reflection on the tableau nature and didactic intent of the entertainment. The speaker praises London, "riche and fortunate, / Famed through the Worlde for peace and happinesse," the figure of which "Is heer advaunc't and set in Highest seat, / Beawtified throughly as her state requires" (p. 209). The tableau apparently occurs arranged on a scaffold, for over London appears in "beaten golde" the Royal Arms. Friends make the City happy—Country, Thames, Soldier, Sailor, Science; and she "thankes her God the Author of her peace" and yields herself, her wealth "Unto the person of her gracious Queene, / Elizabeth renowned through the world" (p.

[5] *The Life and Minor Works of George Peele*, ed. David H. Horne (New Haven, 1952), p. 209. All quotations from Peele will be from this edition. See also Horne's discussion of Peele's pageant career, pp. 71-6 and 154-60.

210). The speaker bids the new mayor to help preserve both kingdom and the sovereign, who "Hath put your honor lovingly in trust: / That you may adde to Londons dignity...." In short, the new magistrate should join with all of London's "friends" in maintaining the healthy condition of the body politic. So the mayor has been duly instructed and the queen complimented, but this differs considerably from John the Baptist's "sermon" in the 1568 entertainment.

When London speaks, she too praises the queen, "my peerles mistresse soveraigne of my peace," that "she may ever live and never dye: / Her sacred shrine set in the house of fame, / consecrate to eternall memorie" (p. 211). Each of the other characters in turn offers his service to the city and the sovereign. Magnanimity observes that "All English harts are glad, and well appaide, / in readines their London to defend," and Loyalty offers herself as "The greatest treasure that a Prince can have." Country grants a "rich encrease," and the Thames offers a pleasant stream "where leaping fishes play betwixt the shores." The Soldier, Sailor, and Science stand "well prepar'd and put in redines, / to doo such service as may fitting be ..." (p. 212). Having tendered their services and praise to Elizabeth, these figures join four nymphs who descant further on the glories of the country. As the second nymph says:

So long as Sunne dooth lend the world his light,
     or any grasse dooth growe upon the ground:
With holy flame, our Torches shall burne bright,
     and fame shall brute with golden trumpets sound
         The honor of her sacred regiment:
         That claimes this honorable monument. (p. 213)

The fourth nymph assures us that virtue shall witness the worthiness of the queen and fame shall register Elizabeth's princely deeds. Characters thus punctuate the static tableau with gracious speeches designed to offer a worthy emblem to the queen and implicit instruction to all who hear, no matter how scarce the dramatic action may be. The various voices of the pageant sing a unified song of praise.

To honor John Allot, Fishmonger, his company selected to devise the entertainment Thomas Nelson, about whom we know little other than his being a printer and ballad writer. The 1590 show survives in a printed text known simply as *The Device of the Pageant*.[6] Again the text provides only the speeches, but from them we see that Nelson has placed his emphasis on allegorical figures and personages from actual English history.

[6]Thomas Nelson, *The Device of the Pageant* (London, 1590). All quotations are from this quarto text. For a brief discussion see Robert Withington, "The Lord Mayor's Show for 1590," *MLN* 33 (1918): 8-13.

The opening speeches of the pageant celebrate the glory of the city and commonwealth; and the speaker who rides on a unicorn bids the new mayor: "Rule now my Lord and keepe this Citie well, / reforme abuses crept into the same, / So shall your fame eternizde be for aie, / and London still preserved from decaie" (p. 4). The principle of fame having been alluded to, we, not surprisingly, encounter the embodiment of Fame who sounds her trumpet and speaks, dressed probably in emblematic costume, though Nelson does not indicate. One can expect such figures as Fame to be represented as they typically appeared in iconographical tradition and in other civic pageants, as when Fame reappears in the mayoralty pageants of 1612, 1613, 1615, and 1618. Here in the 1590 show she refers to the peace which England knows, and she must spread the news of peace everywhere "That all may wish with hearts which do not faine, / our roiall peace in England still may raine" (p. 4).

Having sounded the theme of peace, Nelson pursues it through the speeches of Peace of England, Wisdom, Policy, God's Truth, Plenty, Loyalty, and Concord, virtues reminiscent of those civic virtues presented in Elizabeth's 1559 entry into London, the qualities which help sustain a worthy government. Policy notes, for example, that it works to prevent traitorous fact, and "Both Pollicie and Wise-dome will not cease, / Each night and daie for to preserve this peace" (p. 5). God's Truth brings "comfort for your soules content, / which Englands peace doth willingly imbrace," and God's Truth "doth blesse this little land" (p. 5). Plenty cites the material blessings of the country; Loyalty and Concord note the sense of unity and harmony which binds all hearts in devotion to the queen. But these pleasant notes of peace contrast with the harsh voice of Ambition, who "Doth dailie seeke to worke sweete Englands fall, / He never rests, but seekes each time and tide, / How Englands peace might soone be brought in thrall" (p. 6). But the figure representing Commonwealth reacts to Ambition by observing that the government will seek to banish ambition and to guarantee that "this peace may never cease" and thus rid the country of vice.

Nelson next gives this tension between peace and discord, stated in abstract terms, concrete reality by relating it to an actual historical event. The pageant-dramatist chooses the Jack Straw-Wat Tyler rebellion, part of the Peasants' Revolt of 1381, a subject treated also in the play *The Life and Death of Jack Straw* (printed in 1593) and later referred to in Munday's 1616 show, *Chrysanaleia*.[7] The three principal figures, Richard II, Jack Straw, and William Walworth, all appear in Nelson's pageant. The king speaks but two lines asking for Walworth's help in quelling the uprising. And the rebel, Jack Straw, notes that Walworth thwarted the attempt to harm the king, "He being Maior of London then, soone danted all our pride, / He slew me first, the rest soone fled, and then like traitors

---

[7]For a discussion of the use of the legend see my "Jack Straw in Drama and Pageant," *The Guildhall Miscellany* 2, no. 10 (1968): 459-63.

dide" (p. 6). The figure representing Walworth, also speaks noting his achievement:

> I slew Jacke Straw, who sought my kings disgrace,
>   and for my act reapt honors of great price,
> First Knight was I of London you may reade,
>   and since each Maior gaines knighthood by my deede. (p. 7)

Richard II granted many honors to the brave Lord Mayor, and, as Walworth says,
"Fame her selfe still laudeth me therefore" (p. 7). The voice of Fame sounds forth
the achievement of peace; and we have come full circle, for at the beginning of
the show voices rose in praise of peace, and the allegorical manifestation of Fame
appeared.

Nelson has, then, achieved thematic unity and created dramatic interest by
suggesting on both the abstract and concrete levels the forces that operate against
peace. His use of a former Lord Mayor and other historical figures creates an
important first, for almost all mayoralty pageants of the early seventeenth century will include such personages both as compliments to the trade guilds and as
worthy examples to be imitated. A statement in the printed text that follows
Walworth's speech stirs interest: "It is to be understood that sir William Walworth pointeth to the honors wherewith the king did endue him, which were
placed neere about him in the Pageant" (p. 7). This amounts to a "stage direction," and as such we get a further impression of the pageant as a dramatic form.

The year of the great progress entertainment for Elizabeth at Elvetham, 1591,
also becomes the occasion of the final Lord Mayor's Show of the Elizabethan
period for which an extant printed text survives: George Peele's *Descensus Astraeae* (1591), incidentally the first show to have a specific title. From the Sta-
tioner's Register we know that Peele had devised the pageant of 1588, and from
company records we also know that he probably wrote the one for 1595, but neither survives in pamphlet form. This 1591 entertainment, honoring the new
mayor William Webbe, seems rather elaborate and includes, for the first time, a
speech delivered on the Thames as the mayor made his way to Westminster. The
speaker congratulates the mayor on his office, bids him beautify the city with
good deeds and keep his oath "inviolate for thy soveraignes hope, / Vertues pure
mirror, Londons great mistresse …" (p. 219). The speech asks the mayor to "go
in peace happie by sea and land, / Guided by grace, and heavens immortall hand"
(p. 219). The mayor has to be satisfied with this speech, for the rest of the pageant clearly honors Elizabeth.

Indeed, the show means to prefigure her in the person of Astraea, as the
"Presenter" makes clear in the opening speech of the main land pageant device.
As Peele had done in the 1585 show, this speech interprets and describes the ac-
tion of the tableau. Astraea stands on the top of the device, carrying her

sheephook and watching her flock, as she notes in her speech. She also keeps watchful eyes on a fountain, "Garded with Graces, and with gratious traines, / Vertues divine, and giftes incomparable" (p. 214). But two clergymen, one representing Superstition and the other Ignorance, intend to corrupt this fountain. As Superstition says, "Stirre Priest, and with thy beades poyson this spring"; but Ignorance realizes the futility of their efforts:

It is vaine hir eye keepes me in awe,
Whose heart is purely fixed on the law:
The holy law, and bootlesse we contend,
While this chast nimph, this fountain doth defend.... (p. 216)

Evil does not succeed because of Astraea (Elizabeth), and the fountain retains its peace and purity against religious corruption. Peele makes effective use of an emblematic stage property around which to suggest the contention between good and evil. Perhaps Peele's technique Thomas Dekker had in mind in part of his contribution to the 1604 royal entry entertainment presented to James, discussed in Chapter Two. At any rate, at the triumphal arch called *Nova Felix Arabia* Dekker included a Fount of Virtue which risks being contaminated by Detraction and Oblivion whose efforts fail, thanks to the presence of the sovereign, this time James.

Astraea preserves the sanctity of the fountain in Peele's entertainment with the help of the three Graces, Euphrosyne, Aglaia, and Thalia (who, incidentally, Dekker also included on the arch mentioned above and who had been at Elvetham earlier in 1591 gracing that pageant with their poetical presence). Euphrosyne suggests that Jove has dispatched Astraea to cure the troublesome evils of the world; he sends her "descended through the sweete transparent aire: / And heere she sits in beautie fresh and sheene, / Shadowing the person of a peerlesse Queene" (p. 216). Aglaia says that this princely dame is "Enrold in register of eternall fame," and Thalia observes that they lend their balm to the "sacred head" of the one who brings happiness throughout the realm. The Graces, popular in the literature and the pictorial arts of the Renaissance, also appear later in Munday's 1609 Lord Mayor's Show. Here in the 1591 pageant the Theological Graces, Faith, Hope, and Charity join them. Charity hopes that happiness may continue in the land and prays to "Great Israels God, spring of all heavenly peace" that angels will watch over the queen, and "O let hir princely daies never have fine, / Whose vertues are immortall and devine" (p. 217). Faith and Hope echo the recognition of Elizabeth's virtue.

As the Presenter's speech notes, Honour also waits upon the throne of the queen, and "in hir bright eies / Sits Majestie: Vertue, and Steadfastnesse / Possesse hir hart, sweet mercy swaies hir sword" (p. 215). Of these qualities only Honour appears in the pageant, and she claims that Astraea's honor shines "As bright as is the burning lampe of heaven" (p. 217) and that her fame spreads throughout the world. At the feet of Astraea sits Champion, "armed with resolution," who helps chastise two Malcontents, "that threat hir honors wracke" (p. 215). Champion himself speaks of his function briefly, noting that he advances his colors in defense of the queen and will not let the "misproud Malecontent" threaten the state of one whose "sacred person angels have in keep" (p. 217). The two Malcontents recognize, as had Superstition and Ignorance, the futility of their efforts; as the second one observes: "No marvell then although we faint and quaile, / For mightie is the truth and will prevaile" (p. 218). This statement epitomizes the theme that pervades the entertainment.

On the back part of the pageant device sits a child representing Nature, "holding in her hand a distaffe, and spinning a Web" (pun on the mayor's name), which "passed through the hand of Fortune and was wheeled up by Time" (p. 218). Time, familiar in civic drama from the first civic pageant of Elizabeth's reign, speaks here in Peele's show:

> Thus while my wheele with ever turning gyres,
> At heavens hie heast serves earthly mens desires,
> I wind the Web that kinde so well beginnes:
> While Fortune doth enrich what Nature spinnes. (p. 218)

Thus each part of the show underscores the beneficial effect of Astraea's descent, one who, though confronted with evil, can with the help of other forces quell the rebellion and cast the seeds of peace across the land.

Peele achieves thematic unity, if not in the same way as Nelson. Instead of historical persons, Peele relies on mythological and allegorical characters. Though all the dramatic possibilities of the fountain remain unexplored, he has given the Lord Mayor's Show a new technique, one which will be duplicated in many other pageants, as also in the Fountain of Self-Love in Ben Jonson's *Cynthia's Revels*. But mainly Peele in this civic drama wants to sing a hymn in praise of Astraea, "our faire Eliza." The Presenter sums up the pervasive sentiment:

> Goddesse live long, whose honors we advance,
> Strengthen thy neighbours, propagate thine owne:
> Guide well thy helme, lay thine annointed hand
> To build the temple of triumphant Trueth.... (p. 215)

Company records indicate that Anthony Munday wrote the final Lord Mayor's Show of the Elizabethan era, the one of 1602, to honor Sir Robert Lee, Merchant Taylor; thus begins Munday's long association with these civic pageants, the subject of the next chapter, an involvement which lasted until 1623. A William Haynes also contributed a speech for the occasion. The full records show, for example, the need for a ship, lion, and camel; and Mr Haynes received payment for apparelling "10 scholars who represented the 9 muses and the god Apollo before my Lord Mayor in Cheapside" (*MSC*, p. 60). Despite a payment to Munday of 30s. "for printing the books of speeches," no extant pamphlet for the pageant survives. He got an additional £30 for providing the apparel for all the children in the pageant. Payments went to painters and carpenters and the person who provided breakfast for the children. This mayoralty pageant cost £747 2s. 10d.—a striking increase over the £317 the Merchant Taylors spent in their previous pageant of 1568. And with the expense of the 1602 show we may see how far the Elizabethan Lord Mayor's Show has come, at least materially; such cost clearly becomes the pattern for the opulent Jacobean and Caroline pageants.

By the time James I ascended the throne, the Lord Mayor's Show had achieved much and had moved increasingly in the direction of a dramatic entertainment, elaborate in spectacle. The days of the simple processional through London had ended, and each company begins to pride itself on its pageant—a healthy rivalry which of course generates expensive productions. A simple measure of the development of the Elizabethan show comes in the material growth from a meager £151 spent in 1561 to an excess of £747 in 1602, a handsome sum that compares favorably with that spent on the typical Stuart pageant. Equally important, printed texts, beginning with the 1585 show, established a practice followed rather consistently in the seventeenth century. The Elizabethan show thus sets an extremely valuable precedent that allows this form of civic pageant to be considered along with other kinds of civic drama. One cannot overstate one of the most significant achievements, namely, the beginning of the association of the regular dramatists with the pageant theater of the streets in the Elizabethan period, an involvement that continues to the closing of the theaters.

Though patently didactic, the Elizabethan mayoralty pageant begins to shake off its initial religious content and move into what become the three basic subject areas of the later pageants: mythology, history, and moral allegory. Its greatest debt to medieval drama derives from the morality play, and these pageants frequently suggest the basic morality tension: the conflict between virtue and vice, especially seen in Peele's 1591 show. In keeping with allegory, the pageant-dramatist uses an emblematic method that becomes the basic tool for all writers of pageant entertainments. Nelson in his 1590 show helps point the way for the ever-increasing use of historical persons and historical legends in the pageants—a significant new direction. The mythological characters reflect the new Renaissance learning and its interest in the classical tradition. Preservation of the state's unity against those forces that would destroy it becomes a pervasive theme; hence, the great concern for the commonwealth, both national and local. Elizabeth herself receives much praise, though, understandably, not the complete apotheosis apparent in the royal entries and progress pageants.

An examination of the Elizabethan Lord Mayor's Show demonstrates that a vast common ground existed among all forms of civic pageantry, the mayoralty pageant sharing with the progress entertainment its predilection for mythology and with the royal entry its historical and allegorical bias as well as its processional form. The developments in the Tudor Lord Mayor's Show essentially parallel those discussed in Chapter One concerning the Elizabethan entries and progresses: well-known dramatists becoming involved, fading of the religious emphasis, preparing of texts. Thematically the different kinds of pageants frequently develop along similar and sometimes coincidental lines. We witness in the Elizabethan period a homogeneous dramatic development no matter the precise form which the civic drama might take. Civic pageantry occurring in different places, at different times, under different auspices nevertheless develops a generic form. This form Stuart and Caroline dramatists build upon, as has been seen in earlier chapters and will be demonstrated anew in the chapters that follow as we study the dramatists who took on the task of shaping a civic entertainment worthy of the new mayor and his guild.

5 *Anthony Munday*

ANTHONY MUNDAY'S ENORMOUSLY VARIED AND PROLIFIC CAREER led almost inevitably to his writing Lord Mayors' Shows; indeed, his spirit broods over almost the entire Jacobean period. For his dramatic productions Munday had earned recognition from Francis Meres who in *Palladis Tamia* cites him as being among "the best for comedy" with the additional compliment that he is our "best plotter." But Munday's interests eventually turn from the public to the pageant theater and such things as his additions to Stow's *Survey of London*. Already we have noted his involvement with the final mayoral pageant of the Elizabethan era and his authorship of an entertainment presented in 1610 in honor of Prince Henry's being made Prince of Wales. In the period 1602-23 Munday had a hand in the production of at least fifteen Lord Mayors' Shows, his participation ranging from merely submitting a proposal to being fully responsible for the pageant; and if we had more information about the shows that took place in the last seven years of Elizabeth's reign, we might be able to assign even more to Munday's credit. Quantitatively, the indefatigable Munday remains unsurpassed in involvement in the Jacobean Lord Mayors' Shows; as such he gives us a good measure of its development and achievement.

Munday became the target for satire, as in the character of "Post-haste" in the play *Histriomastix*. Perhaps the earliest satirical allusion came in *The Case Is Altered*, in which Jonson caricatures Munday in the figure of "Antonio Balladino," Pageant Poet to the city of Milan. In Jonson's play Antonio (alias Munday) appears in the second scene of Act I. In response to Onion's question—"you are not *Pageant* Poet to the City of *Millaine* sir, are you?"—Antonio says: "I supply the place sir: when a worse cannot be had sir."[1] Antonio further incriminates himself by coming out vigorously in favor of using stale, threadbare material. He tells Onion: "I do use as much stale stuffe, though I say it my selfe, as any man does in that kind I am sure." Jonson mocks Munday succinctly but skillfully.

Though Munday received £2 "for his paines" for the 1604 Lord Mayor's Show for which guild records indicate Ben Jonson as the apparent author of the entertainment,[2] his pageant of 1605 becomes the first to survive in a printed text. This show, called *The Triumphs of Re-United Britannia*, sought to honor Sir Leonard Halliday, Merchant Taylor, the new mayor; it has two unique qualities. It

---

[1]*Ben Jonson*, ed. C. H. Herford and Percy Simpson, vol. III (Oxford, 1927).
[2]Malone Society, *Collections III: A Calendar of Dramatic Records in the Books of the Livery Companies of London 1485-1640*, ed. D. J. Gordon and Jean Robertson (Oxford, 1954), p. 63. All quotations from company records will be from this source with occasional modernization of the text.

141

contains the only full-scale treatment of the popular Brutus-in-Albion myth of English history to be found in civic pageantry down to the closing of the theaters. This pageant has the further distinction of having been readied twice for performance, because the scheduled day, 29 October, experienced a storm that did much damage to the preparations. Thus upon request of the company "the same shewes were newe repaired, and caried abroade upon *All Saincts day ...*" (*MSC*, p. 69)—which partially accounts for the total expense of £710 2s. 5d. Two payments to Munday indicate much about the diverse duties usually assumed by the dramatist: £38 for providing apparel for all the children in the "pageant, ship, lion, and camel, and for the chariot," and £6 more for "printing the books of the speeches in the pageant and the other shows ..." (*MSC*, pp. 68-9). A "Mr Hearne," a painter, received £75 "for making, painting, and gilding the pageant, chariot, lions, camel, and new painting and furnishing the ship, and for the furniture for both giants" (p. 68). Here we get a glimpse of the increasingly important role of the artificer in the total production of such pageants, a subject discussed more fully in a later chapter. The £10 paid to "88 porters for carrying the pageant, ship, and beasts" suggests that workers carried the devices in a typical Lord Mayor's Show through the city rather than having them remain stationary, the common practice in the royal entry pageants.

The pageant itself opens with what amounts to a prologue to the several scenes or dramatic vignettes that follow, a conversation between the Master, Mate, and Boy of the ship "called the *Royall Exchange*."[3] Ostensibly they have just returned from a voyage where they have gathered rich spices and silks and now experience amazement at the tumult in London. The Boy says with an implicit pun on the name of the new mayor: "Shall we do nothing, but be idle found, / On such a generall mirthfull Holyday?" (sig. A4ᵛ). Thus the Master orders that they disburse the goods aboard the ship so that they might "adde the very uttermost ... / To make this up a cheerefull Holi-day."

This opening prologue with its embedded allusion to the guild leads to a mute scene involving the appearance of Neptune and his Queen Amphitrita seated upon a lion and camel. They come, Munday says, because they "first seated their sonne *Albion* in this land" (sig. B1). The dramatist explains further: "... in them we figure Poetically, that as they then triumphed in their sonnes happy fortune, so now they cannot chuse but do the like, seeing what happy successe hath thereon ensued, to renowne this Countrey from time to time" (B1).

---

[3]*The Triumphs of Re-United Britannia* (London, 1605), sig. A4ᵛ. All quotations will be from this original edition. There are reprints of the text in John Nichols, *Progresses of King James I*, 565f., and in R. T. D. Sayle, *Lord Mayors' Pageants of the Merchant Taylors' Company in the 15th, 16th, and 17th Centuries* (London, 1931). I have edited all of Munday's pageants in *Pageants and Entertainments of Anthony Munday: A Critical Edition* (New York, 1985). For additional discussion of Munday's pageants see Celeste Turner [Wright], *Anthony Mundy: An Elizabethan Man of Letters*, Univ. of Calif. Pubs. in Eng., vol. 2, no. 1 (Berkeley, 1928).

This "dumb show" prepares the way for the full dramatic treatment of Munday's theme of the renewal of unity under the current king, James. Present in this scene, the mythical Corineus and Goemagot (also at the Temple Bar in the 1559 royal entry), appear "in the shape and proportion of huge Giants, for the more grace and beauty of the show"; they serve as guides to the main pageant device.

The chief stage appears as a "mount triangular" which contains in the supreme place "under the shape of a fayre and beautifull Nymph, *Britania* hir selfe" (sig. B1-B1ᵛ). Seated beneath her, Brutus enables this scene to become the thematic and dramatic center of the entertainment with Munday's exploration of the Brutus myth. The pseudo-history of Brutus's settling of England became an important part of the "Tudor myth" or Tudor interpretation of history; and the Elizabethans took the story quite seriously with just cause since such historians and chroniclers as Matthew Paris, Richard Grafton, John Stow, William Camden, and Holinshed had perpetuated the legend. Many literary works alluded to the story—one recalls the catalogue of British kings from Brutus to Uther Pendragon which Arthur finds in the ancient book "hight *Briton Monuments*" at the House of Alma in canto x of Book II of Spenser's *Faerie Queene*. The most obvious example from contemporary drama can be found in the play, of disputed authorship, called *The Lamentable Tragedie of Locrine* (c. 1595), Locrine, of course, Brutus's eldest son. The play rehearses the traditional story. Brutus's decision to divide his kingdom among his three sons and the consequences of that act form the heart of the story; similar situations occur in some of Brutus's descendants, such as Lear and Gorboduc, also the subjects of dramatic works. The beginning of Munday's 1605 text contains his effort to trace the history of Brutus back to Noah and the Flood; in addition he sketches Brutus's conquest of the island and the subsequent division of the kingdom among his sons.

Children deliver the speeches for this scene, "according to their degrees of seating in the Pageant" (sig. B2ᵛ). The figure Britannia complains that she would still be known as Albion but for the conquest of Brutus, who then responds by outlining the advantages that his conquest has brought: taming the wilderness, overcoming the giants in the land, and establishing Troynovant on the Thames. But Loegria, Cambria, and Albania, representing the three divisions of the kingdom, chide Brutus for his decision to sever the kingdom, and they recount some of the consequences. To which Brutus responds with new hope that the separation of the land and the "Weeping so many hundred yeeres of woes" shall be no more; his answer ties to the present sovereign, James I:

> *Albania, Scotland,* where my sonne was slaine
> And where my follies wretchednes began,
> Hath bred another *Brute,* that gives againe
> To *Britaine* her first name, he is the man
> On whose faire birth our elder wits did scan,

Which Prophet-like seventh Henry did forsee,
Of whose faire childe comes *Britaines* unitie.

And what fierce war by no meanes could effect,
To re-unite those sundred lands in one,
The hand of heaven did peacefully elect
By mildest grace, to seat on *Britiaines* throne
This second *Brute*, then whom there else was none.
Wales, England, Scotland, severd first by me:
To knit againe in blessed unity. (sig. B3ᵛ)

This exposition of James's claim to the throne and his reconciliation of the parts of the kingdom serve the dramatic theme of unity; thus while the Tudors may take credit for uniting the warring houses, James and the Stuart line reunify the severed kingdoms. There had been a suggestion of this role of James in the speech by Zeal at Fleet street in the royal entry pageant of 15 March 1604 (see Chapter Two).

After Brutus sketches this new union, his three sons, Locrine, Camber, Albanact, represented in the pageant, speak in turn and submit their kingdoms to the unification of the whole. The new day hailed and applauded, the one personating Troynovant "incites fair *Thamesis*, and the rivers that bounded the severed kingdoms, (personated in faire and beautifull *Nymphs*) to sing *Paeans* and songs of tryumph, in honor of our second *Brute*, Royall King *James*" (sig. B2). So Thamesis, Severn, and Humber join in a universal song of praise of the sovereign. This "scene" thus closes, having sounded the essential theme of the entertainment, that the kingdom must remain physically and spiritually one—a theme adumbrated throughout Shakespeare's history plays.

The next part of the entertainment celebrates the trade guild by presenting seven former kings—Edward III, Richard II, Henry IV, Henry V, Henry VI, Edward IV, and Henry VII—all connected in some way with the history of the company. They pass forth in a chariot preceded by Fame "that attends on *Britaines* Monarchy, / Thus reunited to one state againe ..." (sig. C1). Each figure speaks in turn, revealing his contribution to the company's welfare. A vacant place remains in the chariot with the hope that James will eventually accept the freedom of the Merchant Taylors. Other pageant writers will continue this particular method of complimenting the company and the mayor.

The festivities close with the re-appearance of Neptune and Amphitrita, this time with speaking roles. Neptune praises the king who has set "this wreath of Union" on Britain's head, "Whose verie name did heavenlie comfort bring, / When in despaire our hopes lay drooping dead ..." (sig. C2). And Amphitrita suggests a graceful bridge between the Elizabethan and Jacobean eras:

Our latest Phaenix whose dead cinders shine,
In Angels spheres, she, like a mother milde,
Yeelding to Nature, did her right resigne
To times true heyre, her God-son, and lov'de childe,
When giddy expectation was beguilde:
And Scotland yeelded out of *Teudors* race,
A true borne bud, to sit in *Teudors* place. (sig. C3)

These two characters thus echo the earlier theme and praise of James. In the final speech Neptune directs his attention to the mayor, offering a challenge and moral instruction, suggesting that there will be a true "holiday" when Justice dominates, and when sin receives punishment, "When good provision for the poore is made, / Sloth set to labour, vice curbd every where ..." (sig. C4).

Most of the elements of the pageant serve to re-inforce one another, the historical legend of Brutus and its application to James providing the focus. The "stage properties" underscore its significance, such as the prominence of Britain's Mount with the attendant figures in appropriate costume. No other Lord Mayor's Show centers quite so thoroughly on a single historical legend, and it helps provide a unifying structure for the show even if flagrantly propagandistic. Historical and mythological figures alike posit the importance of the new unity of the island, assuming that without such cohesiveness discord and civil strife would erupt. Clearly here the pageant theater of the streets explores themes common to the public stage, just as the opening tableau in the coronation pageant of 1559 had established a precedent through the tangible genealogical tree of the Tudors and the spoken verses celebrating the end of civic strife. Only under conditions of political stability can Neptune's instruction to the new mayor have much value.

To honor the mayor, Sir Thomas Campbell, the Ironmongers engaged Munday in 1609 to devise a pageant, which he called *Camp-bell or the Ironmongers Faire Field*. Unfortunately, the absence of sheet A of the only extant text renders our knowledge of the entertainment incomplete. Company records, however, provide considerable information and supplement Munday's pamphlet. We learn, for example, of the planned action on the river by the following entry: "A Whale with a Blackamore in his Mouth with Musick and casting water out of his ffynnes, and fyer out of his mouth and rowed private A Mer Mayd coming his tresses in a looking glass with lady Thamesis couched on his ffynes and each of them their speeches."[4] The Ironmongers set up supervisors to guide the necessary preparations, all reminiscent of plans for other kinds of civic pageants, especially the royal entries. According to the records, they would pay Munday £45 for his services, including providing apparel for the children and giving the company "500 bookes printed of the speeches ..." (*MSC*, p. 73).

[4]Malone Society, *Collections III*, p. 75.

In early November shortly after the performance of the pageant, the guild called Munday before the Ironmongers' Court, with the following charges made against him: "that the children weare not instructed their speeches which was a spetiall judgment of the consideration, then that the Musick and singinge weare wanting, the apparrell most of it old and borrowed, with other defects ..." (MSC, p. 76). No clearer example exists in civic pageantry of the discrepancy between the planning and the execution of a dramatic show, and one can only wonder how many times performances might have been faulty. Small surprise that Munday's plea for an additional £5 the company denied later in November. Perhaps anticipating such trouble, Munday writes in his text: "... our time for preparation hath bene so short, as never was the like undertaken by any before, nor matter of such moment so expeditiously performed."[5] He registers a further complaint about the "weake voyces" of the children which "in a crowde of such noyse and uncivill turmoyle, are not any way able to be understood, neither their capacities to reach the full height of every intention, in so short a limitation for study, practise, and instruction." Such excuses fell on deaf ears within the sponsoring company, however, as this guild at least zealously watched over the performances.

Munday's allegorical presentation of the kingdom with the virtues that support it helps unify and offers a thematic motif present in a number of previous civic entertainments. Personifying the virtues necessary for a good government dates from at least 1559, when Elizabeth saw the "seat of worthy government" situated at Cornhill and containing such virtues as Pure Religion, Love of Subjects, Wisdom, and Justice. Occupying Jonson's tableau on the arch at Fenchurch in the 1604 royal entry, similar virtues supported Monarchia Britannica. Munday presents as the main device an island portraying the land of Happiness where "true Majesty holdeth her government ..." (sig. B1), richly garnished with all sorts of jewels, and in its midst a golden field wherein stands Majesty's watchtower. Here Munday creates an idealistic, golden world, based on the metaphorical relationship between this created microcosmic world and the real state.

All of the allegorical figures in this device have emblematic costume, following the general practice of the pageant writers. Majesty, for example, "hath a costly vaile of golde Tinsell on her head, and thereupon her Crowne imperiall, a Mownd in her left hand, and a golden Scepter in her right" (sig. B1). The figure of Religion sits nearby, dressed in pure white and "holdes a rich Booke in one hand, and a silver rod in the other, as her Ensignes of good reward and encouragement ..." (B1). Nobility and Policy also accompany Majesty; and Munday comments: "These are not unapt attendants, to be ever in presence of Soveraigne Majestie" (sig. B1ᵛ). On the lowest level of this arrangement Memory holds a

---

[5]Camp-bell or the Ironmongers Faire Field ([London, 1609]), sig. B2ᵛ. All quotations are from this fragmentary text.

"Table Booke with a silver pen still ready to write," and Vigilancy carries a "Bell and an houre Glasse ..." (B1ᵛ). Tranquility, "that ever blessed Companyon of all Royall Kingdomes ..." (B1ᵛ), dressed in red and carrying a palm branch in one hand and a wreath of flowers in the other, sits behind Majesty.

The three Graces, already used by Peele in his 1591 Lord Mayor's Show and by other dramatists, appear also with the allegorical virtues. Munday assigns to the Graces, Aglaia, Thalia, and Euphrosyne, the qualities of Cheerfulness, Peacefulness and Happiness, dressed, respectively, in crimson, "willowe collour," and purple. Munday adds another dimension to their meaning: Euphrosyne "sitteth in a golden Cave, holding a faire shield wherein *Fame* triumpheth over *Death*. The second [Thalia] holdes another Shield, wherein *Eternity* treadeth upon *Hell* and the *Devill*, and the first [Aglaia] hath her Shield, wherein *Tyme* sits sleeping, his houre glasse layd along and not running, and his Scithe broken in two peeces" (sig. B2). The idea of having the Graces carry emblematic shields Munday may have borrowed from Dekker, who in King James's passage through London in 1604, had placed the Graces, appropriately costumed, at the pageant at Soperlane End holding "in their handes pensild Shieldes; upon the first was drawne a Rose: on the second, three Dyce: on the third a branch of Mirtle. Figuring Pleasantnesse. Accord. Florishing." Not at all uncommon, the pageant writer might borrow a basic device from someone else.

Two figures accompany the mayor and offer interpretation: St. George, mounted on a dragon, and St. Andrew, seated on a unicorn—"united now in everlasting amitie." Should there be any doubt of the allegorical import of this pageant, St. Andrew's words make the meaning quite explicit. He says as he surveys the scene: "Those seaven royall and unparalled Vertues, that are this lifes best glory, and the futures Crowne, do make it seeme a Feild of heavenly happiness" (sig. B3). And he suggests that the seven virtues may foretell "seaven gladsome and fayre nourishing yeares of comfort...." St. George offers an interpretation of the pageant also and concludes on this instructive note: "But loyall hearts, spirits of courage, and hands inured to warre or peace, are the best walles about it [the island], as defensive against invading Envie, or homebred trecherie, as offensive to any hot spleene of Malignitie" (sig. B3ᵛ). Thus the speakers make a moral application of what has been visually displayed, a technique as old as civic pageantry itself. Having in his 1605 show illustrated the need for union of the kingdom, Munday in 1609 presents a visual and verbal statement of the virtues that ought to surround any government, with the allegory clearly pointing to the commonwealth of Stuart England.

Though no extant text exists for the 1610 show, records of the Merchant Taylors indicate Munday as the author who along with the artificer Grinkin received over £200 for part of their services (*MSC*, p. 79). A boy got paid eight shillings for his representation of "Merlin in the Rock," and that about sums up all we know of the nature of the pageant. Clearly it must have been an elaborate spectacle because the total cost exceeded £805. Fortunately a text survives for the 1611 Lord Mayor's Show, which Munday wrote to honor Sir James Pemberton, Goldsmith; he calls the show *Chruso-thriambos. The Triumphes of Golde*. The records of the company reveal that John Lowen, actor of the King's Men, played the role of Leofstane in the pageant; thus he joins Burbage, who in the previous year had performed in Munday's show honoring Prince Henry, as a participant in civic pageantry. At such moments the line separating the regular stage from the street theater blurs more than usual. Lowen, himself a Goldsmith, agreed in conference with Munday to play the role and that he "should provide a horse and furniture for himselfe and the horse ..." (*MSC*, p. 81).

Placing the emphasis again on history, Munday presents former Lord Mayors who had been vital in the history of the company—one recalls Nelson's use of William Walworth in the 1590 Lord Mayor's Show. But this familiar tableau device serves only secondary importance, the principal significance of the entertainment residing in its dramatic action. The new mayor gets rather directly involved in this action, and Munday provides a semblance of plot, at least more than seen in his previous shows.

The river entertainment and the land pageant both allude to the Goldsmiths. In fact, boats ostensibly filled with ingots of gold and silver accompany the mayor on his journey on the Thames. An Indian king and queen, Chiorison and Tumanama, also appear, having "brought into England ... no meane quantity of *Indian* Gold...."[6] On land they ride on "two Golden Leopardes, that draw a goodly triumphal Chariot." Munday describes the nature of the main device: "On a Quadrangle frame, of apt constructure, and answerable strength, we erect a Rocke or Mount of Golde, in such true proportion, as Art can best present it ..." (sig. A4). This mount contains various persons performing the tasks of mining and refining the metal, such as near the top *Chthoon* or *Vesta*, "the breeding and teeming Mother of al Golde, Silver, Mineral, and other Mettals ..." (sig. A4ᵛ). On her right hand sits her daughter *Chrusos* (Gold) and on the left *Argurion* (Silver) linked to her "Chaire of State with a Chaine of Gold ..." (sig. B1). "Two beautifull Ladies," Antiquity and Memory, attend them. While this land pageant clearly refers to the guild and its mythological heritage, it serves little instructional purpose.

But our interest lies with the other figures and other activities of the entertainment. The new mayor, Pemberton, at Baynard's Castle meets Leofstane, a Goldsmith, by whose person Munday means to portray Sir Henry Fitz-Alwin, the first Lord Mayor of London. After a speech of welcome, Leofstane leads the

---

[6]*Chruso-Thriambos. The Triumphes of Golde* (London, 1611), sig. A3ᵛ. There are two editions of this pageant both published in the same year. For the purposes of quotation I have used the copy in the Huntington Library which is probably the first edition; the second is found in only one extant text in the Library of Trinity College, Cambridge.

mayor to a tomb; and they see there also a chariot which contains figures representing Richard I and King John, both largely responsible for instituting and establishing the office of Lord Mayor. History has come, so it seems, to lend its sanction to the activities of the day.

The chief dramatic action occurs at the tomb where Leofstane encounters Time, a familiar figure in civic pageantry or in Shakespeare's *The Winter's Tale*, who develops a history of the Lord Mayors, especially those Goldsmiths who have served as mayor. Time asserts that he has brought Leofstane to this moment and requests: "As thus I turne my Glasse to Times of old, / So tune thine eares to what must now be told" (sig. B3). He further reviews the establishment of the office of mayor during the reigns of kings Richard I and John. Finally, Time reveals that in the tomb lies one Nicholas Faringdon, four times Lord Mayor; and he calls him forth: "Arise, arise I say, good *Faringdon*, / For in this triumph thou must needs make one" (sig. B3ᵛ). The "resurrection" Munday completes in this "stage direction": "*Time striketh on the Tombe with his Silver wand, and then Faringdon ariseth*" (B3ᵛ). Munday breaks down the notion of a still-life tableau with such action and thereby brings us further in the direction of vital dramatic action.

Puzzled, Faringdon responds to the beckoning call of Time: "Cannot graves containe their dead, / Where long they have lien buried, / But to Triumphs, sports, and showes / They must be raisd?" (sig. B4); but Time explains the occasion to Faringdon's delight: "To heare the tale that *Time* hath told, / Since those reverend daies of old, / Unto this great Solemnity ..." (B4ᵛ). As the three figures move throughout the city, they address the new mayor, Leofstane giving a long explanation of the device of the Mount of Gold. Finally the entertainment closes with speeches that night at the mayor's gate where Leofstane dwells on the meaning of Pemberton's name; and Time asserts "that such a goodly name, / Requires bright actions, from pollution free, / In word and deede to be alike ..." (sig. C3ᵛ). But the newly arisen Faringdon, speaking with the authority of one who has visited the land of the dead, closes the event with challenging and instructive words:

> You are a Gold-Smith, Golden be
> Your daily deedes of Charitie.
> Golden your hearing poore mens cases,
> Free from partiall bribes embraces.
> And let no rich or mighty man
> Injure the poore, if helpe you can.
> The World well wots, your former care
> Forbids ye now to pinch or spare,
> But to be liberal, francke, and free,
> And keepe good Hospitality,
> Such as beseemes a Maioraltie,

Yet far from prodigality. (sig. C4)

In effect Faringdon urges the new mayor to follow Aristotle's golden mean (all the more appropriate for a Goldsmith). In a sense the pageant thus moves from the abstract to the concrete: from the misty regions of the Mount of Gold to representations of actual historical figures called forth by Time to the closing pointedly moral advice which applies concretely to the new mayor, James Pemberton. In short, the allegorical method of giving the intangible idea concrete form works.

In 1612 the Merchant Taylors chose Thomas Dekker as the one to prepare the Lord Mayor's Show, and in 1613, the Grocers chose Thomas Middleton (both discussed in following chapters). But in 1614 Munday's fellow Drapers called upon him to direct the pageant for the installation of Sir Thomas Hayes. The show, which Munday called *Himatia-Poleos. The Triumphes of Olde Draperie*,[7] does not differ markedly from his earlier pageants. Scant company records provide little supplementary material. At the end of his text, however, Munday singles out the work of Rowland Bucket and offers praise to this "exact and skilfull Painter ..." (pp. 18-19)—the first time in one of his texts that Munday grants the artificer such recognition. A considerable portion of the first part of the pamphlet offers an apology for having been led astray by Stow to call Henry Fitz-Alwin (Leofstane) a Goldsmith in the 1611 show when in fact he belonged to the Drapers. Appropriately, then, Fitz-Alwin appears again in the 1614 pageant honoring the Drapers.

In addition to Fitz-Alwin, Munday includes another former mayor, Sir John Norman, a mayor in the mid-fifteenth century and allegedly the first to go to Westminster by barge. Munday places him on the water in a boat "with the seaven liberall Sciences (all attired like graceful Ladies) sitting about him ..." (p. 8). Norman greets the mayor with a speech and later assists in explaining the devices of the show. A group of "sweet singing youths, ... each having a silver Oare in his hand" "sing a most sweet dittie of *Rowe thy Boate Norman*, and so seeme to rowe up along to *Westminster*, in honour of our Lord Maiors attendance" (p. 10). These former mayors lend their blessing to the festivities and also remind the new mayor of some of his noble predecessors.

Fitz-Alwin sits with several other figures in a chariot, "drawn by two golden pelletted Lyons, and two golden Woolves" (p. 6). Munday also represents the person of Richard I, surrounded by personified figures of several English cities. "Those Citties are disciphered by their Eschuchions of Armes, and that their best advantage ever ensued by making of woolen Cloathes, for the continuall maintenance of *Englands* Draperie" (pp. 6-7). Munday does not enumerate the cities

---

[7] *Himatia-Poleos. The Triumphes of Olde Draperie* (London, 1614). All quotations will be from this original edition.

except London, "sitting neerest unto himselfe [Richard], as chiefe Mother and matrone of them all" (p. 7). London wears a triple crown of gold, "under battelled or branched with Cloudes, and beames of the Sunne, being the Armes of the *Drapers* Societie ..." (p. 7). Pageant writers regularly personified a city—Peele in one of his shows presents London, as does Middleton in his 1613 pageant. In his speech to the mayor Fitz-Alwin sets forth the illustrious past of the company.

Munday also uses a mount which represents "the whole estate of *Londons* olde Draperie." In the most eminent place sits *"Himatia,* or Cloathing, as Mother, Lady and commaundresse of all the rest, who by their distinct emblemes and properties ... doe expresse their dutie and attendance on so gratious a person ..." (p. 7). Several figures appear industriously performing the various functions of preparing woollen clothes. Also *"Peace, Plentie, Liberalitie, Councell* and *Discreet Zeale,* doe supporte the florishing condition of *Himatiaes* Commonwealth, and strive to prevent all occasions which may seeme sinister or hurtfull thereto" (pp. 7-8). Unfortunately, Munday does not describe these allegorical personages, but we can safely assume their emblematic costumes.

As a final event a "goodly Ramme or Golden Fleece" appears with a Shepherd sitting by it, and the Shepherd addresses the mayor. The Golden Fleece formed part of the heraldry of the Drapers' Company, and Munday will develop the Jason-Golden Fleece story in succeeding pageants. The closing speech of the entertainment gives the usual charge to the mayor to prepare for "envies stormes" and to practice "vertue, zeale, and upright heed ..." (p. 17). On the whole the pageant rather feebly echoes Munday's preceding show of 1611, displaying little of its inherent dramatic interest.

The Drapers succeeded again in 1615 in selecting the mayor, this time Sir John Jolles, and asked Munday to devise the entertainment which he called *Metropolis Coronata, The Triumphes of Ancient Drapery.* History, moral allegory, and mythology all help shape the pageant. Again, company records yield little useful information.

The presentation on the Thames becomes the most elaborate of any of Munday's water shows to date. A boat, the first device on the river, carries Jason and his companions, Hercules, Telamon, Orpheus, Castor, Pollux, Calais, and Zethes. They sit around him "attired in faire guilt Armours, bearing triumphall Launces, wreathed about with Lawrell, Shields honoured with the Impresse of the Golden fleece, and their heads circled with Lawrell, according to the manner of all famous Conquerors."[8] Much of the attention focuses on Medea, "whose love to *Jason,* was his best meanes for obtaining the Golden fleece" (sig. A3ᵛ-A4). To illustrate the "fiery zeale of her affection towards him, she sitteth playing with his love-lockes, and wantoning with him in all pleasing daliance ..." (sig. A4). The

[8]*Metropolis Coronata, The Triumphes of Ancient Drapery* (London, 1615), sig. A4. Quotations will be from this edition. There is a reprint in Nichols, III, 108f.

boat moves "by divers comely Eunuches, which continually attended on *Medea*, and she favouring them but to passe under the fleece of Golde, had all their garments immediatly sprinkled over with golde...."

Another barge, this one in the shape of a whale (one recalls similar constructions in some of the Elizabethan progress pageants), contains the figures of Neptune and Thamesis. Not surprisingly, the redoubtable and seemingly ubiquitous Henry Fitz-Alwin also appeared in the boat. In fact, seated around him "eight royall Vertues" bear the "ensignes" of former Drapers who served as mayor. The allegorical figures of "*Fame* triumphing in the top, and *Time* guiding the way before" (sig. A4ᵛ) crowd in also. In a lengthy speech Fitz-Alwin salutes the mayor, offers interpretation of the water pageant and suggests a "morall application" of the display:

> *Your Honour may make some relation*
> *Unto your selfe out of this storie,*
> *You are our* Jason, *Londons glorie,*
> *Now going to fetch that fleece of Fame,*
> *That ever must renowne your name....*
> *No Monsters dare confront your way.* (sig. B1ᵛ)

The new mayor should consider that "all this faire and goodly Fleete" do attend upon him and offer their services to him. By moral analogy he becomes linked with the mythical Jason and may draw strength from that association.

The first device which greets the mayor on land after his return from Westminster is another ship, "stiled by the Lord Maiors name, and called the *Joell*, appearing to bee lately returned, from trafficking Wool and Cloth with other remote Countryes ..." (sig. B2ᵛ). Guiding the "Chariot of Mans Life" Time, who, though not having a dramatic function as in 1611, describes this chariot which contains a globe supported by the four Elements, emblematically costumed, and which runs on seven wheels "describing the seven ages of man ..." (sig. B4). The chief pageant, which provided the name of the entertainment, the Monument of London, includes the figure of London, "The ancient Mother of the whole Land," and her Twelve Daughters—i.e., the Twelve Companies of London. Raised about London "as supports to *Londons* flourishing happinesse, and continuance of the same in true tranquillitie," four "goodly Mounts" bear "Emblemes of those foure especiall qualities, which make any Commonwealth truly happy" (B4)—Learned Religion, Military Discipline, Navigation, and Homebred Husbandry. This may call to mind the figure of Majesty in the 1609 show and the virtues that surrounded her. It also recalls Middleton's London's Triumphant Mount from his 1613 mayoral pageant. Munday again concentrates on the well-being of the commonwealth and the virtues conducive to it.

The festivities of the day concluded with the appearance of a figure from English pseudo-history, Robin Hood, accompanied by a number of his men "all clad in greene, with their Bowes, Arrowes and Bugles, and a new slaine Deere carried among them" (sig. B3). At the close of the sixteenth century Munday had written two plays dealing with the subject of Robin Hood: *The Downfall of Robert Earl of Huntingdon* and *The Death of Robert Earl of Huntingdon* (the latter written in collaboration with Henry Chettle). Munday suggests a reason, though historically inaccurate, for Robin Hood's appearance: he is son-in-law by marriage to none other than Henry Fitz-Alwin.[9] Robin Hood and his men talk and sing; and finally Robin Hood speaks to the new mayor:

> *Since Graves may not their Dead containe,*
> *Nor in their peacefull sleepes remaine,*
> *But Triumphes and great Showes must use them,*
> *And we unable to refuse them;*
> *It joyes me that Earle* Robert Hood,
> *Fetcht from the Forrest of merrie* Shirwood,
> *With these my Yeomen tight and tall,*
> *Brave Huntsmen and good Archers all:*
> *Must in this joviall day partake,*
> *Prepared for your Honours sake.* (sig. C1ᵛ)

The mayor has been duly welcomed by these figures out of the mythical past: Jason and Robin Hood, and Fitz-Alwin adds his voice as one representing former days; appropriately Time also appears. But Munday fails to achieve much thematic unity here, little connection existing among the various parts of the pageant. Those pageants that make the greatest claim on our interest in them as drama convey a sense of integrity and wholeness—missing here in the episodic tableaux of this show. The most skilful pageant-dramatists let instruction and compliment serve their artistic and dramatic purposes, thus rising above the simplest demands of civic drama, as Munday himself demonstrates in the following pageant.

Munday continues his monopoly on the Lord Mayor's Show again in 1616 when he prepared *Chrysanaleia: The Golden Fishing* to honor John Leman, Fishmonger. Clearly this becomes one of his best productions, having considerable thematic unity and a significant dramatic action. In December 1616, Munday

---

[9]One is struck with this inaccuracy because Munday himself in his Robin Hood plays had called the father-in-law of Robin Hood "Fitzwater." And now, completely ignoring his own work, he links Fitz-Alwin and Robin Hood. Malcolm Anthony Nelson, "The Robin Hood Tradition in English Literature in the Sixteenth and Seventeenth Centuries" unpublished dissertation (Northwestern, 1961), discusses Munday's several corruptions of the Robin Hood tradition, see p. 181.

appeared before the court of the company asking for an additional £10 in "grati-
fication" for the two hundred extra books which he had and for some spoiling of
the costumes, and the court decided "that he shall have v^{li} xv^s gyven unto him
which he is content thankfully to accept in full satisfaction of all his demaundes"
(*MSC*, p. 91). Considerable interest attaches to this civic pageant by the magnificent contemporary drawings preserved by the Fishmongers' company—the most
extensive set of such drawings for any Lord Mayor's Show down to the closing of
the theaters and comparable in value to the drawings of the 1604 royal entry.
These pictures confirm the rich visual spectacle described by Munday[10] (*see* figures 9-12).

The first device, used both on water and on land, honors the company, a
fishing boat called the "*Fishmongers Esperanza*, or Hope of *London*...."[11] (*See*
figure 10.) It may pass, Munday says, "for the fishing Busse, wherein Saint *Peter*
sate mending his Nets, when his best Master called him from that humble and
lowly condition, and made him a Fisher of men" (sig. B1ᵛ). But if this be a bit far
fetched, we may take the boat for one of the ordinary vessels that daily "enricheth
our kingdome with all variety of fish the Sea can yeelde ..." (B1ᵛ). In the boat a
number of fishermen "seriously at labour" draw in their nets filled with fish and
bestow them "bountifully among the people."

A dolphin continues the allusion to the guild; and because this "Fish inclined
much (by nature) to Musique," Arion rides on its back, himself having been
"saved so from death, when Robbers and Pirates on the Seas, would maliciously
have drowned him" (B1ᵛ). Arion and the dolphin had earlier appeared in an
Elizabethan Lord Mayor's Show and at the famous pageant at Kenilworth in
1575.

The next pageant contains "an especiall Morality" and has considerable
symbolic interest. It presents a lemon tree (pun on the mayor's name) "in full
and ample forme, richly laden with the fruite and flowers it beareth," and at its
root "a goodly *Pellicane* hath built her nest, with all her tender brood about her"
(B2) (*see* figure 11). Fully aware of the traditional symbolic meanings of the pelican, Munday draws an analogy between it and the new mayor: "An excellent type
of government in a Magistrate, who, at his meere entrance into his yeares Office,
becommeth a nursing father of the Family: which, though hee bred not, yet, by
his best endevour, hee must labour to bring up" (B2). The mayor truly answers
the emblematic meaning if "his brest and bowels of true zeale and affection, are
alwaies open, to feed and cherish them...." In short, the mayor must exercise
love and compassion in discharging his duties, the mute testament of this device.

---

[10]These drawings are preserved and reproduced in a text of the pageant edited by John Gough Nichols, *Chrysanaleia, The Golden Fishing* (London, 1844).

[11]*Chrysanaleia* (London, 1616), sig. B1. All quotations are from this seventeenth-century edition.
Reprints in John Nichols, *Progresses of James*, III, 195f., and in the text cited in footnote #10.

In addition, the Five Senses "in their best and liveliest representations" appear because the lemon tree aids in restoring and comforting man's senses.

The dramatic and thematic focus of the entertainment centers on the device of "a goodly Bower, shaped in forme of a flowrie Arbour" which stands in St. Paul's churchyard. Within this Bower a Tomb resides whereon rests the figure of Sir William Walworth, twice Lord Mayor in the fourteenth century and also a participant in Nelson's 1590 Lord Mayor's Show (*see* figure 9). The whole conceit, Munday says, "aimeth at that tempestuous and troublesome time of King *Richard* the Second" (sig. B2ᵛ)—specifically the Jack Straw-Wat Tyler rebellion. The body of Walworth five knights surround; they assisted him in protecting the king and defeating the rebels. *London's Genius*, "a comely Youth, attired in the shape of an Angell, with a golden Crowne on his head, golden Wings at his backe, bearing a golden Wand in his hand, sits mounted on Horsebacke by the Bower ..." (sig. B3). The arrival of the new mayor translates this tableau into action.

The Genius speaks to Walworth: "*Thou Image of that worthy man. / ... Though yet thou sleep'st in shade of death; / By me take power of life and breath*" (sig. B4ᵛ). A note in the margin of the text describes the action: "Here the *Genius* strikes on him with his wand, whereat he begins to stir, and comming off the Tombe, looks strangely about him." With this and the several blasts of trumpets Walworth resurrects, all in the pattern of Faringdon in Munday's 1611 show. In his speech Walworth takes note of his company's history and the occasion that brings the present festivity. The legend of Walworth who "manfully defended and preserved" the crown epitomizes the celebration of the guild as in a dramatic revival he comes forth to lend his presence as a tangible reminder of the company's glorious heritage.

Munday continues his allusion to the Walworth story in the last device of the entertainment, a chariot "drawne by two Mare-men, and two Mare-mayds ..." (sig. B3ᵛ) (*see* figure 12). In the highest place of eminence sits "the triumphing Angell, who that day smote the enemy by *Walworths* hand, and laid all his proud presuming in the dust." With one hand the angel holds on the crown of King Richard, who sits beneath her, "that neither forraine Hostilitie, nor home-bred Trecherie should ever more shake it"; in the other hand she holds a striking rod, signifying: "*By mee Kings reigne, and their enemies are scattered*" (sig. B3ᵛ). The forefront of the chariot contains Royall Virtues, "as Truth, Vertue, Honor, Temperance, Fortitude, Zeale, Equity, Conscience, beating down Treason and Mutinie" (sigs. B3ᵛ-B4). The moral (and political) conflict between virtue and vice inheres in these allegorical characters, and the arrangement reminds us of similar tableaux in both the 1559 and 1604 royal entries in London. On the rear and sides of the chariot sit other personified virtues: Justice, Authority, Law, Vigilancy, Peace, Plenty, and Discipline, "as best props and pillers to any Kingly estate" (sig. B4). Munday adds that these figures "are best observed by their severall Emblems and properties, borne by each one, and their adornments answerable to them in like manner." Here, as in other shows, Munday represents allegorically the virtues vital to a government's welfare. By implication Walworth champions the cause of virtue in its struggle against political and moral vice.

In the afternoon when the mayor returns to St. Paul's, all the devices locate near the Little Conduit in Cheapside, and there Walworth describes and interprets, helping make explicit what has been symbolically implied. For example, he notes that the pelican "speakes ingeniously / The Character of your authoritie: / ... fostring her brood: / Though with the deare expence of her owne blood" (sig. C3). Referring to his own valorous deeds, Walworth says: "I made them [the rebels] stand, / And, in my Soveraigns sight, there I strooke dead / Their chiefest Captaine and commanding head" (sig. C3). In similar fashion he explicates all the elements. The festivities close with a graciously poetic speech again by Walworth spoken at night which begins: "Phoebus *hath hid his golden head* / In Thetis *lappe. And now are spred* / *The sable Curtaines of the night,* / *Our Evenings purpose to delight*" (sig. C4). He develops the metaphor of marriage also, suggesting that this day marks the wedding of the mayor to London. Finally Walworth offers a type of benediction: "*May your Fame,* / *Crowne still their ancient worthie name* / *To all posteritie*" (C4).

Munday has adopted the structural movement from the abstract to the concrete again—generally characteristic of his best efforts. He gains additional unity by having every element of the entertainment refer to the Fishmongers in some way. The examples of the fishing boat and Arion on a dolphin allude to the company and imply something of the industry and dignity of the guild. The lemon tree-pelican device symbolizes the charity and compassion that ought to prevail. Through the dramatic resurrection of Walworth and the concluding chariot we gain a realistic, actual example of strength and courage that should be imitated. This glorious incident from the history of the company also carries ramifications regarding the preservation of the state, a constant thematic concern of Munday's.

Middleton won out in the competition for the 1617 show, but Dekker and Munday both received "consolation prizes"; Munday got £5 "for his paines in drawing a project for this busynes which was offered to the Comyttees" (*MSC*, p. 93). This illustrates the competitive nature of the Lord Mayor's pageants. Nevertheless, in 1618 Munday devised the show for the Ironmongers honoring Sir Sebastian Harvey, and he named it *Sidero-Thriambos or Steel and Iron Triumphing*. The company records provide generous information concerning the preparations for the pageant and the dealings with Munday and his associates. Apparently the performance pleased everyone, for on 2 November we find this entry: "In Consideracion of Anthony Mundyes good performance of his business undertaken and of spoyling of his Pageant apparaile by the foule weather it was agreed to give him three powndes as a free guift of the Companie besides and above the Contract" (*MSC*, p. 96). John Grinkin, familiar for his participation in the production of earlier pageants, exists among those who assisted with the show, as does Munday's son, Richard.[12] The distinguished career of Gerard Christmas as artificer has its beginning here (discussed in a later chapter). The total cost of £523. 11s. 9d. seems a bit low considering that the show of 1617 cost over £882. An interesting historical footnote accompanies this pageant: Sir Walter Ralegh's execution took place on the same day as the Lord Mayor's Show, Aubrey says, so "that the pageants and fine shewes might drawe away the people from beholding the tragoedie of the gallants worthies that ever England bred" (*MSC*, p. xiii)—certain testimony to the popularity of these street entertainments.

In keeping with the honored company, Munday constructs for the first device an island which has on it a mine. "Therein *Mulciber*, the God of *Mynes* and *Mettals* ... sheweth his personall attendance, with divers of his one-eyed *Cyclops* about him."[13] These figures actively engage in the various mining processes. At the four corners of the isle four "beautifull *Nymphes* or *Graces*" reside, named "*Chrusos*, *Argurion*, *Calcos* and *Sideros*, figuring the foure ages of the world, and habited according to their true Carracters and natures" (sig. B1ᵛ). Though the Golden Age, Silver Age, and Bronze Age each formerly held sway, they have now given way to the Iron Age, which Munday says parenthetically is the age "wherein wee live." One can speculate that perhaps Munday drew inspiration from Thomas Heywood's series of plays on the four ages of the world, written between 1611 and 1613. Jupiter also appears on the island, "mounted upon his Royall Eagle, with his three-forked Thunderbolt in his hand ..." (sig. B2)—a description that corresponds with Jupiter's appearance in Shakespeare's *Cymbeline*. In the pageant he wears a suit of armor that had originally been intended for Mars but given to him by Mulciber "because hee so graciously vouchsafed, to bee personally present in this Triumph, as Patron of all their pains, and protector from foule-mouthed slander and detraction" (sig. B2). The presence of Jupiter, the highest of the gods, personally compliments the mayor. Furthermore, he embodies the allegorical concept of Protection. A conversation between a Master Gunner and his Mate at the Cannon located near the mine celebrates the achievements of the Ironmongers.

An ancient British Bard guides the way to the Mount of Fame, the second principal device of the show. Obviously in the most eminent place on this mount stands the allegorical figure of Fame, "seeming as if shee sounded her Golden Trumpet, the Banner whereof, is plentifully powdred with Tongues, Eyes and Eares: implying, that all tongues should be silent, all eyes and eares wide open, when *Fame* filleth the world with her sacred memories" (B4). Fame shows the mayor the other personages which accompany her "for more honourable solem-

---

[12]For further discussion see my "Anthony Munday's Son, Richard," *American Notes and Queries* 7 (1969): 115-17.
[13]*Sidero-Thriambos* (London, 1618), sig. B1. Quotations are from this text.

nity of this generall Triumph; presaging a happy and successefull course to his yeare of government" (sig. B4). Munday draws on a long and extensive use of Fame in civic pageantry before this show. Here Fame serves as a reminder that the leaders of state must perpetuate the noble heritage from which they have come, for Fame with her eyes and tongues will pass on to future generations a record of the conduct of the magistrate.

The figure of Expectation sits below Fame on the right and suggests "that there will be more then ordinary matter expecte from him ..." (B4ᵛ). Hope sits on the other side, and reminds the mayor that his father had also once been mayor and "left such sensible instructions to his Sonne, as cannot but edge his temper the more keenely, and quicken his spirits the more industriously" (sig. B4ᵛ). Justice and Fortitude, also present, tread down the figures of Ambition, Treason, and Hostility, "which seeke the subversion of all estates ..." (sig. C1). And to assist the mayor in his struggles against these vices, "they sit gyved, and manacled together in Iron shackles, purposely made and sent from the *Ironmongers Myne*, to binde such base villaines to their better behaviour" (sig. C1). Munday thereby connects the two main devices of the show.

A final group of personages appears on this Mount of Fame, including Fame's two "sober Sisters," Fear and Modesty, "both vailed, but so sharpe-sighted, that they can discerne through the darkest obscurities, when any disorder threatneth danger to *Majesty*, or to his carefull Deputie" (sig. C1-C1ᵛ). Should the two become aware of any danger, they inform Vigilancy and Providence, who sit close by. These in turn awake Care "to ring the Bell in the *Watch-Tower*," which in turn calls forth Courage and Counsel, "that every one may have imploiment, for safe preserving the Mount of *Fame*" (sig. C1ᵛ). These Virtues will readily aid the mayor as he faces the sundry trials of his office. The allegorical message to the magistrate sounds clearly: he must summon forth these different virtues to bear him up in the unstinting conflict with vice.

In deliberately archaic style the Bard addresses the new mayor in the afternoon as he goes to St. Paul's, and he holds out this hope: "Honor, Heale and Happinesse, / Give aw yer actions gud successe" (sig. C3). Similarly at night the Bard gives his "parting" to the mayor: "That Justice, Zeale and Payetie, / Mayne shine in yee with Mejesty, / That he wha puts yee in thilke trust, / Mey finde yer rule sa true and just ..." (C3ᵛ). This pageant lacks the sense of action contained in the previous show of 1616; instead, the allegorical tableau serves as the chief means of expressing the themes with the Bard's speeches being set pieces rather than action intersecting the still-life scene.

One of Munday's comments in this pamphlet deserves special attention, for in it he sets forth a veritable *ars poetica* for the pageant-dramatist. He writes: "For better understanding the true morality of this devise, the personages have all Emblemes and Properties in their hands, and so neere them, that the weakest capacity may take knowledge of them; which course in such solemne Triumphes hath alwaies beene allowed of best observation ..." (sig. C1ᵛ). Munday realizes that he works with a plastic art creating a *tableau vivant*, with an essential visual element. With little time for dramatic development, the allegory must be understood readily: hence the emblematic method. At times it seems as if some of these figures in civic pageants have merely stepped from the pages of the popular emblem books, a subject discussed fully in a later chapter.

Munday's last contribution to civic pageantry came in 1623 in the form of the water show performed on the Thames in honor of the mayor, but Middleton had responsiblity for the rest of the entertainment. Munday called his part *The Triumphs of the Golden Fleece*. Essentially he reaches back into the file and pulls out the same device which he had used in the 1615 show. Again we find a boat with Jason, Medea, and others in it, most of them carrying shields bearing the impress of the Golden Fleece, and for this boat Munday received £35, according to company records. Munday adds: "Wee suppose this Argoe to be returned from *Colchos*, purposely to honor this Triumphall day, by the rare Arte of *Medea* the Enchantresse...."[14] In this performance six tributary Indian kings attend Medea, "holding their severall dominions of *Medea*, and living in vassalage to her" (sig. A4ᵛ). They row the boat, "wearing their Tributarie Crownes, and Antickely attired in rich habiliments." Munday continues to be fascinated by the Jason-Golden Fleece story; and on a more practical level, it has a direct relationship to the Drapers' Company, to which he himself belonged.

Through Munday's involvement with the Jacobean Lord Mayor's Show we learn more about the details of their planning and preparations; especially do we learn of the pageant-dramatist's duties, ranging from being responsible for the children's breakfasts to providing apparel to having the books printed to planning the speeches and action of the entertainment. We also begin to learn something of the role and responsibilities of the artificers, a crucial development discussed in Part Three of this book. Such information largely did not exist for the Elizabethan Lord Mayor's Show.

Munday makes an important contribution to the mayoral pageantry by his concentrated use of history. He alone explored the Brutus myth of English history and gave it dramatic life in London's streets. Building upon the precedent of Nelson's 1590 show, Munday constantly relies on the presence of former Lord Mayors in his pageants; indeed he brings to these pageants a historical sense of continuity.

His unique "resurrection" scenes in the 1611 and 1616 shows suggest a kinship to the regular theater in which a number of plays contained such events— *The Winter's Tale* to name a famous example. By including such action Munday helps open the Lord Mayor's Show even further in the direction of action, and we shall see other dramatists taking their inspiration from Munday's efforts at pro-

---

[14]*The Triumphs of the Golden Fleece (London*, 1623), sig. A4. Citations are to this text.

ducing dramatic as well as thematic interest. At times his civic drama achieves a sophisticated level in the use of allegory and symbolism, an art that he obviously understands well. He makes skilful use of certain stage properties to reinforce his allegorical intent.

Munday may be forgiven his propagandistic excesses especially in the 1605 show and somewhat in the 1616 one, for such remains a crucial part of civic drama which seeks to venerate the noble past while celebrating the present. Thematically he insists on the necessity of the unity of the kingdom, a motif implicit in most of his productions. A strong corollary to this theme occurs: a representation of the virtues necessary to preserve the sanctity of the commonwealth, a theme sounded in other civic pageants of other times as well. Allegory becomes his chief method for presenting that particular theme as the abstract concept takes on flesh. A brief reflection on history plays of Renaissance drama will suggest another kinship that Munday's pageants share with the regular stage. The qualites that become alive and viable in the streets may have similar vitality in the Globe.

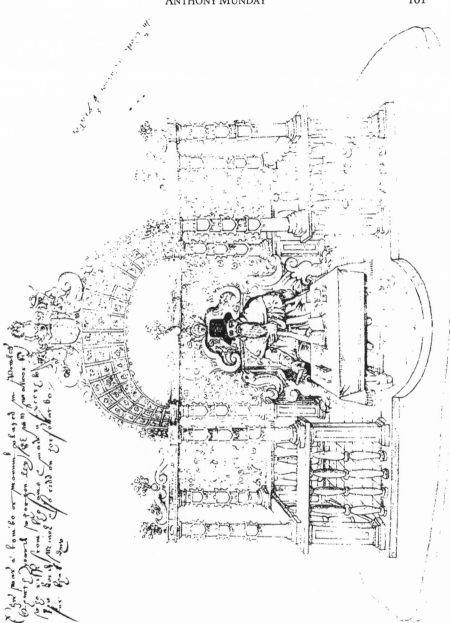

Figure 9. The Bower and Tomb of William Walworth in Munday's 1616 Lord
Mayor's Show. Figures 9-12 are from J. G. Nichols, ed., *The Fishmongers Pageant
1616* (London, 1844), and are based on manuscript drawings in the possession of
the company. Courtesy of the Kenneth Spencer Research Library, University of
Kansas.

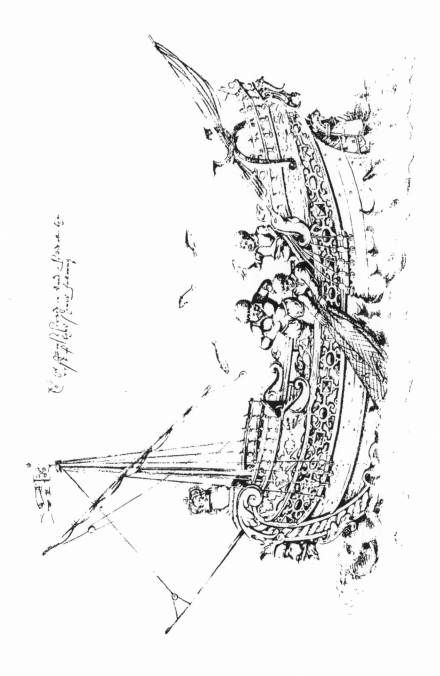

Figure 10. Fishing boat device in Munday's Lord Mayor's Show. Courtesy of the
Kenneth Spencer Research Library, University of Kansas.

Figure 11. The lemon tree pelican device in Munday's Lord Mayor's Show. Courtesy of the Kenneth Spencer Research Library, University of Kansas.

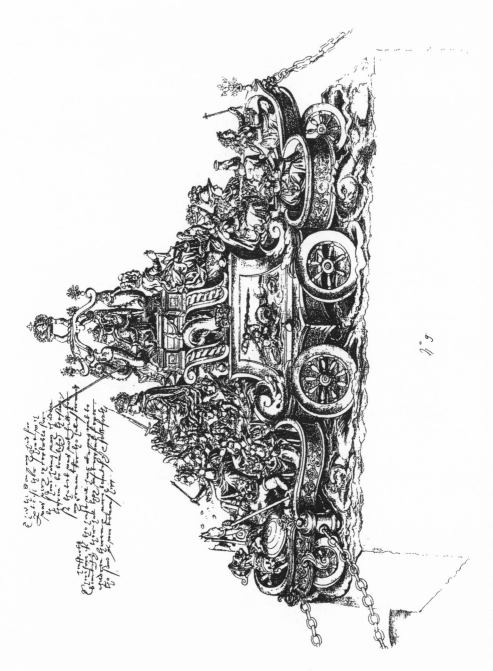

Figure 12. The pageant chariot of Richard II and the Royal Virtues in Munday's Lord Mayor's Show. Courtesy of the Kenneth Spencer Research Library, University of Kansas.

6 *Thomas Dekker*

WRITING NEAR THE BEGINNING of the text of his first Lord Mayor's Show, Thomas Dekker offers a statement which captures some of the traditional feelings about civic pageants:

> *Tryumphes*, are the most choice and daintiest fruit that spring from *Peace* and *Abundance*; *Love* begets them; and *Much Cost* brings them forth. *Expectation* feeds upon them, but seldome to a surfeite, for when she is most full, her longing wants something to be satisfied. So inticing a shape they carry, that *Princes* themselves take pleasure to behold them; they with delight; common people with admiration.[1]

Dekker underscores the "civic" nature of these pageants, their expense, and the political atmosphere that gives them impetus—peace and abundance. The relative stability and increasing wealth of the late Tudor and early Stuart period certainly played a major role in the blossoming of the civic drama of the streets. Dekker also testifies to the intensity of man's desire for such entertainment; and by 1612 when he penned the statement, he could not lack for evidence.

By the time Dekker wrote his first Lord Mayor's Show, he had already made a major contribution to English civic pageantry with his portion of the 1604 royal entry entertainment for King James (discussed in Chapter Two), demonstrating therein that he understood quite well the challenges, demands, and limitations placed on a pageant-dramatist. We cannot be surprised, therefore, to find him involved with mayoral pageantry. Also, his play *The Shoemakers' Holiday* illustrates his knowledge of and interest in former mayors of London. The 1612 entertainment comes in the period of highest achievement of the Jacobean Lord Mayor's Show—the second decade of the seventeenth century, and Dekker's pageant stands as an excellent example of the level of achievement in that period. His remaining mayoral entertainments 1627, 1628, 1629 (texts exist only for the last two), of course come at the beginning of the reign of Charles I and afford us an opportunity for comparison; we shall notice that no real innovations or major changes occur in the form or content of Dekker's Caroline shows.

Dekker's most significant contribution to mayoral pageantry comes doubtless from his effort to impose on the somewhat nebulous form of the show a mo-

---

[1] *The Dramatic Works of Thomas Dekker*, ed. Fredson Bowers (Cambridge, 1958), III, 230. All quotations will be from the Bowers edition and will be cited by volume and page number.

rality play structure: not just the usual concern with moral theme, but rather an attempt to add dramatic value by giving the conflict between virtue and vice a significant, dramatized tension, not a merely visual statement. Whether this represents a conscious effort to imitate the medieval morality play cannot of course be determined. But much of Dekker's drama reflects at least an indebtedness to morality drama in terms of his interest in and use of allegorical figures. *Old Fortunatus* (1599) serves as a good example, for here Dekker freely mixes allegorical and realistic characters. Indeed, Fortune, complete with her wheel, enters in the first scene of the play, and she remains throughout as one of the principal characters in the drama. By Act I, scene iii, Vice and Virtue, appropriately costumed, begin their struggle to win the allegiance of those involved in the action of the play. In true morality drama fashion they vie for the soul of Andelocia in IV.i.; Virtue reminds him: "The path that leades to *Vertues* court is narrow, / Thornie and Up a hill, a bitter jorney, / But being gon through, you find all heav'nly sweetes ..." (IV. i. 200-10). Ultimately, as we might expect, Virtue triumphs, and the action of the play closes with a hymn to Virtue's honor. In his *The Whore of Babylon* (1607), Dekker presents the figures Time, Truth, and Plain-Dealing, among others. In fact, much of the play may be regarded as a historical allegory; for Dekker says in the "Lectori" to the play: "*The Generall scope of this Dramaticall Poem, is set forth (in Tropicall and shadowed collours) the Greatnes, Magnanimity, Constancy, Clemency, and other the incomparable Heroical vertues of our late Queene*" (II, 497). As noted in an earlier discussion, the opening dumb show of this play parallels the confrontation between Time, Truth, and Elizabeth during the 1559 royal entry pageant. With such a background small wonder, then, that Dekker turned to this allegorical technique in his mayoral pageants.

To honor Sir John Swinnerton, Merchant Taylor, Dekker wrote his first show, *Troia-Nova Triumphans* (1612), a quite elaborate affair with a total expenditure of £978. 12s. 11d., one of the more expensive mayoral pageants of the seventeenth century. Part of the elaborateness of the show doubtless derives from the anticipated presence of both Prince Henry and Frederick, Count Palatine, future husband of Elizabeth, the daughter of James I and Anne. According to the company records Dekker and a Mr Hemynges were paid £197 "for the devise of the Land shewes, being a Sea-Chariott, drawne by two sea-horses, one Pageant called Neptunes Throne, with the seven liberall sciences, One Castle called Envies castle, One other Pageant called vertues Throne, and for the printing of the bookes of the Speeches, and for the persons, and apparell, of those that went in them...."[2] In his text Dekker complains about the tradition of porters who typically carried the devices through the city; referring to the "fish" on which the tritons ride in front of Neptune's chariot, Dekker says: they "are not (after the

[2]Malone Society, *Collections III*, p. 85.

old procreation), begotten of painted cloath, and browne paper, but are living beasts, so queintly disguised like the natural fishes, of purpose to avoyd the trouble and pestering of Porters, who with much noyse and little comlinesse are every yeare most unnecessarily imployed" (III, 233). Thus certain changes in production techniques are taking place.

In the pageant Dekker exercises excellent dramatic control of his material, given the inherent limitations of the civic drama form; a distinguishable dramatic movement occurs as well as the usual thematic concern. We witness a dramatic confrontation between the forces of good and evil, which has theatrical tension, not just tableau representation. Dekker carefully orchestrates the show to a dramatic climax when the power of virtue triumphs. Allegorically we have something which resembles the movement of medieval morality drama from sin to salvation. Like Munday, Dekker offers us a coherent dramatic action, not merely theatrical spectacle.

On the south side of St. Paul's the first land pageant awaits the arrival of the new Lord Mayor. The device, a sea chariot, contains as the principal figure Neptune, "his head circled with a *Coronet* of silver *Scollup-shels*," and in "his hand he holds a silver *Trident*, or *Three-forked-Mace* ..." (III, 232). Sitting at Neptune's foot, *Luna* (the Moon), "governesse of the sea," holds the reins of the horses in her hands. Other sea figures sit in the chariot or go before it. When the mayor arrives, Neptune greets him with a speech of welcome in which he initially professes to be puzzled about the occasion of such noise and acclamation, but he soon realizes that in the mayor's honor "*all these* Rites *are done*" (p. 233). But the welcoming speech does not conclude with these rather traditional words; instead, Neptune offers a moral interpretation, obviously setting the stage for the morality action that follows. Neptune bids the mayor:

> *Goe therefore on, goe boldly: thou must saile*
> *In rough Seas (now) of* Rule: *and every* Gale
> *Will not perhaps befriend thee: But (how blacke*
> *So ere the* Skyes *looke) dread not* Thou *a* Wracke,
> *For when* Integrity *and* Innocence *sit*
> *Steering the* Helme, *no* Rocke *the* Ship *can split.* (pp. 233-4)

In this metaphorical journey the mayor serves of course as the pilot, who, Neptune adds, if "sound / To himselfe (in Conscience) nere can run-a-ground" (p. 234). Even a mythological character fulfils a "moral" function for Dekker as Neptune prepares the way for the "rough seas."

The "morality drama" advances another step with the second device, the Throne of Virtue where in the most eminent place sits Virtue, "her temples shining with a *Diadem* of starres, to shew that her *Descent* is onely from heaven: her roabes are rich, her mantle white (figuring *Innocency*) and powdred with starres of gold, as an *Embleme* that she puts upon *Men*, the garments of eternity" (p. 235). Even as Moses lifted up the serpent in the wilderness, so the pageant lifts up Virtue, exalted, ready to draw all people unto her. Accompanying Virtue, the Seven Liberal Sciences appear as ready guides to Virtue; they wear loose robes "for *Knowledge* should be free," and "Every one carrying in her hand, a *Symbole*, or *Badge* of that *Learning* which she professeth" (p. 235). This Throne, a chariot, moves by four horses on which ride Time, Mercury, Desire, and Industry, all costumed according to their usual iconographical representation.

With this presentation of Virtue and her retinue Dekker prepares for the actual confrontation between this force of good and the force of evil, Envy. We can look back to Dekker's contribution to the royal entry of 1604 and see inherent there this conflict between Virtue and Envy. In the most prominent place on the arch at Fleet street Dekker had placed Justice, who incidentally appears as the final speaker in the 1612 Lord Mayor's Show. Directly under Justice sat Virtue, "inthronde, her garments white, her head crowned ..." (II, 295). Also included in the tableau arrangement Envy, "unhandsomely attirde all in blacke, her haire of the same colour, filletted about with snakes," "stood in a darke and obscure place by her selfe, neere unto *Vertue*, but making shew of a fearefulnesse to approach her and the light ..." (p. 295). This static grouping implies the ancient conflict between Virtue and Envy; and in the Lord Mayor's pageant Dekker has, seemingly, taken that earlier idea, breathed life into it, and transformed it into a dynamic and dramatic presentation, a presentation both verbal and visual. This example emphasizes the interconnections between various forms of civic pageantry, especially the royal entry and the mayoral pageants.

When the mayor approaches her throne, Virtue salutes him as one of her own and gives him much moral and political advice. He must be, she says, "stirring" and "resolute," and should "*Set* Plenty *at thy* Table, *at thy* Gate / Bounty, *and* Hospitality ..." (p. 237). When storms come, the mayor must "*Shelter with spred armes, the poor'st* Citizen." In his ministrations he need not "*feare the Stings of* Envy, *nor the* Threates / *Of her invenomd Arrowes, which at the* Seates / *Of those Who Best Rule, evermore are shot....*" This image of Envy Dekker explicitly develops in the next "scene," skilfully offering links between the various segments of the pageant. Under the sheltering wing of Virtue, the mayor moves to face the struggle of vice and virtue for his allegiance.

The abstract conflict between Virtue and Envy gains concrete reality in the next device, the action at which represents a type of "dramatic climax" for the whole pageant. Near the Little Conduit in Cheapside stood the *Forlorne Castle* where on the battlements appeared Envy "as chiefe Commandresse of that infernall *Place* ..." (p. 238). Helping guard the castle are Envy's boon companions—Ignorance, Sloth, Disdain, Oppression. Enlarging somewhat on the 1604 portrait of Envy, Dekker describes the present figure: "her selfe being attired like a *Fury*, her haire full of Snakes, her countenance pallid, meagre and leane, her body naked, in her hand a knot of Snakes, crawling and writhen about her arme" (p. 238). She thus counters in a striking way the appealing presentation of Virtue.

Envy's troops have arrows to shoot at Virtue (making literal the metaphor used by Virtue in her previous speech to the mayor); and Riot and Calumny, the giants, stand at the gates of the castle to block Virtue's passage. But overcoming the obstacles, Virtue "onely holding up her bright shield, dazzles them, and confounds them, they all on a sudden shrinking in their heads, untill the *Chariot* be past ..." (p. 238). This dazzling brightness of Virtue recalls a statement made by Virtue to Vice in Dekker's *Old Fortunatus*: "... *Vice* th'art a foole, / To fight with me, I suffred you awhile, / T'ecclips my brightnes, but I now will shine, / And make you sweare your beautie's base to mine" (V. ii. 298-301). The bright shield of Virtue might also remind us of Arthur's brilliant shield in Spenser's *Faerie Queene*, especially effective in his battle with Orgoglio in Book I. In Dekker's pageant the evil forces shoot their arrows into the air where they burst into fireworks "as having no power to do wrong to so sacred a Deity as *Virtue.*" In her frenzied speech Envy tries to rally her forces: "*Stop, stay her, fright her, with your shreekes, / And put fresh bloud in* Envies *cheekes*" (p. 239). But such panic Virtue's words of assurance counter: "*On, on, the beames of* Vertue, *are so bright, / They dazle* Envy: *On, the* Hag's *put to flight.*" Hanging close by Virtue, the mayor comes through safely, "as it were, through the jawes of *Envy* and all her Monsters" (p. 240). Dekker says: "And this concludes this Triumphant assault of *Envy*: her conquest is to come" (p. 239). The climax of the drama has been reached, but not the complete resolution.

Having survived the encounter with vice, the mayor comes to the Cross in Cheapside where the fourth device stands, the *House of Fame*, functioning as a sort of "house of Holiness" in terms of the thematic development of the pageant. In the upper seat of this House "sits *Fame* crowned in rich attire, a Trumpet in her hand, &c." (p. 240). Dekker seems to assume that we know the common properties of Fame; indeed, she has been represented in a number of civic pageants, including the portrayal of Fame on the Soper-lane arch in the 1604 entertainment where Dekker gives a full description:

A Woman in a Watchet Roabe, thickly set with open Eyes, and Tongues, a payre of large golden Winges at her backe, a Trumpet in her hand, a Mantle of sundry cullours traversing her body: all these Ensignes desplaying but the propertie of her swiftnesse, and aptnesse to disperse Rumors. (II, 276)

Accompanying Fame in her house, several kings, princes, and noblemen appear who have been free of the Merchant Taylors; Fame alludes to them in her speech. Also, "A perticular roome being reserved for one that represents the person of *Henry* the now Prince of *Wales.*" Dekker sets aside a room for Henry because some five years earlier he had accepted the freedom of the guild; also the gesture offers praise for the eighteen-year-old prince who was already carving out his niche in the House of Fame. Unfortunately, Henry could not be present to accept the adulations—he was deathly ill. In fact, on 6 November, a few short days after the pageant, he died, and Dekker's placing him in the household of Fame seems almost prophetic. Surely the elegiac volumes that followed his death secured forever his place in the House of Fame.[3]

When the mayor arrives, he receives welcome to "Fames high Temple" and admonition: *"here fix fast / Thy* footing; *for the* wayes *which thou hast past / Will be forgot and worne out ..."* (p. 240). If he would be successful in his duties, he should gird himself in Virtue's influence which resembles strong armor; Fame asserts: "She [Virtue] *guides thee,* Follow *her. In this* Court *of* Fame / *None else but* Vertue *can enrole thy* Name." The mayor should gain instruction from the examples of the worthy people who fill Fame's *"Voluminous booke."* Fame closes her speech by echoing the moral theme of the pageant: "... *win then that prise / Which* Vertue *holds up for thee,* And *(that done) /* Fame *shall the end crowne, as she hath begun"* (p. 242). The mayor has now been shown the path to salvation. A song that concludes this scene underscores the sense of "salvation" that has been gained:

> *So shall* Swinerton *nere dye,*
> *But his vertues upward flye*
> > *And still spring*
> > *Whilst we sing*
> *In a* Chorus *ceasing never,*
> *He is living, living ever.* (p. 244)

This fourth scene, which offers the dramatic "resolution," finishes when the entourage returns to St. Paul's after the ceremonies at the Guildhall. Virtue and Envy lock in battle again, Envy still desperately trying to rally her troops. But Virtue knows that *"the* Hag's *put to flight"* (p. 245). Routing the forces of Envy comes when the virtuous characters discharge their pistols at the evil ones. The conquest has now come.

As the day closes and the civic drama ends, the figure of Justice stands before the mayor's gate to bid him farewell. Appropriately Justice speaks after Virtue has sealed her victory over Envy—justice having been done. Justice promises to sit beside the mayor's gate for the duration of his term *"To guid thee* In *and* Out: *thou shalt commit / (If* Shee *stand by thee) not* One touch of wrong ..." (p. 245). She knows the mayor is secure, *"Yet men (like great ships) being in storms, most*

---

[3]For additional discussion see my "Prince Henry and English Civic Pageantry," *Tennessee Studies in Literature* 13 (1968): 109-16; also E. C. Wilson, *Prince Henry and English Literature* (Ithaca, 1946).

neere / To danger, when up their sailes they beare." Justice urges the mayor to be impartial in his dealings with the citizens, rich and poor alike, and reminds him:

Thy Conscience *must be like that* Scarlet Dye;
One fowle spot staines it All: *and the quicke* Eye
Of this prying world, will make that spot thy scorne. (p. 246)

He should use the golden collar of his office "*to knit /* Mens hearts *in* Love...." "*Knowing the pathes of* Others *that are gone*" should offer him knowledge, teaching him what to do. Finally Justice hopes that the mayor "*May be as old in* Goodnesse *as in* Yeares" (p. 246). The mayor stands ready to take his place in the real world, having been nurtured through the moral conflict of the day and having been strengthened by such figures as Virtue, Fame, and Justice.

As should be evident now, the structure of this pageant closely resembles the dramatic development of a typical medieval morality play, following the comic pattern from encounter with evil to victory. No mayoral pageant up to 1612 has such structure, though Munday clearly moves in that direction. Nor does any other one so closely involve the participation of the mayor; no mere spectator, here the mayor experiences an active struggle for his allegiance. It all adds up to good theater with dramatic unity being achieved despite the obstacles.

The pageant's thematic unity works well also, and some of the links between the "scenes" have been noted. From the outset, as if preparing for the subsequent action, Neptune warned the mayor that he will sail in rough seas of rule, and the conflict between Virtue and Envy demonstrates just how rough that voyage can be. Fortunately, and not surprisingly, Virtue triumphs in the climactic battle with Envy and thus may bring the mayor into the sanctity of Fame's house where we catch something of a vision of things past and things to come. But the mayor must descend from the rarefied atmosphere of the House of Fame back into the mundane world, and here Justice stands by his gate ever-ready to aid and strengthen him. She will guide him, thus assuring his salvation, as he endures the storm-tossed seas of government. Like Everyman, the mayor may be secure in the knowledge that he has gained; and his Good Deeds may follow him to the grave, validating the words of the song in Fame's temple—"*He is living, living ever.*"

Unfortunately, this high point of achievement of 1612 Dekker did not duplicate in his other mayoral pageants, those written in the early years of Charles's reign. For one thing, the dramatist abandons the morality structure that offered such unity in favor of the more traditional pattern of mayoral shows—the staging of rather loosely connected tableaux. No other pageant-dramatist affords us a glimpse at the possible development in two different historical periods: Munday is exclusively Jacobean (in terms of extant texts); Middleton, with one exception—the 1626 pageant—also wholly Jacobean; while Heywood, the last major

pageant-dramatist, exclusively Caroline. Whether one wants to classify the Dekker of the late 1620s as "decadent," less satisfaction derives from his pageant efforts of that period. Perhaps he merely suffered the all but inevitable "sameness"
that frequently occurred in any such dramatic form.

According to Dekker's own testimony in his *Wars, Wars, Wars* (1628), he
wrote the 1627 mayoral entertainment, but no text survives. In 1628, however,
the Skinners used Dekker's pageant, *Britannia's Honor*, to celebrate the inauguration of Sir Richard Deane. For his services Dekker received £23, and Gerard
Christmas, the artificer, got £150, with total expenses exceeding £700. Though
the pageant lacks the morality drama structure, it nevertheless performs its didactic function. The first device, located appropriately on the Thames, has as its
chief figure Amphitrite, queen of the seas and Neptune's wife. The use of Amphitrite follows, in a way, logically from the 1612 show, which opened with the appearance of Neptune. In the 1628 show she sits on an artificial rock "habited to
her State; a Mantle frindg'd with silver crossing her Body: Her hayre long, and
dishevelled; on her head, a phantasticke dressing made out of a Fishes writhen
shell, interwoven with Pearle ..." (IV, 83). Surrounding her, mermaids swim in
the water, and figures represent the Trent, Humber, and Severn rivers. The presence of Amphitrite may be in partial debt to Munday's *The Triumphes of Re-
United Britannia*, the 1605 Lord Mayor's Show, in which both Neptune and Amphitrite have significant roles, especially at the end of the pageant. For Dekker,
Amphitrite functions to offer a speech of welcome and praise, though she promises to make "*Smooth way Before you* [the mayor], *on This Glassy Floore, / Usher-
ing your glad Arrivall to the Shore*" (p. 84). A speech in French Dekker prepared
to deliver to the queen should she be in attendance.

Recapturing something of the title of the first mayoral pageant, Dekker calls
the first device on land *New Troyes Tree of Honor* with the chief figure as London
"with an ornament of Steeples, Towers, and Turrets on her head ..." (p. 86). Further, in her left hand "she holds a golden Truncheon ... to shew that shees a
Leader and *Conductresse* of a *Mighty People*: Her *Right Hand* (thrusting through
the *Arbor*) takes hold of a Tree, out of which spread *Twelve Maine* and *Goodly
Branches*," symbolizing the twelve major guilds of London (p. 86). In many respects this representation of London parallels her appearance in other civic pageants, especially Middleton's 1613 show. Accompanying London in Dekker's
pageant, Minerva and Bellona intimate "that both *Artes* and *Armes*, are (in a high
degree and fulnesse of honor,) nurc'd up and maintain'd by and in the City ..."
(p. 86). Placed around the Tree of Honour stand certain allegorical figures,
emblematically presented, who help bring glory and strength to the city. Peace
has a dove on her fist and a palm branch in her hand, not unlike the depiction of
her in Dekker's contribution to the 1604 royal entry. Also Religion appears "in a
white glittering roabe, with a Coronet of Starres on her head, holding in one
hand, a Booke open, in the other, a golden ladder, (embleme of prayer, by whose

steppes wee climbe to Heaven)" (p. 87). Other figures include Civil Government in a robe full of eyes, Justice with her sword, Learning with a book, Industry with a golden hammer and a compass, and Honour dressed in scarlet.

In her speech to the mayor, London refers to herself as the mayor's "second Mother." She bids him take note of her Tree of Honour and guard its boughs. While his gates will open to entertain the rich, he should "Remember *at the same* Gate *stands / The* Poore, *with crying Papers in their hands* ..." (p. 88). He should "*Kisse* Peace" and "*let* Order *ever steere the Helme....*" The speech closes with London's metaphorical instruction:

> *You are your* Soveraignes Gardner *for one yeare,*
> *The* Plot *of* Ground, *y'are trusted with, lies here,*
> (*A* Citty,) *and your* care *must all bee spent,*
> *To prune and dresse the* Tree of Government.
>   *Lop off* Disorders, Factions, Mutiny.... (p. 88)

The sea metaphor of Neptune in the 1612 show has been transformed into a correspondence between the body politic and the garden, certainly familiar to us from Shakespeare's *Richard II*, which this passage closely echoes. Whether the mayor be viewed as pilot or gardener, the message remains the same: to him London entrusts the care and nurture of government, and positive action must be taken to ensure the integrity of the state against disruptive forces.

In a chariot that celebrates the Skinners' company Fame compliments the guild and addresses the mayor, but her meager role here contrasts sharply with her dramatically significant function in the 1612 pageant. Such a contrast forms a telling measure of the qualitative difference between these two civic dramas. In another device Britannia complements the earlier appearance of London, "Majestically attirde, fitting to her Greatnesse" (p. 91). She occupies the most eminent seat in her Watch-Tower with eight silver columns, pendents, and two angels standing on pillars. In addition, the "Capitals and Bases of the Pillars are Gold, and are Emblemes of the two Houses of *Yorke* and *Lancaster*: once divided, but now Joyned into One Glorious Building, to Support this Royal Kingdom, and Consequently This Citty." This historical allusion recurs several times in civic pageantry from the 1559 royal entry to Dekker's incidental reference. Just a few years earlier, in 1624, John Webster had also dealt with this theme in his Lord Mayor's Show, *Monuments of Honor*. Thus even in Stuart times the remembrance of the achievement of the Tudors remains a viable theme in civic drama.

Britannia herself had been a significant part of Munday's 1605 entertainment noted above, in which she engaged in dialogue with Brutus, mythical settler of England. This may be further evidence of Dekker's familiarity with Munday's pageant. Dekker surrounds Britannia with Magnanimity, "with a drawne Sword," a Shipwright, Victory "with a Palme Tree," and Providence, "with a

Trumpet, ready to Foresee Dangers, and awaken Men to meete them" (p. 91).
Dekker includes these figures because they serve as "Watch-Towers, and
Lanthornes, in the Nights of Feare and Trouble, to Guard the Kingdome, and in
the Kingdome, This Citty" (p. 92). The Watch-Tower also contains representations of several former English kings who had in some way been associated with
the office of mayor of London.

Because Amphitrite, London, and Fame had already spoken, Britannia feels
that she cannot remain silent. Like London before her, she begs the mayor to
"*Heare then a* Mothers *Counsell* ..." (p. 93). She invokes the sea metaphor: "*You
are Come / Aboard a* Goodly Ship ... / ... High Admirall / You are to All That
Fleete, which Thus you Call / To sayle in This vast Ocean*" (p. 93); and, "*Your
Owne Hands steere the Helme, But Strongly Steere, / And spite of stormes, be stoute
when you stand There.*" The mayor should use his sword to "*Kill, and Keepe /
Vices (like Slaves) in Awe....*" The call to be admiral of the ship of state involves
the recognition that he must be stern and resolute in the never ceasing war
against vice. Finally, Britannia implores him to read a "*Lesson of my love*" and so
be led by love through the perilous journey. London's plea that the mayor be a
faithful Gardener of the realm now joins Britannia's hope that he will be a wise
Pilot.

Dekker makes the last device of the pageant the Sun's Bower, an arbor "in
which the *Sunne* sits, with golden Beames about his Face; an Attire glittering like
gold; and a mantle bright as his garment, fringed with gold, his haire curled and
yellow" (p. 93). Around him appear persons representing the four seasons, "in
proper Habiliments" (p. 94). Beneath them a wilderness contains "many sorts of
such *Beasts*, whose rich Skinnes serve for *Furres....*" Perhaps the idea of using the
Sun and the Seasons came to Dekker from his earlier masque-like play, *The Sun's
Darling* (1624). Raybright, the sun's darling, has rejected the opportunities offered by each season and instead has fallen prey to Folly and Humour. In the
closing moment of the drama Sun appears and points out the play's allegorical
meaning, especially how man should disdain vice and follow the virtuous pattern
of nature that will give him health and youth. In the pageant Sun addresses the
mayor and reports on his travels, primarily that everywhere he goes he encounters turmoil and disorders of all sorts, "*that Hellish brood of Warres* ..." (p. 94).
Peace can be found only in England, the blessed land "*That seest fires kindling
round, and yet canst stand / Unburnt for all their flames....*" The message to the
mayor implies: preserve the peace that graces the land—the instruction of London and Britannia should help on that score.

Though having slight dramatic action, this pageant suggests a certain logical
development in what takes place. One might call it "cosmic" development; that
is, the movement from sea (Amphitrite) to land (London and Britannia) to sky
(Sun), from microcosm to macrocosm, for the Sun views the whole universe and
from his unique vantage point perceives the peace and order that reign in Eng-

land. A strong emphasis occurs here, unlike the 1612 show, on the problems of the commonwealth and the necessity for preserving its unity—a theme shared with many other pageant writers. Instructional value abounds, but theatrical interest wanes.

When the Ironmongers sought to honor the mayor, Sir James Campbell, in 1629, they again chose Dekker to prepare the entertainment, which he called *London's Tempe*. Special interest for the 1629 show comes from the eye-witness account and drawings by Abram Booth, secretary to the delegation of the Netherlands East India Company who had come to London to try to settle the differences between his company and the English East India Company of which the new mayor was a member.[4] Booth's small sketches of six devices the editors reproduce in the Malone Society, *Collections V*, plates I-VI; with the drawings for Munday's 1616 pageant they constitute the only visual records we have of Lord Mayors' Shows from 1558 to the closing of the theaters.

As with Dekker's previous pageants, this one also opens with a sea-figure, this time Oceanus, who provides the initial welcome on the river. He sits "Triumphantly in the Vast (but Queint) shell of a silver Scollup, Reyning in the heads of two wild Sea-horses ..." (IV, 103). He wears a diadem on his head and bears a golden trident in his right hand. Could he summon all the rivers of the world, Oceanus tells the mayor, "*they would weepe out there eyes, / Madde that new* Troys *high towers on tiptoe rize / To hit Heavens Roofe* ..." (p. 104). Further, "*That minion of the world / Venice to Neptune,—A poore Lantscip is, / To these full Braveries of Thamesis*" (p. 105). This praise of London over the festivity-filled city of Venice had also been sounded a few years earlier in John Webster's 1624 Lord Mayor's Show.

A "Proud-swelling Sea" constitutes the second device; and riding upon its waves, a sea lion carries Tethys, wife to Oceanus, "for why should the King of waves be in such a glorious progresse without his Queene, or she without him?" (p. 105). The two devices on the river also come to land where a third joins them; it consists of an ostrich "cut out of timber to the life, biting a horse-shoe." But Dekker fails to exploit these situations for any dramatic or thematic possibilities.

Because the show honors the Ironmongers, the fourth scene presents a *Lemnian Forge* with Vulcan and his servants, the Cyclops. "A fire is seene in the Forge, Bellowes blowing, some filing, some at other workes.... As the Smiths are at worke, they sing in praise of Iron ..." (p. 106). Cupid and Jove also appear near the forge. Cupid has "on his head a curld yellow haire," wings at his back; and he bears a bow and quiver—"Golden and silver arrowes, are ever and anon reached up to him, which hee shoots upward into the aire, and is still supplied with more from the Forge" (p. 107). In an appropriate exalted position sits Jove

---

[4]Malone Society, *Collections V: A Calendar of the Dramatic Records in the Books of the London Clothworkers' Company*, ed. F. P. Wilson (Oxford, 1959), p. 6.

"in a rich *Antique* habite, a long white reverend hayre on his head, a beard long and curld: A Mace of Triple fire in his hand burning" (pp. 107-8).

The tableau gains additional vitality by the conversation between Vulcan and Jove. In fact, Jove interrupts the work of the ironsmiths to speak of the contribution that iron makes to the lives of all. He also asks the workers to fashion thunderbolts for his use, "*For Vices (mountain-like) in black heapes rize, / My sinewes crack to fell them ...*" (p. 108). Idiot pride, Ambition, Avarice, War—"*Shall not* Jove, *beate downe such Impieties?*" And Jove asks further:

> *Ist not high time, Ist not true Justice then*
> (Vulcan) *for thee, and thy tough Hammer-men*
> *To beate thy Anvile,—and blow fires to flames*
> *To burne these Broodes, who kill even with their Names?* (p. 108)

To which Vulcan affirmatively replies: "*Yes, Jove, tis more then Time.*" Jove closes the exchange with a lengthy speech that notes the value of iron both materially— "*How would the Corne pricke up her golden Eares: / But that Iron Plough shares, all the labour beares / In Earth's strange Midwiffry?*"—and morally: "*By irons strong Charmes / Ryots lye bound:—Warre stops her rough Allarmes*" (p. 109). Clearly iron becomes vital in the pursuit of both peace and plenty; and in addition to celebrating the company, this scene recalls the constant struggle against vice.

Possibly Dekker took some of his inspiration for the presentation of Vulcan and Jove from Munday's *Sidero-thriambos*, the 1618 mayoral show, also designed to honor the Ironmongers. As we recall, the first device contained an island called *Lemnos* that had a mine where Mulciber and his Cyclops worked. They fashion products out of iron to the continual fall of their hammers "in sweet Musicall voyces." Also Jupiter appears with his "three-forked thunderbolt" made for him by Mulciber. Such close parallels suggest indebtedness rather than coincidence.

The fifth device gives the pageant its name, *London's Tempe*, "or *The Field of Happinesse*; thereby reflecting upon the name of *Campebell* [the new mayor], or *Le Beu Champe, A faire and glorious field*" (p. 109). It has the design of an arbor, "round about furnished with trees and flowers: the upper part with severall fruites: Intimating that as *London* is the best-stored Garden in the Kingdome for Plants, Herbes, Flowers, Rootes, and such like; So, on this day it is the most glorious Citty in the Christian world" (p. 110). Again it seems possible that Dekker glanced back to Munday's pageant, particularly his 1609 show, *Campbell or The Ironmongers Faire Field*, written to honor Thomas Campbell, father of the 1629 mayor, James Campbell. Munday's garden, containing Majesty's Watch-Tower, had quite opulent trees and fruit of pure gold. And St. Andrew at the close of the show suggested that the virtues that populate the garden "do make it seeme a

Feild of heavenly happines." Dekker's tableau thus seems to strain continuity to the point of duplication.

In Dekker's fair field Titan serves as the chief figure and the speaker, accompanied by Flora, Ceres, Pomona, Spring, and Summer. Offering instruction, Titan bids the mayor to pursue a just pace so that all who follow "*may with Pride, / Say, None like you did Noblier quit the Place*" (p. 110). And "*since Honors Zodiac is your sphaere, / A shrub to you must be the tallest Pine, / On poore and rich you Equally must shine.*" Titan also indicates that the mythological figures that accompany him bring appropriate gifts to the mayor, recalling similar incidents in some of the progress pageants.

Finally appears Apollo's Palace "because seven persons representing the seven liberall Sciences are richly Inthroned in this Citty" (p. 111). The persons, dressed in loose robes, hold in their hands "Escutcheons, with Emblemes in them proper to every one quality." This representation parallels Dekker's treatment of the Liberal Sciences in the 1612 Lord Mayor's Show. Twelve silver columns support the structure, and on the top four gold columns support a square tower. Of course, Apollo stands as the "chiefe person; on his head a garland of bayes; In his hand a Lute." This traditional emblematic representation of Apollo can be seen in John Squire's *The Tryumphs of Peace*, the 1620 mayoral pageant, where Apollo sits at the top of Mount Parnassus under a laurel tree playing his harp. In his address to the mayor in Dekker's show Apollo takes notice of the festive scene and the happiness of the citizens and bids the mayor to "Go on in your full glories; whilst *Apollo*, and these Mistresses of the Learned Sciences, waft you to that Honourable shore, whither Time bids you hasten to arrive" (p. 112).

With the full blessing of Apollo and the Liberal Sciences, the mayor finally at night arrives at his own gate where Oceanus bids him farewell and wishes: "*Peace therefore Guard your bedds: / In your yeares Zodiacke may you fairely move, / Shin'd on by Angels, blest with goodnes love*" (p. 112). This becomes a type of benediction. Between the speeches of Oceanus that open and close the entertainment, the pageant has repeatedly made the mayor conscious of his guild, has welcomed him to his new post, and has offered instruction. And Jove reminds us that the struggle between the forces of good and evil continues, requiring the active support of the company in behalf of virtue. But on the whole, the show suffers from its lack of unity, either thematic or dramatic; scenes tend to be vaguely strung together with little pursuit of the dramatic possibilities. Even thematically, no coherent, cohesive theme binds together the disparate parts. And the obvious reliance on some of Munday's pageants suggests less than full creative imagination brought to the task.

Perhaps the pageants of 1628 and 1629 should be viewed as Dekker's "dotages." Although rich in spectacle, they contain little dramatic "soul." Weighed against the 1612 entertainment, they suffer sorely. All of which does not bode well for the mayoral pageants of the Caroline period. Dekker in his late shows completely ignores the genuine contribution he had made; namely, the morality play structure of the 1612 show. If we had but that Jacobean pageant, we would have to regard Dekker as a successful pageant-dramatist, for he solved the problem of achieving dramatic unity while maintaining a consistent thematic purpose. Doubtless the 1612 show inspired the efforts of Thomas Middleton in his pageant of 1613. We should not stretch Dekker out any longer on this tough rack of comparison, except to say that by the late 1620s perhaps his creative interest and energy no longer stirred at such civic occasions.

7 *Thomas Middleton*

By THE SECOND DECADE OF THE SEVENTEENTH CENTURY Thomas Middleton had already become well-established as a comic dramatist with such achievements as *A Trick to Catch the Old One*, *Michaelmas Term*, and *A Chaste Maid in Cheapside* behind him. Many of his city comedies of course take the urban life of London for their inspiration. We have noted earlier, in Chapter Two, his brief excursions into the civic pageant form: the speech of Zeal at the Fleet street arch in James's 1604 royal entry entertainment and *Civitatis Amor* (1616), written to celebrate the creation of Charles as Prince of Wales. But from 1613 to his death Middleton becomes intimately involved with the production of mayoral pageants, writing a total of seven, a number equalled by Thomas Heywood in the 1630s, and surpassed only by Anthony Munday.[1] By 1620 he becomes the official Chronologer for the City of London, thus ensuring his close connection with the affairs of the city. Toward the end of his dramatic career (and his life) Middleton produced his two best-known tragedies: *Women Beware Women* and with Rowley *The Changeling*. All the while he was also writing civic pageants, reminding us again of the inherently close relationship between the street theater and the regular stage when the same dramatists write for both.

Like Dekker, Middleton's first Lord Mayor's Show (1613) emerges as his finest and his most elaborate with a total cost of some £1,300—the most expensive mayoral pageant of the Renaissance. The planning and preparations for the entertainment which Middleton called *The Triumphs of Truth* become clear in the records of the Grocers' company whose member also named Thomas Middleton became mayor. Interestingly, Anthony Munday received £149 for "the devyse of the Pageant and other shewes, and for the appareling and fynding of all the personages in the sayd shewes (excepting the Pageant) ..."[2] John Grinkin's commendable efforts as artificer Middleton cites at the end of his text—the first time an artificer has been singled out for praise in conjunction with a Lord Mayor's Show.

Doubtless taking a cue from Dekker's 1612 entertainment, Middleton shapes his pageant around a morality conflict: the struggle between Truth and Error with the title of the show indicating the eventual outcome.[3] In many respects the

---

[1]See R. C. Bald, "Middleton's Civic Employments," *Modern Philology*, 31 (1933): 65-78. Bald finds little to praise in Middleton's pageants.
[2]Malone Society, *Collections III*, p. 87. All quotations from company records will be from this source.
[3]For further discussion see Sheila H. Williams, "Two Seventeenth Century Semi-Dramatic Allegories of Truth the Daughter of Time," *The Guildhall Miscellany*, 2, no. 5 (1963): 207-20. Others have pur-

pageant may be regarded as a peripatetic morality play as the conflict follows the movements of the mayor throughout the city, resulting in a skillfully handled allegory rich in color and spectacle as the competing forces vie for the mayor's allegiance. Though the typical morality play structure informs the arrangement of events, the pageant lacks the sort of "dramatic climax" as found in Dekker's show of the previous year, for Error remains to the end a potent force until finally destroyed. A symbolic structure also operates here, subsumed in the conflict between light and darkness, whose contrasting images permeate throughout the pageant in various ways. Middleton could just as easily have named the show "The Triumphs of Light"; thus a dual level of metaphor works: the personification of the battle between virtue and vice (Truth and Error) and the clash between light and darkness. Each metaphorical structure expands and enhances the other.

Watching over the events appears London, "attired like a reverend mother, a long white hair naturally flowing on either side of her; on her head a model of steeples and turrets," holding in her hand a key of gold.[4] While thus personified, London also literally exists in the citizens who line the streets to observe the dramatic presentation. London greets the new mayor in the morning, offering him the counsel of a mother whose virtues she sees epitomized in this son. She warns him, however, of the cares and responsibilities of his office, urging him to go forward "In ways of goodness," disdaining "all titles / Purchas'd with coin, of honour take thou hold / By thy desert, let others buy't with gold ..." (p. 238). The key she holds symbolizes his task: "This place is the kings's chamber; all pollution, / Sin, and uncleanness, must be lock't out here, / And be kept sweet with sanctity, faith, and fear." The allegorical portrayal of the struggle to keep sin and uncleanness locked out emerges here, thus assuring the sanctity of the city. London's welcoming speech therefore helps establish the moral tone of the civic drama.

---

sued the connection between Dekker's 1612 pageant and Middleton's first; see, for example, Theodore B. Leinwand, "London Triumphing: The Jacobean Lord Mayor's Show," *Clio* 11 (1982): 137-53; Sergei Lobanov-Rostovsky, "*The Triumphes of Golde*: Economic Authority in the Jacobean Lord Mayor's Show," *ELH* 60 (1993): 879-98. Two additional essays particularly focus on the immediate political context of *Triumphs of Truth* and other Middleton pageants, emphasizing the mercantile nature of these pageants and their purpose and the office of mayor: Raymond D. Tumbleson, "The Triumph of London: Lord Mayor's Day Pageants and the Rise of the City," in *The Witness of Times: Manifestations of Ideology in Seventeenth Century England*, ed. Katherine Z. Keller and Gerald J. Schiffhorst (Pittsburgh, 1993), pp. 53-68; and A. A. Bromham, "Thomas Middleton's *The Triumphs of Truth*: City Politics in 1613," *The Seventeenth Century* 10 (1995): 1-25. Bromham in particular sees the pageant as responding to a decadent Stuart court by extolling the virtues of the city, and finds a political subtext in the pageant's presumed response to the wedding of Robert Carr and Frances Howard.

[4]*The Works of Thomas Middleton*, ed. A. H. Bullen (London, 1886), VII, 236. All quotations will be from this edition.

Having taken his oath, the mayor returns to the city where at Baynard's Castle Truth's Angel waits to greet him on horseback—"his raiment of white silk powdered with stars of gold; on his head a crown of gold ..." (p. 239). Already the image of light finds expression in the use of gold. The symbolic representation of Zeal who accompanies Truth further enhances the light image: dressed "in a garment of flame-coloured silk, with a bright hair on his head, from which shoot fire-beams, ... his right hand holding a flaming scourge, intimating thereby that as he is the manifester of Truth, he is likewise the chastiser of Ignorance and Error" (pp. 239-40). The Angel informs the mayor: "I am Truth's Angel, by my mistress sent / To guard and guide thee" (p. 240); and he assures that he stood by as the mayor took the oath and "close behind thee / Stood Error's minister, that still sought to blind thee, / And wrap his subtle mists about thy oath...." Fortunately, the Angel's light "expell'd her blackest spite ..." (p. 240). All of this serves as a moral warning to the mayor that his "care's but begun, / Wake on, the victory is not half yet won...." This "invisible" battle that has occurred, as "offstage," prepares the way for the realistic, tangible encounter between the opposing forces of light and darkness, and dramatically we become aware that the victory is "not half yet won."

But the Angel and Zeal assure the mayor of their moral aid, and together they guide him to Paul's-Chain where Error waits to assault him. Error has emblematic costume: "his garment of ash-colour silk, his head rolled in a cloud, over which stands an owl, a mole on one shoulder, a bat on the other, all symbols of blind ignorance and darkness, mists hanging at his eyes" (p. 241). Particularly gruesome appears the portrait of Envy who accompanies Error—she is "eating of a human heart, mounted on a rhinoceros, attired in red silk, suitable to the bloodiness of her manners! her left pap bare, where a snake fastens...." The persuasive tempting argument of Error may remind us of the sort of logic that confronted Spenser's Sir Guyon in the Cave of Mammon, and it suggests the psychological subtlety that Middleton gives to Error, as opposed to the more straightforward, blustery force of Envy in Dekker's 1612 pageant. Three basic appeals come in the argument: first, flattery of the mayor, then an appeal to his appetites and desires, and a call for liberation from the constricting, confining bonds of Truth. Error calls the mayor "My glory's sweetheart" and says that "I was dead / Till I enjoy'd thy presence ..." (p. 241). Distorting the imagery of the pageant, Error claims that he has become "all of light" now that the mayor has arrived. In offering material gain by deceitful methods, Error urges the mayor: "let thy will and appetite sway the sword; / Down with them all now whom thy heart envies, / Let not thy conscience come into thine eyes ..." (p. 242). The mayor, offered "power and profit," needs only to get rid of that "poor, thin, threadbare thing call'd Truth" who impoverishes the city (p. 243). Her way seems straight and narrow and toilsome; but Error knows a hundred "with delight and pleasure, / Back-ways and by-ways ..." (p. 243): the temptation in the wilderness all over again as Error promises to show the mayor a paradise regained. The crowning and ultimately deceiving blow comes when Error boasts to the mayor: "This of thy life I'll make the golden year ..." (p. 243). But "golden" connotes pure, true, virtuous, and ideal, whereas Error really offers only a few ephemeral pleasures that finally lead man into darkness, not light. We recall the House of Pride covered in golden foil though built on a sandy hill. The "golden" offer of Error counters his own dark oppression, and in this instance the physical appearance gives the lie to his meretricious words.

In such a "naive allegory," as Northrop Frye might call it, the symbolic appearance counts as very important, and this we see when Zeal drives back the evil forces to make way for Truth whose portrait counters the presentation of Error. Truth comes in a garment of white satin, making her appear "thin and naked, figuring thereby her simplicity and nearness of heart to those that embrace her ..." (p. 244). And Middleton continues, scrupulous in his emblematic detail: she wears a robe of white silk filled with the eyes of eagles, "showing her deep insight and height of wisdom": over her head rests a "milk-white dove, and on each shoulder one, the sacred emblems of purity, meekness, and innocency"; she treads upon serpents, "in that she treads down all subtlety and fraud"; as witness of "her eternal descent" she wears a diadem of stars on her forehead; on her breast she has a pure round crystal indicating "the brightness of her thoughts and actions"; as further signs of light she carries a sun in her right hand and a fan filled all with stars in her left (p. 244). No other pageant-dramatist, nor Ben Jonson in the masque for that matter, gives greater evidence of understanding the traditional iconographical presentation of allegorical figures. Not merely a portrait, however, it has a dramatic function: to sharpen the contrast between good and evil.

Zeal not only drives back the furies, but his speech offers an interpretation of the symbols connected with Truth's appearance; no one in the audience need wonder at its meaning. Counterposing the previous speech of Error, the words of Truth offer an antidote to the cunning speech. Truth bids the man who has been raised by faith and love not to be "led, / In ignorant ways of insolence and pride ..." (p. 245)—do not succumb to flattery. But the mayor must "first subject thy will, / ... though that elf / Of sin and darkness, still opposing me, / Counsels thy appetite to master thee" (p. 246). Only one way exists, not various and deceiving ways. Finally, Truth presses her cause: "Forsake me not, that can advance thy soul: / I see a blessed yielding in thy eye; / Thou'rt mine; lead on, thy name shall never die" (p. 246), which echoes the refrain of the song in Dekker's 1612 show: "He is living, living ever." Though the battles may continue, Truth has destroyed the tempting arguments of Error and offers to the yielding mayor eternal blessings, not meaningless earthly baubles.

With the verbal conflict over for the moment Truth in her chariot with her "celestial handmaids, the Graces and Virtues" leads the mayor to St. Paul's churchyard, Zeal and the Angel accompanying as well as Error "following as near as it can get ..." (p. 246). By keeping the entourage together in the processional Middleton achieves a dramatic unity, making it easy for the audience at any particular spot to surmise what has happened. In the churchyard rest five islands that had appeared earlier on the water but now gather in this place, occupied by five persons representing the Five Senses, "at their feet their proper emblems,— ... an eagle, a hart, a spider, an ape, a dog" (p. 247); Middleton fails to make clear the significance of this tableau, though it does somewhat obliquely refer to the struggle to maintain control of the senses, the appetite, as depicted in the fight for the mayor's soul; but Middleton does not press the point. Suddenly a ship appears having "neither sailor nor pilot, only upon a white silk streamer these two words set in letters of gold, *Viritate gubernor,*—I am steered by Truth" (p. 247), but containing aboard a King of Moors, his queen, and two attendants. The King's speech offers a justification for his appearance in this entertainment. Referring to his dark physical appearance, he explains: "However darkness dwells upon my face, / Truth in my soul sets up the light of grace ..." (p. 248)—again the basic conflict of imagery. It seems that this King of Moors and his queen had been converted to Christianity by English merchants travelling in their land; thus they have arrived "in blessed time / To do that mistress service, in the prime / Of these her spotless triumphs, and t'attend / That honourable man, her late-sworn friend" (p. 249). Truth steers their ship "as our souls must be." Error, annoyed that his "sweet-fac'd devils" have also forsaken him, has his work cut out for him. This scene closes with the appearance of Time, Truth's father, with his hourglass, wings, and scythe; perhaps we recall their joint presentation in the 1559 London royal entry pageant. Enjoying the spectacle of the victorious Truth, Time claims: "O, I could ever stand still thus and gaze!" (p. 250). But Time must press on to bless his daughter and these triumphs, and he promises the mayor that he will bring him weekly to St. Paul's where he will hear "Truth's celestial harmony ..." (p. 250).

The next event, one of the most spectacular of the pageant, again dramatizes allegorically the battle between Truth and Error. When the procession reaches the Little Conduit in Cheapside, it finds the device of London's Triumphant Mount shrouded over with "a thick, sulphurous darkness, it being a fog or mist, raised from Error ..." (p. 251). Furthermore, four of Error's disciples, Barbarism, Ignorance, Impudence, and Falsehood, sit at the dark corners trembling when Truth approaches, she appalled that Error has stained "this Triumphant Mount, where our delight / Hath been divinely fix'd so many ages" (p. 251). But the dark clouds recede, chased away by Truth's fan of stars: "Vanish, infectious fog, that I may see / This city's grace, that takes her light from me!" (p. 252). The cloud of darkness then transmutes into a "bright-spreading canopy, stuck thick with stars, and beams of gold shooting forth round about it ..." (p. 252). On the mount London sits in the place of greatest honor and above her Religion with the proper emblems of "her sanctity, watchfulness, and zeal." On the right hand of Religion appears Liberality and on the left, Perfect Love "wearing upon his head a wreath of white and red roses mingled together, the ancient witness of peace, love, and union, wherein consists the happiness of this land ..." (p. 252). Emblematically costumed, other virtues populate the triumphant mount and support London: Knowledge, Modesty, Chastity, Fame, Simplicity, and Meekness. The speech given by London defines the crucial thematic development of the pageant. She first thanks Truth for redeeming her lost sight, then warns the mayor of the roughness of his journey and sketches the differences between Truth and Error: the multiple ways of Error lead to a wide hell-mouth that man finds "close, dark, and strait, for hell returns no men," but Truth's one sacred way opens into the breadth of "whole heaven" and the length of "eternal day ..." (p. 254). Good works perfect the path of salvation, as London notes: "But first observe what work she here requires, / Religion, knowledge, sanctity, chaste desires; / Then charity, which bounty must express / ... Honour and action must together shine ..." (p. 255). Here on the Triumphant Mount the mayor gains a vision of what must be done in order to equip himself in the constant struggle with vice; in short, he must put on the whole armor of Truth.

Twice more in the progress through the city Error causes the mists to descend on the Mount and shroud its beauty, and each time the light of Truth drives away that darkness; thus the conflict continues to rage. Eventually London calls upon Perfect Love to offer words of ethical advice, the anagogical issue having already been settled. He banishes from this feast of joy "All excess, epicurism, both which destroy / The healths of soul and body ..." (p. 257). The "golden advice" London sums up in the closing remarks: "He that desires days healthful, sound, and blest, / Let moderate judgment serve him at his feast ..." (p. 258). As with other figures in other civic pageants, the moral instruction recalls some version of Aristotle's golden mean.

That night as the entertainment draws to a close, the various devices accompany the mayor to his gate where London, using the light image throughout her speech, tells the mayor that we cannot "call this night, if our eyes count / The glorious beams that dance about this mount ..." (p. 258). Truth, interrupting her father Time, offers the closing words confident in the mayor's "salvation." She urges him to meet his tasks with goodness, join greatness with grace; and she reminds him:

> I've set thee high now, be so in example,
> Made thee a pinnacle in honour's temple,
> Fixing ten thousand eyes upon thy brow;
> There is no hiding of thy actions now,
> They must abide the light, and imitate me,
> Or be thrown down to fire where errors be. (p. 260)

He should have faith in his heart and plenty in the hall; love in his walks, but justice in his state; zeal in his chamber and bounty at his gate (p. 261). With the sound of triumphant trumpets Zeal appears and calls attention to Error's chariot standing nearby which Zeal desires to burn "in divine wrath." Receiving the sanction of Truth, Zeal shoots flame from his head and sets on fire the chariot of Error "and all the beasts that are joined to it" (p. 262)—a gloriously spectacular and theatrically exciting ending of the war between Truth and Error.

The cause of dramatic unity gains greatly by the movement of all devices throughout the processional; thus the audience at almost any point has a chance to understand the dramatic action. The persistent appearance of the chief antagonists, Truth and Error, makes immediately available to the spectators the essential conflict of the allegory. Suffused with moral instruction, the pageant owes an apparent debt to medieval morality drama both in structure and content. And the constant verbal and visual reference to conflicting light and dark imagery serves to unify the entertainment. Thematically, the show moves along several paths: literally, we see a struggle for the mayor's soul; the vicious battle between Truth and Error informs the allegory; figures outline the path to salvation; and the moral instruction illustrates how that salvation can be perfected in good works. The moments at London's Triumphant Mount constitute the dramatic high point of the pageant, and from that visionary mount we descend confident of the impending destruction of evil and more certain than ever that only light can extinguish darkness, only Truth can dispel Error.

After this highly successful Lord Mayor's Show of 1613, ranking with the finest of the Stuart period, understandably the Grocers in 1617 look to Middleton again, Munday having written the shows of 1614, 1615, and 1616. The pageant, called *The Triumphs of Honour and Industry*, unfortunately, does not measure up to the excellence of the 1613 one, and Middleton resembles Dekker in this respect. The more traditional, more conservative theater elements of other civic pageants gain control here, resulting in a rather undistinguished work. But, nevertheless, for his services Middleton received the handsome sum of £282 as his responsibilities included devising the entertainment, paying for the construction work and costumes, and finding personages for the shows.[5] Munday and Dekker, who both entered the competition, had to settle for £5 and £4 respectively for their pains. Total cost exceeded £882; the extravagance of the Grocers continues.

The fullest eye witness account of a Lord Mayor's Show concerns this 1617 pageant and survives in the account of Horatio Busino, chaplain to the Venetian Ambassador, Piero Contarini, preserved in the *Calendar of State Papers Venetian*.[6] In addition to corroborating Middleton's text, Busino's report captures

---

[5] *Collections III*, p. 92.
[6] For a further discussion of this valuable source see my "Venetian State Papers and English Civic Pageantry, 1558-1642," *Renaissance Quarterly* 23 (1970): 37-47.

much of the color of the total scene as he and the Ambassador first view the show on the Thames and then move to a vantage point in the city in order to watch the processional. He notes the river scene: "The ships were beautifully decorated with balustrades and various paintings. They carried immense banners and countless pennons. Salutes were fired, and a number of persons bravely attired played on trumpets, fifes and other instruments."[7] As his eye gazes on the crowds lining the streets, he reports: "It was a fine medley: there were old men in their dotage; insolent youths and boys ...; painted wenches and women of the lower classes carrying their children, all anxious to see the show" (p. 60). The diverse nature of the audience comes alive in Busino's report. His vivid account of the visual spectacle includes his annoyance at the presence of "two ugly Spanish women ... perfect hobgoblins ..." (p. 60). He takes note of the members of the company in their full livery who line the streets, the City Marshal on horseback trying to keep the route clear, and "men masked as wild giants who by means of fireballs and wheels hurled sparks in the faces of the mob and over their persons, but all proved unavailing to make a free and ample thoroughfare" (p. 61). The first "stages," Busino reports, moved by griffins, lions, camels, or other large animals, "laden with bales from which the lads took sundry confections, sugar, nutmegs, dates and ginger, throwing them among the populace" (p. 61).

Busino's description of the first pageant corresponds closely with Middleton's; the Italian writes: "The first pageant represented a lovely forest with fruit on the top of its trees and peopled with children in Indian costume, with the black tress falling from the back of the head ..." (p. 61). Middleton observes that these Indian figures cease their labors and begin to dance about the trees. This scene gives way to "a rich personage presenting India, the seat of merchandise" (VII, 298). Sitting on the top of an "illustrious chariot," India has as companions Traffic and Industry, all emblematically costumed. Other allegorical figures, Fortune, Wealth, Virtue, Grace, and Perfection, also appear, bearing their traditional symbolic properties. In her speech Industry asserts that she is "the life-blood of praise: / To rise without me, is to steal to glory ..." (p. 298); and her comments prepare the way for the next device, the "Pageant of Several Nations," on the top of which a laurel tree, "the leaves spotted with gold ..." (p. 300). About this tree sit six celestial figures: Peace, "holding a branch of palm"; Prosperity, a laurel; Love, "two joined hands"; Unity, "two turtles"; Plenty, "holding fruits"; and Fidelity, "a silver anchor" (p. 300). Speeches come from figures representng several nationalities, including a Spaniard of whom Busino writes: "He kept kissing his hands, right and left, but especially to the Spanish Ambassador, who was a short distance from us, in such wise as to elicit roars of laughter from the multitude" (*CSP Ven*, p. 62).

---

[7]*Calendar of State Papers Venetian, 1617-1619* (London, 1909), XV, 59.

To the chief device of the entertainment, the "Castle of Fame or Honour," Industry "brings her sons unto in their reverend ages" (p. 302). Reward and Justice keep a seat in front of the Castle for George Bowles, the new mayor whom the pageant honors. The arms of former Grocer mayors also appear on the device. Thematically, this tableau constitutes the chief instructional part of the show as evinced especially in the speeches of Reward and Justice. Justice sketches what must be done in order for the new mayor to occupy the reserved spot:

Justice must flow through him before that be;
Great works of grace must be requir'd and done
Before the honour of this seat be won.
A whole year's reverend care in righting wrongs,
And guarding innocence from malicious tongues,
Must be employ'd in virtue's sacred right
Before this place be fill'd: 'tis no mean fight.... (p. 303)

Offering their support to the mayor in his efforts to achieve the seat of honor, other virtues station themselves about the Castle—Truth, Antiquity, Harmony, Fame, Desert, Good Works, Honour, Religion, Piety, and Commiseration, each bearing some symbolic property.

The several devices gather at the gate of the mayor that night, and Honour from the top of the castle speaks, reminding the mayor that "we should upward seek our crown ..." (p. 306). "All I desire for my grace and good / Is but to be remember'd in your blood, / With honour to accomplish the fair time / Which power hath put into your hands" (p. 306). He further bids the mayor to open his bounty to the citizens, "For bounty 'twas ordain'd to make that clear, / Which is the light of goodness and of fame ..." (306). Thus the pageant closes, the mayor and the guild having been praised and instructed; but dramatic interest remains negligible, for Middleton abandons the much more theatrical form of his 1613 show and uses instead the simplest form—loosely connected tableaux. One could wish that Busino's reportorial skills had been lavished on a better civic pageant.

After an interval of a year in which Munday prepared the mayoral show, the Skinners selected Middleton to write the pageant to honor Sir William Cockayne, Skinner, which he entitled *The Triumphs of Love and Antiquity* (1619). Guild records reveal that Munday, Middleton, and Richard Grimston "poettes, all shewed to the table their severall plottes for devices for the shewes and pagente against Symon and Judes tide and each desired to searve the Companie" (*MSC*, p. 99). This account, dated 1 July 1619, demonstrates again the competitive nature of civic pageantry in what must have been a typical procedure for the guild.

Though much less elaborate in both spectacle and structure than the 1613 show, this 1619 pageant captures at least some of the earlier pageant's thematic development. On the river a lengthy speech of welcome from Love reminds the mayor that "Men's loves will last to crown thy end of days ..." (VII, 316); and it encourages the mayor to be diligent in good works during his brief tenure. Love also senses a note of victory in the present festivity:

> Methinks I see oppression hang the head,
> Falsehood and injury with their guilt struck dead,
> At this triumphant hour; ill causes hide
> Their leprous faces, daring not t'abide
> The brightness of this day; and in mine ear
> Methinks the Graces' silver chimes I hear. (p. 317)

The entertainment thus presumes the mayor's victory over evil forces instead of presenting the actual dramatic confrontation between opposing powers as in the 1613 pageant; but the mayor should be made fully aware of some of the dangers that will beset him while in office.

The first land device contains a wilderness occupied by numerous fur-bearing beasts, an allusion to the company; but Middleton lifts the tableau above the level of simple compliment by including Orpheus who has "over his head an artificial cock, often made to crow and flutter with his wings" (p. 318)—a visual pun on the mayor's name. In an important speech Orpheus offers wise words from one who achieved order out of chaos, taming the wild beasts with his harmony. Orpheus urges the mayor to disdain the flatterers and instead follow only virtue; then he develops a metaphorical interpretation of the visual scene. The wilderness, Orpheus says, represents—

> The rude and thorny ways thy care must clear;
> Such as the vices in a city sprung,
> As are yon thickets that grow close and strong; ...
> Just such a wilderness is a commonwealth
> That is undrest, unprun'd, wild in her health.... (pp. 319-20)

But an answer comes to this incivility: by "fair example, musical grace," harmonious government can be achieved; thus it may be said that "Every wise magistrate that governs thus, / May well be call'd a powerful Orpheus" (p. 320). One recalls Munday's technique in the use of the pelican in his 1616 show as applied to the qualities that the mayor should adopt. For Orpheus the cock represents the vigilancy that the magistrate must maintain; also the bird sounds a warning before it strikes, thus exercising justice, and the mayor should exhaust all possibilities before the harshness of the law be tried against an individual. With the reconciling virtues of an Orpheus, the mayor may tame the wilderness of the government; he becomes a wise gardener, a metaphor used by Dekker in his pageants.

At the device located at the Little Conduit in Cheap stands a "Sanctuary of Fame" crowned with twenty-six "bright-burning lamps," alluding to the twenty-six aldermen of the city. The speaker Example links the tableau with the previous one by asserting that from that "rough wilderness" the mayor now moves to the reward—"a chief seat / In Fame's fair Sanctuary, where some of old, / Crown'd with their troubles, now are here enroll'd ..." (p. 322). He will enter Fame's book provided that he safely creates order out of the wilderness; such a reward recalls Dekker's 1612 pageant where the besieged mayor goes to the House of Fame. Thematically, though certainly not dramatically, both pageant-dramatists share a common purpose.

From the "Parliament of Honour" Anitquity addresses the mayor as his entourage moves toward the Guildhall. She reminds him that she keeps "all the records of fame," preserving all good works "that after-times may see / What former were, and how they ought to be / Fruitful and thankful, in fair actions flowing ..." (p. 323). Visual symbols provide examples of those of the company who left behind a good report. Thus this tableau complements the previous one, offering both instruction and challenge. The mayor should be careful "to bring forth deeds / To match that honour that from hence proceeds" (p. 324).

The several devices accompany the magistrate to his house that evening, and from the "Triumphant Chariot of Love" Love closes the pageant with a speech. Because Love opened the entertainment, he appropriately closes it: "For love is circular, like the bright sun, / And takes delight to end where it begun ..." (p. 330). Posing the question of what the mayor must do, Love answers:

That which in conscience ought to be requir'd;
O, thank 'em in thy justice, in thy care,
Zeal to right wrongs, works that are clear and fair,
And will become thy soul, whence virtue springs,
As those rich ornaments thy brother-kings. (p. 330)

The speech ends with the use of the marriage metaphor—the city (bride) awaiting the mayor (bridegroom)—an appropriate metaphor for Love. So, the civic drama closes, with a tight control of thematic development and significant links between the tableaux—a decided improvement over the 1617 show. But no dramatic tension exists, since the pageant starts with assumptions that had been dramatically realized in the more successful 1613 pageant. Middleton, however, seems content not to repeat the morality play structure of that show, relying instead on a much more conventional presentation.

Though Middleton becomes City Chronologer in 1620, John Squire wrote the Lord Mayor's Show; but in 1621, when the Drapers sought to honor Sir Edward Barkham, they selected Middleton to prepare the pageant, which he did with the assistance of Christmas and Munday again, the three of them receiving

£140 for their services (*MSC*, p. 101). Varying the title from the formula of his previous shows, Middleton names this one *The Sun in Aries*. The pattern of development resembles the 1619 entertainment, but with a bit more elaborate devices.

In Paul's Churchyard waits the Chariot of Honour with many worthies in it, such as Jason and Hercules. As a true son of honor, Jason speaks; and the sea metaphor governs much of his speech as he observes that the mayor has set sail for a year's voyage bound for justice, "A coast that's not by every compass found ..." (VII, 340). On the basis of his own experience Jason can with authority say:

There is no voyage set forth to renown,
That does not sometimes meet with skies that frown,
With gusts of envy, billows of despite,
Which makes the purchase, once achiev'd, more bright.
State is a sea; he must be wise indeed
That sounds its depth, or can the quicksands heed.... (pp. 340-341)

Just as Jason received assistance from his fellow argonauts, so can the mayor of his "worthy brethren, some of which have past / All dangerous gulfs, and in their bright fames plac'd, / They can instruct and guide thee ..." (p. 341). Having drawn an example from the mythical past—Orpheus—in the 1619 show, Middleton now brings forth Jason, urging the mayor to imitate his courage as he embarks on the year of service.

Further on, a Tower of Virtue, "which for the strength, safety, and perpetuity, bears the name of the Brazen Tower" (p. 341), awaits the mayor in all its gilded splendor. Fame, Antiquity, and six knights serving as Virtue's standard-bearers occupy the device. From the tower Fame "properly adorned" greets the mayor, welcoming him to Virtue's fortress that celebrates its brightness as a discerner of Truth. The six warders, Providence, Watchfulness, Wisdom, Constancy, Zeal, and Care, "keep the watch-tower sure, / That nothing enters but what's just and pure ..." (p. 343). The pageant honors the example of Fitz-Alwin as a servant of Truth and Justice. But along the path of the processional rests "one in a cloudy ruinous habit, leaning upon the turret, at a trumpet's sounding suddenly starts and wakes, and, in amazement, throws off his unseemly garments" (pp. 344-5). Transformed by the appearance of the noble guests, this anonymous figure emerges from "ruin's womb." Round about this character sit "figures of illustrious princes crown'd"—two Henries, Edward, Mary, Elizabeth, and James (p. 345). This quasi-"resurrection" may recall a similar event in Munday's 1611 and 1616 pageants, and also it suggests the light of Truth changing that which is dark, a recurring image in Middleton's pageants. A speaker challenges the mayor to preserve the city's peace begun by Henry VII and increased by all to James—"from Henry that join'd Roses, / To James that unites king-

doms, who encloses / All in the arms of love, malic'd of none ..." (p. 346). The
celebration of the Tudors and James recalls Munday's 1605 pageant, which so
clearly honored the new king as well as the mayor.

The light imagery continues in the next device, a mountain "artfully raised
and replenished with fine wooly creatures; Phoebus on the top, shining in a full
glory, being circled with the Twelve Celestial Signs" (p. 346). The speaker Aries
notes that Phoebus' rays "cheer and ... illumine good men's ways"; and those
who have dared to behold his globe have departed "tried all like gold ..." (p.
347). Light refines men, and only those who do "deeds of night" flee the sunbeams. This mountain, Aries suggests, may be viewed as resembling "magistracy's seat and grace; / The Sun the magistrate himself implies," and the sheep,
the flock of citizens (p. 347). The mayor's duty becomes to "cheer oppressed
right with looks of love," just as the sun spreads its light and gladness "over the
drooping creatures...."

That night at his gate the mayor encounters again the Brazen Tower and in
addition the "triple-crowned Fountain of Justice," supported by the virtues that
assist the mayor in discharging his office—Justice, Sincerity, Meekness, Wisdom,
Providence, Equality, Industry, Truth, Peace, Patience, Hope, Harmony, "all illustrated by proper emblems and expressions ..." (p. 348). For example, Wisdom
has a serpent, Meekness a dove, Hope a silvered anchor, and Truth a "fan of
stars, with which she chases away Error"—part of her equipment in the 1613
show as well. Fame delivers the closing speech from the Brazen Tower, noting the
Fountain and its meaning:

Behold yon Fountain with the tripled crown,
And through a cloud the sunbeam piercing down;
So is the worthy magistrate made up;
The triple crown is Charity, Faith, and Hope,
Those three celestial sisters; the cloud too,
That's Care, and yet you see the beam strikes through;
A care discharg'd with honour it presages
And may it so continue to all ages. (p. 349)

The pageant which began with the "secular" example of Jason moves quickly in
its dramatic development to the moral and spiritual examples of the virtues that
light man's path and specifically support the government. Virtue can penetrate
the darkness of care, as it does in one tangible example in the pageant, and bring
about transformation, all dramatically anticipated in the 1613 Lord Mayor's
Show.

For the third time the Grocers sought the services of Middleton, and he
wrote *The Triumphs of Honour and Virtue* (1622) to celebrate the inauguration of
Sir Peter Proby. Middleton and Christmas again collaborated on the show, the

two of them receiving £220 for their various wide-ranging services (*MSC*, p. 104). But the pageant itself comes across as more a pastiche of former shows than anything strikingly original.

As in his two earlier shows for the Grocers, Middleton includes an allusion to the trade of the company in foreign lands; thus the first device Middleton calls the "Continent of India, a triumph replenished with all manner of spice-plants and trees bearing odour ..." (VII, 358). A black person representing India and called the Queen of Merchandise occupies the most eminent seat, attended by other Indians and three men who are dressed like merchants. Above the trees appears a sun "in brightest splendour and glory." This light contrasts with the black queen; and her speech, resembling the one made by the King of Moors in the 1613 pageant, picks up this imagery. She claims: "I'm beauteous in my blackness," for "living waters" brought by the English merchants now flow through her (p. 358). She has found the "savour of eternal life, sweet Truth, / Exceeding all the odoriferous scent, / That from the beds of spices ever went ..." (p. 359). Possessing considerable wealth, she has come to know that "All wealth consists in Christian holiness," the knowledge of which has come through English merchants who first enlightened her. The sun that shines over this device may be regarded as the Sun of Justice that drives away the mists that would interfere with its power. Just as the light of Truth has come to this Queen, so the sun of Justice comes to cheer the land.

Near the Little Conduit in Cheap the Chariot of Fame awaits the mayor; and Antiquity, "a grave and reverend personage with a golden register-book in his hand," speaks (p. 360). The lengthy speech recalls "things sprung from Truth," mainly noble persons worthy of remembrance in the book of fame. Building upon this speech, the next device, the Throne of Virtue, illustrates the virtues of the worthies. Beneath Antiquity sits Authority, "placed between Wisdom and Innocence, holding a naked sword, a serpent wound about the blade thereof, two doves standing upon the crossbar of the hilt, and two hands meeting at the pummel, intimating Mercy and Justice ..." (p. 363). Magistracy, also present, holds in his hand a golden key, "signifying both the key of Knowledge and of Confidence...." When the mayor moves to this Throne, its chief deity, Virtue, addresses him, pleased that Power has come to Virtue, for she has the ability to raise Power; those who think otherwise build "the empire of their hopes on sand" (p. 364). Virtue chooses to yield to the one who seeks her,

> nor does it wrong
> Great Power to come to Virtue to be strong,
> Being but a woman, merciful and mild:
> Therein is Heaven with greater glory stiled
> That makes weak things, as Clemency and Right,
> Sway Power, which would else rule all by Might. (p. 364)

When Power and Virtue join, then the city benefits and the magistrate is complete.

That night the Throne of Virtue has with it the Globe of Honour, a rather spectacular machine which suddenly opens and flies into eight parts revealing eight persons "most gloriously decked, representing (as it were) the inward man, the intentions of a virtuous and worthy breast by the graces of the mind and soul, such as Clear Conscience, Divine Speculation, Peace of Heart, Integrity, Watchfulness, Equality, Providence, Impartiality, each exprest by its proper illustration" (p. 365). Mists hover near the Globe showing that the "brightest day has its overcastings," and "worldly mists oftentimes interpose the clearest cogitations, and yet that but for a season ..." (p. 365). About the four corners reside the Cardinal Virtues, Wisdom, Justice, Fortitude, and Temperance. From this *"unparalleled masterpiece of invention and art"* Honour speaks, congratulating the mayor that he has taken the right path, having come by Virtue. He bids him behold this Globe, which, when closed, represents the world with its "Adventures, dangers, cares, and steepy ways ..." (p. 366). All of which cause man to mount to "heavenly cogitations"; the eight parts can be found by the wise who open their hearts to these "eight beatitudes." Honour stands atop the Globe with his foot fixed "on this orbicular ball, / Over the world expressing my command ..." (p. 367). The pageant has clear allegorical implications: conveyed by Virtue, the mayor may be exalted to the position of Honour, embracing the eight virtues of the "inward man." In this sense the pageant moves the mayor thematically from worthy examples of the past to the position of achieving a victory over the world.

In a final collaborative effort, Munday and Middleton prepared the Lord Mayor's Show of 1623, designed to honor Martin Lumley, Draper. Munday's part comprised the water entertainment which he called *Triumphes of the Golden Fleece* (discussed in Chapter Five) that included Jason, Medea, and the Argonauts on the Thames. The land entertainment, printed in a separate text, Middleton entitled *The Triumphs of Integrity*. The artificer Christmas again assisted Middleton, and together they received £150 for their work (*MSC*, p. 105). Payments also include one for Munday, as well as an additional £3 paid to Middleton "for the making of a Breakfast and fyer for the Children of the Pageants" (*MSC*, p. 106). Total cost for this civic drama exceeded £707. Such expense and preparation did not, however, rescue the show from the sameness of pattern to which Middleton had fallen victim.

Waiting for the mayor in Paul's Churchyard, the device called the Mount Royal contains "certain kings and great commanders, which ancient history produces, that were originally sprung from shepherds and humble beginnings ..." (VII, 386). The speaker observes that on this Mount one can "find fair Virtue, and her name, / From low, obscure beginnings, rais'd to fame, / Like light struck out of darkness ..." (p. 387). And the speaker reminds us of a truth recounted time and again in morality drama: "... 'tis virtuous strife / That makes the complete Christian, not high place, / As true submission is the state of grace: / The path to bliss lies in the humblest field ..." (p. 387). From the hands of Virtue these shepherds have risen to exalted positions. Though not a shepherd, the mayor has likewise become lifted up, presumably by his own virtuous qualities.

Building upon this reflection into the past, the device in Cheapside offers a chariot called "Sacred Memory," which contains "the register of all heroic acts and worthy men" associated with the guild. Under allegorical figures sit the representations of famous men, such as Fitz-Alwin who sits "figured under the person of Government; John Norman under the person of Honour; Francis Drake, Victory; Simon Eyre, Charity; Richard Champion and John Milborne, Bounty; Richard Hardell and John Poultney, Justice and Piety." From the chariot Memory speaks, enunciating the common denominator of those men represented here: they all bent their powers to goodness. Many try to erect great buildings in order to raise their names, but these "more truly wise built up their fames, / Erected fair examples, large and high, / Patterns for us to build our honours by ..." (p. 390). The example of Fitz-Alwin gets special praise, for he understood that one must lay up treasures in heaven, not on earth. Those qualities that define a magistrate Memory outlines: a fair, noble soul, wisdom, care, and "upright justness to the oath ..." (p. 391). Such a person gladly goes into the palace of Sacred Memory.

The next device, called the Crystal Sanctuary, contains the Temple of Integrity "where her immaculate self, with all her glorious and sanctimonious concomitants, sit, transparently seen through the crystal ..." (p. 391). This temple also opens at "fit and convenient times"; it has columns of gold and battlements of silver. The wholeness and clearness of Integrity constitute the theme of the speech from this crystal sanctuary. Integrity points out to the mayor: "'Tis all transparent what I think or do, / And with one look your eye may pierce me through; / There's no disguise or hypocritic veil ..." (p. 392). Having no conflict between appearance and reality, Integrity claims that she is "One that is ever what she seems to be...." She warns the mayor that his acts will be open to public scrutiny; therefore, he should be translucent "and leave worthy tracts / For future times to find, thy very breast / Transparent, like this place wherein I rest" (p. 392).

As a final tableau Middleton presents the "thrice-royal Canopy of State, ... the Imperial Crowns cast into the form and bigness of a triumphal pageant, with cloud and sunbeams" which spread like a canopy over the "deified persons" under it (p. 393). These divine persons represent the Eight Beatitudes, which may recall the appearance in the initial civic pageant of Elizabeth's reign of these same Beatitudes, thus underscoring a basic continuity in civic drama though sixty-four years separate these events. To enhance the device further Middleton includes the king's motto, *Beati pacifici*, set in "fair great letters near the uppermost of the three crowns ..." (p. 394). The speaker assures the mayor that these blessings that the kingdom enjoys come as a result of the efforts of "that royal peace-maker our king ..." (p. 394). Interpreting the static tableau, the speaker suggests that the three crowns may represent the celestial graces, Faith, Hope, Charity. Or they may signify "those three kingdoms, sway'd by the meek hand / Of blest James, England, Scotland, Ireland ..." (p. 395). Invoking a familiar image, the speaker says that the cloud that swells beneath the crowns may imply "Some envious mist cast forth by heresy, / Which, through his happy reign and heaven's blest will, / The sunbeams of the Gospel strikes through still ..." (p. 395). The light of Truth keeps conquering Error's darkness, though a decade removed from the 1613 pageant that dramatically gave us the image. By the Beatitudes we should understand "The fulness of all blessings to this land, / More chiefly to this city...." Clearly the mayor ought to imitate the example of the peace-loving king and see that these blessings continue to pervade the land, no matter the occasional clouds of evil. Thus from the beginning of the pageant various historical persons help illustrate the path the mayor should follow: the path to salvation—true submission forged out of a virtuous strife, a just soul, transparency, and after these things the function of a peace-maker. Thematically, we connect to the 1613 pageant, except there it had a dramatic life, not simply static visual and verbal statement.

The mayoral pageantry of the Jacobean period closes with Webster's 1624 show, there being no entertainment in 1625. Opening the Caroline period, Middleton's *The Triumphs of Health and Prosperity* (1626) seeks to celebrate the inauguration of Cuthbert Hacket, Draper. Because of "the ill performance" of the pageant, the guild delayed payment to Middleton and Christmas (*MSC*, p. 110). A later account in the company records shows a payment of £125 to the two men "for makinge and setting out of the Pageantes and Shewes ..." (*MSC*, p. 110). The amount of the payment seems a bit low in comparison to other pageants, but it is diffcult to tell exactly what the dramatist and artificer got beyond their expenses. The overall level of expenditure for this entertainment shows total costs of slightly over £545.

The first device that greets the mayor on land Middleton calls the Beautiful Hill or Fragrant Garden, structured on a platform shaped like a hill, adorned with all kinds of flowers and sheep grazing nearby—reminiscent of a similar device in Middleton's 1621 show. On the top of the mount appears an "artificial and curious rainbow, which both shows the antiquity of colours, the diversity and nobleness, and how much the more glorious and highly to be esteemed, they being presented in that blessed covenant of mercy, the bow in the clouds ..." (VII, 404). By this garden Middleton means to symbolize London, "the flowers intimating the sweet odours of their virtue and goodnesses, and the fruits of their works of justice and charity, which have been both honourable brothers and bounteous benefactors of this ancient fraternity ..." (p. 404). The sheep, of course, allude to the Drapers. The anonymous speaker refers to the recent eclipse—the plague—which produced showers of tears in the garden. But mercy, symbolized in the rainbow, followed the darkness; and now all flourishes: "The garden springs again; ... / ... barns crack with store ..." (p. 405). Echoing words of the earlier 1619 pageant, the speaker asks what's required of the mayor: "That which in conscience ought to be desir'd; / Care and uprightness in the magistrate's place, / And in all men obedience, truth, and grace" (p. 405).

The Sanctuary of Prosperity, the second device, has hanging on its top arch the Golden Fleece that prompts the memory of Sir Francis Drake, "who never returned to his country without the golden fleece of honour and victory ..." (p. 406). The four columns suggest the Cardinal Virtues, "the especial upholders of kingdoms, cities, and honourable societies." The speaker makes the connection between the dauntless courage of Jason and the accomplishments of Drake, "England's true Jason, who did boldly make / So many rare adventures, which were held / For worth unmatch'd, danger unparallel'd ..." (p. 406). Just as Jason and Drake became successful sailors, the speaker reminds the mayor that he sets out on a year's voyage and warns him: "Nor on these seas are there less dangers found / Than those on which the bold adventurer's bound; / For rocks, gulfs, quicksands, here is malice, spite, / Envy, detraction of all noble right ..." (pp. 406-7). But by the "compass of a virtuous name" he may safely gain the shore. From Dekker's 1612 pageant onward the sea metaphor becomes a favorite with the pageant-dramatists as a means of expressing and anticipating the conflicts that the mayor will face. Always, a concomitant assurance of victory occurs so long as the mayor remains virtue's man.

Passing from this tableau, the mayor encounters the Chariot of Honour—"On the most eminent seat thereof is government illustrated ..." (p. 407). Repeating the technique of the 1623 show and the device of Sacred Memory, Middleton here associates several former mayors with allegorical virtues: Government connects with Fitz-Alwin; John Norman, with Munificence; Simon Eyre, Piety. Upon the lions that draw the chariot two figures present Power and Honour. The memory of the previous mayor gets recalled because of his good qualities and also because there had been no entertainment to honor him, for "triumph was not then in season" because of the death of James I. In his speech Government likens the city to the heart of the country; the head being, of course, the sovereign, the eyes the "councillors of state," the lips, the clergy and judges, and the arms, the defensive part of men. Clearly the entertainment illustrates the city's "heart," the source of life; and this city "hath been / In former ages, as in these times, seen / The fountain of affection, duty, zeal, / And taught all the cities through the commonweal ..." (p. 409). The speech gains strength by the representation of former mayors, excellent examples of the "heart" in operation.

A Fountain of Virtue joins the Fragrant Garden to bid farewell to the mayor. The speaker interprets the presence of the garden:

Mercy's fair object, the celestial bow,

As in the morning it began to show,
It closes up this great triumphal day,
And by example shows the year the way,
Which if power worthily and rightly spend,
It must with mercy both begin and end. (p. 410)

The year ahead offers various challenges and opportunities including time "To treasure up good actions fit for heaven." The various elements of the pageant evoke the theme of the renewal of the city as it recovers from previous trials, with the unmistakable implication that the mayor must continue this process of renewal, mercy being skilfully applied to secure the healing grace of this city. In a sense, two processes of salvation occur, one collective and one personal; i.e., one for the city and the other for the mayor. The rainbow symbolically links the two in hope, and the historical examples point the way to victory over adversity. Together the mayor and the city may continue to bring home the Golden Fleece, no matter the dangers.

While most of Middleton's Lord Mayors' Shows must be judged as thoroughly adequate, competent examples of such civic drama, they fail to exploit the theatrically exciting pattern of the 1613 pageant with its dialogue, dramatic conflict, vivid and consistent imagery, thematic development, and integrated allegory. Instead, Middleton goes the way of Dekker, lapsing back into what become veritable formulas for arranging a Lord Mayor's Show. Even his morality structure of the 1613 entertainment seems in all probability an adaptation of Dekker's 1612 effort. He may ring all sorts of changes on what particular virtue triumphs in a given year, but the structure remains nearly always the same. An inveterate pageant-goer might have justifiably felt that he had seen all this somewhere before. Fortunately, the 1613 pageant looms large in our memories when the others begin to fade into an undistinguishable whole.

Though Middleton makes no startling innovations in form, he does make a worthy contribution to the development of the Jacobean show. No other pageant-dramatist so consistently follows through on a pattern of imagery as Middleton; time and again, without being obtrusive, he presents both visually and verbally the conflict between light and darkness, a tension of symbolic import. This becomes his particular way of symbolizing the struggle for the victory of Truth and Virtue over men and nations. Indeed, we could view his whole pageant output as a vast morality play, thematically considered at least. A person comes up against the forces of Evil and Error, but Truth leads to the triumphant mount; and the path to salvation gains by encounters with Honour, Love, Fame, and Integrity—all confirming that the "salvation" will be manifest in good works as the individual creates harmony out of the wilderness or sails the rough seas of life. Even Jason, Orpheus, and Aries add their instructive parts to this thematic development. Like Milton, Middleton "cannot praise a fugitive and cloistered virtue unexercised and unbreathed, that never sallies out and sees her adversary." This viable moral theme pervades Middleton's civic pageants, though only once does it get fully realized dramatically. At other times we have to be satisfied with static tableaux which give testimony to the human battle; always Middleton's predilections and assumptions clearly put one on the comic path to salvation.

8 *John Squire, John Webster, John Taylor*

JOHN SQUIRE (1620) AND JOHN WEBSTER (1624) interrupted Middleton's monopoly on the Lord Mayor's Show of the closing years of the Jacobean period. And in the next decade John Taylor in 1634 broke the string of successive mayoral pageants written by Thomas Heywood, the subject of the next chapter. Of the known authors of Lord Mayors' Shows in the seventeenth century to the closing of the theaters these three men became the only dramatists to write only one pageant each. In a sense these three authors stand out for their non-involvement in civic drama since of the texts that survive Munday wrote seven and part of an eighth Lord Mayors' Shows, Dekker three, Middleton seven, and Heywood seven. With a discussion of the shows of Squire, Webster, and Taylor we complete the study of the Jacobean show and prepare the way for an analysis of Heywood's pageants.

I. JOHN SQUIRE

We know little of Squire other than his one excursion into civic pageantry in which he wrote *Tes Irenes Trophaea or The Tryumphs of Peace*, celebrating the inauguration of Sir Francis Jones, Haberdasher (1620). Some fourteen years later James Shirley explored a similar theme in his elaborate masque, *The Triumph of Peace* (1634), a court occasion rather than a civic spectacle. Records of the Haberdashers reveal that Squire and the artificer Francis Tipsley received £180 for their services out of a total expenditure of £750. 8s. 6d. (*MSC*, p. 100). Squire extols the craftsmanship of Tipsley at the close of the text of the pageant. The rather apparent influence of morality drama on Middleton's pageants does not seem obvious here, though Squire's entertainment contains the usual sort of moral instruction. *The Tryumphs of Peace* has essentially a dual structure with the first part taking place on the Thames dominated by mythological figures, and the second, on land, governed by allegorical characters. Also, as a corollary to this division, the pageant moves from simple entertainment (mythological part) to serious instruction (allegorical).

On a sea chariot drawn by sea horses rides Oceanus, a figure to be used by Webster in 1624 and by Dekker in the 1629 show, "his head wreath'd with segges, one hand grasping a *scepter* of green reeds, to shew his potent sway within his watery dominions; and the other curbing the forward fearcenesse of his *horses....*"[1] His hair and beard "hung like the careles emblem of a reverend age" over his body, itself covered with a mantle of sea green taffeta, "lymd with waves and fishes" (sig. A3ᵛ). Following Oceanus, a ship carried Aeolus, god of the winds, who filled "their sailes with prosperous *gusts*"; at each corner sat figures representing the four parts of the world: America, Africa, Asia, and Europe, "each of them inviting their trade unto their coasts." Asia appeared dressed in a habit of peach colored satin, a coronet on her head, and a censer in her hand; Africa, "*a blackmoore* in a naked *shape*, adorned with *beads*, and in her hand the branch of a *Nut-megg-tree*"; America, as a "tawny Moore," wearing a crown of feathers, carrying a bow and arrows; Europe, in a robe of crimson taffeta, "on her head an imperiall crowne conferred on her by the other three as *Empresse* of the *earth*, and holding in her hand a cluster of grapes, to signifie her full swolne plenty" (sig. A3ᵛ). Though this costuming may have been original with Squire, a masque written by Thomas Campion presented at the marriage of the Earl of Somerset and Lady Frances Howard in 1613 had contained very similar figures as shown in Campion's description: "*Europe* in the habit of an Empresse, with an Emperiall Crowne on her head. *Asia* in a Persian Ladies habit, with a Crowne on her head. *Africa* like a Queene of the Moores, with a crown. *America* in a skin coate of the colour of the juyce of Mulberies, on her head laye round brims of many coloured feathers, and in the midst of it a small crowne...."[2] Rather than indebtedness, this example may illustrate again the interconnections of the several dramatic forms, especially regarding iconographical representation.

In his speech to the mayor Oceanus reminds us of his vast power, and he comes as a representative of the "watery deities" to add honor to this occasion. He says: "*And now with a desire that outstrips* / Imagination, *I am come to see,* / *And wonder at the* state *which I now find* ..." (sig. A4). So long as the moon determines the tides and the shipman "*throwes to heaven his boone* / *For safe returne*," Oceanus shall attend these ships to their coasts. Similarly, Aeolus promises to unite the seas and winds and send home the ships "*and take delight* / *To play with gentle murmures on your sailes*" (sig. A4ᵛ). Though these figures offer welcome and protection to the mayor, they might in the hands of Munday, Dekker, or Middleton, have had an explicitly moral instructional role, or at least found the occasion for a metaphor linking the sea to the mayor's tenure of office. But Squire had no such purpose.

The second device on the river presents Mount Parnassus with Apollo and the Muses, a tableau used in the royal entry in Antwerp in 1582 as well. Squire carefully assigns to each of the Muses an appropriate property; for example, Clio has books with her, Euterpe plays on a flute recorder, Terpsichore on a lute, Ura-

---

[1]*Tryumphs of Peace* (London, 1620), sig. A3. All quotations will be from this seventeenth-century edition. Reprint in Nichols, *Progresses of King James*, IV, 619f.
[2]Percival Vivian, ed., *Campion's Works* (Oxford, 1909), p. 152.

nia wears a robe decked with stars. Apollo, who sits on top of the mount "in a robe of cloth of gold, under a laurell tree" plays on a harp (sig. B1). As a fitting companion to this gathering, Mercury, familiar to us in several civic entertainments, such as the Norwich pageant of 1578, stands on the backside of the mount "listning to their harmonious straines" (sig. B1). When the mayor returns to land, Euterpe and Terpsichore meet him in Paul's Churchyard with a pleasant song, recalling songs from some of the progress entertainments:

We Muses of the pleasant hill,
That bath within the Thespian spring,
That did direct the Grecians quill,
Who of olde *Pelius* sonne did sing.
We that *Amphion* did inspire,
With admired straines and layes,
And did infuse a sacred fire,
In both these to gaine the Bayes.
We *Appolloes* hand-mayds nine,
Come to meet thee on the way,
that unto thy honours shrine,
Wee might dedicate this day. (sigs. B1ᵛ-B2)

Simple, innocent praise to the mayor as these harmonious forces come to bless this day. Interestingly, the text includes the musical notation, a most unusual occurrence in a pageant text.

The first tableau on land consists of a structure that forms an Egyptian pyramid where in a drawing appear the shires of England; "on the top sat a princely *Majesty* acootered in a robe of purple velvet furred with *Ermines*, on his head hee wore an Imperiall Crowne, and in his right hand a *scepter* ..." (sig. B2ᵛ). Lying at his feet, a "*Lyon* couchant ... did demonstrate his power in reconciling fearcenesse unto a willing servitude...." Figures representing Dukes, Earls, Barons, Marquises, dressed in Parliament robes, sit under Majesty. Streamers include arms of the four kingdoms; before the device written on a scroll the motto *Respublica Beata*, "and round about it ran the *Ocean*." The tableau parallels in several respects Majesty's island in Munday's 1609 Lord Mayor's Show. Seeming to support the pyramid in Squire's device appear City in a scarlet gown, holding two golden keys, Country in rustic habit, Law habited like a judge, Religion attired like a Bishop carrying a book in his hand. The allegorical representation of the virtues or qualities that support and sustain a kingdom dates back at least to the initial civic pageant of Elizabeth's reign.

The next scene primarily honors the company, for it presents the patron saint of the guild, Catherine of Alexandria, the first time since the early Elizabethan Lord Mayors' Shows that a pageant represented the patron saint of the

company, but Heywood in the 1630s will also include this Catherine in his
shows. On the top of a mount under a canopy lined with stars Squire gives us
Catherine dressed in a snow white gown, holding in one hand a book, in the
other a sword pointing downward, "it being the instrument that in death sealed
her the fruition of immortall rest; her head circuled with a crowne of *gold*, which
did intimate her *princely* descent; and at her feete lay a broken *wheele* ..." (sig.
B3). These details correspond with her frequent portrayal in Renaissance art.
Further, she has attending her twelve maids each bearing a shield "upon which
were portrayed *Catherin Wheeles*, and within them the *Motto* to the *Companies
armes, Serve and obay*" (sig. B3). Completing the tableau, servants busily work
with wool, and a shepherd keeps his sheep behind the mount. Having shown the
qualities that support Majesty, Squire depicts the source of mystical support for
the guild.

At the upper conduit in Cheapside a chariot, "painted full with *houre-glasses*,
and *sun-dialls*, the fore-wheeles were two *Globes*, and the hinder wheeles were
like two Church *dialls* ..." (sig. B3ᵛ), greets the mayor. Seated upon an hourglass,
Time holds a sickle and a crutch; a giant representing the Iron Age supports the
hourglass. This chariot bears a striking resemblance to the one that conveyed
Time in Munday's 1615 pageant, even to the point that both contain the four
Elements whose costume Squire describes. For example, the robe of Fire is flame-
colored, Air's lined with clouds and shapes of birds, Water's with waves and fish,
and Earth's with grass and flowers. Also emblematically costumed, the Seasons
draw the chariot, moving Time along. Time speaks, showing the spacious world
the age he bears. He has descended from "*mans first dayes the age of gold*"
through the silver and bronze ages to the present Iron Age, "*this last prop of the
world that doth sustaine, / My ponderous glasse and me* ..." (sig. B4). A similar
theme, the movement of the world to the Iron Age, occurs in Munday's *Sidero-
thriambos* (1618), and of course forms the subject of Heywood's plays on the ages
of the world. Time comes in this triumphant chariot to show the love he bears to
the mayor and the guild. And he promises—

> ... *if that with* honor'd *care,*
> *Thou execute thy charge, then shall thy urne,*
> *Be reverenced, and thither shall repaire,*
> *A blessed* memory *that never dies*.... (sig. B4)

Time promises immortality in a vein similar to the song in Dekker's 1612 pageant or the speech of Truth in Middleton's 1613 show. But it always rests upon
the mayor's faithful and virtuous execution of his duties. How closely also Shakespeare links the theme of Time and the granting of immortality in his sonnets.

The thematic center of this mayoral show comes in the tableau that greets
the mayor further along his route to St. Paul's, in succinct form the allegory of

the triumph of peace. Under a pyramid sat "sacred *Peace*"; "on her head she wore a wreath of olives, in her right hand a palme, her robe was of white taffaty, limm'd with the mappe of *England* ..." (sig. B4ᵛ). On her lap rests a model of London and on her shield the arms of the Haberdashers. At her feet "lay warre in compleat armes upon Speares, Launces, foulded ensignes; and leaning on *an Unbrac't drum*...." The visual spectacle of war lying at the feet of Peace recalls Jonson's arch at the Temple Bar in the 1604 royal entry. Here Peace dominates, and Mars lay at her feet "groveling," with the implements of war shattered. The dependence on allegorical tableaux in both the royal entry and mayoral pageant forms ensures some similar presentations, especially when dramatists attempt to express the same theme.

Speaking to the mayor and the audience, Peace explains her background:

> *I am* Peace
> *That my long* Pilgrimage *did never cease,*
> *From the first minute of the aged* World,
> *Untill I found this* Iland; *for being hurld*
> *Out of each region by rebellious* War,
> *(Which now lies bound my* Vassall*) like a* star,
> *Whose unfixt glory glides from spheare, to spheare,*
> *I wandred up and downe....* (sig. B4ᵛ)

Peace pleaded to be recalled from earth, but finally she found England whose people embraced her, "*And* Joyntly *all of them delivered* War, / *Fetterd in chaines to be my* prisoner ..." (sig. C1). Because Peace dwells in the land and in the city by divine decree, the challenge comes to the mayor: "*then have a care,* / *To see me safely kept....*" He should use his will to guarantee the survival of Peace in the commonwealth. As she has triumphed in the past, Peace should continue to prevail; such becomes the thematic imperative of the pageant.

At the mayor's house that evening the theme of peace echoes again as a vigorous but submissive War addresses the mayor. He recounts in vivid detail how he has, mounted on the back of horror and bathed in blood, driven Peace from many lands. For example, he taught the Romans "*to immortallize,* / *Their names by their great acts, and to refine,* / *Their meane creation by the sacrifize,* / *Of their owne blood to* Warre *and to my shrine* ..." (sig. C1ᵛ). But once-powerful War yields to sacred Peace and to the mayor, now admitted to his office by Time. Ready to aid the cause of Peace with his might, War tells the mayor "*that if times should cease,* / *To be unto this land as now they are,* / Warre *might restore againe the Palme to* Peace" (sig. C1ᵛ). The veracity of this pledge becomes symbolically assured when after the speech Peace conducts the Lord Mayor into his house, "*and* Warre *stood with fire and sword to defend his gates*" (sig. C2).

Squire maintains good control of his diverse material, with meticulous attention to emblematic detail; he sustains a high level of interest throughout the show, including the imaginative theatrical touch at the end with Peace and War. The various parts of the pageant cohere nicely as we move from simple welcome of the mayor by the mythological characters to a more serious consideration of how the commonwealth (city) can survive. In retrospect, however, even the mythological figures sound a motif of peace as Oceanus and Aeolus promise a tranquil and safe voyage to the ships, and the lyric presence of Apollo and the Muses underscores the achievement of harmony, a type of reconciliation. Catherine, herself a victim of evil, offers a divine sanction to the cause of peace as she reminds the guild of their motto, serve and obey. Majesty can be said to dwell in a *respublica beata* only when Time brings to pass the victory of Peace over War. But when the mayor and citizens embrace Peace and imprison War, the land becomes secure—so will be their immortal fame, for those who cause lions and lambs to lie down together shall be remembered as the blessed peacemakers, the children of God.

II. JOHN WEBSTER

Best known to us for his two powerful tragedies, *The Duchess of Malfi* and *The White Devil*, John Webster nevertheless near the end of his dramatic career turned his efforts to civic pageantry, resulting in the Lord Mayor's Show of 1624, *Monuments of Honor*, designed to grace the installation of Sir John Gore, Merchant Taylor, the company of which Webster was himself a member. The account in the guild records indicates the arrangement made with Webster and others and also his duties:

> Item paid to John Webster the Poet and to John Terry Painter, Wm Patten and George Lovett for the device making painting and gilding all the land and water shewes Pageantes, Chariott, Greene men and theire fier workes Apparrell Porters to carry them, ... the some of Two hundred threescore and Tenn poundes.... (*MSC*, p. 107)

In spite of Dekker's comment in the 1612 pageant, porters obviously still transport some of the devices. Apparently satisfied with the production, the company awarded an additional ten pounds "by way of Gratuity," and the total cost of £1,099. 5s. 11d. places the show among the most costly of the Stuart period and indicates something of the opulence of the entertainment.

While the allegorical theme of peace provided the content for Squire's pageant and the theme of integrity dominated Middleton's 1623 show, Webster achieves thematic unity by exploring the problem of honor, how it has been accomplished. The main technique for revealing this theme centers on the use of historical persons who exemplify honor, and the pageant moves toward a culmination in the last device which represents honor at its apogee. Historical representations have become common in mayoral pageantry, especially with Munday, and Middleton's 1623 pageant gives an immediate foretaste of the way in which Webster will handle his material.

Riding in a barge on the river, the sea figures of Oceanus, Thetis, Thamesis, and Medway, recall the opening of Squire's show. In addition, another water device appears: "a faire Terrestiall Globe, Circled about, in convenient Seates, with seaven of our most famous Navigators: as, Sir *Francis Drake*, Sir *John Haukins*, Sir *Martine Furbisher*, Sir *Humfery Gilbert*, Captaine *Thomas Cavendish*, Captaine *Christopher Carlile*, and Captaine *John Davis*."[3] Explaining the conjunction of these two spectacles, Webster says: "that in regard the two Rivers pay due Tribut of waters to the Seas, *Oceanus* in gratefull recompence returnes the memory of these seaven worthy Captaines, who have made *England* so famous in remotest partes of the world" (p. 317). In welcoming the mayor, Thetis likens the city of London to Venice in terms of pageant entertainment, but Oceanus quickly responds that "Venice *had [ne'er] the like* ..." (p. 318). The city itself thus appears as a "monument of honor." As he interprets the water scene, Oceanus takes note of the navigators seated about the globe: "*So many worthies I could adde at Seas, / Of this bold Nation, it would envy strike, / Ith' rest ath' World, who cannot shew the like* ..." (p. 319). The path thus opens to a dramatic representation of honor, and the technique of achieving such resides in the show on the water.

Appropriately, the first device on land, located in St. Paul's Churchyard, Webster calls the Temple of Honour, "the Pillars of which are bound about with Roses, and other beautifull Flowers ..." (p. 319). Presiding over this Temple and occupying the most eminent position, *Troynovant* awaits "in rich Habilaments," and "beneath her, as admiring her peace and felicity" sit figures personating five important cities: Antwerp, Paris, Rome, Venice, and Constantinople. The verbal prominence of London enunciated by Oceanus on the river now gains concrete visual representation. And beneath these cities sit five famous scholars and poets: "Sir *Jeffery Chaucer*, the learned *Gower*, the excellent *John Lidgate*, the sharpe-witted Sir *Thomas Moore*, and last as worthy both Souldier and Scholler, Sir *Philip Sidney* ..." (p. 319). (One notes with interest Webster's selection, especially the absence of Shakespeare.) Of these poets Troynovant says: "*These beyond death a fame to Monarckes give, / And these make Cities and Societies live*" (p. 320). The presence of Troynovant in Webster's pageant may remind us of the full treatment of the Brutus story in Munday's *The Triumphs of Re-United Britannia* (1605), an entertainment that also honored a Merchant Taylor and that Webster

---

[3]*The Complete Works of John Webster*, ed. F. L. Lucas (London, 1927), III, 317. All quotations will be from this edition. Reprint in Sayle, p. 116f.

could easily have known. The inclusion of the poets is unique in civic pageantry and especially a figure from such recent past as Sidney, who addresses the mayor and reveals how the poets relate to the pursuit of honor: "*To Honour by our Wrightings Worthy men / Flowes as a duty from a judging pen, / And when we are emploid in such sweet praise, / Bees swarme and leave their honey on our bayes ...*" (p. 320). Thus the poets undergird the state by exalting the honorable achievements of her members, clearly also the aim of pageant-dramatists.

Before the mayor meets a chariot filled with kings who have been members of the guild, he encounters John Hawkwood, himself a former Merchant Taylor and valiant soldier during the reign of Edward III. Hawkwood speaks and observes that despite his low birth he achieved great eminence and brought credit to the company—another example of honor fulfilled. The Chariot of Kings, drawn by four horses, bears the arms of the guild: "colored and guilt in several places of it, and over it, there is supported for a Cannopy, a rich and very spatious Pavillion, coloured Crimson, with a Lyon Passant ..." (p. 321). Occupying the chariot sit the eight kings who have been free of the company: Edward III, Richard II, Henry IV, Henry V, Henry VI, Edward IV, Richard III (who Webster says was a bad man but a good king), and Henry VII. This device seems to look back to Munday's 1605 pageant which also had a chariot filled with kings connected with the guild, but there only seven kings—Richard III conspicuously absent. Webster has the chairs of the Lancastrian kings garnished with artificial red roses, the others with white, "but the Uniter of the devision and houses, *Henry* the Seaventh, both with White and Red, from whence his Royall Majesty now raigning tooke his *Motto* for one peice of his *Coyne, Henricus rosas regna Jacobus*" (p. 322). The figure of Edward III speaks and notes the honor that these kings have brought to the company; and he bids them: "*Let all good men this sentence oft repeate, / By unity the smallest things grow great*" (p. 322). To which all the kings respond as a single chorus: "*By unity the smallest things grow great.*" Webster adds: "And this repetition was proper, for it is the Companies Motto: *Concordia parvae res crescunt*" (p. 322).

Unifying the kingdom by Henry VII who ended the War of the Roses recalls a theme familiar in several civic pageants as well as in Shakespeare's history plays. Middleton and Dekker both allude to the theme, and Munday gives a rather full treatment in the 1605 pageant as he also portrays James in the role of unifier—the second Brute. In civic drama the theme of unity by the Tudors finds an early symbolic representation in Elizabeth's coronation royal entry in London in January 1559; there on a street corner the union appeared in a genealogical tree and got verbal expression by the child who addressed the queen. Such reconciling of disparate forces constitutes, of course, a notable "monument of honor," rightfully belonging in a pageant devoted to embodying the theme of honor.

After several figures and a lion and camel all alluding to the company, Webster presents one of the main devices called the *Monument of Charity and Learn-*

ing, fashioned "like a beautifull Garden with all kind of flowers, at the foure Corners foure artificiall Bird Cages, with variety of Birds in them: this for the beauty of the Flowers, and melody of the Birds, to represent a Spring in Winter ..." (p. 323). Such an ideal setting, a microcosmic garden, forms the natural place for the exaltation of Charity and Learning. Under an elm tree in this device sits a figure representing Sir Thomas White, a former mayor and Merchant Taylor who built the college of St. John the Baptist at Oxford. Webster gives considerable detail, not altogether accurate, of how White came to select the precise spot for the college. On one hand of White "sits *Charity* with a Pellican on her head, on the other *Learning* with a booke in one hand, and a Lawrel Wreath in the other ..." (p. 324). Behind these allegorical figures twelve additional personages represent some twenty-four cities to which White had been benefactor and a model of the college. Both of the allegorical figures have of course been presented in the expected emblematic detail, common to several other pageants; Learning speaks and interprets the tableau, thus fulfilling the function of the verses of the typical emblem. Of Sir Thomas White Learning says:

> ... *Truth can testife*
> *His merrit, whilst his Faith and Charity*
> *Was the true compasse, measur'd every part,*
> *And tooke the latitude of his Christian heart; ...*
> *And may the Impression of this figure strike*
> *Each worthy Senator to do the like!* (p. 325)

This historical figure thus offers a worthy precedent for all to follow as Charity and Learning help govern his actions.

To the memory of another historical personage, the late Prince Henry, the final device, the *Monument of Gratitude*, refers, forming the pageant's most elaborate tableau. We recall that Dekker's 1612 show had preserved a special room in the House of Fame for the prince whose actual presence had been anticipated. In Webster's device four pyramids stand upon an artificial rock with all sorts of precious stones suggesting "the riches of the Kingdome Prince *Henry* was borne Heire to," and the pyramids, as monuments for the dead, "that hee is deceased ..." (p. 325). Surmounting this "rests halfe a Celestiall Globe, in the middest of this hangs the Holy Lambe in the Sun-beames, on either side of these, an Angell; upon a pedestall of gold stands the figure of Prince *Henry*...." Clearly the visual arrangement dramatizes Henry's prominence not only in this tableau but for the whole entertainment. Several allegorical personifications of his virtues surround the prince. Magistracy, for example, tending a bee hive, represents his gravity in youth; Liberality with a dromedary shows his speed in gratifying his followers; Navigation demonstrates his interest in ships; Unanimity, who carries both a group of lilies and a sheaf of arrows, suggests that the prince loved both the nobility and the commonalty "with an intire heart." With their emblematic signs, Industry, Chastity, Justice, and Obedience illustrate other qualities. Also appear Peace "sleeping upon a Canon, alluding to the eternall Peace he now possesses," and Fortitude, with a "Pillar in one hand, a Serpent wreath'd about the other, to [express] his height of minde, and the expectation of an undaunted resolution" (p. 326).

Bringing the various elements of the tableau together, a figure named Amade le Graunde notes that they salute Prince Henry, "*fames best president, / Cald to a higher Court of Parliament, / In his full strength of Youth and height of blood.*" Understandably the pageant celebrates Henry because of his link with the Merchant Taylors, but more important because of the qualities he embodies. Thus le Graunde can say:

> *Such was this Prince, such are the noble hearts,*
> *Who when they dye, yet dye not in all parts:*
> *But from the* Integrety *of a Brave mind,*
> *Leave a most Cleere and Eminent Fame behind.* (p. 327)

The memory of the prince transcends his death; his example waits to be imitated by those who would also leave behind a monument of honor.

This apotheosis of Henry some twelve years after his death demonstrates something of the popularity and adulation he enjoyed and forms part of the elegiac outpouring that followed his untimely death. In 1613 Webster had contributed a funeral elegy, called *A Monumental Columne.* The poem opens:

> The greatest of the Kingly Race is gone,
> Yet with so great a reputation,
> Layd in the earth, we cannot say hee's dead,
> But as a perfect Diamond set in lead,
> (Scorning our foyle) his glories do breake forth,
> Worne by his Maker, who best knew his worth.... (p. 275)

And of course those glories break forth in the Lord Mayor's Show of 1624. Elsewhere in the elegy Webster says that "Fames lips shall bleed, yet nere her trumpet fill / With breath enough" to celebrate the prince's virtues fully (p. 281). Throughout the poem Webster refers to Henry's virtuous traits, claiming, "He well became those vertues which grac'd him" (p. 276). Indeed this statement would be a fitting summary or motto for the portrayal of the prince in the pageant, as if Webster has sought to give dramatic life in a symbolic tableau to the sentiments of the poem. Even the image of the diamond gets concrete realization in the precious stones adorning the rock of the tableau. The civic drama tangibly manifests the monumental column of honor erected in the prince's memory.

Implied moral instruction exists in Webster's pageant, but the more overt indebtedness to morality drama as in Middleton's shows does not. Webster has a different approach and reveals considerable imagination in its conception. He seizes upon the theme of honor to which all the elements of the pageant cohere. Though for a Falstaff honor may be but a word, a mere scutcheon, for Webster it forms the culmination of man's historic achievements and thus becomes the informing principle for the pageant. A straight-line development occurs leading to the final tableau that epitomizes all that Webster wishes to say on the subject. Oceanus points to honor by the examples of the courageous and famous sailors; the poets sing the praises of honor; the achievement of unity also leads to a path to honor as the kings illustrate; surrounding oneself with Charity and Learning creates a certain way to achieve honor as exemplified in Sir Thomas White. All of which serve to bring us to the thematic high-point: the portrayal of Prince Henry in whose person reside the attributes that assure honor. The path away from the prince becomes one of imitation for those who would appropriate his virtues, this best precedent of Fame.

III. JOHN TAYLOR

A decade after Webster's show John Taylor, the Water Poet, also addressed himself to the issue of honor in his 1634 Lord Mayor's Show, *The Triumphs of Fame and Honour*, designed for the inauguration of Sir Robert Parkhurst, Clothworker. In the text of his pageant Taylor explains something of the division of labor between himself and Norman: "... onely the Speeches, and illustrations which are here printed I doe justly challenge as mine owne, all the rest of the Composures and Fabricks were formed and framed by the ingenious and industrious M'r *Robert Norman* Citizen and Painter of London, who was indeed the prime inventor prosecuter and finisher of these works...."[4] Obviously the artificer has achieved new levels of responsibility by the 1630s (a subject to be discussed more fully in Chapter Ten). The evidence, however, does not lead necessarily to Williams' conclusion "that Norman rather than Taylor was responsible for the ideas expressed in the show."[5] Taylor's own testimony lays claim to more than that.

If we compare Taylor to Squire and Webster, then his Lord Mayor's Show more nearly resembles Squire's, making use primarily of allegorical figures to elucidate the pursuit of fame and honor. Webster's reliance on historical examples does not operate here. But like both Squire and Webster, Taylor opens his

---

[4]John Taylor, *The Triumphs of Fame and Honour* (London, 1634), sig. B4. All quotations are from this text.
[5]Sheila Williams, "A Lord Mayor's Show by John Taylor, the Water Poet," *Bulletin of the John Rylands Library* 41 (1959): 508.

entertainment with mythological sea figures who attend the mayor on the river. Thetis, whom Webster had also used, and Thames greet the mayor in a boat, Thetis "being habilimented in a mantle of sea-Greene, with a corronet of shels of divers sorts of sea-fish on her head with a great whelk-fish in her hand with adornments of strange fishes and other significant representations," and Thames "having on her head a Chaplet of green Reeds, Flowers and Rushes, and about her feet deck'd with Sedge, Bulrushes, and Flaggs ..." (sig. A5-A5ᵛ). Thetis has come, she explains, to grace this day and her daughter Thames. Together they gain assurance "that Heaven will ever blesse / Your stores, who doe her injuries redresse, / *Thetis* and Thames, their services shall shew / To you, as long as they doe ebb and flow" (sig. A6). With this promise the mayor can move forward to accept the challenges of the pageant.

Upon the mayor's return to land Time and Mercury wait for him in St. Paul's Churchyard—both had been included in Squire's show, and Time of course regularly appeared in civic pageants. Time, dressed in a blue robe, carries a scythe, while Mercury has his caduceus and wings on his head "to signifie quicknesse of Invention, Acutenesse of wit, and Volubility of tongue with Eloquence of speech" (sig. A6ᵛ). Having attended many such triumphs of London's mayor, Time can with authority claim that he has never been better pleased than this day. The mayor has achieved the honor of this office because he ever loved Truth, Time's daughter; thus Time says: "I doe command her, still with you t'abide, / Doe you defend her, she shall be your guide: / For truth-sake *Time* shall be your servant still: / And in your just commands, obey your will" (sig. A7). Mercury has brought wit and eloquence to the poet and quick invention to the "Artists that these pageants fram'd ..." (sig. A7). Attaining fame and honor comes assured with the promised help of Time and Truth.

More elaborate, the next device takes the form of a city representing London, "with walls, Battlements, Gates, Churches, Towers, Steeples and lofty Buildings, and some Antique shapes here and there on the tops of the highest Edifices ..." (sig. A7). Perhaps it resembles the arch at Fenchurch street in the 1604 royal entry, which contained the city carved in miniature atop the arch designed by Jonson. Also depicted in Taylor's arrangement, shops portray people working with cloth and the allegorical figures Antiquity, Record, Memory, and Wisdom. The person of London appears as "an ancient Matron in a civill grave robe with her haire long hanging downe in trammels dishevelled behind her backe ..." (sig. A7ᵛ). Munday, Middleton, Dekker, all represented the city of London, and in Webster's show she appeared as Troynovant. Counting herself the queen of cities, London in Taylor's pageant contemplates the way of the world and what has happened to other once noble cities; she knows why she survives:

Turke, Pope, and war, beare here no rule or sway,
For I one God, one King, one Law obey;

Ther's my security, and my state doth stand
Supported by the unsupported hand,
These are the meanes and instruments whereby
We rise to Honour, painfull Industry. (sigs. A7ᵛ-A8)

London exists therefore as a signpost along the road to honor, even if she seems a bit smug about her success.

The way has thus been prepared for the device of the Tower of Honour on the top of which sits a figure, apparently Majesty, in "royall robes, with a majestique Impalement on his head, a scepter in one hand, and a Ball in the other ..." (sig. A8). Under him sit figures representing a Lord Mayor who has Honour placed at his right hand, a Bishop with Piety, a Lawyer with Power, and a Captain with Victory. This arrangement bears a close resemblance to the first land pageant in Squire's show in which Majesty had the support of City, Country, Law, and Religion. In Taylor's tableau below the Mayor sits an apprentice and by him Obedience; below the Bishop, a scholar and with him Patience; under the Lawyer, a clerk and by him Diligence; beneath the Captain, a common soldier and by him Virtue "which shews that by vertuous actions and true industry meane men have ascended and may be raised to Honourable places ..." (sig. A8ᵛ). The Cardinal Virtues also appear at the corners of the device. The speech of Honour has one basic theme: man may make the ascent to Honour through his own efforts:

All such as will true Honours seat ascend,
Must doe (as these have) first obey and bend:
For though Humility to man seemes low,
The fruit of it as high as Heaven doth grow....
Thus Humble service is advanc'd and rear'd
To Honours seat, obey'd, belov'd and fear'd. (sig. B1)

Honour reminds the mayor that his "faith and Honour are in marriage joynd / By oath this day, which no man can unbinde...." By his industry and virtuous deeds man through humility may approach this Tower of Honour; the qualities that support Majesty here stand ready to assist. Securing honor, man can be assured of fame.

Before the mayor moves to the final device, someone stops him in Cheapside, one personating Endymion who in former days "did keepe / Upon th'Arcadian hils" his "harmeles sheepe ..." (sig. B2). His appearance represents something of a dramatic interlude and functions primarily to praise the guild. The pageants of Heywood will afford more opportunity to study such planned interruptions. Endymion brings a bit of the Arcadian world of the Elizabethan progress entertainment with him as a dance follows his speech. He explains that for his "sake the Swaines doe still prefer / The booke ycleap'd the shepherds

Kallender"—an apparent allusion to Spenser. Nevertheless, he appears riding on a golden ram, the celestial sign "come from the Zodiack to adorne your fame" (sig. B2). He wishes for the mayor "prosperous windes, and happy tides" that eventually the wool may be turned to cloth "and Cloth by transformation, / Be turn'd to gold, that you may say with joy, / That *Jasons* fleece (to yours) was but a toy" (sig. B2ᵛ). From Endymion's implied alchemical metaphor we may extrapolate and envision the whole pageant as demonstrating the transformation of man's achievement of honor into fame.

On fame the final tableau concentrates, for at the mayor's gate that night stands "an ancient Monument of Fame ..." (sig. B3). Fame with her usual accoutrements occupies a prominent position in this device, itself covered with ensigns of former Lord Mayors of the Clothworkers whom "Fame revives, sounding their praises, and inforceth *Time* to revive their noble Memory, encouraging his Lordship to follow them in all their Honourable actions ..." (sig. B3). The speaker Time observes his paradoxical nature: he gives and takes away, "Builds and throwes downe, and ruins and erects ..." (sig. B3ᵛ). But Time alone cannot make fame or immortality, and the examples of the former mayors demonstrate that their own virtuous actions lead to fame. To the new mayor Time offers wisdom and a challenge:

> Tis truly said, that man that rules his passions,
> Doth conquer more, than he that conquers Nations.
> As you have rul'd your selfe, let it appeare
> In ruling London this ensuing yeare,
> So you, with *Time* shall be together blest,
> And *Time* shall bring you to Eternall Rest. (sig. B4)

On this ethical note the civic drama concludes, as Time repeats a theme earlier stated: man must first rule himself and with humility and industry move in the direction of honor and fame.

Of the three Lord Mayors' Shows considered here, Taylor's may be the least interesting dramatically, his being the rather conventional pattern of set tableaux. This serves to suggest again that after the second decade of the Jacobean period few real innovations occur in the pageant form, which should not be surprising since to a greater or lesser degree the same can be said of other dramatic forms. The occasion, the processional route, involvement of the guilds all conspire to assure a rather conservative theatrical approach to such street pageants. The presentation of Endymion in Taylor's show serves as about the only thing that breaks the stereotype form. Clear instruction follows about the means of attaining honor and fame, and the physical structures of a tower and a mount underscore the thematic significance of these qualities. But Webster had demonstrated effectively how one can add a touch of realism to this emblematic drama by using figures representing actual historical characters in conjunction with allegorical ones to embody the theme. Taylor primarily uses allegory as the pageant follows a path that illustrates how to achieve honor and subsequent fame; Time and London offer the opportunity and place for the effort to attain these virtues, Time promising eternal rest if man governs first himself and then others wisely. In such an atmosphere a person stands ready to scale the heights of all virtues.

9 *Thomas Heywood*

LIKE SEVERAL PAGEANT-DRAMATISTS BEFORE HIM, THOMAS HEYWOOD also turned in his last productive years to civic pageantry, and a study of his Lord Mayors' Shows in the 1630s closes the saga of these civic entertainments of the period 1558-1642. By 1630 writing pageants was about the only thing Heywood had not done; by his own testimony he lays claim to having written whole or in part some two hundred and twenty plays, a record which even the indefatigable Anthony Munday would be hard pressed to match. And his *Apology for Actors* remains one of the few such theoretical statements between the time of Sidney and Dryden. Despite the several critical studies made of Heywood's work, little attention has been devoted to his pageant career;[1] but surely this part of his long and fruitful involvement in the literary world ought no longer be passed over.

Though he came late to pageant writing, Heywood had long been familiar with other pageants. For example, in Chapter One we noted how the end of Part I of his *If You Know Not Me* (1605-6) resembles in several details the actual coronation royal entry of Elizabeth in 1559. And in 1631, the year of his first mayoral pageant, he published *Englands Elizabeth*, a prose study of her reign, which contains an accurate account of that first civic pageant of the Elizabethan age. The lengthy poem, *Troia Britanica or Great Britaines Troy* (London, 1609), among its various subjects and allusions, contains in Canto VIII reference to the entertainment of King Christian of Denmark which occurred in 1606. And in Canto IV, stanza 40, an allusion occurs to the entry of James I who "without threatned armes or rude hostility" received entertainment "With zeale, with loyall thoughts, and harts unfeined" (p. 87).

A picture of Heywood's immense erudition emerges from a study of his civic drama, especially classical learning, which at times takes him on rather esoteric paths. Sometimes this learning appears in the opening of his pageant texts where he may, for example, trace the office of mayor back to the Romans; in this respect he resembles Munday who, thoroughly antiquarian, delighted in specifically stating the year Brutus set foot in Albion, how many years after the Flood, how many years after the world began. Like Ben Jonson and others, Heywood doubtless plumbed the redactions of the mythographers for much of his information; nevertheless, his assimilation of the materials of antiquity is admirable, and the

---

[1]A. M. Clark, *Thomas Heywood: Playwright and Miscellanist* (Oxford, 1931) discusses the pageants, pp. 112-18; Michel Grivelet, *Thomas Heywood et le Drame Domestique Elizabethain* (Paris, 1957), has only a brief mention on pp. 87-8; F. S. Boas, *Thomas Heywood* (London, 1950), discusses the pageants pp. 147-53, but shows no awareness of the 1638 and 1639 Lord Mayors' Shows.

whole subject of his classicism begs for a full study. More than any of the other
major pageant-dramatists Heywood depends on mythology and classical learning. Of the major writers we can simplify and say that Munday primarily relies
on history, Middleton on moral allegory, and Heywood on mythology—the differences more matters of degree, not kind.

Heywood adds an innovation in the Lord Mayor's Show by creating a type of
"anti-masque"—he, in fact, uses that term in one of his texts. This presentation
aims at the vulgar, he says, concerned only with visual spectacle. Most often, he
does not describe specifically what makes up the action or "scene," content rather
to dismiss it as unimportant. This "anti-masque" occurs in the shows of 1632,
1633, 1635, and 1637; Taylor used such an interrupting action in his 1634 show,
as noted in the previous chapter, though Taylor's relates more to the pageant's
development than the incidents in Heywood. In addition to this something
"new" that Heywood brings to these mayoral pageants, he also recaptures one of
the older elements: the use of the guild's patron saint—a device common to the
early Elizabethan Lord Mayors' Shows and one that Squire had also used in his
1620 entertainment.

In his seven pageants Heywood develops a structure that typically places the
main tableau near the conclusion of the entertainment so that the thematic development proceeds logically to this moment. Summarizing and interpreting
become the functions of the last speech of the pageant; as such these final
speeches serve the cause of unity. Though nothing in Heywood resembles the
morality structures of the 1612 and 1613 pageants, nor the "resurrection" action
of the 1611 and 1616 shows, considerable variety and dramatic interest reside in
Heywood's civic dramas, and generally he handles his material well. Heywood
escapes some of the monotony that frequently plagued Middleton's entertainments because he chose to place his emphasis on mythology rather than moral
allegory, which seems to have limited possibilities for variety.

The most significant fact that emerges from the company records for the
1631 pageant comes in the payment to the artificer Gerard Christmas of £200
"for pageants and shewes" (MSC, p. 121). No mention appears of Heywood,
though he clearly wrote the show, which he called Londons Jus Honorarium, dedi-
cated to George Whitmore, Haberdasher. The entry in the guild records reflects
the growing prominence of the artificer, especially in the 1630s when he achieves
a status unmatched in earlier decades—a subject to be discussed more fully in
Chapter Ten. At the end of the text Heywood commends the work of Christmas.

Dependent upon his classical knowledge, the first scene, presented on the
river, consists of two "craggy Rockes" between which the barges must pass; "these

are full of monsters, as Serpents, Snakes, Dragons, etc....."[2] Heywood means to depict in these rocks the ancient dangers of *Scylla* and *Charibdis*, compounded by the tempting Syrens placed on the rocks. But these obstacles Ulysses overcame "who by his wisedome and pollicy ... preserved himselfe and his people ..." (sig. B1). In his representation here Heywood means to embody "a wise and discreete Magistrate." Appropriately, Ulysses, the conqueror of these dangers, speaks and offers instruction to the mayor, assuring him that "ther's a way to scape." To avoid Scylla and Charibdis the mayor should

> *Keepe the even Channell, and be neither swayde,*
> *To the right hand nor left, and so evade*
> *Malicious envie (never out of action,)*
> *Smooth visadgd flattery, and blacke mouthd detraction,*
> *Sedition, whisprings, murmuring, private hate,*
> *All ambushing, the godlike Magistrate.* (sig. B1ᵛ)

Remembering that the sweet tones of the Syrens come "from foule brests," the mayor need only follow the example of Ulysses: "... *doe but stop your eare / To their inchantments, with an heart sincere ...*" (sig. B2). Ulysses subsumes the theme in his comment: "*But shunne th' extreames, to keepe the golden meane.*" Following such a temperate course the mayor can, like Ulysses, be wise and discreet. And the ethical advice here helps establish the instructional tone for the pageant.

Obeying Aristotle's golden mean had been suggested before in mayoral pageants—in Middleton's 1613 show and Munday's 1611 one, to cite two obvious examples. But Heywood, who apparently frequently plagiarized from himself, had interpreted Scylla and Charibdis with regard to this ethical position in his earlier prose work, *Gunaikeion: or, Nine Books of Various History Concerning Women*, published in 1624. In this omnium-gatherum Heywood says that these rocks epitomize the struggle between virtue and vice, and the meaning comes from Aristotle's *Ethics*, which posits that virtue exists as the mean between extremes. We seek out the middle course, "for mans life is nothing else but a continuall navigation betwixt divers molestations on one hand, and tempting and unlawfull pleasures on the other...."[3] Further in this book Heywood also discusses the incident of Ulysses and the Syrens indicating how Ulysses overcame their temptations, saving himself and his men and causing the destruction of these evil ones (pp. 364-5). The dramatic form of the pageant allows this inter-

---

[2]Thomas Heywood, *Londons Jus Honorarium* (London, 1631), sig. A4ᵛ. All quotations are from this quarto edition. The texts of all of Heywood's pageants can now be found in my edition: *Thomas Heywood's Pageants: A Critical Edition* (New York, 1986).
[3]*Gunaikeion* (London, 1624), p. 42.

pretation and the application to the mayor to come alive, charting the course by which the mayor may escape the vices that will assault him.

Greeting the mayor on land, the device located in Paul's Churchyard consists of a "greene and pleasant Hill" that contains a "faire and flourishing tree, furnished with variety of faire and pleasant fruite"; under the tree sits a woman "of beautifull aspect, apparrelled like Summer: Her motto, *Civitas bene Gubernata* ..." (sig. B2). The theological virtues, Faith, Hope, and Charity, serve as her attendants. Hanging on the tree, sentences express "the causes which make Cities to flourish and prosper: As, *The feare of God, Religious zeale, a Wise Magistrate, Obedience to rulers, Unity, Plaine and faithfull dealing ...*" (sig. B2ᵛ). At the bottom of the hill "sitteth old Time, and by him his daughter Truth, with this inscription; *Veritas est Temporis Filia ...*" (sig. B2ᵛ). Heywood thus duplicates many of the details of the scene at the Little Conduit in Cheapside of the 1559 royal entry pageant which contained two contrasting hills, representing a flourishing and a decaying commonwealth; Time and Truth also appeared.[4] (The striking relationship between this scene of these two pageants separated by some seventy-two years will be discussed further in Chapter Eleven.) In his speech Time observes that the scene represents "*Emblems of a City governd well; / Which must be now your charge*" (sig. B3). The mayor must "*bravely stand / To oppose vice*" and thereby defend Time's daughter, Truth. Suddenly Time pauses in his speech, picks up a withered branch and observes: "*See you this withered branch, by* Time *o're growne / A Cities Symbole, ruind, and trod downe. / A Tree that bare bad fruit* ..." (sig. B3ᵛ). And Time then enumerates the qualities that lead to such a ruined city, all of this in sharp contrast to the hill and flourishing tree that the audience witnesses. As the chosen leader, the mayor should see that a condition of health prevails in the city—a perpetual summer, like the figure on the hill. The symbolism of this tableau Heywood skillfully handles with the verbal instruction closely supported by the visual spectacle.

Appearing in the upper part of Cheapside, a chariot stands with two beasts placed before it on whose backs ride Justice and Mercy; but the chief figure in the chariot consists of one personating London, surrounded by representations of other cities such as York, Bristol, Oxford—all distinguished by their shields. London hopes that her "two Coacht Ladies," Justice and Mercy, may ever smile on all the cities. In accounting for her success, London says that the secret resides in her motto, "Serve and obay"—the motto of the Haberdashers as well. With such obedience cities flourish and help make "*unanimous peace content and joy* ..." (sig. B4ᵛ). Understandably, the scene urges the mayor to perpetuate this harmonious atmosphere; thus Heywood has moved from an abstract avoiding of vice allegorized in the representation of Ulysses, through the virtues that sustain

[4]Sheila Williams, "Two Seventeenth Century Semi-Dramatic Allegories of Truth the Daughter of Time," *Guildhall Miscellany* 2. no. 5 (1963): 218.

a city, to the specific case of London. As if to remind us of the dangers, the rocks and the syrens and other monsters, "beeing in continuall agitation and motion, some breathing fire, others spowting water," appear after the chariot (sig. C1).

Near the great Cross in Cheapside stood the *Palace of Honour*, "a faire and Curious structure archt and Tarrest above, on the Top of which standeth *Honour*, a Glorious presens, and richly habited ..." (sig. C1). In front of this palace rests Catherine, patron saint of the company, which recalls her presence in Squire's 1620 pageant. Here she invites the mayor to the Palace and explains her properties: "... *nor is this my Wheele, / Blind Fortunes Embleame ... / Mine is the Wheele of* Faith, *(all wayes in motion) / Stedfast in* Hope, *and Constant in Devotion*" (sig. C2). She bids the mayor to gain a "*treasure beyond valew, ... trew Caelestiall grace, / Ayme first at that ...*" (sig. C2ᵛ). At the moment Catherine points to Honour who can give further instruction to the mayor. Honour knows the difficulty of the way to her, and she enumerates how some persons gravitate to her. Reflecting doubtless on what has been presented, she tells the mayor: "*You through a Wildernesse of Seas, / Dangers of wrack, Surprise, Desease / Make new descoveryes, for a lasting story / Of this our Kingdomes fame and Nations glory ...*" (sig. C3). If he would know the way to this Palace of "*peace, rest and blisse,*" he need only follow Honour's advice: "'*Tis plaine, God, the* King Serve *and* Obay" (sig. C3). This tableau becomes the thematic focus of the pageant; for having come this far, the mayor stands ready to be received into Honour's household.

At the mayor's gate that night Ulysses appears and ties together the whole entertainment by underlining its allegorical intent. He explains that the wisdom of a Ulysses may guide the mayor and steer him through all dangers; Time with the support of Truth will help him re-establish "*This Ancient* Citty *in her pristine Youth*"; the flourishing London will shine in the mayor's Justice and Mercy (sig. C4). Under these conditions Honour invites the mayor to her palace. The unity and consistency of the pageant's thematic development gain skillfull assistance by this closing speech. Much like Middleton, Heywood focuses on moral instruction, and each tableau serves that end. The dramatic events come together on the concern for the preservation of the city (commonwealth), a challenge which the mayor, instructed and guided as he has been, must meet, navigating a temperate and middle course through the dangers that would obstruct or deter him.

Electing the mayor again in 1632, the Haberdashers once more turned to Heywood, who responded with *Londini Artium & Scientiarum Scaturigo: or, London's Fountaine of Arts and Sciences*,[5] celebrating the installation of Nicholas Raynton. And again company records show a payment of £190 to Christmas for the pageants (*MSC*, p. 122), whose work Heywood at the end of the text commends. The pageant itself follows basically the structure of the 1631 show, though Heywood depends more on his classical learning than in the previous

---

[5](London, 1632). All quotations will be from this text.

entertainment. He introduces for the first time a scene wholly visual in its appeal that develops into what he calls an "anti-masque."

Opening the entertainment, Arion appears on the river "with his Harpe in his hand, riding upon the backe of a Dolphin ..." (sig. A4ᵛ). From the halcyon days at Kenilworth in 1575 to Munday's 1616 Lord Mayor's Show to the year 1632, Arion keeps reappearing in civic pageants; and in Heywood's drama he links with two more familiar figures, Oceanus and Amphitrite. After a lengthy and learned discussion of the principal events in Arion's life, Heywood gives us Arion's speech, directed to the river Thames. Cataloguing various rivers of the world, Arion contends that none seems fairer than the Thames, which, despite its many favorable attributes, does truly transcend all others because it gives rise to "*this Day the Honour and the State / Of this thy Great and God like Magistrate*" (sig. B1ᵛ). And he bids the mayor: "*this Day to be invested / The Head of al these, passe on unmolested, / In your great Inauguration proceede ...*" (sig. B2). Mainly this initial tableau contributes by singing the praises of the community.

The first land show has Saint Catherine, patroness of the guild, who, of course, had been present in the previous year's entertainment: "Crowned as being a Queene, bearing a Wheele in her hand, full of sharpe cutting Irons, the Embleame of her Martyrdome ..." (sig. B2). Several allegorical figures accompany her: Humility, Truth—"which scaleth the Heavens, ... maintaineth Justice, governeth Cities, kils Hatred, cherisheth Love, and discovereth Treasons"—Zeal, and Constancy, "All which are necessary in a Magistrate, as needfull in a Martyr ..." (sig. B2ᵛ). In her speech St. Catherine explains her presence, taking special note of her banner which bears the company's motto, and she bids the mayor "*behold, and view*" her attendants. She closes:

> *Doe it in Zeale, in Truth, and all submission,*
> *That their be found no crosse interposition*
> *Betwixt* Power *and* Obedience, *so shall all*
> *Arts, Mysteries, and Trades Mechannicall,*
> *Thrive, prosper, and increase, so long as they*
> *Honour the King, the Magistrate obey.* (sig. B3)

As in the 1631 show, so here the theme of obedience sounds, and it gains special force by being enunciated by the martyred saint.

Mythology affords the content of the next tableau that depicts *Andromeda* tied to a rock, ready to be devoured by a sea-monster, "but rescued by *Perseus* the Sonne of *Jupiter* and *Danae*, who is mounted upon a *Pegasus*, or Winged-horse ..." (sig. B3). Perseus has a harp, a crooked sword, and shield "with a *Gorgons* head figured therein." Heywood states the meaning: "In *Perseus* are comprehended all the prime Vertues acquired in a Noble Magistrate: In *Andromeda* Chastity and *Innocence*" (sig. B3ᵛ). We may, Heywood says, check Ovid for more details. Or perhaps we could refer to Heywood's *Troia Britanica*, where in Canto VI, especially stanzas 21 and 27, Heywood recounts the story of Perseus' courage; similarly in *Gunaikeion*, pp. 39-40, incidents occur of Perseus' heroism. In the pageant the story of Perseus becomes an allegory of what the mayor ought to be and do. Perseus explains in his speech that Andromeda embodies Chastity and Innocence *"which Divine ayde / Is ready to assist still from above, / By one or other of the Sonnes of* Jove" (sig. B3ᵛ). Among the ranks of Jove's sons stands the new mayor who must "Perseus *like, / Keepe that ... Sword still drawne, ready to strike; / Making such Monsters of ... Justice tast, / Who insidiate the Innocuous and the Chaste.*" The mayor should put on the whole armor of Perseus whose sword symbolizes impartial justice and his winged-horse "Celerity and Speed." Bidding the mayor to put on these garments of strength and courage, Perseus issues his last challenge: *"Strive you to imitate what I have done, / Since you this day, are* Perseus *and* Joves *sonne"* (sig. B4). The story of Perseus thus becomes an effective allegory for shadowing forth the role and duties of the mayor; Heywood follows an ancient tradition of allegorizing myths, making them relevant to the present moment. And the example of Perseus adds to the example of Ulysses of the previous pageant in a sort of cumulative portrait based on mythology of what the mayor ought to be.

The first Heywood "interruption" occurs in the next land show, being Heywood says, "more Mimicall then Materiall, and inserted for the Vulgar, who rather love to feast their eyes, then to banquet their eares ..." (sig. B4). He offers no description of what it might have been. Perhaps unwittingly Heywood points the direction for the later Lord Mayors' Shows which by the beginning of the eighteenth century dropped the speeches and became more a parade than a civic pageant, as it has traditionally been defined. Not the first pageant-dramatist to be so aware, Heywood recognizes that the verbal elements fight sometimes a losing battle against the elaborate visual spectacle.

Taking a different approach to the definition of the mayor's task, Heywood presents an elephant with a castle on its back, guided by an Indian speaker. The elephant becomes a natural symbol for sketching something of the mayor's role. The castle borne on the elephant's back suggests the strength that the mayor must have to shoulder the burdens of the city, burdens that would *"Make* Atlas *shrinke beneath"* them (sig. B4ᵛ). The understanding, judgment, wisdom, and retention of the elephant the Indian commends to the mayor and says:

Yet such an Elephant *we hope to finde*
Of you, both in th'ability of Minde
And strength of Arme, by that incouragement
The former passage of your life hath lent.... (sig. C1)

In years to come Fame shall recall the story of how the mayor has "*borne up in her pristine Glory / This flourishing City*...." This beast thus functions as a symbol that evokes the qualities that the mayor should possess, and the tableau joins the religious example of Catherine and the mythological Perseus in an effort to encourage and challenge the mayor in his journey ahead.

The final tableau consists of the "*Scaturigo* or Fountaine of Vertue, from which all Arts and Sciences are watered"; about the fountain twelve persons represent the twelve major guilds of London (sig. C1). But Heywood adds no further description. The technique of a fountain dates from at least Peele's 1591 Lord Mayor's Show, and most pageant-dramatists have used it in some way. The unidentified speaker finds the number twelve significant in many ways: twelve Caesars of the Julian line, twelve signs of the zodiac, twelve disciples, and, of course, twelve companies of which the mayor serves as chief. From these guilds "*the Inundant* Scaturigo *growes, / Which through our Kingdomes large Dominions flowes* ..." (sig. C1ᵛ). London is the mother, and the mayor "*of all her Sonnes now eldest Child*...." Being heir to her good works, the mayor must "*incourage still / Those pious Acts, and by Example fill / Voide places with the like*...." With a final reminder of the company's motto, serve and obey, the speech closes. Though this tableau should be the thematic focus of the pageant, it fails to achieve that end, for other devices contain inherently much more interest.

That night Arion closes the entertainment with a speech that reminds the mayor of what has been seen. Underscoring the meaning, Arion says:

Next, how your Queene-like Saint directs the way
For you to rule, for others to obey.
Then to be cal'd Joves *Sonne you have the Grace,*
And that in Perseus *figured is your Place.*
That in this able Elephant's *implyde*
Your Strength to beare, your Judgement to decyde.
Last, that you are the Spring and Fountaine made
To water every Science, Art, and Trade.... (sig. C2)

Heywood achieves here the connection of such disparate and diverse elements into a meaningful whole, and Arion's speech helps show this inter-relatedness. When the mayor has been instructed by the examples of Catherine, Perseus, and the elephant, then he becomes ready to assume the cares of maintaining the Fountain of Virtue.

Heywood continued his dominance of the Lord Mayors' Shows in the decade of the 1630s by being selected to prepare the pageant of 1633, honoring Ralph Freeman, Clothworker; he named it *Londini Emporia, or Londons Merca-*

tura.[6] Scant company records do include a meeting of Gerard Christmas with members of the guild for purposes of planning the show. Again Heywood at the end of the text praises the work of Christmas, who for the last time serves as artificer; he dies in 1634, and the work passes to his sons. Heywood also commends the company "for their affaillity and courtesie, especially unto my selfe being at that time to them all a meere stranger, who when I read my (then unperfect) Papers, were as able to judge of them, as attentively to heare them ..." (sigs. C1-C1ᵛ). Heywood sketches here something of the procedure of preparing the entertainment. Like the previous two pageants, this one combines several elements with the main tableau dependent on allegorical figures, but the others reliant on mythological tradition.

After a lengthy discussion of the history of merchants, including references or quotations from Plutarch, Aristotle, Plato, Socrates, and Horace, Heywood describes the water show which consists of a "Sea-chariot, beautified and adorned with shel-fishes of sundry fashion and splendor ..." (sig. A4ᵛ). Drawing the chariot, two griffins allude to the arms of the guild. Seated in the front with water nymphs about him, *Thamesis* "seemeth asleepe, but at the approach of the Lord Maiors Barge, he rowzeth himselfe as being newly wakend from a Dreame" and speaks to the mayor (sig. A4ᵛ). An analogy between the griffins who have the head of eagles, a lion's body, and wings, and the mayor becomes the focus of the speech. The eyes of an eagle suggest that the mayor "*must always have an Eagles eye / To out gaze the Sun, and keepe that* Aquilant *sight / To see what's wrong, and to distinguish right*" (sig. B1). He must have the strength, boldness, and fairness of a lion which "*rends and teares*" "*such as strive or shall oppugne his lawes....*" The winged speed of the griffins symbolizes the speed the mayor should apply "*to such as justice neede*" (sig. B1). Having drawn the relationship, Thamesis closes with a welcome to the new mayor. As in the previous year's show, Heywood again uses a natural symbol to define some of the qualities that the mayor will need.

A different metaphor informs the first land device located in Paul's Churchyard: on a hill a shepherd grazes his flock as he sits "upon a Dyall to which his sheepe-hooke is the *Gnomon*, (a Symbole of his care and vigilancy,) ..." (sig. B1ᵛ). But the placid quality of this pastoral scene a wolf challenges, "ready to cease upon his prey...." While the tableau alludes to the Clothworkers, it does much more by making a comparison between this shepherd and the mayor. In his speech the shepherd informs the mayor that the numerous throng of people constitute his "*owne Sheep, this Citty is their fold, / And by your grave descretion they shal best, / Know where to browze by day, by night to rest*" (sig. B2). The mayor's watchful eye must be ready to spy the ravenous wolf, "*Least hee on any of your Flocke should prey*" (sig. B2). Citing the achievements of the clothing indus-

---

[6](London, 1633). All citations are from this original edition.

try occupies most of the remainder of the speech. Finally, the shepherd says: "*Make much Sir of your great Charge, 'tis not mine, / Y'are the true* Shepheard, *I my place resigne*" (sig. B2ᵛ). The mayor is thus the pastor of his flock with all that implies, and the shepherd metaphor joins the seaman and gardener metaphors used by other pageant-dramatists as a means of giving expression to the challenges and responsibilities of the mayor.

In the upper end of Cheapside stands a ship piloted by Mercury, "figured like a young man, fresh coloured and beardlesse: In his right hand holding a Golden Purse, in his left a *Caduzcaeus* ..." (sig. B3). He has wings on his hat and heels, symbolizing his celerity, and behind him a cock denotes "his Vigilancy," much as it had for Orpheus in Middleton's 1619 Lord Mayor's Show. Mercury's speech primarily celebrates the adventures of the merchant-traders as they traverse the globe, and as patron of all trade Mercury appears—a rather different meaning from his representation in Squire's show of 1620 and Taylor's of 1634. Mercury closes: "*Next on your Motto thinke: so happy proove, / Let your trust be in him that reignes above*" (sig. B3ᵛ). Such a moral seems tacked on instead of growing more naturally out of what has been said.

The third show on land "is a Modell devised for sport to humour the throng, who come rather to see then to heare ..." (sig. B3ᵛ)—but Heywood does not describe it except to say that it "consists onely in motion, agitation and action ..."; therefore, a speaker would have been futile, his words being "drown'd in noyse and laughter ..." (sig. B4). Heywood offers a rationale for this interruption: "And without some such intruded Anti-maske, many who carry their eares in their eyes, will not sticke to say, I will not give a pinne for the Show" (sigs. B3ᵛ-B4).

In striking contrast to this "anti-masque" appears the final tableau, "bearing the Title of *The Bower of Blisse*" (sig. B4). Most unlike another Bower by that title—Spenser's in Book II of *The Faerie Queene*—this one does not represent sensual, earthly pleasure. Instead, this one Sir Guyon and Arthur would have gladly preserved. It seems, in fact, a little House of Holiness, or as Heywood says, an "Embleame of that future Happinesse, which not onely all just and upright Magistrates, but every good man, of what condition or quality soever in the course of his life, especially aimeth at ..." (sig. B4). Thus the meaning of the pageant gains universal scope, embracing all men, not merely the mayor. The Bower has as chief occupants the Cardinal Virtues "which are behoovefull unto all who enter into any eminent place or Office." Unfortunately, Heywood does not describe the Bower nor the Virtues; instead, he concentrates on arguing for the interrelationship of these qualities. Much of what he says derives from Cicero and Epictetus, and it leads him to suggest that "*Fortitude* without *Prudence* is but *Rashnes*, *Prudence* without *Justice* is but *Craftines*, *Justice* without *Temperance* but *Tyrany*, *Temperance* without *Fortitude* but *Folly*" (sig. B4ᵛ). The Theological Virtues, Faith, Hope, and Charity, assist in conducting "all such pious and religious Magistrates, the way to the caelestiall Bower of Blisse." In the speech Prudence suggests that the Bower represents but the petty symbols of what will come, the shadows of the eternal reality, for all the virtues will gain a new transcendent quality far beyond their earthly manifestations. The path to the celestial bower Prudence defines:

> *The way to finde which, through these vertues lies*
> *Call'd* Cardinall: *The stepps by which to rise,*
> *These* Graces *shewe,* Faith, Hope, *and* Love *attend you:*
> *Who on their unseene wings shall soone ascend you.*
> *These (when all Earths pompe failes) your prayers shal bring*
> *Where Saints and Angels* Haleluiahs *sing.* (sig. C1)

No other pageant-dramatist deals more explicitly with the means to achieve salvation, which gets concrete realization in the Bower. This tableau stands at the thematic center of the entertainment, illustrating what can be attained through the virtuous life.

Varying from the function of the last speeches in the previous two pageants, Heywood here does not use the concluding speech as a recapitulation and interpretation of the events of the drama; rather it offers to the mayor the blessing of the twelve celestial signs "which may aptly be applied unto the twelve Moneths during the Lord Mayors government" (sig. C1ᵛ). In this night of rest "*Starres and Planits all conspire, / To warme you so by their celestiall Fire* ..." (sig. C1ᵛ). This speech may be viewed then as a logical extension of the Bower of Bliss—Taurus offers strength, the Twins peace, the Celestial Maid advice. On the other hand, the hate and spleen of Cancer should not be found in the mayor's government. The speaker closes:

> *That as* Aquarius *doth his water power*
> *You may your goodnes on this Citty shower,*
> Pisces, *the last of Twelve, the Feete they guide,*
> *From Head to Foot, O may you so provide.* (sig. C2)

The various features of the pageant do not connect well to one another, which may account for the closing speech not attempting a summary. Having been shown the path to salvation in the Bower of Bliss, the mayor gets practical help in his earthly government by the astrological signs. This serves as a fit conclusion to the day's entertainment in which the mayor has been likened to a shepherd, has been instructed by Mercury to put his trust in God, and has seen the divine wonders of the Bower.

As discussed in the previous chapter, John Taylor wrote the 1634 show, but Heywood won out in the competition for the 1635 pageant as he and the Christmas brothers underbid Taylor and Norman. Heywood entitled his entertainment, *Londini Sinus Salutis, or, Londons Harbour of Health, and Happinesse,*[7] and it celebrates the inauguration of Christopher Clethrowe, Ironmonger. The drama focuses on mythological characters with the exception of the tableau that gives the pageant its name, which has allegorical figures that help define the virtues needed in a magistrate.

On the Thames appears a device "partly fashioned like a Rock, and beautified with sundry varieties, and rarities ..." (sig. A4ᵛ); but Heywood gives no further description of the structure, although occupied by the "Three Caelestiall Goddesses, *Juno, Pallas, Venus* ..." (sig. A4ᵛ). The symbolic meaning of each the speech given by Venus notes as these three come dispatched from Jupiter to honor the day's triumph. Venus explains that Juno brings state and power to the mayor; and Pallas, "*who, from* Joves *brain / Derives her selfe, and from the highest straine / Of all the other gods, claimes her descent, / Her Divine Wisedome, doth this day present*" (sig. A5). But Venus born of the seas brings a gift equal to theirs, "*that which shall lift / You up on voyces, and from the low frame / Of sordid Earth, give you (above) a name* ..." (sig. A5). The love she offers will help fix the mayor's name "*in an eternall spheare*" (sig. A5ᵛ). And Venus points the way to attain this goal by interpreting the emblems that the figures bring: "*Take* Juno *for your guide, / Maintaine her Peacocks riches, not her pride* ..."; "*Observe next* Pallas *Owles, and from them take / This notion; you must watch even as they wake* ..." (sig. A5ᵛ). Such forms the path to wisdom. Venus herself has as emblems of her love swans and turtles, and Cupid also attends her. All three mythological figures had been discussed in Heywood's *Gunaikeion*; in fact, he notes in that source that swans draw Venus's chariot and peacocks, Juno's (p. 8). With the blessings of Power, Wisdom, and Love, the mayor readies to embark on his year in office.

Waiting for the mayor on land, a tableau depicts Sagittarius, one of the celestial signs; and at the four corners of the device appear other "signs"—Virgo, Ariadne, Cassiopeia, and Andromeda. The speaker, an Astrologian, assures the mayor of the command over the companies. Also the Astrologian finds symbolic importance in Sagittarius whose bow, he says, forms a "*perfect Emblem ment / Of Divine* Justice ..." (sig. A6ᵛ). The "moral" of the emblems implies that "*All* Justice *should be mixt with lenitie* ..." (sig. A7). Concluding the speech, the Astrologian presses the point forcefully:

> *O mixe then*
> Mercy *with* Justice, *Interweave againe*
> Justice *with* Mercy; *so shall you in your state,*
> *Not Starres alone, but the gods Imitate;*
> *So shall your Terrene body, in the end, ...*
> *Above the spheares, shine to eternitie.* (sig. A7)

[7](London, 1635). All references are to this text.

To the virtues singled out in the device on the river the mayor should add justice tempered with mercy; these celestial signs point the way to transcendence of the earthly sphere, to the achievement of immortality, a theme sounded in several previous civic pageants.

The next device becomes an interlude "contrived onely for Pastime, to please the vulgar ..." (sig. A7). But a tableau follows which presents a Castle equipped with the necessary pieces of ordnance and such "Persons as are needfull for the defence of such a Citadell ..." (sig. A7ᵛ). Appropriately, Mars serves as the chief occupant; his long history and traditional garb Heywood recounts in considerable detail. Mars comes, he says, "*To heighten these brave Triumphs of Renowne,*" and he resides by the castle to demonstrate the power he brings (sig. A8). At the proper moment a piece of ordnance fires. Mars delivers a long section of praise on the various useful functions of iron, strongly reminiscent of a similar speech made by Jove in Dekker's *London's Tempe* (1629), which also honored the Ironmongers. No art, craft, faculty, or trade can exist without iron, he insists. After reminding the mayor of his metal sword, Mars says:

> Justice *would cease,*
> *If (as in Warre) it were not us'd in Peace:*
> *Power makes it yours, your wisedome now direct you;*
> *Whilst Peace stayes heere,* Mars *shall abroad protect you.* (sig. B1)

Mars as the guardian of peace may remind us of the closing of Squire's *The Tryumphs of Peace* (1620). The assurance of peace thus joins the other qualities—power, wisdom, love, justice and mercy—previously presented to the mayor in the mythological scenes on the river and on land. These tableaux pave the way for the one that gives the pageant its title.

The *Sinus Salutis* or harbor of health and happiness forms a "sculpture" adorned "with eight several persons, representing such vertues as are necessary to bee imbraced by all such Majestrates" who after the storm-tossed seas hope to anchor in the safe port (sig. B1). Again Heywood follows the pattern of not describing what these qualities look like, their portrayal, or what emblematic properties they bear; instead, he digresses on each—only seven in spite of his saying eight—citing all sorts of ancient writers as the sources for his information. Heywood commends the virtues of Fortitude, Gentleness, Candour, Philosophical Patience, Placability, Humanity, and Zeal. Embracing these qualities, the speaker suggests, constitutes the steps that mount a mayor to the height, and such virtues imply the course he must sail. These attributes "*being harbour'd in your honour'd brest, / Shall (maugre shelves and rocks) your passage cleare, / And bring you to the* Port, *to which you steare* ..." (sig. B3). Being the city's chief citizen, the mayor should lead by a steadfast course; eventually all may know the "salvation" of the blessed harbor. The closing speech that night by Mars reviews what has been promised the mayor by the various characters including himself offering protection "*untill / Hee, which shall all your upright Actions blesse, / Conduct you to your Port of Happinesse*" (sig. B3ᵛ). The several tableaux fit together well and logically with the thematic climax centering on the *Sinus Salutis*, in its own way a "Bower of Bliss." The pageant implies the sea or journey metaphor that shapes the terms of the ultimate goal of the port; these many virtues steer the mayor, and he must guide the state until it also gains the safe harbor.

No record exists of a Lord Mayor's Show in 1636; but in 1637 when the Haberdashers sought to honor Richard Fenn, they chose Heywood, and he responded with *Londini Speculum: or, Londons Mirror*.[8] As in the previous pageant, the Christmas brothers assisted in the production, and their services Heywood commends at the end of the text. From this show to the last one of which texts survive before the closing of the theaters Heywood dominates civic pageantry. The structure of *Londini Speculum* closely parallels the arrangement of tableaux of most of Heywood's pageants with the scene that gives the entertainment its title coming last.

Before Heywood comes to the water show in his text, he delivers a learned history of the development of London and the office of mayor, including a discussion of Brutus and Troynovant. Riding on the river "*on a Scallop, which is part of his Lordships Coate of Armes, drawne in a Sea-Chariot*," St. Catherine appears, patron saint of the guild and previously presented in Heywood's other pageants honoring the Haberdashers. She comes, she tells the mayor, as a representative of the gods, especially Mercury who had addressed the council of the gods. Because he cannot be present for the festivities, Neptune has loaned his best sea-horses to pull Catherine's chariot. With the promise of the gods to watch over the mayor, the speech ends.

Located in Paul's Churchyard, the first device on land stands "being outwardly *Sphericall* and *Orbicular*, yet being opened it quadrates it selfe just into so many *Angles* as there be Scepters, over which his Sacred Majesty beareth title: namely, *England, Scotland, France*, and *Ireland* ..." (sig. B4ᵛ). The chief figure Pythagoras speaks and dilates on the significance of the number four. Heywood had earlier observed in his *Gunaikeion* that the Pythagorists hold four to be a sacred number even swearing "*By the holy number of foure, which lends to the soule an eternall nature* ..." (p. 58). In the pageant Pythagoras observes the prominence of four—the seasons, divisions of the day, ages of man, the elements, the humors, the winds. Further, "*All Morall vertues we in foure include, / As Prudence, Justice, Temperance, Fortitude*" (sig. C1ᵛ). The globe, Pythagoras says, represents the king's power, "*And yours beneath Him, in the* number foure" (sig. C2).

---

[8](London, 1637). All quotations are from this edition.

An "anti-masque" follows, "devised onely for the vulgar ..." (sig. C2). Paralleling somewhat the 1635 show, the next device offers an "*Imperiall* Fort," with the chief occupant Bellona, while others stand ready to defend the fort. As the chief general of the metropolis, Bellona says, the mayor should be the prime governor of this fort which symbolizes the chamber of the king. In such a fortress the theological virtues, the Graces, Piety, Zeal, Peace, all have residence; these war with Pride, Arrogance, Sloth, Vanity, Profaneness—Heywood does not make it clear if these various qualities gain representation in any visual way. Nevertheless, the allegory implies that the strong fort under the mayor's command serves to ward off those who would assault it—the vices.

Heywood decorates the main tableau "with glasses of all sorts: the persons upon or about it are beautifull Children, every one of them expressing their natures and conditions in the impresaes of their shields," each representing some quality of the optic sense (sig. C3ᵛ). Heywood explains that "Sight is the most soveraigne sence, the first of five, which directeth man to the studdy and search of knowledge and wisedome ..." (sig. C3). The speaker Opsis claims that the device represents London's mirror and the glass reveals what "*the spacious Universe might see / In her, what their great Cities ought to be* ..." (sig. C3ᵛ). The various qualities of sight offer instruction to the mayor: seek out deserving men, cast the powerful eye on the poor wretch, take counsel first and pause with meditation before judging a cause, view future dangers, let every cause be searched, look out for the security of the people, and finally, "*cast thine eyes backe upon all things past*" (sig. C4). In London one appreciates the internal vision:

> *Divine* Astraea *here in equall scale*
> *Doth ballance* Justice, Truth *needes not looke pale,*
> *Nor poverty dejected, th' Orphants cause,*
> *And Widowes plea finde helpe....* (sig. C4)

The mayor's task becomes to preserve such a London, to maintain that healthy vision that looks on man's needs.

Briefly that night Pythagoras recounts for the mayor what he has seen and why: St. Catherine would remind him of the world of care he will confront in his office; the globe implies what the king owes to the kingdoms; the fort displays the mayor's military honors; and "Londons Mirrour, *that all men may see / What* Magistrates *have beene, and ought to be*" (sig. C4ᵛ). But Pythagoras's speech cannot redeem the pageant's lack of much thematic unity—the elements remain rather disparate and non-integrated. The only obvious link occurs between the fort and the device of the "mirror," both of them reflecting on qualities of the city. The various elements remain vignettes rather than integrated drama.

When the Drapers made plans in 1638 to honor Maurice Abbot, the new mayor, they selected Heywood to prepare the entertainment, which he did in conjunction with the Christmas brothers. For "making and setting out of Five Pageants" the artificers and Heywood received £170 plus an additional £10 for "the Companies well liking it ..." (*MSC*, p. 127). Total cost for the show, *Porta Pietatis*, exceeded £747. In the entertainment the dramatist emphasizes the achievements of the company, omits the "anti-masque," and again has a central tableau that epitomizes the theme of the show.

On the Thames Heywood offers Proteus in a sea-chariot attended "with divers Marine Nymphs and Sea-goddesses, etc."[9] Proteus, the "first, or most ancient of the Sea-gods, the Sonne of *Oceanus* and *Thetis*," rides on a tortoise, and Heywood includes a discussion of his history. Speaking to the mayor, Proteus claims that he can assume many shapes, sometimes a bull, a serpent, or fire, all of which have symbolic relevance for the mayor who must have the strength of a bull, the wisdom of the serpent to discern error, and the quality of fire that "sunders *and* divides *the* drosse *from* Gold ..." (sig. B1). The double-nature of the tortoise suggests that the guild trades both on land and on sea. Proteus hopes that the trading ports will prosper and that the mayor may heighten their fame so that "*future Story / Above all other States may crowne her glory*" (sig. B1ᵛ).

On a platform "adorn'd with Flowers, Plants, and Trees bearing sundry Fruits" stands a shepherd surrounded by his flock, "some feeding, others resting in severall postures ..." (sig. B1ᵛ). (In 1633 Heywood had presented a similar scene.) Here the shepherd in addressing the mayor praises the sheep for their many beneficial qualities—no other animal can with them truly compare. Furthermore, the shepherd suggests that the sheep represents an emblem of patience and of profit; thus great honor belongs to the company and to the mayor "*for whom this triumph's made*" (sig. B2ᵛ). This theme of praise for the guild continues in the second land device which presents a rather different animal, a rhinoceros, accompanied by an Indian, reminiscent of the use of an elephant in the 1632 show. In this 1638 pageant the Indian speaks, drawing the analogy between the rhinoceros and the office of mayor:

> [the animal] *to all Beasts of prey, who rend and teare*
> *The innocent heards and flocks, is foe profest,*
> *But in all just defences armes his crest.*
> *You of this wildernesse are Lord, so sway,*
> *The weake may be upheld, the proud obey.* (sig. B3ᵛ)

As in the earlier pageant, Heywood intends the animal as a natural symbol with the additional metaphorical view that the state as a wilderness needs the mayor's strength to be equal to the task of supporting the weak and helpless.

---

[9]*Porta Pietatis, or, The Port or Harbour of Piety* (London, 1638), sig. A4. All references are to this original edition.

In describing the third land show that consists of a fully equipped ship, Heywood refers to his tract on ships and navigation published the previous year in which he praised the great ship being built for Charles I.[10] The speech from the ship celebrates the trading industry, "*And through an* Hellespont *who would but pull, / Steere, and hoise saile, to bring home golden Wooll?*" (sig. B4). The young sailor also has advice for the mayor, informing him that he must have good sight to see into each strife with impartiality. And in a striking image, the sailor tells the mayor that he must—

> *be feather'd now all o're:*
> *You must have feathers in your thoughts, your eyes,*
> *Your hands, your feete; for he that's truely wise*
> *Must still be of a winged apprehension*
> *As well for execution, as prevention.* (sig. B4ᵛ)

The principal tableau comes in the last one, entitled *Porta Pietatis, The Gate of Piety*, which, Heywood explains, "is the doore by which all zealous and devout men enter into the fruition of their long hoped for happinesse ..." (sig. B4ᵛ). In this device structured like a temple resides Piety, "upon her head are certaine beames or raies of gold, intimating a glory belonging to sanctity; in one hand an Angelicall staffe, with a Banner; on the other Arme a Crosse Gules in a field Argent ..." (sig. C1). Including more description of the emblematic detail than in other pageants, Heywood also describes those who accompany Piety. On one side "sits a beautifull Childe, representing *Religion*, upon whose Shield are figured *Time*, with his daughter *Truth* ..." (sig. C1). Another figure represents the Virgin, patroness of the guild, crowned and in her hand a fan of stars. Next to her the Theological Graces each have a shield containing an appropriate "motto." Zeal "whose Escutchion is a burning Hart," Humility, and Constancy also appear in the tableau. This citadel or tower, Piety says, illustrates "*the way to blisse, guirt with a ring / Of all those Graces that may glory bring*" (sig. C1ᵛ). Religion, "*shining in her pure truth*," stands ready to aid the mayor, as do the other virtues cited by Piety. The mayor should "*proceede in that faire course you have begun*," seeking to gain a crown (sig. C2). Having passed through Piety's gate, the mayor stands ready to govern the metropolis. The allegorical tableau demonstrates a path to salvation and the virtues that ought to attend the mayor. Heywood presents a variation of the Bower of Bliss and the *Sinus Salutis* tableaux with a similar allegorical theme in all three dramatic presentations. Closing this 1638 pageant, Proteus at night reviews what has been seen, offering summary interpretation and reminding the mayor that "Piety *doth point You to that Starre, / By which good*

---

[10]Thomas Heywood, *A True Description of His Majesties Royall Ship* (London, 1637). Another edition followed in 1638.

Merchants steere ..." (sig. C2). Each device in the pageant aids the thematic development as Heywood moves us toward the *Porta Pietatis*, for each scene offers something in the way of personal instruction to the mayor, frequently invoking a natural symbol to vivify the point. In a sense, the year that lies ahead of the mayor constitutes an opportunity to perfect his "salvation," Proteus and others having pointed the way. His path remains secure so long as he navigates from the star of Piety.

The story of the Lord Mayor's Show ends with Heywood's 1639 pageant, *Londini Status Pacatus*, the last such entertainment before the Restoration. The show Heywood designed to honor Henry Garway, Draper, and the company records indicate a payment of £196 to Heywood and the Christmas brothers, with a total expenditure of £787. 3s. 4d. (*MSC*, p. 129-30). This civic drama, heavily indebted to mythology and Heywood's understanding of the ancients, nevertheless contains the central tableau that gives the pageant its title; thus Heywood continues to follow essentially the same structural pattern as in his other mayoral shows.

Mounted in a sea-chariot, "his habit suiting with the nature of the river, in his right hand a seven-forked Scepter," a figure represents "the ancient River Nilus...."[11] Two crocodiles draw him, and he addresses the mayor on the Thames. After a long catalogue of various rivers throughout the world, the speaker claims that "*none of these compare with aged Nile ...*" (sig. B1). But more important, symbolic meaning attaches to this scene. Recalling that its floods meet the needs of the land, Nilus says bluntly, "*So Magistrates ... / ... ought to the distrest ...*" (sig. B1ᵛ)—out of the overflow of their bounty and concern the needs of men will be met. The seven-forked scepter symbolizes the seven liberal arts maintained by the mayor and indicates the city's "magnitude and worthinesse" (sig. B1ᵛ). The crocodiles that accompany Nilus represent the evils that he must curb and tame; in these various ways Nilus symbolizes attributes that the mayor ought to have, and this water tableau lends its part to the allegory of attaining a peaceable estate.

On land awaiting the mayor a square structure contains at its corners the four Seasons and Janus as the chief occupant, "every one habited agreeable to his propriety and condition" (sig. B1ᵛ). As usual, Heywood cannot resist a learned discussion of Janus's history. This presentation of Janus may recall the Temple of Janus located at Temple Bar, part of Ben Jonson's contribution to the 1604 royal entry for James I. Heywood suggests that the "fixt bases" on which Janus stands admonish all men of honor "to be constant in all their courses; but especially in the establishing and maintenance of true Religion ..." (sig. B2). The golden key that he holds shuts up the year past and opens the year future; "it may also be an

---

[11]*Londini Status Pacatus: or, Londons Peaceable Estate* (London, 1639), sig. A4ᵛ. All citations are to this text.

Embleme of noble policy to unbosome and bring to light their trecherous devises and stratagems, who seeke to undermine and supplant the prosperity of a faire and flourishing Common-weale" (sig. B2). Even the bar in his left hand symbolizes the fortitude required in a good magistrate as he tries to suppress vice and encourage virtue. In his speech Janus also offers an interpretation of his emblematic properties. With one face he looks back "*least good Acts done / Might be obscur'd in darke oblivion*," and with the other he looks forward "*to see what's to doe; / Both for Gods Honour, and your Countryes to*" (sig. B2ᵛ). To the mayor Janus resigns the seasons and the twelve months, and he bids the mayor to use the golden key "*to set wide / Those Prison gates, where many a soule hath dide, / Starv'd by th' Oppressors curelty ...*" (sig. B3). He expresses confidence that none knows better than the mayor "*What Mercy is; or when to use the Sword.*" To the qualities of Nilus the mayor must now add the attributes of Janus. Appropriately, Heywood offered an earlier interpretation of Janus in *Gunaikeion*; in this work Heywood says that Janus uses his golden key to open the Temple of Peace (p. 226)—certainly in the pageant he points in the direction of *Status Pacatus*.

Continuing the illustration of peace, the next device presents Orpheus with his harp, "seated in a faire Plat-forme, beautified with pleasant Trees, upon which are pearcht severall Birds, and below Beasts of all sorts, ... all imagined to be attentive to his Musick" (sig. B3). This microcosmic garden of a golden world corresponds metaphorically to the "peaceable and blest estate" of the present kingdom. Heywood's presentation of Orpheus recalls a similar portrayal by Middleton in the 1619 show, and he served as the subject of Canto VII in Heywood's *Troia Britanica*. In the pageant Orpheus recounts many of his achievements, such as calming the flooding rivers, taming the wild beasts, causing lions and lambs to come "*together coucht in love*," charming the trees, and moving the stones to his "*Harps sweet sound ...*" (sig. B3ᵛ). Yet an achievement in harmony greater than all this, greater than the music of the spheres, can be found in the mayor, an "Orpheus *who can doe all these ...*" (sig. B4). With the powers of his office he can violence halt and protect his people, rich and poor alike. Even "*Trees rooted in selfe-will*" and senseless stones may be changed into life through the power of such wisdom. But the accomplishment of unanimous hearts, plenty, increase, and all blessings that wait on peace, "*Proves sweeter Musicke then e're* Orpheus *made*" (sig. B4). Such a divine concord makes possible arriving at a peaceful estate.

In a salute to the company Heywood offers the next device which consists of a chariot drawn by two camels on whose backs Indians ride; in the chariot Jason and Medea symbolize respectively, healing and counsel. Reviewing the achievements of her husband, Medea praises the sheep as being one of the most useful animals to man. Men small and great make use of the wool provided by the sheep. The camels that pull the chariot represent the far-flung travels of the mayor and "*may the world perswade / The rich Commerce and noblenesse of your*

Trade" (sig. C1ᵛ). Jason and Medea have appeared in a number of mayoral pageants, especially ones devoted to honoring the Drapers. After the appearance of the chariot came a ship "decored with the Armes of the nine Companies of Merchant-adventurers, of which his Lordship hath bin, and is at this present free ..." (sig. C1ᵛ). The press of time caused the speech to be omitted.

The final tableau culminates and expands what has preceded it, portraying the "calamities of War, and the blessednesse of peace, *Status Pacatus* ..." (sig. C2). Though not offering much description, Heywood notes that in "one part thereof are exprest to the life, the figures of *Death, Famine, Sicknesse, strage* [slaughter], etc. in the other *Prosperity, Plenty, Health, Wealth*, but especially the free and frequent Preaching of the Word and Gospell" (sig. C2). Good government forms the ground of peace, Heywood maintains, "asking no lesse wisedome to preserve it, then valour to obtain it...." To give visual reality to the allegorical conflict between war and peace Heywood includes a company of artillery men "to expresse Warre" and "the Livery and gown-men being the Embleme of Peace" (sig. C2ᵛ). The *Genius of the City* gives the speech with its graphic depiction of the ravages of war—blood-drenched earth, rushing of routed troops, clashing of arms, "*flying, crying, dying*" (sig. C3). A horrible time—

> When *pinching need*
> *Of food, hath forc'd the famish'd Mother feed*
> *On her 'fore-starved Babe; and* Hunger *raves*
> *So fiercely*, Men eate men out of their Graves.... (sig. C3)

Houses, palaces, temples disintegrate, and "*those Towers / That with the* Clouds *did late* alliance *boast*" fall down, reminding us of Prospero's vision of the dissolution of the "cloud-capp'd towers, the gorgeous palaces, / The solemn temples...." Though other nations currently experience such calamities, "*this* sole-happy Isle" enjoys "calme Peace, / Prosperity, *and* Plenty *with* increase / *Of all* concatinated Blessings ..." (sig. C3ᵛ). The challenging task ahead becomes to preserve the peace that graces the land. For such an undertaking the examples of Nilus, Janus, and Orpheus could be invaluable; so the closing speech of the pageant reminds the mayor, hoping that the happiness of this peaceful state may last long.

Fortunately Heywood's mayoral pageant career ends with this fine example, for he has with good control of his material welded the various elements of the pageant together. The mythological figures with their symbolic properties prepare the way for the thematic climax, the *Status Pacatus* tableau which presents the tension between war and peace, graphically illustrated and vividly discussed by the Genius of the City. Tightly organized, this civic drama has few loose ends. An awesome challenge has been given the mayor, as well as the audience: ensure the progress of peace as dramatically revealed in this "triumph of peace." But from our vantage point in history we can look back with an irony doubtless un-intended by Heywood to this celebration of peace on this favored island, given the turmoil and civil strife that soon gripped the nation a few years after Hey-wood's pageant. And this "insubstantial pageant" fades into a harsher reality where men experience torment by conflicting desires and needs, and peace goes into exile.

Though Heywood has no pageant with the dramatically exciting form of Dekker's 1612 show and Middleton's 1613 pageant, he does on the whole avoid the sameness which plagued their later efforts. Admittedly Heywood follows a similar structure in each of his entertainments, but he nevertheless achieves a satisfactory variety. Much of this diversity results from his intense interest in and use of mythology and ancient traditions. His texts bristle with evidence of this erudition, and one imagines at moments that the shadow of Ben Jonson can be seen lightly falling across the pages. In the entertainments themselves such figures as Ulysses, Perseus, Janus, Orpheus, Mercury, Venus, Juno, Pallas, Mars, and Proteus play crucial roles, offering instruction or themselves as examples that ought to be imitated. Like Francis Bacon, Heywood understands the allegorizing of classical stories, and his mythological characters fulfill a thematic role conso-nant with the moral structure of the pageant. Thus they prepare the way for such tableaux as the Bower of Bliss, *Sinus Salutis*, *Porta Pietatis*, and *Status Pacatus*, where the moral theme culminates, sketching the way to gain a transcendence of this earthly life.

The "anti-masque" device Heywood does not exploit very thoroughly, but it does represent something a bit different in civic pageantry and may point to the later eighteenth-century complete focus on visual spectacle and abandonment of speeches. At any rate, Heywood senses no artistic conflict between his "interlude" and the rest of the pageant. The rise of the artificer reaches completion in the 1630s in which he actively negotiates with the company, and the dramatist seems to slip into a secondary position—all to be discussed in the next chapter. Hey-wood also differs somewhat from his fellow pageant-dramatists in his scant at-tention to emblematic detail; he seems to sacrifice such description for learned discussions of mythological figures or for references to writers of antiquity. The fault may lie with his preparation of the text rather than with the entertainment itself, for sufficient evidence exists to demonstrate that Heywood understands traditions of iconography that helped shape the visual qualities of most civic pag-eants.

In two of his most satisfactory Lord Mayors' Shows, the 1631 and 1639 ones, Heywood focuses on a dramatic conflict between evil and virtuous forces that ultimately affects the condition of the commonwealth. Ulysses in the 1631 pag-eant reveals some of the dangers that will attend the mayor and urges on him a temperate course. And on the beautiful hill, symbolizing a city well-governed, Time picks up a withered branch, tell-tale symbol of a decadent state, and underscores the effects of the conflict between virtue and vice. In order to arrive at the peaceable estate dramatized in the final pageant the mayor has to grapple with the problem of conflict that sometimes leads to horrendous war. After witnessing the tableau of *Status Pacatus*, one cannot doubt that war must be avoided at all costs, such are its horrible effects. The cumulative instruction given the mayor, the examples of mythological characters, and the personification of virtues stand the mayor in good stead to preserve the sanctity, the security, the integrity of the state. Consciously or not, Heywood sounds a theme of considerable relevance to his time; unfortunately, bad fruit grows in the garden of the state, and it spoils the stability and affluence so necessary for the production of civic pageants. Sad indeed comes the entry in company records in 1640: "... their is noe publike show eyther with Pageats or uppon the water" (*MSC*, p. 131).

Before it closed along with other drama, the Lord Mayor's Show had made great progress from its earliest days in the opening years of Elizabeth's reign through the reign of Charles I. The simple, inexpensive processional with perhaps but one pageant device has been surpassed by costly, complex, and highly sophisticated dramas, taking place regularly in the streets of London. While the other civic pageant forms, the progress entertainment and the royal entry, may suffer an eclipse in the Stuart reign, the Lord Mayor's Show retains its vitality, satisfying the public demand for entertainment. The civic pageant focus has clearly shifted from the sovereign to the chief citizen of London, and the drama prepared for the occasion of the mayor's inauguration achieves its own status as a dramatic form to be reckoned with. With major dramatists preparing the pageants, the printing of texts, active involvement of the guilds, and generous expenditures, little remained to impede the development of the mayoralty shows.

Dekker reminds us that these entertainments spring from peace and abundance: "*Love* begets them; and *Much Cost* brings them forth." When these conditions change, the shows languish and eventually perish. War and Parliament break off the continuous line from the early days of Peele and Nelson through the major achievements of the second decade of the seventeenth century to Heywood's sustaining power of the 1630s. The street theater must await its revival in the Restoration.

Part three

Pageants:
Body and Soul

IN HIS SATIRICAL ATTACK ON INIGO JONES, Ben Jonson comes to the heart of the issue that divided these two workers in the court masque. He writes in his poem "An Expostulation with Inigo Jones":

> O Showes! Showes! Mighty Showes!
> The Eloquence of Masques! What need of prose
> Or Verse, or Sense t'express Immortall you?
> You are the Spectacles of State! Tis true
> Court Hieroglyphicks! and all Artes affoord
> In the mere perspective of an Inch board! ...
> Oh, to make Boardes to speake! There is a taske
> Painting and Carpentry are the Soule of Masque.
> Pack with your pedling Poetry to the Stage,
> This is the money-gett, Mechanick Age![1]

Painting and carpentry make up, of course, elements of the "body" of the masque or of a civic pageant, while the poetry and allegorical themes constitute the "soul," a distinction also made in the emblem books. The quarrel between Jonson and Jones centers on the problem of the relative importance of the body and the soul, or the relative importance of poet and architect.[2]

Thomas Dekker in the text of his contribution to the royal entry entertainment of James I in 1604 also makes the distinction between the poetical soul and the mechanical body. Having already acknowledged that "hard words" alone would "breake" the audience and send their minds "a wooll-gathering," Dekker recognizes the desire for some sort of harmonious reconciliation between spectacle and theme; and he observes:

---

[1] *Ben Jonson*, ed. Herford and Simpson (Oxford, 1947), VIII, 403-4.
[2] For a discussion see D. J. Gordon, "Poet and Architect: The Intellectual Setting of the Quarrel between Ben Jonson and Inigo Jones," *Journal of the Warburg and Courtauld Institutes* 12 (1949): 152-78.

By this time Imagine, that *Poets* (who drawe speaking Pictures) and *Painters* (who make dumbe Poesie) had their heads and hands full; the one for native and sweet Invention: the other for lively Illustration of what the former should devise: Both of them emulously contending (but not striving) with the proprest and brightest Colours of Wit and Art, to set out the beautie of the great *Triumphant-day*.[3]

The key of course assumes a peaceful and mutually beneficial working together of painter (body) and poet (soul). Dekker adds further:

Many dayes were thriftily consumed, to molde the bodies of these Tryumphes comely, and to the honour of the Place: and at last, the stuffe whereof to frame them, was beaten out. The Soule that should give life, and a tongue to this *Entertainment*, being to breathe out of Writers Pens. The Limmes of it to lye at the hard-handed mercy of Mychanitiens. (II, 257-8)

The chapters that follow deal with these two essential elements of any civic pageant: body and soul. This discussion will afford a means of looking back over the pageants already studied in order to analyze common problems or ideas that link many of them.

---

[3] *The Dramatic Works of Thomas Dekker*, ed. Fredson Bowers (Cambridge, 1955), II, 257.

10 *Body: Men and Machines*

A NUMBER OF CRAFTSMEN work together to bring life to the "body" of the pageant, as do committee members who preside over the planning and preparation for the civic dramas. Principally this chapter focuses on that group of workers whom we may call artificers—the chief artisans involved with the physical aspects of the pageant, instrumental in causing the "word" to take on flesh. Making the total scene possible was the financing of these pageants, and representative examples will illustrate how it worked. A survey of the major stage properties and machines will provide a glimpse at the products of the artificers and the expenditures.

This study of the artificers concentrates on the Jacobean and Caroline periods, for in the Stuart era sufficiently full records provide an understanding of the function of the chief artificer. And such a study centers also on the Lord Mayors' Shows and the royal entries, there being, so far as I know, little evidence relevant to the progress pageants. As we move from the opening of James's reign to the 1630s, we see an emerging importance of the artificer's role in the production of civic pageants until finally he becomes more crucial in negotiations with the guild than the dramatist. But the internecine war that plagued the masque did not occur in the street pageants where a harmonious relationship prevailed between body and soul.[1] Scores of names associate with the physical preparation of the pageants; but in order to have a manageable approach, I have selected those artificers who appear with some frequency or who get recognition in the pageant texts.

Stephen Harrison rises to prominence in the royal entry pageant, being responsible for the architecture in the 1604 entertainment for James I. As mentioned in Chapter Two, Harrison, in addition to his duties as artificer, prepared the magnificent folio, *The Arches of Triumph*, providing a pictorial record of the seven arches erected throughout London. In his text Dekker alludes to the work of Harrison as placed over all the other craftsmen: "the sole Inventor of the Architecture, and from whom all directions, for so much as belonged to Carving, Joyning, Molding, and all other worke in those five Pageants of the Citie (Paynting excepted) were set downe."[2] Though unspecified, a payment to Harri-

---

[1]See Jean Robertson, "Rapports du Poète et de l'Artiste dans la Préparation des Cortèges du Lord Maire (Londres 1553-1640)," in *Fêtes de la Renaissance*, ed. Jean Jacquot (Paris, 1956), I, 265-77.
[2]*The Dramatic Works of Thomas Dekker*, ed. Fredson Bowers (Cambridge, 1955), II, 303. All quotations from Dekker are from this edition. For discussion of Harrison's work, see my "Pageants, Masques, and Scholarly Ideology," *Practicing Renaissance Scholarship*, pp. 164-92.

son for his work exists in the city records, as noted in Chapter Two. Only one other royal entry show has very full records regarding the workmen, the 1633 Edinburgh pageant for Charles I. Though many names appear throughout the records, no single person emerges as the chief artificer, and no one gets mentioned in the pageant text. But at least in 1604 Harrison stands out as crucial to the total production, and he has helped perpetuate his own memory through his book of engravings. To the mayoral shows our attention must turn for the rest of the story of artificers in civic pageants.

For a thirty-five year period, 1604-39, we can trace the involvement of several artificers repeatedly concerned with the production of Lord Mayors' Shows or who received praise by the dramatist at the end of the pageant text. The discussion of the artificers begins with John Grinkin and closes with Gerard Christmas and his two sons; following such a path will reveal the developments that come in the role of the artificer in the Stuart era. Though we know little of the 1604 Lord Mayor's Show because no extant text survives, the records of the Haberdashers indicate Ben Jonson as the deviser, making one of his rare excursions into this form of civic pageantry.[3] A payment appears for John Grinkin: "Item paid to John Grinkin for the Pageant, Lion, mermaides, Chariott and other thinges 046. 00. 0" (*MSC*, p. 62). Considering that Jonson received £12, Grinkin fares rather well. An earlier mention of Grinkin occurs in company records, though not concerned with pageants: "The earliest known reference which appears to be to him is that in the Court Book of the Carpenters' Company, the 7th of January 1586, whereby Adam Ramshaw is 'to deliver unto John Grinkin two new Joystes which he promiseth to paye and deliver accordinglie.'"[4]

Grinkin worked fully in the 1609 Lord Mayor's Show, honoring the new mayor Sir Thomas Campbell, Ironmonger, written by Anthony Munday and called *Camp-bell or the Ironmongers Faire Field*. An entry of 17 October in company records spells out the agreement made with the artificer:

His agreement made to make the dragon and unicorne and paint the same and to fynd the Armor sheildes and Coparisons ... besides he is to make and furnish two Estriches of silver to draw the Chariot of the Bellfield/. and to make the frame, frutages trees and fountaine and garnishing to the same belonginge, more also the maine Pageant with a golden feild, and an Ocean about it with Mermaides and Tritons artificiallie moovinge, and a majesticall throne upon the topp of the ffeild with iij majesticall diadems and other thinges answerable to the modell therof

---

[3]Malone Society, *Collections III: A Calendar of Dramatic Records in the Books of the Livery Companies of London 1485-1640*, ed. Jean Robertson and D. J. Gordon (Oxford, 1954), p. 63. References to company records are generally to this source and are cited as *MSC* within the text.
[4]J. H. P. Pafford, ed., *Chruso-thriambos* (London, 1962), p. 53.

this day left with the Companie the same all to be done [in oyle] and he
to have for the same xlv^li/. (*MSC*, pp. 73-4)

Not only does this specify Grinkin's duties, but also it reveals something of the
sophistication of the machinery used in such street pageants and it supplements
Munday's text. After the performance on 29 October, Grinkin received £45 according to records dated 3rd and 6th of November; but a minor problem occurred: "whereas it was petitioned for recompence towards the pavement broken
in Christchurch att the tyme of the fforme for the shewes making it is conceived
that the same is parcell of the sayd Grinkins bargaine and hee to amend the
same:/" (p. 77). Months later Grinkin made his own petition: "John Grinkin
payntersteyner petitioning some further recompence for his paynes is allowed for
the setting upp of the Shewes in the Hall five shillings:/" (p. 78). This note of August 1610 reminds us that occasionally some of the devices used in the entertainments eventually found a place in the hall of the company or perhaps the
Guildhall.

Though no extant text remains of the 1610 show, the Merchant Taylors' Accounts give evidence that Munday again served as the author; and several payments to Grinkin appear: "£126 to Mr. Grinkin, the painter, for making, painting, and gilding the pageant, chariot, 3 lions, 2 unicorns, a camel, 2 giants, new
painting the ship ..." (*MSC*, p. 79). He got an additional 6s. 8d. "for his colours"
and 12s. "for guns that he bought for the ship, and for his men's attendance upon
the pageant, chariot, and the other shows ..." (p. 79). Thus with these accounts
and others we can at least salvage something regarding the details of this lost
show.

Again in 1611 Munday and Grinkin joined in the production of *Chruso-
thriambos*, celebrating the installation of Sir James Pemberton, Goldsmith. Seemingly, each man, dramatist and artificer, conducted his own negotiations with the
company. The agreement with Grinkin, dated 7 September 1611, called for him
to provide the following:

> ... the Tomb for ffarington the Maior, properties for Tyme, the
> Chariott and the two Kinges drawne with two Leopardes, the Orpherie
> drawne by two unicornes with places to contayne Justice and her two
> daughters on the top, and for Dunstone ... ffor this Grinkin is to have
> uppon the sufficient performance thereof the somme of lxxv^li. (*MSC*, p.
> 81)

Other details included gold and silver wedges and workmen ostensibly refining
gold at a forge. The agreement tacks on at the end this stipulation: "And yf he
shall [fayle in the well doing thereof] satisfie the expectation in the well doing
thereof the Companie will be pleased to have further consideration of his care

and paynes therein to be had./" (p. 81). Again these records corroborate the printed pamphlet by referring to personages like Faringdon, the former Lord Mayor "resurrected" at his tomb by Time and Leofstane (apparently the "Dunstone" in the entry).

Though Thomas Middleton, the dramatist for the 1613 pageant which he called *The Triumphs of Truth*, received £40, the ubiquitous Anthony Munday, in charge of many of the arrangements, got £149, and John Grinkin the artificer, the handsome sum of £310. But the account in the Grocers' Charges of Triumphs reveals that Grinkin's payment included his expenditures:

> Paide to John Grynkin Payntersteyner for the making of the Pageant, Senate howse, Shipp, errors and truthes Charryottes, withall the severall beastes which Drew the [them?], The five Ilandes, and for all the Carpenters worke, paynting, guilding, and garnishing of them with all other thinges necessarrye reddye for the Children and Players to to [sic] sytt in…. (*MSC*, p. 88)

How much of the sum went beyond Grinkin's expenses unfortunately cannot be determined; nevertheless, he clearly occupies a place of increased responsibility as he assumes the charge of so many projects and workers. Apparently pleased with his work, Middleton acknowledges the aid of Grinkin at the end of the pamphlet: "… the whole work and body of the Triumph, with all the proper beauties of the workmanship, most artfully and faithfully performed by John Grinkin; and those furnished with apparel and porters by Anthony Munday, gentleman."[5] From his first mayoral pageant Middleton begins the practice of citing and commending his chief assistants, perhaps revealing something of the close relationship between poet and artisan.

For the entertainment of 1618, Munday's *Sidero-thriambos*, Grinkin again served as the chief artificer. An entry in the Ironmongers' records for 9 October 1618 notes the arrangement: "it is now agreed that Anthony Mundy with whom the Committees are contracted for the pageant shall have xx^{li} payed him and John Grinkin xx^{li}, in parte of payment of the worke by them to be done according to the agrement of the sayd Committees./" (*MSC*, p. 94). And a few days before the show, 26 October, Edward Atkinson assisted, "appointed to attend with his Carpenters tooles upon Grinkin to mend the Pageant …" (p. 95). According to an entry on 27 October Grinkin received an additional £5 for his services; and one final account also refers to finances: "More paid Munday and Grinkin in parte of the Pageants 0040 00 00"; and, "More paid them in full payment 0025 00 00" (p. 97). We note the striking contrast between the payment of Grinkin in

[5]*The Works of Thomas Middleton*, ed. A. H. Bullen (London, 1886), VII, 262. All quotations from Middleton are from this edition.

1618 and the £310 he received in 1613, doubtless reflecting his responsibilities and the materials that he provided. In fact, the Ironmongers spent only £523 while the Grocers in 1613 had spent about £1,300. The 1618 pageant included two other helpers: Gerard Christmas, his long career discussed below, and Anthony Munday's son, Richard, who provided some banners.

On the basis of evidence in the Haberdashers' Triumphs Accounts of a payment to Grinkin of £54 for his silk works Pafford asserts plausibly Grinkin's involvement with the 1620 mayoral pageant written by Squire. The Haberdashers' Yeomanry Account includes the record of a payment to Francis Tipsley and Squire of £180 "for the Pageants" (*MSC*, p. 100), but no mention of Grinkin. At any rate, Grinkin passes from active participation in the production of mayoral pageants. Pafford notes his extensive employment by Lord William Howard from 1618 to 1621 for whom he mended and painted pictures. "There was a self-portrait of him in the collection of Charles I which passed to that of James II. It cannot now be traced, and may not have survived."[6] Through Grinkin's career as artificer in civic shows we learn something about the variety of tasks such a person might perform, the wide range of his responsibilities, and the commensurate differences in pay. The ever-increasing responsibility and prominence for the artificer become obvious, reaching their high point in 1613 for Grinkin. In other words, Grinkin establishes a precedent upon which other artisans can build.

We know disappointingly little about Rowland Bucket who deserves attention here for his work with two Lord Mayors' Shows. For his artistry he gained recognition at the end of the descriptive pamphlets for the 1614 and 1617 shows, but we know nothing else. Munday's *Himatia-Poleos* (1614) closes with praise for Bucket—the first time in his pageant career that Munday makes such a statement:

> To conclude, as the severall Inventions (with all their weaknesses and imperfections) were mine owne: so the worth and credit of their performance (if any may waite on so meane a businesse) belongeth to the exact and skilfull Painter Maister *Rowland Bucket*, whose care, diligence, and faithfull dealing I must needs commend, and should wrong him overmuch if I did not give him due praise to his merit.[7]

Unfortunately, we cannot know precisely what Bucket did to earn such praise nor even his financial reward.

A similar story occurs in Middleton's 1617 show, *The Triumphs of Honour and Industry*, where at the close of the text Middleton writes:

---

[6]Pafford, *Chruso-thriambos*, p. 53.
[7]Anthony Munday, *Himatia-Poleos* (London, 1614), sigs. C3ᵛ-C4.

No sooner the speech is ended but the Triumph is dissolved, and not
possible to scape the hands of the defacer; things that, for their quaint-
ness (I dare so far commend them), have not been usually seen through
the City; the credit of which workmanship I must justly lay upon the
deserts of master Rowland Bucket, chief master of the work.... (VII,
307)

Middleton also mentions Henry Wilde and Jacob Challoner who assisted, but
Bucket clearly serves as the chief artificer. With Bucket we can only make infer-
ences: he was obviously a capable and skilled craftsman, he generated praise for
his artistry, and he occupied a prominent position in the production of the entertainments. Beyond this we cannot go.

Robert Norman, another artificer, generates little information. The *Diction-
ary of National Biography* includes a Robert Norman (fl. 1590), noted as a
mathematical instrument maker and the author of *The New Attractive, containing
a short discourse of the Magnes or Lodestone* (1581), a book often reprinted in the
sixteenth and seventeenth centuries. The preface refers to Norman as "the expert
artificer," which makes one wonder if this Robert Norman and the one associated with the Lord Mayors' Shows may be the same person. Whatever the identity, Williams offers an incomplete picture, when she says of our Norman:
"Nothing is known of this Norman except that he assisted Garret Christmas in
preparing *Britannia's Honor* in 1628."[8] Indeed he assisted Christmas, the man in
charge of the production matters for Dekker's 1628 show, and he received something over £28 for his services (*MSC*, p. 113); but nearly ten years earlier he had
also assisted Christmas in Middleton's *The Triumphs of Love and Antiquity*
(1619) for which he shared in the recognition from the dramatist:

... yet not without a little leave taken to reward art with the comely
dues that belong unto it, which hath been so richly expressed in the
body of the Triumph with all the proper beauties of workmanship, that
the city may, without injury to judgment, call it the masterpiece of her
triumphs; the credit of which workmanship I must justly lay upon the
deserts of master Garret Crismas and master Robert Norman, joined-
partners in the performance. (VII, 331-2)

Norman's duties or contributions remain unspecified, but his place in the production seems obviously important. He may also be the person referred to in an
entry in the Domestic State Papers dated 7 October 1622: "Warrant for delivery

[8]Sheila Williams, "A Lord Mayor's Show by John Taylor, the Water Poet," *Bulletin of the John Rylands
Library* 41 (1959): 507.

of stuff to Robt. Norman, one of the Prince's Hunstmen, for his livery."[9] Unfortunately, his identity remains uncertain, and one can only be tantalized by these occasional references.

About Norman in 1634 we can be quite certain, for he worked with John Taylor in mounting the mayoral pageant, *The Triumphs of Fame and Honour*. In the Clothworkers' Account books we find mention of an item paid for a dinner for a meeting "at the hall a seconde tyme to treate with Zachary Taylor and Robert Norman about the Pageantes the some of xxviij^s ij^d."[10] But no payment appears for the actual duties of Norman. Nevertheless, the pageant-dramatist leaves no doubt about Norman as the chief artificer, as noted previously:

> It were shamefull impudence in mee to assume the invention of these Structures and Architectures to my selfe, they being busines which I never was inured in, or acquainted with all, there being little of my directions in these shewes; onely the Speeches, and illustrations which are here printed I doe justly challenge as mine owne, all the rest of the Composures and Fabricks were formed and framed by the ingenious and industrious M'r *Robert Norman* Citizen and Painter of London, who was indeed the prime inventor prosecutor and finisher of these works, with the assistance of *Zachary Taylor* a quaint and well knowne curious Carvar, which being gracefully accepted and approved of, after good CHRISTMAS, the authors may be the more merry at the next.[11]

Clearly with this show the artificer assumes the larger responsibility, with the poet, by his own admission, playing a secondary role. This corresponds with the pattern happening generally in the production of these shows in the 1630s as we shall see also in the example of Christmas and his sons.

The final chapter of Norman's participation with the civic pageants comes in 1635 and reveals much about the negotiations with the company, this time the Ironmongers. He again collaborated with John Taylor as shown in this entry of 2 October in the Ironmongers' Court Books: "Robert Norman and John Taylor presented to the Court their project of 5 pageantes for the Lord Maiors shewe for which they demanded 190^{li} and under that price they would not undertake it" (*MSC*, p. 122). But their effort failed, because the team of Thomas Heywood and John and Mathias Christmas underbid them by £10, and the company went for the lower bidder. For their project and invention the Court decided to pay Nor-

---

[9]*Calendar of State Papers Domestic, 1619-1623*, X, 453.
[10]Malone Society, *Collections V: A Calendar of Dramatic Records in the Books of the London Clothworkers Company*, ed. Jean Robertson (Oxford, 1959), p. 14.
[11]John Taylor, *The Triumphs of Fame and Honour* (London, 1634), sig. B4. Note the allusion to Gerard Christmas.

man and Taylor twenty shillings; and in the Ironmongers' Registers occurs this entry: "Pd to Mr Norman and Taylor for their paines in drawing a draught of the pageantes 01 00 00" (p. 124). Nevertheless, from the simple task of painter and early assistant to Christmas Norman moved to a place of considerable prominence, actively joining the dramatist in negotiation and perhaps surpassing him in significance in the 1634 show.

With the career of Gerard Christmas and his sons, John and Mathias, we learn even more about the role of the artificer in civic pageantry, and this family has a unique involvement in the mayoral shows. For one thing no other father-sons team serves as artificer for any civic entertainment; furthermore, no one else has as long an association with the pageants as the Christmas family—a twenty-one year span from 1618 to 1639. Writers consistently and universally single them out for praise whether Middleton, Dekker, or Heywood. By tracing this family's involvement in the production of the mayoral shows, we shall learn not only about this particular family; but, more important, we shall get an additional and very valuable picture of the relationship between poet and architect in civic pageantry.

Robertson notes the importance of the career of Gerard (or Garrett) Christmas, but she makes no attempt to follow it chronologically. At one point she says of Christmas: "Il apparaît pour la première fois comme faiseur de *pageants* en 1619 lorsque Middleton rend hommage à l'habileté de Garrett Christmas et Robert Norman."[12] But I would place Christmas's beginning in the previous year, 1618, when he assisted with Munday's show.[13] As noted above, John Grinkin served as the principal artificer; but the records of the Ironmongers' Court Books show Christmas's involvement: "It was now by erection of hands Committed to Mr Nicholas Leate and Mr William Canning to deal with Christmas about the devise of a cannon for the Show" (*MSC*, p. 94). Three more entries itemize the amounts paid to Christmas for the cannon. From this modest beginning he gained increasing importance in the overall production of the pageants. And Middleton calls attention to him in the Lord Mayor's Show of 1619, where at the close of the pamphlet Middleton singles out the effort of both Norman and Christmas, "joined-partners in the performance."

On four more occasions Christmas assisted Middleton, in the production of the mayoral pageants for 1621, 1622, 1623, and 1626. In 1621 the Drapers' Wardens' Accounts record: "Item paid to Mr Thomas Middleton Garrett Christmas and Anthony Monday by Agreement for makinge and settinge out of the Pag-

[12]"Rapports du Poète," p. 275.
[13]R. C. Bald says that "In 1616 Middleton worked for the first time with Garret Christmas ..." ("Middleton's Civic Employments," *MP* 31 (1933): 73). Surely this is a mistake, for there is no evidence of their association before 1619. The date 1616 is probably a printer's error, and there is another one in Bald's footnote #26 where the date of *Civitatis Amor* appears as 1619 instead of 1616.

eantes and showes ..." the sum of £140 (*MSC*, p. 101). Presumably the three worked out some sort of distribution of the money. In addition, Christmas got three pounds "to paie for the hyer of a barne in Whitecrosstreete for the tyme when the Pageantes weare makinge" (p. 103). This information underscores Christmas as the main artificer, and it also specifies some of his duties. At the close of his account of *The Sun in Aries*, Middleton applauds the work of Christmas: "For the frame-work of the whole Triumph, with all the proper beauties of workmanship, the credit of that justly appertains to the deserts of master Garret Crismas, a man excellent in his art, and faithful in his performances" (VII, 350). Middleton says much the same thing in his *Triumphs of Honour and Virtue* (1622) when he notes: Christmas "an exquisite master in his art, and a performer above his promises" (p. 367). The year 1622 became especially profitable for Middleton and Christmas, for they received £220 "for orderinge overseeing and wrytinge of the whole devise ... printinge of 500 bookes, ... and for all the Carpenter and Carvers worke payntinge guyldinge and garnishinge of them ..." (*MSC*, p. 104) . This account from the Grocers' Charges of Triumphs reminds us of the typical responsibility of the poet and his assistant to have printed the commemorative books describing the pageant.

In 1623 Middleton and Christmas got £150, according to the agreement with the Drapers (*MSC*, p. 105). Christmas received additional money "for the hiring of boardes to make a place for the making of the Pageant," and his men got paid "when the wardens went to see the Pageants" (p. 106). Praise belongs to Christmas, Middleton says in *Triumphs of Integrity* (1623): "For all the proper adornments of art and workmanship in so short a time, so gracefully setting forth the body of so magnificent a Triumph ..." (VII, 395-6). As we have noted, Anthony Munday also assisted in this mayoral pageant by writing a water scene performed on the Thames which he describes in his pamphlet, *The Triumphs of the Golden Fleece*.

Not until 1626 did Middleton and Christmas collaborate again, but Middleton refers to Christmas in language strikingly similar to the 1623 statement. In 1626 in *The Triumphs of Health and Prosperity* Middleton commends Christmas, "a man not only excellent in his art, but faithful in his undertakings," "For his fabric or structure of the whole Triumph, in so short a time so gracefully performed ..." (VII, 411). For their efforts the two received £135 according to the records of the Drapers company, but not without some difficulty. An entry in the guild records suggests the cause of the delay: "Item the paymente of Mr Middleton and Mr Christmas for the Pageantes and of others for the fireworkes and providinge of Chambers beinge hetherto putt of in regarde of the ill performance thereof is nowe referred to the Wardens Batchellors of this Company ..." (*MSC*, p. 110).

Earlier in 1626 both Middleton and Christmas had apparently been involved with the futile effort to prepare a royal entry pageant for Charles I, a subject discussed in Chapter Three. But word came to the Aldermen in January 1626 "of abuses and badd workmanshipp in and about the contrivinge and payntinge of the Pagentes"; therefore, the Aldermen established a committee to "veiwe the Pagentes also the Crosse in Cheape, and the worke done in the Exchange, and sufficientlie to informe themselves of the abuses any waie committed in and aboute the workmanshipp thereof...."[14] On 8 June 1626 the Aldermen consider the case of Christmas and the money disbursed to him "for the fynishing of the three pageantes, and for the performance of the shewes," intended for the king's entry. The record states further: "It is thought fitt and soe ordered the said Mr Chrismas and Mr Middleton referring themselves unto this Court, that noe further moneyes shalbe paid unto either of them, but that Mr Chrismas shall forthwith cause the said Pagentes to bee taken downe, and to have the some for his full satisfaccion."[15] Bald's suspicion of possible peculation on the part of Christmas and Middleton[16] seems rather tenuous especially in the light of the entry of 22 June in the records of the Aldermen in which they take into consideration the "humble petition" of Christmas "who now wholy submitted himselfe unto this Court to abide theire order this Court is pleased to give him the some of c^{li} over and above what alreadie hee hath received...."[17] The year 1626 seems to have been fraught with difficulty for Christmas and Middleton, but the evidence from the city records suggests that the Aldermen became sufficiently satisfied with the work of Christmas.

No extant pamphlet describes the 1627 Lord Mayor's Show; however, the Haberdashers' Yeomanry Account clearly states that Christmas got £200 "for the Pageants and shewes" (*MSC*, p. 112). Apparently he assisted Thomas Dekker with the pageant, for in the dedication to *Wars, Wars, Wars* (1628) Dekker expresses pleasure at having written the entertainment for the mayor in 1627. And the next two years Christmas again worked with Dekker.

Christmas's relationship with Dekker especially reveals information about the position of the artificer. For example, from the Skinners' Renter Wardens' Accounts we learn that Dekker received £23, Christmas £150, and Robert Norman, painter, in excess of £28 for the 1628 Lord Mayor's Show (*MSC*, p. 113). This unusual account tells us about the money distribution among the people responsible for producing the pageant; one can reasonably conjecture this as a typical pattern. Undoubtedly Christmas had to pay for most of the materials from his sum. At the close of the pamphlet, *Britannia's Honor*, Dekker says of the devices of the pageant: "They are not Vast, but Neate, and Comprehend as much Arte for Architecture, as can be bestowed upon such little Bodies. The commen-

[14]Corporation of London, *Repertory*, XL, fol. 84-4^b.
[15]Ibid., fol. 243.
[16]"Middleton's Civic Employments," pp. 75-6.
[17]Corporation of London, *Repertory*, XL, fol. 268.

dations of which must live uppon Mr. *Gerard Chrismas* the Father, and Mr. *John Chrismas* the Sonne" (IV, 95). This becomes the first mention of one of the Christmas sons in the civic entertainments. Dekker again utilized the services of the father for the 1629 show, *London's Tempe*. According to the Ironmongers' Court Books Dekker and Christmas offered their talents for £200, but the company considered this an "overvalue"; however, agreement finally came for the sum of £180 (*MSC*, p. 115). Christmas also had to take care for the provision of breakfast for the child actors (p. 116), for which he got an additional £1. Duties for the artificer obviously ranged at times quite widely. Dekker says: "Thus much, his owne worth, cryes up the Workman (Master *Gerard Chrismas*) for his Invention, that all the peeces were exact, and set forth lively, with much Cost" (IV, 112). Dekker and Christmas have in their association successfully joined together "to set out the beautie of the great *Triumphant-day*."

The association of Gerard Christmas and Thomas Heywood appears also an apparently harmonious and productive one, and during this association with Heywood the work passes from father to sons because of Gerard's death in 1634. Nevertheless, the father served as the artificer for three of Heywood's pageants— 1631, 1632, 1633. The records, the Haberdashers' Yeomanry Account, indicate that for 1631 Christmas received £200 "for pageants and shewes" (*MSC*, p. 121) and £190 "for Pageants" in 1632 (p. 122). Interestingly, in neither year does the name of Heywood get mentioned in the company records, suggesting Christmas as in charge of negotiations with the company. At the close of the text of *Londons Jus Honorarium* (1631), Heywood says:

> The maine show, being performed by the most excellent in that kind, Mr. *Gerard Christmas*, who hath exprest his Modals to be exquisite, as having spared neither Cost nor care, either in the Figures or ornaments. I shall not neede to point unto them to say, this is a Lyon, and that an Unicorne, etc. For of this Artist, I may bouldly and freely thus much speake, though many about the towne may envie their worke, yet with all their indevor they shall not be able to compare with their worth.[18]

This praise of Christmas's work follows in the 1632 pageant with equal recognition of his artistry:

> So he who found these Pageants and showes of Wicker and Paper, rather appearing monstrous and prodigious Births, then any Beast ... in the least kind imitating Nature; hath reduc't them to that sollidity and substance for the Materialls, that they are so farre from one dayes washing to deface them, that the weathering of many Winters can not im-

---

[18]Thomas Heywood, *Londons Jus Honorarium* (London, 1631), sig. C4ᵛ.

peach them: and for their excellent Figures and well-proportioned lineaments, (by none preceding him) that could bee sayd to be paralleld....[19]

In 1633 no mention of actual payment appears in the company records, but an entry for 19 September 1633 in the Clothworkers' Court Books shows that a conference occurred with Gerard Christmas "towchinge the providinge of such Pageantes as shalbee" on the day of the installation of the Lord Mayor.[20] In the pageant text Heywood applauds Christmas: "... I am of opinion that there is not any about the towne who can goe beyond him, of whom I may boldly speake, that as Art is an helpe to nature, so his experience is, and hath beene an extention to the tryall and perfection of Art...."[21] No other pageant writer has been so abundant in praise of Gerard Christmas as Heywood. Obviously their relationship remained harmonious, and apparently Christmas assumed new status and responsibility in dealing with the trade company. Robertson suggests that this rise in importance came about without friction: "Sans doute Christmas payait-il Heywood d'une façon équitable, en échange de quoi le poète reconnaissait dans son livret sa dépendance à l'égard de l'artiste. L'habileté de Christmas et son respect de la parole donnée faisaient l'objet d'autant d'éloges que son art. On a l'impression qu'il demeurait un artisan digne de confiance."[22]

A new chapter in the career of the Christmas family begins in 1634. On 24 March a petition entered on the behalf of Gerard Christmas to the Lords of the Admiralty appears:

Petitioner has been established in his place these 20 years, under warrant of the Earl of Nottingham then Lord Admiral, and for his service there is due to him 400 l., which has been due these 16 years. Having brought up his two sons John Christmas and Matthias Christmas in the said art, and being aged, sick, and with a charge of ten children, petitioner prays that his two sons before mentioned may be jointly admitted into his place.[23]

In a few days Gerard Christmas died; his career as an artificer in civic pageants and as a carver in the navy thus ended. Fortunately, the two sons gained admission into their father's place as carver to the navy as shown in their work on the

---

[19]*Londini Artium & Scientiarum Scaturigo* (London, 1632), sig. C2ᵛ.
[20]Malone Society, *Collections V*, p. 12.
[21]*Londini Emporia* (London, 1633), sig. C2.
[22]"Rapports du Poète," p. 277.
[23]*Calendar of State Papers Domestic, 1633-1634*, p. 521.

"great ship,"[24] and they also succeeded in their father's stead in the Lord Mayors' Shows in the four remaining pageants of Heywood.

The Ironmongers' Court Books for 1635 give a most interesting account of how the company devising the pageant selected Heywood and the Christmas brothers. It reminds us of the usual procedure of competition in determing the author. As mentioned above, the company chose John Christmas and Heywood because of their low bid over Robert Norman and John Taylor. Interestingly, the agreement with the Ironmongers John and Mathias Christmas signed but not Heywood (*MSC*, p. 123), and the payment of £180 went to John Christmas (p. 124). In the text of *Londini Sinus Salutis* Heywood closes with praise of the two sons and remembrance of the father:

> These Frames, Modells, and Structures, were Fashioned, Wrought, and Perfected, by the Two Artists JOHN, and MATHIAS CHRISMAS; Successors to their Father, Mr. GERALD CHRISMAS, late disceased, as well in the Exquisite performance of his qualitie, as in his true sincerite, and honesty; of whom I may confidently speake, as no man could out-vie him in these Workes, which hee underwent, so none could out-match him in his word, For anything hee undertooke....[25]

Heywood, obviously, expresses satisfaction with the artistry of the sons as with the accomplishment of the father.

The only reference to the Christmas brothers and their work in the 1637 pageant occurs in the pamphlet, *Londini Speculum*, which gives Heywood's description. Here Heywood again refers to Gerard, "a knowne Master in all those Sciences he profest...."[26] Of the sons Heywood says further: "My Opinion is, that few Workemen about the Towne can parallel them, much lesse exceede them. But if any shall either out of Curiosity or malice taxe their ability, in this kind of Art, I referre them to the Carving of his Majesties *Great Ship* lately built at *Woolwitch*, which Worke alone is able both to satisfie *Emulation*, and qualifie *Envie*" (sig. C4ᵛ). Entries in the *Calendar of State Papers Domestic* provide much information about the "great ship" and also reveal the involvement of John and Mathias Christmas. In a pamphlet printed in 1637 in which he traces the history of shipbuilding from ancient times to the present building of the royal ship for King Charles, Heywood gives us additional commentary on this great ship. Near the end of the document he singles out various workmen for praise and includes the Christmas brothers, "the Sonnes of that excellente Workeman Master *Gerard*

[24]On 19 April 1634 they were admitted to their father's place according to the *Calendar of State Papers Domestic*, p. 558.
[25]*Londini Sinus Salutis* (London, 1635), sig. B3ᵛ.
[26]*Londini Speculum* (London, 1637), sig. C4ᵛ.

Christmas, some two yeares since deceased, who, as they succeed him in his place, so they have striv'd to exceed him in his *Art*...."[27] Heywood's constant remembrance of the father becomes a touching and fine tribute to him, obviously implying great rapport between them. The sons, too, find much favor in his eyes be it for their work for his pageants or their work for the navy.

The entries for 1638 and 1639 in the records of the Drapers relevant to the pageants closely parallel each other. In 1638 the account reads thus:

> Item paid to John Christmas and Matthew Christmas by agreement for making and setting out of five Pageants or showes as by the printed booke they are particularly described ... and to discharge M[r] Thomas Hayward the Poet for writing the booke and furnishing the Company with 500 bookes the some of Clxx[li] and of the Companies well liking it, x[li].... (*MSC*, p. 127)

The agreement of 1639 corresponds almost word for word except the men received £196 (p. 129). From these records the Christmas brothers clearly assume primary responsibility for the production, even to the extent of paying the poet from their fees. At the close of the descriptive pamphlets Heywood again dutifully salutes their efforts. In *Porta Pietatis* (1638) he writes:

> I will not speake much concerning the two Brothers, M[r] *John* and *Mathias Christmas*, the Modellers and Composers of those severall Peeces this day presented to a mighty confluence, (being the two succeeding Sonnes of that most ingenious Artist M[r] *Gerard Christmas*) to whom, and whose Workmanship I will only conferre that Character, which being long since (upon the like occasion) conferr'd upon the Father, I cannot but now meritedly bestow upon the Sonnes: Men, as they are excellent in their Art, so they are faithfull in their performance.[28]

This high praise continues in *Londini Status Pacatus*, the 1639 Lord Mayor's Show, where Heywood says of the brothers: "I can onely say thus much: their workeman-ship exceeds what I can expresse in words, and in my opinion their performance of what they undertake, is equall at least, if not transcendent over any's who in the like kind shall strive to parallel them."[29] With these words of commendation from Heywood a large and important chapter in the history of English civic pageantry closes. The year 1639 marks the end of Heywood's pag-

[27]*A True Description of His Majesties Royall Ship* (London, 1637), sig. G4. See the critical edition of this text prepared by Alan R. Young (New York, 1990).
[28]*Porta Pietatis* (London, 1638), sig. C2[v].
[29]*Londini Status Pacatus* (London, 1639), sig. C4.

eant career; it marks the end of his profitable association with the Christmas family; it marks the end of mayoral pageantry until the Restoration.

We witness in the pageants from 1618 to 1639 not only a fascinating story of one family's involvement but also the steady rise in importance of the artificer, all confirmed in the examples of the other artificers as well. Robertson rightly claims: "Sans aucun doute cette promotion de l'artiste était due au succès de Garrett Christmas."[30] In less skilful hands the role of the architect might have remained nominal, but Christmas—father and sons—brought artistic talent and apparently congenial personalities to the task and thus earned new importance. In a sense the artificer becomes by the 1630s analogous to the modern-day producer: he negotiates, he oversees, he gets paid and in turn pays others. And certainly during Heywood's tenure as pageant-writer, the Christmas family dominates the negotiations with the trade company. The poet-dramatist begins to slip into the background, though the pronounced break between poet and artificer observed in the development of the court masque does not materialize in the civic pageant. The Christmas family of course provides continuity for a twenty-year period in the mayoral entertainments—small wonder that they achieved a prominence unknown to their predecessors.

The various planning committees established by the cities or by the guilds complemented the work of these artificers. Throughout the preceding chapters we have noted something of the preparations made especially for the royal entry and the Lord Mayors' pageants, and a selective review will underscore the importance of these groups in helping establish the "body" of the civic pageant. Particular attention will focus on the financing of these civic shows.

Typically for the royal entry the aldermen or some governing body of the city would establish the necessary committees to plan all the details of the pageant, including raising the necessary money. We recall that for the 1559 London entry entertainment the City of London set up several groups to prepare the city for the queen's processional. For financing the entry of Mary, Queen of Scots, into Edinburgh in 1561 the city government decreed "that ane generall extent be set and lyftit of all the nychtbouris of this burgh, bayth merchant and craftisman, to the quantite of the said sowme of iiij m.merkis, and with all deligence to be collectit and debursit for the releif of the creditouris, furnissaris of the necessaris of the said banquet triumphe and propyne."[31] This direct involvement of the citizens underlies the civic nature of pageantry and suggests again a link to medieval drama.

As noted in Chapter Two, the planning for the entertainment for James I in London ranged quite extensively; from the outset the city determined to spend

---

[30]"Rapports du Poète," p. 275.
[31]Anna J. Mill, *Mediaevel Plays in Scotland*, St. Andrews University Publication, no. XXIV (Edinburgh & London, 1927), p. 189.

some £2,500 to be "paide and disbursed by all the severall companies halles and corporacions within this Cittie...."[32] Several more assessments called for £400 being specifically set aside for the pageants, the amount to be "leavied by all such of the severall Companyes within this Cyttie as heeretofore weare assessed to contribute ..." (*Journal*, XXVI, fol. 163). For example, the city expected the Merchant Taylors to raise £37 for this expenditure, the Haberdashers £28, the Mercers £32, the Grocers £34, the Goldsmiths £32, etc. From the ranks of these guilds the money would be raised in a manner doubtless similar to that of the Lord Mayors' Shows. We recall also the dismantling of the "bodies" of the pageants and their being offered for sale "at the best and highest rates" to the best benefit of the companies "as contributed towardes the charge of them" (fol. 186). By the time all assessments had been made, the city had anticipated debts of £4,100 for this entertainment. Selected members of the Painter-stainers had the task of viewing the pageants to be sure the city had gotten good value for its investment. Interestingly, the Wardens of the Brewers' company refused to pay £50 for the pageant, leading to their confinement to the ward until they made at least partial payment.[33] This resistance appears several times in other civic pageants as either guilds or individual members balked at the expense. For example, in 1606 when King Christian IV of Denmark made an official entry into London, the city levied the sum of £1,000 against the companies,[34] but the Goldsmiths resisted their assessment of £80, which they considered excessive. Thus they decided to offer "three score pounds ... till the Wardens shall see fit to make further payment. The Clerk, in the meantime, to represent to the Lord Mayor how hard the Company take it that they are rated so high above other Companies...."[35]

While the Audits in the city of Bristol contain an account of the expenses for Queen Anne's visit there in 1613, they offer no clear indication for raising these sums. But at Wells, which Anne also visited in 1613, we get a good idea of the financial arrangement for the body of the pageant. A committee oversees the preparations, and "every companie to bee Contributorie as they have binne in tymes past to the shewes aforesaid."[36] Another entry indicates that every guild and every man within the company "shall Contribute such somme and sommes of money towardes the said shewes as shalbee agreed uppon amongst themselves"; failure to pay could result in "paine of imprisonment and there to lie till such severall rate bee payde and satisfied" (fol. 377). The city maintained a strong posture in assuring itself that the debts for such civic drama would be met.

[32]Corporation of London, *Journal*, XXVI, fol. 78.
[33]Corporation of London, *Repertory*, XXVI, pt. 2, fol. 290-90[b].
[34]*Journal*, XXVII, fol. 73[b].
[35]Walter Prideaux, *Memorials of the Goldsmiths' Company, 1335-1815* (London, 1896), I, 106.
[36]Wells, *Acts of the Corporation 1553-1623*, fol. 376.

The failure of Charles I to make his scheduled royal entry into London in 1626 caused considerable frustration and consternation, as discussed in Chapter Three. And we have seen above the payments made to Gerard Christmas for work that had to be torn down, the body failing to gain a soul. The sense of loss increases with the elaborate but futile efforts and planning of the committees established by the city as in earlier royal entries. They had the task "to consider what course and meanes they conceave most fittest to be taken for the levyinge and raysinge of moneys already disbursed or to be disbursed...."[37] The debts for this intended pageant hang on; thus in September 1627 another group must determine what has been disbursed and "to advise and consider, howe and what manner, the same moneys may most fittly be raised and collected, and repaid to the Chamber...."[38] Reporting a month later, the committee reveals a debt of some £4,300 outstanding, but it does make a proposal for securing the necessary money. Precedent suggests that formerly such expense came "borne and raysed, by and out of the severall Companies of this Citty according as they were rated for the provision of Corne"; thus the present debt may be "nowe likewise raised and leavyed of the sayd Companies accordinge to the proporcion of tenne thowsand quarters of Corne as each Companie is rated at to provide ..." (fol. 163). One may logically take this as the principal way of scheduling the assessments in the earlier entries, such as the 1559 and 1604 ones. Again the Goldsmiths hesitate to pay their fee of nearly £157 until the city pays its debts to the guild, for they had assisted the city in lending money to King Charles.[39]

For the elaborate festivities in Edinburgh in 1633 the city had to secure over £41,000 to defray the expenses of the coronation, banquet, and civic pageant. Wherever one looks—in London, Edinburgh, Bristol, Wells—one constant emerges: the cities incurred financial obligation to present an appropriate civic entertainment for the sovereign, and that economic burden rested squarely on the shoulders of the guilds. From these selected examples we learn not simply of the magnitude of the expense, but also of the methods for meeting such encumbrances. While we can know little about the financing of the progress pageants and must assume that typically the nobleman whose estate the sovereign visited incurred the expenses for dramatic entertainments, we do know a great deal about the economic arrangements for the Lord Mayors' Shows; to them our attention now turns as we shall see how the guilds met the demands for the "body" of the pageant.

Almost any year can be selected, especially from the Jacobean period forward to 1640, and one can get an excellent example of the planning made by the guilds for the civic pageants designed to honor the new mayor of London. Active nego-

---

[37]Corporation of London, *Journal*, XXXIII, fol. 182.
[38]*Journal*, XXXIV, fol. 159[b].
[39]Prideaux, I, 147.

tiation would take place between the dramatist and the company and increasingly, as noted above, with the chief artificer. Expenditures ranged over such items as costume apparel for the actors, printing the book of speeches, services of the dramatist and many other workers chiefly concerned with the body, providing breakfast for the child actors on the day of the show, porters to carry some of the devices about the city, numerous banners and streamers, chariots, "green men" with fireworks who might clear the path for the procession, musicians, removing obstacles (such as signs) out of the scheduled route—all such expenses appear in the records for the 1604 Lord Mayor's Show where we find a typical example of that repeated many times.[40]

To meet the increasing expense for the production of the mayoral pageants the guilds had to assess their members, and this becomes a crucial function in the preparation for the shows. When the Goldsmiths made their plans for the 1611 entertainment, they decided that the Bachelors of the company—the chief source of revenue for most of the pageants—should "each of them ... paye fyve poundes unto the two Treasurers" in order to help "towardes the defraying of the common charge of the pageantes ..." (*MSC*, p. 83). Also the "yeomanry of the company did likewise make apparance before Mr Wardens and willinglie consented to undergoe anye reasonable charge for the performance of the busynes and triumphe upon occasion of the succeeding Lord Maior" (p. 80).

Several entries among the records of the Drapers confirm something of the pattern seen in the 1611 show. For Munday's 1614 mayoral pageant, the Wardens of the Drapers had power to "admit twenty-one freemen to the Livery over and above the Master Bachelors of the year ... These were to pay 20 marks each...."[41] In addition they ordered eighty Bachelors to attend the procession, "forty dressed in foynes who were to contribute £5 towards the general charge, and forty dressed in budge who were to pay £3; while those excused from attending in foyne were to pay £12, and those excused from attending in budge £6" (p. 7). Similarly in 1626, ten persons of the yeomanry gained admission into the livery in order to help defray the expenses of the pageant, and "what moneyes shall fall shorte with the moneyes arysinge be the present yeomandryes stocke and to be raysed out of the yeomandry by fines for and aboute the intended service togeather with the moneyes received for admittance into the livery shall all of yt be ymployed to performe the sayd Showes and tryumphes" (*MSC*, pp. 109-10). And in the last two Lord Mayors' Shows before 1642, Heywood's 1638 and 1639 ones, the Drapers again used the method of elevating members to the Livery in order to assist in meeting the costs of the pageants. Thus the company follows a consis-

---

[40]Malone Society, *Collections III*, pp. 62-8.
[41]A. H. Johnson, *The History of the Worshipful Company of Drapers of London* (Oxford, 1914-22), III, 7.

tent pattern in solving the financial problems, as revealed in these representative examples covering a twenty-five year period.

From 1620 to 1637 the Haberdashers produced five Lord Mayors' pageants with a similar method of defraying the expense in each instance. The guild records for Squire's 1620 show indicate that the committee in charge of preparation needed to choose ninety or a hundred bachelors from the yeomanry to serve, some in foins, some in budge, "and those in foynes to Contribute towardes the Charges of that triumphe v^{li} a peece and those in Budg fyve markes a peece ..." (*MSC*, p. 100). This assessment remains consistent throughout the company's other pageants. But just as the guilds sometimes hesitated to meet their charges for the royal entry shows, so individual members occasionally balked at paying their assessments for the mayoral pageants. An entry in the records of the Grocers for 1613 becomes somewhat typical:

> Paide to William Atkins the Lord Maiors officer for paynes by him taken about suche brothers of this Company as weare disobedient and refused to pay as they were assessed 003. 00. 00.[42]

In December 1630 the Court of Aldermen dealt with the case of three members of the Merchant Taylors who had refused to contribute towards the expenses of the pageant; the account of the Aldermen records:

> And the said Hackshawe being assessed at xxx^s and the said Gore at L^s did in Conformity and obedience to the orders of the said Company by the mediacon of this Court lay downe and pay into the hands of Mr Pratt the M^r of the said Company their said severall moneys But the said Stubbins being assessed at L^s did here in open Court obstinately and wilfully refuse to lay downe his said money notwithstanding that he was oftymes in all loving manner perswaded by Mr Recorder and the Court to doe the same for which cause the said Stubbins was by this Court Comitted to the Comon gaole of Newgate there to remayne untill he Conforme himselfe or other order be taken by this Court for his inlargment.[43]

Later in that same December the case of William Whitehead got similar treatment. Having first refused to pay his levy of 30s., he finally repented and was released (fol. 59-59^b). The fierce determination of the guilds to collect the mem-

---

[42]In Sheila H. Williams, "The Lord Mayors' Shows from Peele to Settle: A Study of Literary Content, Organization, and Methods of Production," unpublished Ph.D. thesis (University of London, 1957), I, 58.

[43]Corporation of London, *Repertory*, XLV, fol. 40^b.

bers' assessments impresses us; but given the frequency and considerable expense of the Lord Mayors' Shows, this zeal seems reasonable.

Out of such planning and such expense arose the bodies of the pageants that the artificers fashioned, and this discussion closes with a review of the most significant stage properties and machines of civic pageantry. The descriptive analysis of the royal entries, progress pageants, and Lord Mayors' Shows has already revealed much about the attention to costume; thus we need only remind ourselves of the great care and attention given to the matter of appropriate costume, usually following traditions of iconographical representation. Like the Shakespearean theater, the pageant theater remains also essentially emblematic, and its properties reflect this approach to dramatic presentation.[44] The representative examples discussed below illustrate the emblematic nature while also making us desire more information about the properties of the Shakespearean stage.

Carrying on a tradition of medieval stagecraft, the pageant theater makes extensive use of some sort of scaffold stage, ranging from the simple scaffold erected in Bristol in 1574 as a place for the oration to the magnificent triumphal arches used in several royal entry pageants. Something of the nature of the scaffold/arch occurs in the description of the 1559 London royal entry where, for example, the arch at Soper lane stretched from one side of the street to the other. It had three gates and over the middle one "wer erected three severall stages, whereon sate eight children as hereafter foloweth."[45] In the front part of the arch "was a convenient standing cast out for a chylde to stande, which did expound the said pageaunt unto the quenes majestie ..." (p. 41). Written across the front of the scaffold stood the name of the pageant, and all "voide places in the pageant wer furnished with prety sayinges, commending and touching the meaning of the said pageant ..." (pp. 41-2). Over the two side "portes" the musicians appeared. The basic structure provides the stage for dramatic presentations for many other pageants, such as the royal entry shows in Edinburgh, culminating in the elaborate arches prepared for Charles I in 1633.

Surveying Harrison's drawings for the opulent triumphal arches of the 1604 London royal entry, one sees again the basic elements of the scaffold stage with two or three gates, the arch itself highly decorated, several niches for the live figures. The "stage" area corresponds to the upper stage level of the Elizabethan theater; and George Kernodle, perhaps pressing the point too much, sees the Shakespearean stage as indebted to several features of the architectural façade of the pageant arch.[46] Understandably, triumphal arches predominate in the royal entry, and some of the stage arrangements for the Lord Mayors' Shows may have

[44]See Glynne Wickham, *Early English Stages* (London, 1963), II, chapter VI.
[45]*The Quenes Majesties Passage through the Citie of London*, ed. James M. Osborn (New Haven, 1960), p. 41.
[46]*From Art to Theatre: Form and Convention in the Renaissance* (Chicago, 1944).

resembled the scaffold/arch, but the descriptions make it difficult to know for certain. Of course, all sorts of changes could be rung on the basic design of the arch; thus many of the devices may have approximated a scaffold arrangement, such as the elaborate tableau in Webster's 1624 pageant honoring Prince Henry, which suggests some type of structured grouping.

Located at the Little Conduit in Cheapside in the 1559 civic pageant, a device of "square" proportion contained two mountains, a stage property used frequently in the civic entertainments. Here in Cheapside the hills contrasted, one green and flourishing, the other barren and desolate, both functioning symbolically to assist the thematic soul. Similarly in Heywood's 1631 Lord Mayor's Show a "greene and pleasant Hill" contains a prospering tree, it too reflecting on the condition of the commonwealth. The principal stage of Munday's 1605 pageant, a "mount triangular," includes the chief figures of Britannia and Brutus seated beneath her and also various children, seated "according to their degrees." On a "quadrangle frame" in the 1611 pageant a "Rocke or Mount of Golde" holds the chief place for Vesta and her companions Chrusos and Argurion. Though not offering much description, both Munday in the 1618 show and John Taylor in the 1634 one include the device of a mountain whose chief occupant is Fame. Several times writers designated the mountain as Mount Parnassus which contained Apollo and the Muses. In both the 1582 pageant in Antwerp and in the tiltyard entertainment in Heidelberg in 1613 the Mount Parnassus structure moved, and a drawing in the French text published in Antwerp shows the mount situated on a cart that could move about the area. In the 1620 mayoral pageant Squire used the mount as a device on the river, probably constructed on some type of barge. Along the route in Edinburgh in 1633 Charles I encountered Mount Parnassus populated by Apollo, the Muses, and ancient worthies of Scotland; trees decorated this mount, and it served as the stage from which Apollo could speak. Basically the mountain device seems a modification of the scaffold/arch; especially the arrangement of characters on the mounts recalls a scaffold grouping.

The castle or tower corresponds to both the arch and the hill, such as the Forlorn Castle in Dekker's 1612 Lord Mayor's Show. This structure, complete with battlements, contains, of course, the fortress of Envy and her companions, and the forces of Virtue must safely get past this property—again the close relationship of body and soul. Mars serves as the chief figure in a castle included in Heywood's 1635 pageant, which has various kinds of ordnance as well as the necessary men to defend such a fort. Of a rather different sort forts had been constructed and used in the entertainments at Bristol in 1574 and at Elvetham in 1591. Britannia in Dekker's 1628 show occupies a watch-tower surrounded by eight silver columns and angels standing on the pillars. Much earlier Munday in the 1609 show offered Majesty who also occupied a watch-tower, square in structure and containing columns, arches, "and other skilfull Architecture."

A prevalent property, the tree or arbor makes its presence obvious from the beginning of the Elizabethan period to the last Lord Mayor's Show at the end of the 1630s. A device in the 1559 pageant captures elements of both the arch and the tree, for the structure has the usual arch form with three gates and stretching from one side of the street to the other. Over the middle section three stages ascend, all arranged as a genealogical tree: out of the white and red roses on the lowest stage emerges one branch leading to the second and a final branch springing upward to the top stage. Such a visual arrangement supports the soul—the uniting of the Lancaster and York houses and the unity achieved by the Tudors. No other civic pageant duplicates this genealogical tree device. Instead, Dekker in the 1604 royal entry garnishes one of his arches with flowers and trees and makes of it a Garden of Plenty, an appropriate place for the allegorical virtues of Peace and Plenty, and the speaker offers the king this bower or garden.

Surviving drawings let us know about the appearance of the lemon tree which Munday uses in the 1616 Lord Mayor's Show: "richly laden" with fruit and flowers, at its roots a pelican has built her nest. Here the stage property constructs a visual pun on the mayor's name, John Leman. Because the fruit of the lemon tree admirably preserves the senses, Munday says, he also includes representations of the Five Senses around the tree. Focusing on a single tree, Dekker in the 1628 show depicts "New Troyes Tree of Honor," out of which spread twelve branches, representing the twelve major guilds of London. Surrounding the tree, virtues help sustain the city. The little sketches for Dekker's 1629 pageant reveal another use of trees, for in this show the dramatist presents an arbor furnished with trees and flowers, all of which corresponds to London as a garden. Taking a different approach, Middleton in the 1619 entertainment depicts a thorny wilderness from which Orpheus derives symbolic meaning. At such moments, we recall again the obvious emblematic nature of the pageant's body.

In order to present his "Monument of Charity and Learning," Webster in 1624 creates a garden complete with various kinds of flowers and bird cages. Beneath an elm tree on this device sits Sir Thomas White, who embodies the qualities that Webster wants to represent. In the final pageants of the Caroline period Heywood utilizes the garden arrangement, offering in 1638 a platform adorned with flowers, plants, and trees bearing fruit as a fit place for a shepherd who watches his flock. Celebrating the peaceful estate, Heywood in his final show presents Orpheus seated on a device decorated with trees, several birds, and other animals. For an age so attuned to metaphor the tree/arbor/garden stage device offered many possibilities for the development and enhancement of the poetic soul of the civic pageant.

Writers made limited use of the fountain device, providing scanty descriptions. For example, the final tableau in Heywood's 1632 pageant, the *Scaturigo* or Fountain of Virtue, gets limited description other than to indicate that twelve persons representing the guilds surround the fountain from which all arts and sciences receive nourishment. Middleton's Fount of Justice in 1621 has an accompanying number of allegorical virtues, with little said of the fountain itself. As early as 1591 Peele had used a fountain in his Lord Mayor's Show where the figures of Superstition and Ignorance try to poison the fountain of truth, but their efforts the virtuous presence of Astraea checks. Similarly a few years later, Dekker, as suggested in an earlier chapter, seems to have adapted Peele's device in the tableau at Soper lane in the 1604 civic pageant. Here on an arch Detraction and Oblivion seek by "their olde malitious intention" to suck the fountain dry, but the king's arrival thwarts them. Vice having been suppressed, the fount then flows with milk, wine, and "balme" through its several pipes. The body clearly responds to the demands of the soul.

Only Anthony Munday uses the property of the tomb, including it in both the 1611 and 1616 Lord Mayors' Shows. In 1611 the former Nicholas Faringdon Time summoned from the tomb, and in 1616 William Walworth had a similar resurrection from the tomb where he lay. In that year the tomb appeared within a "goodly Bower," as the extant drawings make clear. From this stage property Munday provides the unique dramatic experience of the calling forth of these ancient Lord Mayors.

Both Munday and Dekker used a structure resembling a mine as an appropriate device in shows honoring the Ironmongers. In the 1618 pageant Munday includes the mine on an island, the whole structure movable and pulled "by two goodly *Estridges*." At the mine several figures work, some using hammers, others attending the fire, and all singing. At the four corners sit four nymphs embodying the four ages of the world. Placed above the mine, a figure sits personating Jupiter whose "three-forked Thunderbolt" has ostensibly been made from this mine by Mulciber. Similarly, Dekker's mine in the mayoral entertainment of 1629 offers men busy at work at the forge, and includes also Jove in an exalted position and Cupid who has a ready supply of arrows from the mine.

Given the processional nature of most civic pageants, we cannot be surprised that chariots abound. A spectacular example comes in Mercury's coach in the 1578 Norwich entertainment, covered with birds; in the middle stood a tower decked out with golden jewels, and a plume of white feathers emerging out of the top of the tower. On a less spectacular scale, the 1605 mayoral show contained a coach used to transport former English kings; similarly, in Webster's 1624 pageant a chariot conveyed kings with appropriate roses used for the Lancastrians and the Yorkists. Pulled by two "Mare-men" and two "Mare-mayds," the final device of the 1616 pageant consisted of a chariot at whose top sits the "triumphing Angell" who through Walworth drove away the king's enemies. Beneath the angel sits a person representing Richard II whose crown an angel holds on fast. Additional royal virtues occupy the front of the chariot, all obvious from the drawings of this Munday pageant.

The striking Chariot of Time in Munday's 1615 entertainment has on its top a globe supported by the four elements. The Chariot itself runs on seven wheels symbolizing the seven ages of man, drawn by two lions and two sea horses, with Time as the principal figure in the coach. With similar details a chariot greeted the new mayor in Squire's 1620 show: decorated with painted hourglasses and sun dials, the front wheels like globes, and the rear wheels like church dials. Time sits upon an hourglass with his usual emblematic properties while the Seasons draw the coach, appropriately costumed. A modification of the chariot device comes in the numerous boats that appear frequently in the civic pageants, especially the Lord Mayors' Shows. In the same 1615 show mentioned above Munday included one boat on the Thames containing Jason, Medea, and others associated with the Golden Fleece story and another boat drawn on land named for the mayor and allegedly just returned from trading around the world. A fishing boat opens Munday's 1616 entertainment which celebrates the Fishmongers company. Calling the boat *Esperanza*, Munday includes fishermen busily at work, drawing up their nets, and bestowing the fish "bountifully among the people." These various properties help constitute the "body" of civic pageantry, though of course others could be mentioned, but the ones discussed here give a fair picture of the use of such properties in the pageant theater.

Reacting with scorn to the creaking thrones of the public stage, Ben Jonson nevertheless must have delighted in the machines associated with the production of court masques. One cannot fail to be impressed also with some of the machines of the civic pageant stage; quite possibly they offered ideas to the inventors of masques. One recalls the imaginative flying dragon that cast out flames in the waning moments of the Warwick entertainment of 1572. Along the route in Antwerp in 1582, a giant "by cunning" turned his face towards the duke when he passed. One recalls, too, that the Lady of the Lake greeted Elizabeth at Kenilworth by floating forth on a movable island blazing with torches. In that same entertainment Arion later appeared surmounting a twenty-four feet long mechanical dolphin that contained inside of it a consort of musicians. Several machines assist in the descent of various figures; for example, in Edinburgh in 1561, a mechanical device in the form of a cloud opened, and a child representing an angel descended and greeted Queen Mary. Assisting in the welcome of the King of Denmark in 1606 in London, the figure of Concord descended by a "quaint devise," let down in her throne to a lower part of an arch from which she spoke to the two kings. In the festivities in Chester in 1610, Mercury descended from heaven in a cloud, "artificially Winged, a Wheele of fire burning very cunningly"—again making use of similar machinery. One wishes for more details about these mechanical devices but must remain content with the brief references to them.

Both the 1579 and 1590 royal entries in Edinburgh include the device of a globe that opens. For James's new bride, Anne, the globe in 1590 descends and opens into four parts from which a child representing an angel appears. When the presentation finishes, the globe closes and ascends. On the arch at Fleet street in the 1604 London pageant an open globe moved, and in the 1632 mayoral show an orbicular device, probably a globe, opened and "quadrated" itself into four sections representing the kingdoms. But more striking, Middleton's 1622 mayoral pageant produced a globe device that suddenly opened and flew into eight parts, revealing eight persons allegorically representing the virtues of an inward man. Clearly these mechanical bodies serve an essential function in the presentation of the soul.

Shrouded in a thick curtain of silk painted like a cloud, stood the arch at Fenchurch in 1604. But the shroud dispersed—the curtain drawn—when King James arrived, thus revealing a bright new city of London carved in miniature atop the arch. Jonson outlines the allegorical meaning of his action of the body. As part of the battle between Truth and Error in Middleton's 1613 pageant London's Triumphant Mount has similar cover, having been darkened by Error. But the dark cloud—apparently a curtain device—vanishes at the presence of Truth, and it changes into a bright canopy, "stuck thick with stars, and beams of gold shooting forth round about it." Several more times in the course of the drama the mist descends on the mount, only to be chased away by Truth. The body and soul closely unite in such efforts.

One finds an impressive sophistication in the properties and machines of the civic pageant theater, the richness and variety of the "body," all representing a level of achievement not always fully appreciated but firmly established before similar accomplishments on the public stage and in the court masque. These "bodies" came as the result of the careful planning and generous expenditures of the guilds or cities and the skilful work of the artificers. Given the nature of civic pageantry and its dependence on visual appeal, one logically expects such concerted effort focused on the body of the pageant, it providing the means and the place for the soul to come alive. From the "cloud-capp'd towers, the gorgeous palaces, / The solemn temples, the great globe itself," the triumphal arches, and symbolic mountains, our attention turns to the poetic essence of the pageant without which the body remains but an incomplete skeleton.

11   *The Soul*

Eɪᴛʜᴇʀ ʙʏ ꜱᴘᴇᴄɪꜰɪᴄ ᴏʀᴅᴇʀ or through the working of Time's careless hand, the bodies of the pageants suffered defacement, tearing down, sometimes being carted away for resale; at such moments the pageants indeed become insubstantial, leaving not a rack behind. But we can hold in our imagination memories of the civic pageants long after their scheduled or unscheduled destruction. The sense of spectacle lingers, along with visual display, color, the drama of the moment when sovereign or magistrate appeared, and overtones of the thematic intent of this civic entertainment. Motifs, ideas, themes—such constitute the "soul" of civic pageantry. This soul generates the work of the artificers, the finances of the city or guilds, the creation of the body; in a word, it gives additional "meaning" to the day, a meaning that may remain after the shouts have subsided, after the audience scatters, after abandoning the body. If the civic pageants can make an honest claim on our artistic and dramatic interest, then they must contain something that transcends their physical nature.

What follows attempts to sketch the soul of civic pageantry, recognizing that such an effort will be imprecise. Nevertheless, ideas and themes cut across a number of civic entertainments; and they may justifiably be viewed as part of the conglomerate soul, the poetic and dramatic soul. I find that a number of the ideas and motifs that recur over the four decades of pageantry discussed here can be epitomized in allegorical and mythological persons. Because the representation of these persons and their thematic significance closely link with the technique of the popular emblem books, I intend to explore the relationship between emblems and civic pageants, which should help in defining pageantry's soul as well as offering us a different perspective on the interrelationship of civic pageants with other non-dramatic literary and visual traditions. From this discussion we can move to a consideration of other themes not directly parallel to the emblem books but which form part of the poetic essence of civic pageantry. Such themes can be subsumed under the large categories of "national" and "personal," all in keeping with pageantry's "civic" and didactic nature.

As we know, the typical emblem has essentially a tripartite arrangement. It must have a picture, usually allegorical, symbolic, or mythological in content, frequently accompanied by a "word" or "motto," a brief epigraphic summary of the meaning of the illustration. Verses that attempt to bring the picture and motto together and make clear the meaning of the drawing constitute the third element of the emblem. Francis Quarles, chiefly a religious emblematist, says in the "To the Reader" section of his emblem book that

An Embleme is but a silent Parable.... Before the knowledge of letters, God was knowne by *Hierogliphicks*; And, indeed, what are the Heavens, the Earth, nay every Creature, *Hierogliphicks* and *Emblemes* of His Glory? I have no more to say.[1]

Quarles emphasizes the instructional nature of the emblems; this reinforces their allegorical expression, and civic pageantry certainly shares this didactic function. Geoffrey Whitney usefully categorizes the different types of emblems:

... all Emblemes for the most parte, maie be reduced into these three kindes, which is *Historicall, Naturall,* and *Morall. Historicall,* as representing the actes of some noble persons, being matter of historie. *Naturall,* as in expressing the natures of creatures, for example, the love of the yonge Storkes, to the oulde, or of suche like. *Morall,* pertaining to vertue and instruction of life, which is the chiefe of the three, and the other two maye bee in some sorte drawen into this head. For, all doe tende unto discipline, and morall preceptes of living.[2]

We might add the category of mythology to Whitney's list, but perhaps he intended that one of his divisions would subsume mythology, for he certainly uses mythological figures in his own book.

Emblem books, at least in England, look backward in the allegorical tradition toward the morality drama, and they may possibly draw some of their inspiration from the medieval theater. Freeman notes:

Emblem books depended for their existence upon the validity of these allegorical ways of thinking; they depended also upon a close interrelation between the arts of poetry and painting. While poetry was regarded as "a speaking picture" and painting as "dumb poetry", the emblem convention, in which poem and picture were complementary to each other, could flourish.[3]

The same may be said of civic pageantry, for indeed its tableaux frequently resemble animated emblems.

The emblematic method of the pageant-dramatist appears time and again, and any one of the several tableaux stationed throughout the city of London in the 1559 pageant would suffice to suggest this emblematic technique. For exam-

[1]Francis Quarles, *Emblemes* (London, 1635), sig. A3.
[2]Geoffrey Whitney, *A Choice of Emblemes* (Leyden, 1586), "To the Reader." All quotations from Whitney will be from this original edition.
[3]Rosemary Freeman, *English Emblem Books* (London, 1948), pp. 4-5.

ple, at the device at Soper lane on a scaffold arrangement eight children represented the eight Beatitudes, "eche having the proper name of the blessing, that they did represent, writen in a table and placed above their heades."[4] In addition, "Everie of these children wer appointed and apparelled according unto the blessing which he did represent" (p. 41). This, then, constitutes the "picture" of the typical emblem.

The name or motto of the pageant appears inscribed on the forefront: "The eight beatitudes expressed in the .v. chapter of the gospel of S. Mathew, applyed to our soveraigne Ladie Quene Elizabeth" (p. 41). "And all voide places in the pageant wer furnished with pretty sayings, commending and touching the meaning of the said pageant, which was the promises and blessinges of almightie god made to his people" (pp. 41-2). Some of these additional sentences in Latin enhanced the theme of the pageant.

When the queen arrived, one of the children stepped forth and spoke the verses:

Thou hast been .viii. times blest, o quene of worthy fame
By mekenes of thy spirite, when care did thee besette
By mourning in thy griefe, by mildnes in thy blame
By hunger and by thyrst, and justice couldst none gette.

By mercy shewed, not felt, by cleanes of thyne harte
By seking peace alwayes, by persecucion wrong.
Therfore trust thou in god, since he hath helpt thy smart
That as his promis is, so he will make thee strong. (p. 42)

The pageant-emblem thus complete, the observer has been duly instructed. From this pageant one could easily construct a corresponding emblem.

Additional examples could of course be cited, but one needs only recall the descriptions in the earlier chapters to confirm the idea that the methods of the emblem book and civic pageant correspond. To take the matter a step further, we can direct our attention to studying parallels between specific emblems and specific pageants without worrying over the problem of possible indebtedness. The greater indebtedness of both forms goes obviously to iconographical traditions that aid in the problem of visual representation. To facilitate the discussion, I rely primarily on two representative emblem books: Geoffrey Whitney's A Choice of Emblemes (1586), a highly derivative one, and Henry Peacham's Minerva Britanna (1612).

---

[4]The Quenes Majesties Passage through the Citie of London, ed. James M. Osborn (New Haven, 1960), p. 41. All references to this pageant will be to this facsimile edition.

One of the first emblems in Whitney's book portrays Time and his daughter Truth with the appropriate motto "*Veritas temporis filia.*" Time with wings at his back and carrying a scythe busily attempts the rescue of Truth, who has been incarcerated by Envy, Slander, and Strife. The concluding lines of the verses offer hope:

> Yet Time will comme, and take this ladies parte,
> And breake her bandes, and bring her foes to foile.
>> Dispaire not then, thoughe truthe be hidden ofte,
>> Bycause at lengthe, shee shall bee sett alofte. (p. 4)

The association of Time and Truth, of course an old one, Whitney but continues.[5]

Paralleling Whitney's emblem, two presentations put Time and Truth together in the civic pageants, and a number of times the two figures appear separately. Especially reminiscent of the emblem, Time and Truth appear in the 1559 coronation royal entry in London at the tableau located at the Little Conduit in Cheapside. The total scene reinforces the thematic understanding. This device included two hills or mountains. The north hill "was made cragged, barreyn, and stonye, in the whiche was erected one tree, artificiallye made, all withered and deadde, with braunches accordinglye" (p. 46). Under this decaying tree on this barren hill sat a man "in homely and rude apparell crokedlye, and in mournyng maner" bearing the name, *Ruinosa Respublica*, a decayed commonweal. Hanging from the withered tree, tablets expressed the causes for a decaying state: Want of the fear of God, Disobedience to ruler, Blindness of guides, Rebellion in subjects, Flattering of princes, Unmercifulness in rulers.

The other half of this symbolic landscape contained a fair hill, "freshe, grene, and beawtifull, the grounde thereof full of flowres and beawtie, and on the same was erected also one tree very freshe and fayre ..." (p. 47). Under this healthy tree "stoode uprighte one freshe personage well apparaylled and appoynted" who bore the name *Respublica bene instituta*, a flourishing commonweal. This tree contains phrases that suggest the causes of a healthy state: Fear of God, A wise prince, Learned rulers, Obedience to officers, Obedient subjects, Virtue rewarded, Vice chastened. Thus every significant detail of the first hill finds its counter in the other hill, even to the matter of having the first personage sitting and the second standing. Meticulous attention helps establish the two hills as symbolically contrasting parts of the landscape.

[5]See Erwin Panofsky, *Studies in Iconology* (New York, 1962), Chapter 3; and D. J. Gordon, "'Veritas Filia Temporis': Hadrianus Junius and Geoffrey Whitney," *Journal of the Warburg and Courtauld Institutes* 3 (1939-40): 228-40.

An eye-witness account of Il Schifanoya, Venetian Ambassador in London, written to the Castellan of Mantua, confirms the description of the landscape of contrasting mounts. The Italian notes the one hill green and flourishing and the other dry and uncultivated. Il Schifanoya adds: "On the sterile mount there sat another youth dressed in black velvet, melancholy, pale, and wan, under a dry and arid tree, loaded with labels and mottoes indicating the cause of its dryness and sterility, whilst on the green mount conversely the cause of its greenness and fertility were demonstrated."[6] A citizen of London also took note of this pageant and recorded in his diary: "at the lytylle condutt a-nodur goodly pagant of a qwyke tre and a ded, and the quen had a boke gyffyn her ther...."[7]

Of special interest in the total landscape, a cave (also in Whitney's emblem) exists between the two hills from which "issued one personage whose name was *Tyme*, apparaylled as an olde man with a Sythe in his hande, havynge wynges artificiallye made ..." (p. 47). He leads forth his daughter, Truth, "fynely and well apparaylled, all cladde in whyte silke" (p. 47). Truth carries with her the word of Truth, the English Bible, and presents it to Queen Elizabeth after the verses have been spoken. A child stands on the flourishing mount and addresses the queen offering interpretation of the scene:

> The ruthfull wight that sitteth under the barren tree,
> Resembleth to us the fourme, when common weales decay
> But when they be in state tryumphant, you may see
> By him in freshe attyre that sitteth under the baye.
>
> Now since that Time again his daughter truth hath brought,
> We trust O worthy quene, thou wilt this truth embrace. (p. 48)

The Venetian ambassador, doubtlessly correct, offers his interpretation: "The whole implied in their tongue that the withered mount was the past state, and the green one the present, and that the time for gathering the fruits of truth was come ..." (*CSP Ven*, VII, 15).

The symbolism of this pictorial technique operates on two levels. On the more abstract plane, the dramatic tableau points to the causes for any flourishing or any decaying commonwealth. But its meaning ties quite concretely to the historical moment. The barren hill really represents symbolically the reign of Queen Mary, and the fertile mount the hopeful dreams for Elizabeth's rule. Truth can now emerge from the cave, having been oppressed, because the possibility of a fruitful reign has become real. The didactic instruction for the new queen the spoken word accomplishes and also by the pictorial device of contrasting hills.

---

[6]*Calendar of State Papers Venetian* (London, 1890), VII, 14-15.
[7]*The Diary of Henry Machyn*, ed. John Gough Nichols (London, 1848), p. 186.

The message seems clear: turn the back on the barren, unfruitful mount, look unto the freshness of the green hill, use Time to follow the dictates of Truth. We have, as it were, the *aera sub lege* opposed to the *aera sub gratia*.

An adaptation of this landscape technique of the 1559 pageant and the presentation of Time and Truth occurs some seventy-two years later in another civic pageant, Heywood's *Londons Jus Honorarium* (1631). After the new mayor has been entertained on the Thames, he returns to the city and to St. Paul's Churchyard where stands "a greene and pleasant Hill, adorned with all the Flowers of the spring, upon which is erected a faire and flourishing tree, furnished with variety of faire and pleasant fruite,"[8] all strongly reminiscent of one of the hills of the earlier pageant. Under this flourishing tree sits a woman "of beautifull aspect, apparrelled like Summer" who bears the motto, "A City well-governed." Accompanying her, figures represent the theological virtues, Faith, Hope, and Charity, all emblematically costumed. "Amongst the leaves and fruits of this Tree, are inscerted diverse labels with severall sentences expressing the causes which make Cities to flourish and prosper"—Fear of God, Religious zeal, a Wise Magistrate, Obedience to rulers, Unity, Plain and faithful dealing (sig. B2ᵛ).

Although uncommonly close to the Queen Elizabeth entertainment, Heywood's scene lacks the decadent mount, the contrasting hill. At the foot of the hill that Heywood presents sit Time and his daughter Truth with the inscription *Veritas est Temporis Filia*. In a lengthy speech Time interprets the symbolic landscape; he notes, for example:

> This Hill, that Nimph apparreld like the Spring,
> These Graces that attend her, (everything)
> As fruitfull trees, greene plants, flowers of choise smell,
> All Emblems of a City governd well;
> Which must be now your charge.... (sig. B3)

He further bids the mayor to follow and defend his daughter, Truth, and to suppress all forms of evil. Time interrupts his speech by a symbolic action; for he picks up a "leafelesse and withered branch" and then proceeds speaking:

> See you this withered branch, by Time o're growne
> A Cities Symbole, ruind, and trod downe.
> A Tree that bare bad fruit.... (sig. B3ᵛ)

The speech closes with the enumeration of the causes of a ruined city, such as Pride, Malice, Envy, Fraud, Oppression, Neglect of virtue.

[8](London, 1631), sig. B2. All quotations are from this text.

The decaying mount, though not tangibly present in Heywood's landscape, gets implicit representation with the withered branch, and the symbolic contrast thus exists. The causes for a flourishing and for a decadent city obviously occur in opposition to one another. In the midst of the signs of prosperity and life, Time picks up a dead branch and makes the symbolic visual contrast.

In addition to showing Time and Truth together, Whitney also has an emblem in which he depicts Time alone. Here Time seems to be descending from a cloud; naked, he carries a scythe, and has wings at his back. Two people seem to be trying to escape the presence of Time, but this becomes futile, as Whitney observes. On the contrary, he urges, we must use our brief span as well as possible:

> And since, by proofe I knowe, you [Thomas Wilbraham] hourde not up
>   your store;
> Whose gate, is open to your frende: and purce, unto the pore:
> And spend unto your praise, what GOD dothe largely lende:
> I chiefly made my choice of this, which I to you commende. (p. 199)

In this emblem Whitney commends his friend Wilbraham for his wise use of time.

As we recall, when Elizabeth made one of her last progresses, she encountered that appropriately costumed Time at Harefield in 1602. He came with his hourglass stopped and his wings clipped, asserting that he represented the queen's Time. From the first civic pageant to the last one in her reign Elizabeth gets reminded of Time, a theme of course woven throughout much of Elizabethan literature. Time in Munday's 1611 Lord Mayor's Show dramatically struck his wand on the tomb of Nicholas Faringdon and called him forth from death. In the 1620 mayoral pageant Time promises immortality to the mayor if he follows virtue and diligence in discharging his duties. In the final decade before the theaters close, Time appeared to the new mayor in Taylor's 1634 show. Time commends the mayor for loving his daughter Truth: "I doe command her, still with you t'abide, / Doe you defend her, she shall be your guide: / For truth-sake *Time* shall be your servant still."[9] At the conclusion of the pageant Time once again speaks to the mayor, bids him follow virtue and to use his moments wisely:

> Tis truly said, that man that rules his passions,
> Doth conquer more, than he that conquers Nations.
> As you have rul'd your selfe, let it appeare
> In ruling London this ensuing yeare.... (sig. B4)

---

[9]John Taylor, *The Triumphs of Fame and Honour* (London, 1634), sig. A7. All quotations will be from this edition.

Time also reminds the mayor of its paradoxical nature—destroying while building.

Figure 13. Truth, from Peacham's *Minerva Britanna* (London, 1612).

Truth also has devoted to her an entire emblem in which Peacham depicts her as naked with one foot resting on a globe[10] (*see* figure 13). In her right hand she holds a sunburst, in the left, an open book and palm branch. Peacham interprets the meaning of her presentation:

Her nakednes beseemes simplicitie:
The Sunne, how she is greatest frend to light:
Her booke, the strength she holds by historie:
The Palme, her triumphes over Tyrants spite:
     The world she treads on, how in heaven she dwels,
     And here beneath all earthly thing excells.

Of course, Peacham does not originate this portrayal of Truth; he has before him a long history of similar representations.

---

[10]Henry Peacham, *Minerva Britanna* (London, 1612), p. 134. All references are to this original edition.

In three of his Lord Mayors' Shows Middleton presents the figure of Truth, the most elaborate portrait occurring in the 1613 pageant, *The Triumphs of Truth*, where he duplicates but also embellishes Peacham's picture. She wears a "close garment of white satin, which makes her appear thin and naked, figuring thereby her simplicity ...," has a sun in her right hand and in her left, "a fan filled all with stars ... with which she parts darkness, and strikes away the vapours of ignorance."[11] In Middleton's portrayal Truth treads upon serpents "in that she treads down all subtlety and fraud." Interestingly Peacham's picture of Truth has a frame of a border of two serpents intertwined. Peacham may have intended the border merely as decoration; nevertheless, it corresponds with Middleton's association of snakes and Truth. Furthermore, Middleton adds to Truth a diadem of stars, a white dove atop her head, a robe filled with the eyes of eagles, "showing her deep insight and height of wisdom," and on her breast "a pure round crystal, showing the brightness of her thoughts and actions." In the Lord Mayor's pageant of 1617, Middleton places Truth among other allegorical figures at the Castle of Fame; she holds "in her right hand a sun, in the other a fan of stars ..." (VII, 304). In 1621, Middleton says simply that Truth carries the emblem of a "fan of stars, with which she chases away Error ..." (p. 348). These brief descriptions in 1617 and 1621 may merely be a type of shorthand; that is, Middleton may just be assuming the other usual accoutrements of the figure Truth. Understandably, in an age keenly conscious of time and mutability civic drama should reflect this dominant theme sounded in the literature, such as in Spenser and Shakespeare, to cite two obvious examples. The abstract concept of Time gains concrete reality throughout the pageants, and the frequent presence of Truth reinforces the didactic nature of these entertainments.

In an emblem portraying Time and Truth, Whitney also includes the person of Envy, one of the forces that has imprisoned Truth. The picture depicts Envy as eating her heart, her head covered with serpents. Whitney has another emblem devoted exclusively to Envy which makes her especially unattractive (*see* figure 14). She eats snakes—"that poysoned thoughtes, bee evermore her foode" (p. 94)—and wears snakes on her head, "the fruite that springes, of such a venomed braine." Whitney suggests that she has a heart filled with gall, and her tongue "with stinges doth swell."

---

[11]*The Works of Thomas Middleton*, ed. A. H. Bullen (London, 1886), VII, 244. All citations will be to this edition of Middleton.

Figure 14. Envy, from Geoffrey Whitney's *A Choice of Emblemes* (Leiden, 1586).

At the triumphal arch constructed at Fleet street King James could see the figure of Envy, among others, during his coronation passage through London on 15 March 1604. Thomas Dekker describes Envy as being "unhandsomely attirde all in blacke, her haire of the same colour, filletted about with snakes."[12] Having had this experience with presenting Envy, Dekker uses her again, this time in his first Lord Mayor's Show, *Troia-Nova Triumphans* (1612). An important figure, she functions in direct opposition to Virtue, and she serves as commandress of the Forlorn Castle. Her description reveals the traditional portrait: "her haire full of Snakes, her countenance pallid, meagre and leane, her body naked, in her hand a knot of Snakes, crawling and writhen about her arme" (III, 238). Middleton perhaps drew some inspiration from Dekker for his depiction of Envy in the mayoral pageant of 1613, but he intensifies the picture. Envy accompanies Error, "eating of a human heart, mounted on a rhinoceros, attired in red silk, suitable to the bloodiness of her manners! her left pap bare, where a snake fastens; her arms

---

[12]*The Dramatic Works of Thomas Dekker*, ed. Fredson Bowers (Cambridge, 1955), II, 295. All quotations are from this edition.

half naked; holding in her right hand a dart tincted in blood" (VII, 241). Middleton has recovered the detail used by Whitney of Envy eating her heart. In the civic entertainment presented in honor of Prince Henry in Chester on St. George's Day in 1610, Envy, along with others, rode by on horseback. She had a "wreath of snakes about her head; another in her hand, her face and armes besmeared with blood."[13] In a speech Peace indicates that she will "send pale Envie downe to hell with speed, / Where she upon her Snakes shall onely feed ..." (sig. C2ᵛ). The conflict between Envy and the other qualities finally ends when Joy joins the battle against her, forecasting that Envy's "everlasting shame / Shall be still blasted by the Trumpe of *Fame*..." (sig. C4ᵛ). Thus the "ugly Monster, Loves Misanthropos" makes her exit, having been routed by virtuous forces. The moral landscape of the civic pageant bristles with such vicious characters that must be fought against, and we find ourselves in a very old dramatic tradition.

Peacham brings together the qualities of Fame and Virtue in a single emblem designed to honour Sir Thomas Chaloner (p. 35). (*See* figure 15.) Virtue unfolds a scroll and seeks the services of Fame to publish abroad the reputation of the gentleman. Fame stands to the left in the illustration; she wears a robe decorated with eyes, she has wings at her back, and she blows a trumpet. This traditional portrayal pageant writers use.

Interestingly, two pageant dramatists bring Virtue and Fame together, Dekker being the first to make the association in the Lord Mayor's Show presented in the publication year of Peacham's book, 1612. Dekker describes Virtue much more elaborately than Peacham has pictured her; for Dekker, Virtue wears a diadem of stars, "her roabes are rich, her mantle white (figuring *Innocency*) and powdred with starres of gold, as an *Embleme* that she puts upon *Men*, the garments of eternity" (III, 235). Virtue successfully brings the mayor past Envy and the Forlorn Castle, and having done this, "the next and highest honour shee can bring him to, is to make him arive at the house *of Fame* ..." (p. 240). Dekker says that Fame wears "rich attire, a Trumpet in her hand, etc." Perhaps he does not feel it necessary to add further description. Fame delivers a long speech instructing the mayor to follow Virtue, thus fulfilling the function of the verses in the typical emblem. In quite similar fashion Fame functions as one of the chief residents in the Tower of Virtue in Middleton's 1621 Lord Mayor's Show; she addresses the mayor and explains the meaning of the Tower.

[13]*Chesters Triumph in Honor of Her Prince* (London, 1610), sig. A4ᵛ. All quotations are from this text.

Figure 15. Fame and Virtue from Henry Peacham's *Minerva Britanna* (London, 1612).

More frequently, Fame appeared by herself in the pageants. She welcomed Elizabeth to Bristol in 1574; and at the arch at Soper lane King James could see her as one of the main representations, described by Dekker as a "Woman in a Watchet Roabe, thickly set with open Eyes, and Tongues, a payre of large golden Winges at her backe, a Trumpet in her hand ..." (II, 276). Munday uses as one device in his 1618 mayoral pageant the Mount of Fame where she occupies the most eminent place, "seeming as if shee sounded her Golden Trumpet, the Banner whereof, is plentifully powdred with Tongues, Eyes and Eares: implying, that all tongues should be silent, all eyes and eares wide open, when *Fame* filleth the world with her sacred memories."[14] Fame assists in pointing the way to good government for the new magistrate. John Taylor presents Fame in the 1634 Lord Mayor's entertainment, this time with a silver trumpet where at her monument she sounds forth the praises of former Lord Mayors "and inforceth *Time* to revive their noble Memory, encouraging his Lordship to follow them in all their Honourable actions ..." (sig. B3). From Shakespeare's men of Navarre in *Love's Labour's Lost* through numerous civic pageants characters make a concerted effort to achieve fame, and the pageants repeatedly offer examples of noteworthy people out of the past (for example, Prince Henry and many former mayors)

---

[14]Anthony Munday, *Sidero-thriambos* (London, 1618), sig. B4.

who indeed achieved immortal fame, always with the assistance of virtue. To be accepted into the House of Fame, as in Dekker's 1612 pageant, becomes tantamount to achieving a type of salvation, for Fame's voice sounds across the centuries recounting man's accomplishments. Understandably, the pageants place such thematic emphasis on Fame since the dramatic presentation itself functions to assist the propagation of the fame of the country, the city, the guild, the mayor or sovereign.

While Whitney in the statement quoted earlier indicates that "moral" emblems predominate over other kinds, the emblems devoted to mythological subjects nevertheless abound. Similarly in civic pageants mythological figures serve both the functions of spectacle and instruction. Or as Whitney says, all emblems "tende unto discipline, and morall preceptes of living." In his famous letter to Ralegh, Spenser had observed that such a writer as Homer had in the persons of Agamemnon and Ulysses "ensampled a good governor and a virtuous man...." Likewise, Francis Bacon in *The Wisdom of the Ancients* sought to uncover the allegorical meaning that lay hidden underneath many of the mythological fables—the "dark conceits." The parallels between certain emblems and the presentation of mythological figures in the pageants demonstrate how these characters help the didactic intent of the pageant, as they help offer "mirrors for magistrates."

In the first few pages of his book Whitney depicts Ulysses tied to the mast in a boat (*see* figure 16), being enticed with the music of the sirens: "Withe pleasaunte tunes, the SYRENES did allure / Ulisses wise, to listen theire songe ..." (p. 10). Whitney makes clear the moral meaning of this incident from mythology:

Which shewes to us, when Bewtie seekes to snare
The carelesse man, whoe dothe no daunger dreede,
That he shoulde flie, and should in time beware,
And not on lookes, his fickle fancie feede:
    Suche Mairemaides live, that promise onelie joyes:
    But hee that yeldes, at lengthe him selffe distroies.

Figure 16. Ulysses, from Geoffrey Whitney's *A Choice of Emblemes* (Leiden, 1586).

In Heywood's 1631 Lord Mayor's Show we encounter a strikingly parallel presentation. As the new mayor made his voyage on the Thames to Westminster, he found a scene depicting the dangers of any voyage: broken vessels scattered about, and the dangers of Scylla and Charybdis. In addition, "Upon these Rocks are placed the *Syrens*, excellent both in voyce and Instrument ... The morrall intended by the Poets, that whosoever shall lend an attentive eare to their musicke, is in great danger to perish; but he that can warily avoyd it by stopping his eares against their inchantment, shall not onely secure themselves, but bee their ruine ..." (sig. B1). Ulysses addresses the mayor, interpreting the pageant scene in true emblematic fashion. He warns the mayor of all the dangers and especially of the sirens:

> But though their tones be sweete, and shrill their notes,
> They come from foule brests, and inpostum'd throats,
> Sea monsters they be stiled, but much (nay more,
> 'Tis to be doubted,) they frequent the shoare.
>   Yet like Ulisses, doe but stop your eare
> To their inchantments, with an heart sincere;
> They fayling to indanger your estate,

Will from the rocks themselves precipitate. (sig. B2)

Ulysses, in whom Heywood personates "a wise and discreete Magistrate," makes his own experience relevant to the current mayor; the message does not greatly differ from Whitney's.

In one emblem Peacham shows Ulysses in the company of Pallas, wearing a warrior's garb and leading Ulysses by the hand, "That he aright, might in his Journey treade, / And shunne the traine of Error, everywhere ..." (p. 69). The subject of Pallas, the traditional embodiment of Wisdom, must somehow have fascinated Peacham, for he has no fewer than four emblems that include her. In one the forces of Mars and Pallas balance on a set of scales held in a hand extended from the sky; here Pallas, symbolized by the bay and a golden pen, outweighs the cannon, symbol of Mars; and Peacham concludes: "Yet wiser PALLAS guides his [Mars's] arme aright, / And best at home preventes all future harmes ..." (p. 44). Yet another emblem depicts the birth of Pallas springing from the forehead of Jove. In the fourth, Money and Dissimulation trap Pallas in a net, and the emblematist makes a fitting moral. One of Whitney's emblems illustrates the Judgment of Paris which, of course, involves Pallas. Indeed Whitney goes so far as to disagree with Paris's decision and concludes: "But yet the wise this judgement rashe deride, / And sentence give on prudent PALLAS side" (p. 83).

In Dekker's 1628 show, *Britannia's Honor*, Pallas joins other figures around the Tree of Honour. Dekker calls her "Inventresse and Patronesse of Artes, Handy-crafts, and Trades"; she has "Ornaments proper to her quality ..." (IV, 86). Located near her stands Bellona, "goddesse of Warre, in a Martiall habit...." Dekker joins these two much as Peacham had in one of his emblems, though Dekker's interpretation differs somewhat: "both *Artes* and *Armes*, are (in a high degree and fulnesse of honor,) nurc'd up and maintain'd by and in the City." A speech by London at this tree indicates the necessity of making room for both Pallas and Bellona. Heywood in 1635 brings together Juno, Pallas, and Venus as Whitney had in his emblem. For Heywood, Pallas represents *Armes* and *Artes*, and she has with her some owls, a detail not used by the two emblem writers. Venus in a speech explains the meaning:

> ... *you must watch even as they wake:*
> *For all such as the management of state*
> *Shall undergoe, rise earlie, and bed late,*
> *So Wisdome is begot; from Wisedome Love....*[15]

Pageant and emblem writers agree that Pallas, as a representative of Wisdom, serves as a useful guide to all who govern.

---

[15]Thomas Heywood, *Londini Sinus Salutis* (London, 1635), sig. A5ᵛ.

Whitney presents Mercury in two different emblems. In the first he sits by a roadside, wearing a winged helmet and carrying a caduceus. He functions to point the way to the travelling man; and having been shown the way by Mercury, man "never went awrie, / But to his wishe, his jorneys ende did gaine / In happie howre, by his direction plaine" (p. 2). Whitney likens this guidance to God's providence. Mercury appears similarly costumed in the second emblem that Whitney devotes to him; he busily strings a lute, "Which being tun'de, such Harmonie did lende, / That Poettes write, the trees theire toppes did bende" (p. 92).

When Elizabeth made her trip to Norwich in 1578, she encountered a figure personating Mercury in traditional costume. Similarly, Charles I in his coronation passage through Edinburgh in 1633 met Mercury. And in the Lord Mayors' Shows of 1612, 1633, and 1634, Mercury made an appearance, each time dressed appropriately. Heywood in 1633 calls Mercury the "Patrone of all Trade," and in such a role he addresses the mayor. For John Taylor in the pageant of 1634, Mercury has "his Caduceus or charming rod in his hand, with wings on his head to signifie quicknesse of Invention, Acutenesse of wit, and Volubility of tongue with Eloquence of speech. He hath also wings on his feet to signifie his swiftnesse, as Messenger to the Gods" (sig. A6ᵛ). Time, who accompanies Mercury, speaks of Mercury's function: he—

> Hath brought the Poet wit, and Eloquence;
> And quick Invention, likewise he Inflam'd
> Into the Artists that these pageants fram'd,
> That for your future Honour, this may be
> A day of well Compos'd Variety…. (sig. A7)

One cannot get more immediate than to have Mercury inspire the very poet devising the pageant. The guidance of which Whitney had written may take different manifestations, but Mercury inspires whether he guides the traveller or coaxes harmony out of nature or assists the pageant poet.

In one emblem Whitney portrays Apollo dressed in a robe and holding a lute in his right hand, in the company of Bacchus (p. 146). Whitney views them as two necessary forces in life; he does not place one above the other. In another emblem Apollo plays on the lute; and Whitney's four brief lines explain the scene:

> Presumptuous PAN, did strive APOLLOS skill to passe:
> But MIDAS gave the palme to PAN: wherefore the eares of asse
> APOLLO gave the Judge: which doth all Judges teache;
> To judge with knowledge, and advise, in matters paste their reache? (p. 218)

Here Whitney makes the traditional association of Apollo with music and harmony.

Among the various entertainments presented the newly married Prince Frederick, Count Palatine, and Princess Elizabeth, daughter of James I, the procession in the tiltyard at Heidelberg honored them in mid-June 1613. Interestingly, Apollo and Bacchus came into the tiltyard together as Whitney had earlier arranged them. Midas also appeared, "sitting on an *Asse*, hee himselfe having *Asses* eares for comparing *Pan*, to *Apollo*: and next him, miserable *Marsyas*, and a *Saytire*, fleaing of his skin, because he durst contend with *Apollo*, in musicke."[16] John Squire in the 1620 pageant presents Apollo with the Muses on Mount Parnassus, and they also appear in this arrangement in the coronation procession for Charles I in Edinburgh. The pamphlet writer observes: "*Apollo* sitting in the midst of them was clad in Crimson taffeta, covered with some purle of gold, ... his head was crowned with Laurell, with locks long and like gold; hee presented the King with a booke."[17] With a slight alteration Dekker presented Apollo with the Seven Liberal Sciences in *Londons Tempe* (1629). Apollo, "on his head a garland of bayes" and in "his hand a Lute," occupied the chief position (IV, 111) and advised the new mayor: "Go on in your full glories: whilst *Apollo*, and these Mistresses of the Learned Sciences, waft you to that Honourable shore, whither Time bids you hasten to arrive" (IV, 112). Typical of civic pageants, the mythological figure here offers support and moral guidance.

Another figure associated with music is Arion, miraculously saved by a dolphin when some sailors threw him overboard. Whitney recounts the story in picture and verse, being especially distressed at man's inhumanity to man as epitomized in the Arion incident. The picture shows a turbulent sea, the sailors throwing Arion into the water, and a dolphin coming to his rescue. The seamen "rob'd the man, and threwe him to the sea, / A Dolphin, lo, did beare him safe awaie" (p. 144). Arion's beautiful music attracts the dolphin to him.[18]

Arion came floating forth on a mechanical dolphin and sang to Elizabeth as part of the entertainment provided for her during the prolonged stay at Kenilworth Castle in 1575. In honor of the new mayor and especially the Fishmongers' Company, Munday presented Arion, "a famous Musicion and Poet," riding on a dolphin's back, "being saved so from death, when Robbers and Pirates on the Seas, would maliciously have drowned him" (sig. B1ᵛ), in the Lord Mayor's Show of 1616. A speech later in the day explains the emblematic significance of Arion. The most extensive treatment came in the civic entertainment of 1632, *Londini*

---

[16]John Stow, *The Annales, or General Chronicle of England* (London, 1615), p. 922.
[17]*The Entertainment of the High and Mighty Monarch Charles ... Into his auncient and royall City of Edinburgh* (Edinburgh, 1633), p. 15.
[18]Arion is also portrayed in an emblem book of the Caroline period: George Wither, *A Collection of Emblemes* (London, 1635), Book I, Illus. 10.

Artium & Scientiarum Scaturigo, in which Heywood recounts the traditional story. Arion, "with his Harpe in his hand, riding upon the backe of a Dolphin," greets the mayor in a pageant on the Thames.[19] He also gives the concluding speech of the day where he fulfils the function of the verses of an emblem by explaining the allegorical significance of all that the mayor has seen. He closes: "... *you are the Spring and Fountaine made / To water every Science, Art, and Trade; / Observing those, your Honour shall shine bright* ..." (sig. C2). The didactic function of the civic pageant, like that of an emblem, manifests itself clearly.

Figure 17. Orpheus from Geoffrey Whitney's *A Choice of Emblemes* (Leiden, 1586).

The music of Orpheus has a soothing power in nature, and in this traditional role Whitney depicts him (*see* figure 17). Orpehus dominates in a circular arrangement, seated and carrying his harp and surrounded by various kinds of animals. Perhaps Whitney has chosen the circular pattern to underscore the sense of harmony that Orpheus conveys. Besides being able to calm the savage kind of the animal world, Orpheus

... could with sweetenes of his tonge, all sortes of men suffice.

---

[19]Heywood, *Londini Artium* (London, 1632), sig. A4ᵛ.

And those that weare most rude, and knewe no good at all:
And weare of fierce, and cruell mindes, the worlde did brutishe call.
Yet with persuasions sounde, hee made their hartes relente,
That meeke, and milde they did become, and followed where he wente. (p. 186)

Whitney suggests that man can be like Orpheus, if he seeks to be harmonious.

The view of the pageant writers about Orpheus parallels Whitney's concept. Orpheus addresses the new mayor in Middleton's Lord Mayor's Show of 1619, *The Triumphs of Love and Antiquity*; and he explains the device stationed in Paul's Churchyard, saying of the beasts represented there in a thicket:

... by fair example, musical grace,
Harmonious government of the man in place,
Of fair integrity and wisdom fram'd,
They stand as mine do, ravish'd, charm'd, and tam'd:
Every wise magistrate that governs thus,
May well be call'd a powerful Orpheus. (VII, 320)

Anyone who can govern discordant elements may claim the name Orpheus; Whitney had implied much the same thing. Heywood's treatment of Orpheus in the 1639 entertainment virtually reissues Whitney's emblem. Orpheus with his harp sits "in a faire Plat-forme, beautified with pleasant Trees, upon which are pearcht severall Birds, and below Beasts of all sorts," all of whom attend Orpheus's music.[20] He addresses the mayor in words strongly reminiscent of Middleton's:

You are that Orpheus *who can doe all these:*
If any streame beyond its bounds shall swell,
You beare the Trident *that such rage can quell.*
When beasts of Rapine (trusting to their power)
Would any of your harmelesse flocks devoure:
Yours is the sword that can such violence stay.... (sig. B4)

This didactic imperative Whitney, Middleton, and Heywood enunciate: appropriate the qualities of Orpheus and be a wise man, a harmonious ruler.

As a means of separating the two parts of his book, Whitney introduces an emblem of Janus, depicted as a warrior with the customary two faces looking in opposite directions. In one hand he holds what may be a scepter or a key and in the other an object that seems to be a mirror (unclear from the drawing). Whit-

---

[20]Thomas Heywood, *Londini Status Pacatus* (London, 1639), sig. B3. All quotations are from this edition.

ney suggests that Janus bids us review the past year in order to make amends for the coming year. Whitney says further:

> This Image had his rites, and temple faire,
> And call'd the GOD of warre, and peace, bicause
> In warres, hee warn'de of peace not to dispaire:
> And warn'de in peace, to practise martiall lawes:
>   And furthermore, his lookes did teache this somme;
>   To beare in minde, time past, and time to comme. (p. 108)

In the coronation entertainment for King James in 1604, Jonson's device called the Temple of Janus stood at Temple Bar, but Peace serves as the principal figure in the temple at whose feet lies Mars. Though the device honors Janus, he does not appear as an actual live figure. But in Heywood's show of 1639, Janus appears in traditional emblematic garb. At the first land-pageant Janus is the chief figure, accompanied by persons representing the four seasons. Heywood, in the text, briefly traces the history and the meaning of Janus:

> He holdeth in his right hand a golden Key to shut up the yeare past, as never more to come; and open to the yeare future: it may also be an Embleme of noble policy to unbosome and bring to light their trecher-ous devises and stratagems, who seeke to undermine and supplant the prosperity of a faire and flourishing Common-weale. (sig. B2)

Janus addresses the mayor, resigns the seasons to his charge, and bids him to "*spend the* Houres *to inrich future story, / Both for your owne grace and the Cities glory*" because "*none knowes better than your selfe (Grave Lord) / What* Mercy *is; or when to use the Sword*" (sigs. B2ᵛ-B3). For Whitney and Heywood Janus sym-bolically reminds us of the need for an attitude of watchfulness both in private lives and in the body politic.

Coming out of national myth but also historically real, two additional figures received celebration in emblem and pageant. In an emblem that truly belongs in his "historical" category, Whitney exalts the glories of Sir Francis Drake. This emblem, incidentally, we know to be of Whitney's own devising. In the picture a hand, reaching down from a cloud, holds a rope that attaches to a boat perched on a globe, with the motto: *Auxilio divino* (p. 203). Whitney begins the verses by speaking of the accomplishments of Jason, "Who throughe the watchfull dragons pass'd, to win the fleece of goulde." He did this "*By help of power devine.*" Then Whitney likens Drake to Jason:

> But, hee, of whome I write, this noble minded DRAKE,
> Did bringe away his goulden fleece, when thousand eies did wake....

Geve praise to them, that passe the waves, to doe their countrie good.
Before which sorte, as chiefe: in tempeste, and in calme,
Sir FRANCIS DRAKE, by due deserte, may weare the goulden palme.

Small wonder that Whitney writing in 1586 should speak with such adulation of
Drake, and the comparison to Jason seems a natural one.

Drake appears as a figure only once in the civic pageantry of this period, in
Webster's 1624 mayoral show where he sat with six other famous navigators on a
globe. But writers alluded to him several times, all reminiscent of Whitney's emblem. In both 1621 and 1623, Middleton presents some sort of pageant that includes a list of famous members of the Drapers' company, indicating the reason
for remembering these men. Of Drake, Middleton says in 1621: "the son of
Fame, who in two years and ten months, did cast a girdle about the world ..."
(VII, 342). He repeats the idea in 1623. The 1626 pageant, again by Middleton,
makes the comparison of Drake and Jason; and he describes one of the devices,
the "Sanctuary of Prosperity" on

the top arch of which hangs the Golden Fleece; which raises the worthy
memory of that most famous and renowned brother of this company,
Sir Francis Drake, who in two years and ten months did encompass the
whole world, deserving an eminent remembrance in this sanctuary,
who never returned to his country without the golden fleece of honour
and victory.... (VII, 406)

A speech in the Sanctuary makes the association clear:

If Jason, with the noble hopes of Greece,
Who did from Colchis fetcht the golden fleece,
Deserve a story of immortal fame, ...
What honour, celebration, and renown,
In virtue's right, ought justly to be shown
To the fair memory of Sir Francis Drake,
England's true Jason.... (VII, 406)

The speech concludes by likening the mayor's year in office to a perilous voyage
on the sea. By implication, he should draw instruction from the noble example of
Drake. Whatever the matter of actual indebtedness, emblematist and pageant
writer dwell on common ground.

While Whitney could celebrate Drake, Peacham chose another son of
Fame—Prince Henry, elder son of King James. In fact, he dedicates his emblem
book to the prince, and one of the first emblems shows the prince suited out in
his armor complete with lance astride a charger. The adulatory verses conclude

with suggesting that "thy Trophees may be more, / Then all the HENRIES ever liv'd before" (p. 17). This becomes something of the ultimate of compliments to speculate that the prince might be greater than all the previous Henries of English history when one recalls such men as Henry V and Henry VII.

In Dekker's 1612 Lord Mayor's Show Henry resided securely ensconced in a device called the House of Fame to which the new mayor came led by Virtue. The prince occupied a special place because some five years earlier he had accepted the freedom of the Merchant Taylors, the sponsoring guild for this show. But more than that, the gesture essentially praises the eighteen-year-old Henry, already carving out his niche in the House of Fame. As we have noted, although he had planned to attend the show, Henry could not come because of illness, and within a week after the pageant he died. The fullest treatment of Prince Henry in a civic pageant comes twelve years after his death in Webster's 1624 mayoral pageant. In the final device of the entertainment, the Monument of Gratitude, Prince Henry stands on a pedestal of gold surrounded by allegorical figures, each representing some feature of his character—Liberality, Unanimity, Industry, Justice, Peace, and Obedience. These personified virtues constitute a grand compliment to the dead prince. Should the meaning not be clear, Webster has a figure named Amade le Graunde deliver a closing speech which reviews Henry's virtues (this, of course, corresponds to the function of the verses of the typical emblem). The speaker takes special note that the prince leaves "a most Cleere and Eminent Fame behind."[21] Obviously, the lessons and examples of history echo in emblem and pageant alike. These several figures from mythology and actual history serve as exemplars of accomplishment, frequently having crucial thematic roles in the pageants. The role of the mayor could therefore be likened to the examples of a Ulysses, or Orpheus, or Jason—all offering a means of instruction. Collectively these various mythological characters, similarly represented in emblem and pageant, embody "morall preceptes of living," assisting in the fashioning of noble persons "in virtuous and gentle discipline." And on the pageant stage these figures of antiquity and their allegorical meanings have dramatic realization.

The civic entertainments also make some use of "natural" emblems, as Whitney defines them. In his own book Whitney includes an emblem of a pelican feeding her young, and the verses elucidate the symbolic meaning:

The Pellican, for to revive her younge,
Doth peirce her brest, and geve them of her blood:
Then searche your breste, and as yow have with tonge,
With penne proceede to doe our countrie good:
    Your Zeale is great, your learning is profounde,
    Then helpe our wantes, with that you doe abounde. (p. 87)

---

[21] The Complete Works of John Webster, ed. F. L. Lucas (London, 1927), III, 327.

Giving her own blood symbolizes love, and Whitney obviously understands this traditional interpretation of the pelican. The striking emblem of the pelican in George Wither's *A Collection of Emblemes* (1635) depicts the pelican with her young and includes in the distant background a representation of the crucifixion (p. 154)—an appropriate symbolic linking. We recall that near the root of the lemon tree device in Munday's 1616 mayoral show stood a pelican "with all her tender brood about her."[22] She shares her blood with her young, all visually duplicating the typical emblem. In the text Munday discusses the common symbolic interpretations of the bird; and finally he makes the specific correspondence between the pelican and the mayor:

> An excellent type of government in a Magistrate, who, at his meere entrance into his yeares Office, becommeth a nursing father of the Family....
> If his love and delight be such to the Commonwealth, as that of the *Pellican* to her young ones, ... then doth he justly answere to our Embleme.... (sig. B2)

This pageant-emblem isolates one of the qualities that the new magistrate should imitate, summed up in this natural symbol.

Several instances occur in Heywood's pageants where this method of drawing a relationship between the natural emblem and the mayor exists. For example, as a means of commenting on the mayor's responsibilities, Heywood in 1632 presents an elephant which celebrates the virtues of understanding, judgment, wisdom, and strength. The Indian speaker says of the mayor: "*Yet such an Elephant we hope to find / Of you ...*" (sig. C1). A year later Heywood found the griffin to be an appropriate symbol because its eagle eyes suggest the incisive vision that the mayor needs to distinguish right from wrong, its lion body, the strength and boldness needed to oppose the forces of evil, and its wing, the speed with which justice should be administered. Reminiscent of the elephant of the 1632 show, the rhinoceros appears in Heywood's 1638 show; and again an Indian speaker draws the analogy between the animal and the mayor, focusing primarily on this animal's protection of the innocent. While being true to the methods of the emblem books, these natural symbols in the pageants also obviously form significant parts of the total thematic soul of the civic entertainments, joining other elements in the instructional function of this outdoor drama. Duplicating, or at least paralleling, many of the allegorical, mythological, historical, and natural emblems, the civic pageants give them dramatic life, making real what had appeared on the pages of books—adding the third dimension. It should be obvi-

[22]Anthony Munday, *Chrysanaleia* (London, 1616), sig. B2.

ous that frequently the pageants seem animated emblems, combining picture and verbal elements to fulfil a didactic function.

Reflecting a technique of many other dramatists and poets, the pageant-dramatists frequently resorted to metaphor to help define the function of the magistrate or sovereign. We get the traditional idea of a correspondence between the microcosm and the body politic, altogether appropriate in a drama whose soul centers on the "civic" life. The dominance of such stage properties as trees, arbors, and gardens reinforces the garden metaphor, used several times to sketch the responsibilities of the leader of the people. And one recalls the vivid use of this correspondence which Shakespeare made in *Richard II*, the garden scene, Act III, scene iv. In the 1604 royal entry James comes to the arch at the Little Conduit in Cheap, in the fashion of a bower and called *Hortus Euporiae*. This garden had drooped with the sad events of Elizabeth's death, but now renews in the presence of the king. Using the garden metaphor, Vertumnus, the speaker, likens the officials of the city to gardeners who prune and weed out harm; by implication James becomes the chief gardener. Focusing on a tree in the first land pageant of Dekker's 1628 show, the allegorical figure London offers metaphorical instruction to the mayor, reminding him that he serves as the "Soveraignes Gardner" with the function *"To prune and dresse the* Tree *of* Government. / *Lop off* Disorders, Factions, Mutiny ..." (IV, 88). With a slight variation Middleton in the 1619 civic pageant has Orpheus draw the analogy between the represented wilderness and the mayor's task. The thickets symbolize, Orpheus suggests, the thorny ways of vice: "Just such a wilderness is a commonwealth / That is undrest, unprun'd, wild in her health ..." (VII, 320). Order must be created out of this wilderness, and this becomes the mayor's task. No weed must go unnoticed or unchecked, if the state wants to prosper in the best possible way.

Altering the metaphor, Dekker in the 1612 show has Neptune tell the mayor that he must sail *"In rough Seas (now) of* Rule: *and every* Gale / *Will not perhaps befriend thee* ..." (III, 233-4). But no fear occurs if Integrity and Innocence sit steering the helm. Piloting this ship of state, the mayor, if sound in conscience, Neptune says, will never "run-a-ground." In Dekker's 1628 pageant the sea image emerges as Britannia likens the mayor to the Admiral of the State, steering it strongly despite the storms. Jason in Middleton's 1621 mayoral drama picks up the sea metaphor, warning the mayor of the difficulty of the voyage "set forth to renown." Making the analogy, Jason says: "State is a sea; he must be wise indeed / That sounds its depth, or can the quicksands heed ..." (VII, 341). Similarly in Middleton's final Lord Mayor's Show, the 1626 one, the speaker in the Sanctuary of Prosperity compares, as noted earlier, the achievements of Jason and Francis Drake and states the familiar metaphor:

The world's a sea, and every magistrate
Takes a year's voyage when he takes this state:

Nor on these seas are there less dangers found
Than those on which the bold adventurer's bound;
For rocks, gulfs, quicksands, here is malice, spite,
Envy, detraction of all noble right.... (VII, 406-7)

One circumvents the dangers by sailing by "the compass of a virtuous name."

At least two other metaphors help draw the correspondence between the microcosm and the state, especially in suggesting the magistrate's function. Waiting for the mayor in St. Paul's Churchyard in Heywood's 1633 pageant, a hill contains a shepherd who grazes his flock, whose peace a wolf threatens, ready to attack the innocent sheep. In his speech the shepherd makes the relationship between himself and the mayor, informing him that the citizens become his "*owne Sheep, this Citty is their fold....*"[23] Further, the mayor should stand guard against the perils symbolized in the wolf; and the shepherd says finally to the mayor: "*Y'are the true Shepheard, I my place resigne*" (sig. B2ᵛ). Earlier in 1619 Middleton likened the mayor to a bridegroom ready to be received by the city (the bride). Appropriately, this metaphor Love uses in the closing speech of the entertainment:

You are by this the city's bridegroom prov'd,
And she stands wedded to her best belov'd:
Then be, according to your morning vows,
A careful husband to a loving spouse.... (VII, 330)

Several of the speeches of Munday's 1616 show appropriate the marriage metaphor: Walworth at the tomb refers to the day as a "*blessed marriage day*," "*Londons and Lemans* [the mayor's] *wedding day.*" In the closing speech at night Walworth voices the metaphor again:

You[r] mariage Rites solemnized
Bequeathes you to the Bridall bed:
Where you and your chaste wife must rest.
London (it seemes) did like you best, ...
To be her Husband for a yeere.... (sig. C4)

With considerable variety and imagination the pageant-dramatists come to the task of illustrating the relationship of the sovereign or magistrate to the state. The thematic soul gains expression in metaphor, likening the leader to a gardener, a seaman, a shepherd, or a bridegroom, each correspondence carrying with it the implicit sense of responsibility of this leader to weed the garden, sail the rough

[23]Thomas Heywood, *Londini Emporia* (London, 1633), sig. B2.

seas, watch over the flock, and be a loving "husband." Significantly, most of these metaphorical expressions grow out of a reference to the body of the pageant, revealing a harmonious relationship between poet and painter, between body and soul.

Having examined that part of the soul of pageantry made up largely of emblems and metaphors, we may move to a consideration of certain themes that recur throughout the late Tudor and early Stuart periods in the outdoor pageants. Such themes also inform the regular stage and other forms of literature, all colored by a didactic view of the function of literature. It follows logically from what we know of the involvement of the guilds and cities and from the occasions themselves that civic pageantry should have several themes that may be catalogued under the heading of "nationalistic." The greeting and honoring of the sovereign or mayor create in themselves a nationalistic experience, as city and dramatist seek to praise and compliment the present honored guest as well as the past accomplishments of the kingdom. Throughout these civic dramas hymns ring of national praise and national expectation.

Understandably, one dominant thematic concern focuses on the preservation of the sanctity and the security of the commonwealth, usually expressed in terms of the virtues required for such preservation. The initial thread of this theme comes in the 1559 royal entry in London where, for example, Elizabeth, encountered in Cornhill the "seate of worthie governance," which displayed the virtues that support the state: Pure Religion, Love of subjects, Wisdom, and Justice, each visually represented as treading underfoot his opposite vice. While these qualities dominate and supress the evil forces, "So long shal government, not swarve from her right race...." Such virtues establish and maintain the sovereign's control over the kingdom, thus preserving it. As we recall from the discussion earlier in this chapter, Elizabeth saw two hills erected near the Little Conduit in Cheap, one representing a flourishing commonwealth, and the other, a decaying one. From the trees on these hills come the qualities that contribute to either prosperity or decadence. To maintain the commonwealth requires such virtues as Fear of God, A wise prince, Learned rulers, Obedience to officers, Obedient subjects, Lovers of the commonweal, Virtue rewarded, and Vice chastened. Similarly in Heywood's 1631 depiction of a city well-governed, among the leaves on the tree sentences epitomize those virtues that sustain the state: Fear of God, Religious zeal, a Wise Magistrate, Obedience to rulers, Unity, Plain and faithful dealing.

At the arch at Fenchurch in the 1604 pageant James could see the representation of Monarchia Britannica, underneath whom sat Divine Wisdom as crucial to the state. And the daughters of the Genius Urbis—Gladness, Loving Affection, Unanimity, Veneration, Promptitude, and Vigilance—likewise represent allegorically the attributes that assist in maintaining the state. Emblematically costumed, the figures appear in Munday's 1609 Lord Mayor's Show that support the kingdom of "Majesty." Thus Religion, Nobility, Policy, Memory, Vigilancy, and Tranquillity get personified as "apt attendants" to Majesty, offering their qualities to the maintenance of the kingdom. Supporting London in Munday's 1615 show, four "goodly Mounts" contain emblems suggesting the qualities "which make any Commonwealth truly happy"—Learned Religion, Military Discipline, Navigation, and Homebred Husbandry. Crowded into the chariot that carries Richard II in Munday's 1616 pageant, numerous royal virtues sit, plus an angel who has struck down the enemies of the king. Munday makes particular mention of the figures personifying Justice, Law, Authority, Vigilancy, Peace, Plenty, and Discipline, "as best props and pillers to any Kingly estate." Pageant-dramatists call for the traditional idea of maintaining order in the state; upon this principle all other nationalistic interests rest.

In an age nurtured on war and rumors of war, we cannot be surprised that the public theater of the streets should echo time and again the theme of peace, another expression or means of preserving the security of the commonwealth. At Bristol in 1574 Elizabeth and the audience witnessed a three-day battle that saw the defeat of the Fort of Feeble Policy; but the cause of peace gains strength by the courage of the people and the virtuous presence of the queen, who assures peace, war having grown weary of overcoming peace. The battle between the wood-gods and sea-gods at Elvetham in 1591 finally subsides because Elizabeth causes peace, and such battles cannot long rage without feeling the calming and courageous force of the sovereign. Thomas Nelson in the 1590 Lord Mayor's Show embodies Peace as an allegorical figure but notes the challenge to peace such as found in Ambition. And on the realistic level Nelson presents the historical example of the Jack Straw-Wat Tyler rebellion, a certain threat to peace, fortunately overcome through the efforts of William Walworth, then Lord Mayor.

Occupying the dominant places on the arch near the Conduit in Cheapside in the 1604 entertainment, Peace and Plenty sit, emblematically costumed. Sylvanus has, in fact, been dispatched by Peace to bring James to the arch that resembles a garden. The theme of peace Jonson explores further in the Temple of Janus arch. Here resides the chief figure *Irene* or Peace with her usual symbolic properties, and under her feet lies Mars "groveling." Her presence gets reinforced by several handmaids who accompany her: Quiet, Liberty, Safety, and Felicity. This static thematic statement receives dramatic life in the Chester entertainment of 1610 where a vigorous Peace pledges to rid the land of Envy and drive her down to hell. As in the 1604 pageant, Peace joins Plenty in the tiltyard in Chester.

Later in the Jacobean era John Squire celebrated this theme of peace in his 1620 mayoral show, *The Tryumphs of Peace*, a skilfully orchestrated pageant in which the various elements point to the victory and necessity of peace. The abstract concept gains concrete embodiment in a figure personifying Peace with the traditional properties at whose feet lies War, reminiscent of Jonson's portrayal in the 1604 entertainment. As Peace explains to the mayor and the audience, she has wandered about the world despairing of gaining acceptance until she came to England where the citizens captured War and imprisoned him. The challenge to the magistrate remains clear and direct: see that Peace gets safely maintained. That night Peace escorts the mayor into his house while a submissive War stands guard by the gate. The final civic pageant of the Caroline period, Heywood's 1639 show, also focuses on the issue of peace, all culminating in the main tableau, the *Status Pacatus*. Heywood represents in this device the figures of Death, Famine, Sickness and their opposites, Prosperity, Plenty, and Health. Heywood asserts that good government forms the ground of peace. The Genius of the City graphically describes the ravages of war; while other nations experience war, this "sole-happy Isle," this England, enjoys Peace, Prosperity, and Plenty. This expresses the fervent hope that peace may be sustained. From the opening days of Elizabeth's reign to the waning moments of Charles's fateful rule pageant-dramatists have seized upon the national interest for preserving the commonwealth by illustrating the virtues necessary for a prosperous state and by echoing the intense desire for peace. All other matters become of no consequence if something disturbs the integrity of the state or drives peace from the land.

Another manifestation of this national concern, obviously shared by Shakespeare particularly in his history plays, comes in the recurring theme of the union of the warring houses, the uniting of the Lancaster and York houses at the advent of the Tudors. Poets, historians, chroniclers, dramatists alike celebrated the mythic unity and concord forged by the Tudors out of the chaos of war; this also reflects an increasing historical consciousness developed in the Renaissance. Primarily the uniting of the roses emerges as a great moment in history to be savored. The most striking statement of this theme in civic pageantry comes in the coronation royal entry of 1559 where the first device revealed a genealogical tree with figures personating Henry VII and his wife Elizabeth, Henry VIII and his wife Anne Boleyn, and the new queen Elizabeth. The scaffold arch, full of white and red roses, the writer calls "The uniting of the two houses of Lancastre and York." The writer further argues: "… it was devised that like as Elizabeth was the first occasion of concorde, so she another Elizabeth might maintaine the same among her subjectes, so that unitie was the ende wherat the whole devise shotte …" (p. 33). The verses of the child speaker reinforce the meaning of the tableau:

> Therfore as civill warre, and shede of blood did cease
> When these two houses were united into one
> So now that jarre shall stint, and quietnes encrease,
> We trust, O noble Queene, thou wilt be cause alone. (p. 35)

Allegedly Elizabeth spoke and promised to preserve the concord achieved by her ancestors. This initial civic pageant of Elizabeth's reign clearly establishes in the popular mind the dominant theme of the union attained by the Tudors as they overcame war, a theme rehearsed many times in different places and by different means.

Other scattered references in the pageants keep the theme alive. For example, at Elizabeth's entry into Norwich in 1578, St. Stephen's gate had on one side a red rose and on the other a white rose, in the middle the white and red roses united. Verses that explain this "emblem" also appear on the gate; and they sound the basic theme of union: "Division kindled strife, / Blist union quencht the flame: / Thense sprang our noble Phenix deare, / The peareless prince of fame."[24] Several references in Middleton's Lord Mayors' Shows keep the theme securely placed on the pageant stage. Accompanying other allegorical figures on London's Triumphant Mount in the 1613 pageant, Perfect Love wears on her head a wreath of white and red roses mingled together, "the ancient witness of peace, love, and union, wherein consists the happiness of this land ..." (VII, 252). Depicted in the 1621 show, figures represent the two Henries, Edward, Mary, Elizabeth, and James with a speech that challenges the mayor to preserve the peace begun by Henry VII and continued through James: "... from Henry that join'd Roses, / To James that unites kingdoms ..." (VII, 346). In the chariot of kings in the 1624 mayoral entertainment Webster distinguishes the Lancastrian from the Yorkist ones by the use of appropriate roses, but Henry VII who healed the division and united the houses has surrounding him both white and red roses. The figure representing Edward III sounds the theme echoed by the other characters: "*By unity the smallest things grow great.*" Britannia's watchtower in Dekker's 1628 pageant contains "Emblemes of the two Houses of *Yorke* and *Lancaster*; once divided, but now Joyned into One Glorious Building, to Support this Royal Kingdom ..." (IV, 91). Obviously the achievement of the uniting of the houses served nationalistic purposes, even propaganda, for the Tudor sovereigns, but that does not fully explain its persistence as a viable theme on the pageant stage. Well into the Stuart period the pageant-dramatists keep looking back to that auspicious moment in English history because the event underscores the necessity for maintaining unity and concord. To appreciate the theme one need only to recall what happens when the union breaks down, faction set against faction—a subject, as we have seen, discussed by many pageant-dramatists as they seized on the virtue of peace and the horror of war.

From the initial civic pageant of Elizabeth's reign, the coronation royal entry, we encounter a continuing reference to the Brutus myth of English history, also serving nationalistic ends and emphasizing the union of the kingdoms. At Temple Bar Elizabeth could see the "images" of Gotmagot and Corineus, depicted as giants, both crucially involved in the conquering of Albion by Brutus. Here in the pageant they hold in their hands a tablet that summarizes the meaning of the tableaux that the queen has witnessed. Speaking in Peele's 1591 Lord

---

[24]Holinshed, *Chronicles* (London, 1807), IV, 380.

Mayor's Show, the "Presenter" says of Astraea (Elizabeth) that she descends "of the Trojan Brutus line: / Offspring of that couragious conquering king."[25] At the arch at Fleet street in 1604 Zeal (in a speech written by Middleton) addressed James, sounding the note of union by indicating that the four kingdoms "By *Brute* divided, but by you alone, / All are againe united and made *One*, / Whose fruitfull glories shine so far and even, / They touch not onely earth, but they kisse heaven ..." (Dekker, II, 298). Other brief allusions to the Troy legend occur; for example, Dekker entitles his 1612 pageant *Troia-Nova Triumphans*; Webster calls London *Troynovant* in the 1624 show; and in 1628 Dekker includes as the first Land device "New Troyes Tree of Honor."

But, as noted in Chapter Five, the fullest treatment of the myth comes in Munday's 1605 pageant, *The Triumphs of Re-United Britannia*. Here the whole panoply of the story unfolds with the presence of Brutus, and his sons, Locrine, Camber, and Albanact, as well as the giants Corineus and Gotmagot. In several speeches Brutus explains what he achieved for the country, but some complain that he divided the kingdom among his sons and civil strife followed. Nevertheless, cause for new hope exists because, as Brutus observes, Scotland has given rise to "another *Brute*" who comes to unite the kingdom. Therefore, what war could not achieve, the peaceful transition to King James does accomplish: "This second *Brute*, then whom there else was none. / *Wales, England, Scotland*, severd first by me: / To knit againe in blessed unity."[26] And this part of the pageant closes with speeches and songs celebrating the new-found unity. Whether one looks to the actual historical events of the union of the warring houses or to the shadowy regions of myth concerning Brutus, one inevitable fact emerges: the kingdom must be spiritually and physically united no matter to whom the credit goes. Obviously, a civic drama should rehearse such national events and repeatedly direct its thematic attention to the national needs of unity.

Apart from the understandable concerns for the commonwealth, several themes deal more exclusively with the personal life, already anticipated in the relationship of the emblems and the pageants. For instance, any number of figures represented in the entertainments offer personal guidance: characters such as Orpheus, Janus, or Jason or the many former Lord Mayors present worthy examples to be imitated, while giving moral instruction to the mayor and the audience as well. The didactic intention of the pageants thus extends from the problems of statecraft to the individual concerns of those who constitute the body politic.

The theme of transformation weaves throughout the shows but especially in the Elizabethan age and the early Stuart period. Typically we see the transformation wrought by the strange and wondrous power of the presence of the sover-

---

[25] *The Life and Minor Works of George Peele*, ed. David Horne (New Haven, 1952), p. 214.

[26] Anthony Munday, *The Triumphs of Re-United Britannia* (London, 1605), sig. B3ᵛ.

eign—the response to nobility sketched by Spenser and others. We recall that the Hercules figure who greeted Elizabeth in the Kenilworth progress pageant changes into submission as he surrenders his keys and club to this noble person. Being set free from her imprisonment, the Lady of the Lake also appears at Kenilworth. Numerous times the queen's presence transmutes war into peace, all underscoring the general apotheosis of Elizabeth. Lyly's Quarrendon entertainment pursues the same theme. In response to James's arrival, a curtain fell that had shrouded the arch at Fenchurch in the 1604 pageant, and Jonson explains the allegory in terms of the liberating presence of the king who changes the sadness of the country into new hope. At other arches the king causes a fountain to flow again and assists in the flourishing arbor at the Garden of Plenty arch that had formerly languished. The noble person becomes in these civic pageants a type of supreme alchemist capable of mystically transforming sadness into happiness, enslavement into freedom, war into peace, the iron age into the golden world.

Like the men of Navarre in Shakespeare's comedy who desired fame and wanted to circumvent the ravages of time through the formation of the academy, many pageant-dramatists explore the theme of immortality that can give man a final proof against change and mutability. Such immortality derives from man's virtuous deeds—his action as opposed to the program of contemplation set up by Navarre's men. Man's achievement can be seen in the House of Fame in Dekker's 1612 show where the mayor comes, brought through the good offices of Virtue. Man shall never die the song of the pageant concludes:

> But his vertues upward flye
>   And still spring
>   Whilst we sing
> In a Chorus ceasing never,
> He is living, living ever. (III, 244)

Similarly, in the 1613 pageant by Middleton, Truth, who safely brings the mayor past all the pitfalls of Error, promises "thy name shall never die" so long as he follows Truth. Offering immortality in the 1620 show, Time bids the mayor faithfully discharge his duties; having done this, he may receive "A blessed memory that never dies...." For Webster in the 1624 pageant Prince Henry stands out as the example of one who has gained immortality because of his virtues; and such persons of virtuous and noble hearts "when they dye, yet dye not in all parts: / But from the Integrety of a Brave mind, / Leave a most Cleere and Eminent Fame behind" (III, 327). And in the last decade before the theaters closed, Heywood includes in the 1635 show an Astrologian who bids the mayor to mix Justice and Mercy—

> *... so shall you in your state,*
> *Not Starres alone, but the gods Imitate;*
> *So shall your Terrene body, in the end, ...*
> *Above the spheares, shine to eternitie.* (sig. A7)

A transcendence of the mundane world becomes possible for those who exercise virtue and thus work out their own immortality. It follows logically in a drama so preoccupied with the presentation of Time that there should be a corresponding thematic emphasis on the power of man to conquer time, to gain a bit of eternity. Shakespeare, of course, understood the problem well.

A possible dominant ethical pattern presented in these civic dramas derives from the familiar idea of temperance from Aristotle, the mean between extremes. In *Chruso-thriambos*, Munday's 1611 show, the closing speech of the newly arisen Faringdon points clearly to the issue. The speaker urges the new mayor: "... Golden be / Your daily deedes of Charitie"; further, "But to be liberall, francke, and free, / And keepe good Hospitality, / ... Yet far from prodigality" (sig. C4). The middle course must be chosen, the golden mean followed—particularly appropriate in a pageant honoring the Goldsmiths. From London's Triumphant Mount in Middleton's 1613 show Perfect Love offers ethical advice. He banishes all excess and "epicurism," arguing instead: "He that desires days healthful, sound, and blest, / Let moderate judgment serve him at his feast ..." (VII, 258). This ethical theme sounds again in Heywood's *Londons Jus Honorarium*, the 1631 pageant. The dangers of Scylla and Charibdis, graphically represented, the figure portraying Ulysses knows how to steer around. He urges the mayor to keep the even channel, "*be neither swayde, / To the right hand nor left*" and so avoid the evils that lurk there. And Ulysses makes his instruction more explicit: "*But shunne th' extreames, to keepe the golden meane*" (sig. B2). By nature and function conservative, the civic pageants offer the expected ethical advice. Thus the numerous allegorical representations of Temperance gain reinforcement by these explicit statements advocating the moderate course of behavior, for in the mean consists virtue—part of the program for achieving personal virtue. Remiss indeed would be the "soul" of pageantry if no room existed for ethical instruction.

Rounding out the "personal" feature of pageantry's soul and indeed occupying a vast portion of the thematic concern is the eternal conflict between virtue and vice, the ancient *psychomachia* between good and evil. Owing a debt to medieval morality drama, almost all the pageants contain some sort of reference to the moral struggle, and one need only review the pageants to see the theme in action. It might be expressed in mute, visual terms, such as in the 1559 royal entry where in one tableau the virtues hold underfoot their opposite numbers, a technique duplicated in the Temple of Janus arch in the 1604 pageant. Or Munday's 1616 mayoral show offers the example of the royal virtues in the chariot beating down Treason and Mutiny. The conflict gets more dramatic life at Norwich in 1578, for example, where in the open field the battle between Cupid and Chastity takes place. Especially in Dekker's 1612 mayoral show and Middleton's 1613 pageant, both discussed extensively in Chapters Six and Seven, we get an explicit, highly theatrical statement of the conflict between virtue and vice. In 1612 we witness Virtue successfully overcoming the threats of Envy and bringing the mayor safely to the House of Fame, a place of salvation. The running battle between Truth and Error culminates in the eventual destruction of the evil forces in the 1613 pageant, the triumph of truth and light. The allegorical paraphernalia of morality drama gets striking use in these two civic pageants. Occupying the Bower of Bliss in Heywood's *Londini Emporia* (1633), the Cardinal Virtues illustrate the path to the celestial bower: *"These (when all Earths pompe failes) your prayers shal bring / Where Saints and Angels Haleluiahs sing"* (sig. C1). This resembles the ancient voyage of Everyman from the snares of sin to the freedom and assurance of salvation. Whether implied or explicitly dealt with, this antique quarrel between virtue and vice permeates the pageants, forming the most ubiquitous theme of pageantry's soul.

This soul that inhabits and gives life to the body of civic pageantry appears many-sided and multi-faceted, the thematic expression sometimes resembling emblems, sometimes dependent on metaphors, sometimes coming to grips with national issues as well as personal ones. Through it all shines the reflection of the milieu in which this soul first took life. Thus the soul remains optimistic and orthodox, singing the praises of the idealistic achievements and the virtuous hopes of a people. The official occasions that give rise to the pageants dictate a degree of orthodoxy, but the shows escape being naive. For through the prismatic quality of this soul, we may perceive darkness among the light, evil among the good. The pageant-dramatists do not shrink from a realization of the horrors of war or from the reality of evil. They celebrate, of course, the victory over the threatening forces, be they national or personal and inward. But we recall the civil strife among the houses of Lancaster and York, the threat to peace by Jack Straw's rebellion against Richard II, the constant threat to the virtuous life by such challengers as Error and Envy, a contest not restricted by time or place. One could argue that a "comic" vision prevails in the pageants, a perspective that allows for victory, for continuity, for new hope, for an upward movement; thus they share with the medieval dramatic tradition this comic pattern as well as a didactic and instructional function. The phoenix rises from the ashes as the spirit of comedy broods over the pageants, helping give them shape and direction. Though we have traversed several regions of the soul of pageantry, we recognize that this soul emerges greater than the sum of its parts, ineffable and heuristic.

Bibliography

MANUSCRIPTS

Bristol, Council House, Archives
    Chamberlain's Accounts, Mayor's Audits
British Library
    Additional MS. 40885: James Locke, Treasurer, Edinburgh, 1633
    Additional MS. 41499A: Sir Henry Lee's Devices, entertainment, 1575-92
    Egerton MS.2877: Order of show at Greenwich
    Egerton MS. 3320: Drawings for Coronation of Elizabeth
    Harleian MS. 4707: Scottish Collections (Coronation of Charles I in 1633)
    Harleian MS. 6395: Incident at Kenilworth in 1575
    Sloane MS. 3213: Anthony Weldon, James's entertainment in Scotland
Corporation of London Records Office
    City Journals, records of the Common Council
    Remembrancia MS.
    Repertories, records of the Aldermen
    MS. 85.6: Disbursements for the Civil War, 1637-67
Coventry Records Office
    City Annals
Society of Antiquaries
    MS.201: Papers Relating to Progresses of 1627 and 1637
Warwick, County Records Office
    Black Book MS.
Wells, Town Clerk's Office
    Acts of the Corporation, 1553-1623
Folger Shakespeare Library
    MS.L.b.33, MS.L.b.109: Papers of Thomas Cawarden

PRINTED BOOKS: PRIMARY SOURCES

*The Arrivall and Intertainements of the Embassador, Alkaid Jaurar Ben Abdella,
with his associate, Mr. Robert Blake.* London, 1637.
Beschreibung Der Reiss: Empfahung des Ritterlichen Ordens . . . Heidelberg, 1613.
Bruce, John, ed. *Correspondence of Robert Dudley, Earl of Leycester.* London, 1844.
Burel, John. *The Discription of the Queenis Majesties Maist Honorable Entry into
the Toun of Edinburgh.* Edinburgh, 1590.
Calendar of State Papers Domestic, 1558-1642. London, 1856-1887.

Calendar of State Papers Venetian, 1558-1642. London, 1884-1924.

Camden, William. *Annales. The True and Royall History of the Famous Empresse Elizabeth.* London, 1625.

The Letters of John Chamberlain, ed. Norman Egbert McClure. 2 vols. Philadelphia: American Philosopical Society, 1939.

Chesters Triumph in Honor of Her Prince. London, 1610.

Churchyard, Thomas. *The Firste parte of Churchyardes Chippes.* London, 1575.

Clark, A. M. "Two Pageants by Thomas Heywood; 1632, 1633." *Theatre Miscellany.* Oxford: Luttrell Society, 1953.

Collections III: A Calendar of Dramatic Records in the Books of the Livery Companies of London 1485-1640, ed. Jean Robertson and D. J. Gordon. Oxford: Malone Society, 1954.

Collections V: A Calendar of the Dramatic Records in the Books of the London Clothworkers' Company, ed. F. P. Wilson. Oxford: Malone Society, 1959.

Craig, J. T. Gibson. *Papers Relative to the Marriage of King James . . . with the Princess Anna of Denmark.* Bannatyne Club. Edinburgh, 1828.

Daniel, Samuel. *The Civil Wars,* ed. Laurence Michel. New Haven: Yale University Press, 1958.

Dekker, Thomas, *The Dramatic Works of Thomas Dekker,* ed. Fredson Bowers. 4 vols. Cambridge: Cambridge University Press, 1953-61.

The Entertainment of the High and Mighty Monarch Charles . . . into his auncient and royall City of Edinburgh. Edinburgh, 1633.

Extracts from the Records of the Burgh of Edinburgh 1604 to 1626, ed. Marguerite Wood. Edinburgh: Oliver & Boyd, 1931.

Extracts from the Records of the Burgh of Edinburgh 1626 to 1641, ed. Marguerite Wood. Edinburgh: Oliver & Boyd, 1936.

Fairholt, F. W. *The Civic Garland: A Collection of Songs from London Pageants.* London, 1845.

Gascoigne, George. *The Complete Works of George Gascoigne,* ed. John W. Cunliffe. vol. II. Cambridge: Cambridge University Press, 1910.

Goldwell, Henry. *A briefe declaration of the shews, devices, speeches, and inventions, done and performed before the Queenes Majestie, and the French Ambassadours.* London, 1581.

Grosse, Francis. *The Antiquarian Repertory,* 4 vols. London, 1808.

Harrison, G. B. *A Second Jacobean Journal Being a Record of Those Things Most Talked of during the Years 1607 to 1610.* London: Routledge & Paul, 1958.

Harrison, Stephen. *The Arches of Triumph.* London, 1604.

Heywood, Thomas. *Englands Elizabeth Her Life and Troubles.* London, 1631.

———. *Gunaikeion: or, Nine Books of Various History Concerninge Women.* London, 1624.

———. *If You Know Not Me, You Know Nobody, Parts I & II,* ed. Madeleine Doran. Oxford: Malone Society, 1934.

———. *Londini Artium & Scientiarum Scaturigo: or, Londons Fountaine of Arts and Sciences*. London, 1632.

———. *Londini Emporia, or Londons Mercatura*. London, 1633.

———. *Londini Sinus Salutis, or, Londons Harbour of Health, and Happiness*. London, 1635.

———. *Londini Speculum: or, Londons Mirror*. London, 1637.

———. *Londini Status Pacatus: or, Londons Peaceable Estate*. London, 1639.

———. *Londons Jus Honorarium*. London, 1631.

———. *Porta Pietatis, or, The Port or Harbour of Piety*. London, 1638.

———. *Thomas Heywood's Pageants: A Critical Edition*. Ed. David M. Bergeron. New York: Garland, 1986.

———. *Troia Britannica: or, Great Britaines Troy*. London, 1609.

———. *A True Description of His Majesties Royall Ship*. London, 1637.

Holinshed, Raphael. *Holinshed's Chronicles of England, Scotland, and Ireland*, vol. IV. London, 1807.

The Honorable Entertainement gieven to the Queenes Majestie in Progresse, at Elvetham in Hampshire. London, 1591.

Jonson, Ben. *Ben Jonson*, ed. C. H. Herford, Percy and Evelyn Simpson. 11 vols. Oxford: Clarendon Press, 1925-52.

The Joyfull Receyving of the Queenes most excellent Majestie into hir Highnesse Citie of Norwich. London, 1578.

The Joyfull Returne, of the Most Illustrious Prince Charles . . . from the Court of Spaine. London, 1623.

Kemp, Thomas. *The Black Book of Warwick*. Warwick, 1898.

King Charles His Entertainment, and Londons Loyaltie. London, 1641.

The King of Denmarkes Welcome. London, 1606.

La Joyeuse & Magnifique Entree de Monseigneur Francoys. Antwerp, 1582.

A Letter: Whearin, part of the entertainment untoo the Queens Majesty, at Killingwoorth Castl, . . . is signifed. London, 1575.

Lithgow, William. *Scotlands Welcome to Her Native Sonne, and Soveraigne Lord, King Charles*. Edinburgh, 1633.

Lyly, John. *The Complete Works of John Lyly*, ed. R. Warwick Bond. Oxford: Clarendon Press, 1902.

The Diary of Henry Machyn, Citizen and Merchant-Taylor of London, ed. John Gough Nichols. London, 1848.

The Magnificent, Princely, and most Royall Entertainments given to the High and Mightie Prince . . . Frederick . . . and Elizabeth. London, 1613.

The Marriage of the two great Princes, Fredericke . . . and the Lady Elizabeth. London, 1613.

Middleton, Thomas. *The Works of Thomas Middleton*, ed. A. H. Bullen. Vol. VII. London, 1886.

Mill, Anna Jean. *Mediaeval Plays in Scotland*. Edinburgh and London: Blackwood, 1927.

Munday, Anthony. *Camp-bell or The Ironmongers Faire Field*. London, 1609.

——. *Chruso-thriambos, The Triumphes of Golde*. London, 1611.

——. *Chruso-thriambos*, ed. J. H. P. Pafford. London: privately printed, 1962.

——. *Chrysanaleia: The Golden Fishing*. London, 1616.

——. *Chrysanaleia*, ed. John Gough Nichols. London, 1844.

——. *Himatia-Poleos, The Triumphs of olde Draperie*. London, 1614.

——. *Londons Love, to the Royal Prince Henrie*. London, 1610.

——. *Metropolis Coronata, The Triumphes of Ancient Drapery*. London, 1615.

——. *Pageants and Entertainments of Anthony Munday: A Critical Edition*, ed. David M. Bergeron. New York: Garland, 1985.

——. *Sidero-thriambos or Steele and Iron Triumphing*. London, 1618.

——. *The Triumphs of Re-United Britannia*. London, 1605.

——. *The Triumphs of the Golden Fleece*. London, 1623.

Naile, Robert. *A Relation of the Royall . . . Entertainement, given to . . Queene Anne, at the renowned Citie of Bristoll*. London, 1613.

Nelson, Thomas. *The Device of the Pageant*. London, 1590.

Nichols, John Gough. *London Pageants: Accounts of Fifty-Five Royal Processions and Entertainments*. London, 1837.

Nichols, John. *The Progresses and Public Processions of Queen Elizabeth*. 3 vols., new edition. London, 1823.

——. *The Progresses, Processions, and Magnificent Festivities, of King James the First*. 4 vols. London, 1828.

The Order and Solemnitie of the Creation of the High and mightie Prince Henrie, Prince of Wales. London, 1610.

Ovatio Carolina, The Triumph of King Charles. London, 1641.

Overall, W. H. *Analytical Index to the Series of Records Known as the Remembrancia*. London, 1878.

The Passage of our most drad soveraigne lady Quene Elyzabeth through the citie of London to Westminster the daye before her coronacion. London, 1559.

Peacham, Henry. *Minerva Britanna or a Garden of Heroical Devises*. London, 1612.

Peele, George. *The Life and Minor Works of George Peele*, ed. David H. Horne. New Haven: Yale University Press, 1952.

Pena, Juan Antonio de la. *A Relation of the Royall Festivities . . . made by the King of Spaine at Madrid*. London, 1623.

Pollard, A. W. *The Queen's Majesty's Entertainment at Woodstock 1575*. Oxford: Clarendon, 1910.

Quarles, Francis. *Emblemes*. London, 1635.

Queen Elizabeth's Entertainment at Mitcham, ed. Leslie Hotson. New Haven: Yale University Press, 1953.

The Queenes Majesties Entertainement at Woodstock. London, 1585.

The Quenes Majesties Passage through the Citie of London to Westminster the Day before her Coronacion, ed. James M. Osborn. New Haven: Yale University Press, 1960.

Robarts, Henry. *The Most royall and Honourable entertainement of the famous and renowned King, Christiern the fourth.* London, 1606.

The Royall Passage of her Majesty from the Tower of London, to her Palace of Whitehall. London, 1604.

Sawyer, Edmund, ed. *Memorials of Affairs of State in the Reigns of Queen Elizabeth and King James I.* 3 vols. London, 1725.

de la Serre. *Histoire de l'Entree de la Reyne mere du Roy tres-chrestien dans la Grande Bretagne.* London, 1639.

Shakespeare, William. *The Complete Works of Shakespeare,* gen. ed., Alfred Harbage. New York: Penguin, 1969.

Somers, Lord. *A Collection of Scarce and Valuable Tracts, etc.,* 13 vols., 2nd ed. London, 1809-15.

The Speeches and Honorable Entertainment given to the Queenes Majestie in Progresse, at Cowdrey in Sussex. London, 1591.

Speeches Delivered to Her Majestie this Last Progresse, at the Right Honorable the Lady Russels, at Bissam, the Right Honorable the Lorde Chandos at Sudley, at the Right Honorable the Lord Norris, at Ricorte. Oxford, 1592.

Squire, John. *Tryumphs of Peace.* London, 1620.

Stow, John. *The Annales, or Generall Chronicle of England.* London, 1615.

Taylor, John. *Englands Comfort, and Londons Joy.* London, 1641.

————. *Heavens Blessing and Earths Joy.* London, 1613.

————. *The Triumphs of Fame and Honour.* London, 1634.

A True Discourse of all the Royal Passages, Tryumphs and Ceremonies, . . . at the Mariage of the High and Mighty Charles . . . and Lady Henrietta Maria. London, 1625.

A True Reportarie of the Most Triumphant, and Royal Accomplishment of the Baptisme of . . . Frederick Henry. Edinburgh, 1594.

Vivian, Percival, ed. *Campion's Works.* Oxford: Clarendon, 1909.

Walker, Sir Patrick. *Documents Relative to the Reception at Edinburgh of the Kings and Queens of Scotland 1561-1650.* Edinburgh, 1822.

Webster, John. *The Complete Works of John Webster,* ed. F. L. Lucas. London: Chatto and Windus, 1927.

Weldon, Anthony. *The Court and Character of King James Whereunto is now added the Court of King Charles.* London, 1651.

Whitney, Geoffrey. *A Choice of Emblemes.* Leyden, 1586.

Wilson, Arthur. *The History of Great Britain, being the Life and Reign of King James the First.* London, 1653.

Wither, George. *A Collection of Emblemes.* London, 1635.

PRINTED BOOKS AND ARTICLES: SECONDARY SOURCES

Anglo, Sydney. "The Court Festivals of Henry VII: A Study Based upon the Account Books of John Heron, Treasurer of the Chamber." *Bulletin of the John Rylands Library* 43 (1960): 12-45.

———. "The London Pageants for the Reception of Katherine of Aragon: November 1501." *Journal of the Warburg and Courtauld Institutes* 26 (1963): 53-89.

———. *Spectacle, Pageantry, and Early Tudor Policy*. Oxford: Clarendon Press, 1969.

Bald, R. C. "Middleton's Civic Employments." *Modern Philology* 31 (1933): 65-78.

Bennett, Josephine Waters. "Churchyard's Description of the Queen's Entertainment at Woodstock in 1592." *Modern Language Notes* 55 (1940): 391-3.

Bergeron, David M. "Actors in English Civic Pageants." *Renaissance Papers 1972* (1973): 17-28.

———. "Anthony Munday: Pageant Poet to the City of London." *Huntington Library Quarterly* 30 (1967): 345-68.

———. "Anthony Munday's Son, Richard." *American Notes & Queries* 7 (1969): 115-17.

———. "Charles I's Royal Entries into London." *The Guildhall Miscellany* 3, no. 2 (1970): 91-7.

———. "Charles I's Edinburgh Pageant (1633)." *Renaissance Studies* 6 (1992): 173-84.

———. "The Christmas Family: Artificers in English Civic Pageantry." *ELH* 35 (1968): 35-64.

———. "Civic Pageants and Historial Drama." *Journal of Medieval and Renaissance Studies* 5 (1975): 89-105.

———. "The Elizabethan Lord Mayor's Show." *Studies in English Literature* 10 (1970): 269-285.

———. "Elizabeth's Coronation Entry (1559): New Manuscript Evidence." *English Literary Renaissance* 8 (1978): 3-8.

———. "The Emblematic Nature of English Civic Pageantry." *Renaissance Drama* NS 1 (1968): 167-98.

———. "Gilbert Dugdale and the Royal Entry of James I (1604)." *Journal of Medieval and Renaissance Studies* 13 (1983): 111-25.

———. "Harrison, Jonson and Dekker: The Magnificent Entertainment for King James (1604)." *Journal of the Warburg and Courtauld Institutes* 31 (1968): 445-8.

———. "Jack Straw in Drama and Pageant." *The Guildhall Miscellany* 2, no. 10 (1968): 459-63.

———. "King James's Civic Pageant and Parliamentary Speech in March 1604." *Albion* 34 (2002): 213-31.

———. "Medieval Drama and Tudor-Stuart Civic Pageantry." *Journal of Medieval and Renaissance Studies* 2 (1972): 279-93.

———. "Middleton's Moral Landscape: *A Chaste Maid in Cheapside* and *The Triumphs of Truth*." In `Accompaninge the players': Essays Celebrating Thomas Middleton, 1580-1980,* ed. Kenneth Friedenreich. New York: AMS Press, 1981. 133-46.

———. "Middleton's *No Wit, No Help* and Civic Pageantry." In *Pageantry in the Shakespearean Theater.* Athens: University of Georgia Press, 1985. 65-80.

———, ed. *Pageantry in the Shakespearean Theater.* Athens: University of Georgia Press, 1985.

———. "Pageants, Patrons, and Politics." *Medieval & Renaissance Drama in England* 6 (1993): 139-52.

———. "Pageants, Masques, and Scholarly Ideology." In *Practicing Renaissance Scholarship.* 164-92.

———. *Practicing Renaissance Scholarship: Plays and Pageants, Patrons and Politics.* Pittsburgh: Duquesne University Press, 2000.

———. "Prince Henry and English Civic Pageantry." *Tennessee Studies in Literature* 13 (1968): 109-16.

———. "Representation in Renaissance English Civic Pageants." *Theatre Journal* 40 (1988): 319-31.

———. "Stuart Civic Pageants and Textual Performance." *Renaissance Quarterly* 51 (1998): 163-83.

———. "Symbolic Landscape in English Civic Pageantry." *Renaissance Quarterly* 22 (1969): 32-7.

———. "Thomas Dekker's Lord Mayor's Shows." *English Studies* 51 (1970): 2-15.

———. "Thomas Middleton and Anthony Munday: Artistic Rivalry?" *Studies in English Literature* 36 (1996): 461-79.

———. "Venetian State Papers and English Civic Pageantry, 1558-1642." *Renaissance Quarterly* 23 (1970): 37-47.

Black, J. B. *The Reign of Elizabeth 1558-1603.* Oxford: Clarendon, 1959.

Boas, F. S. *Thomas Heywood.* London: Williams and Norgate, 1950.

Bradbrook, M. C. *The Rise of the Common Player: A Study of Actor and Society in Shakespeare's England.* London: Chatto & Windus, 1962.

Brennecke, Ernest. "The Entertainment at Elvetham, 1591." In *Music in English Renaissance Drama,* ed. John H. Long. Lexington: University of Kentucky Press, 1968. 32-56.

Bronham, A. A. "Thomas Middleton's *The Triumphs of Truth*: City Politics in 1613." *The Seventeenth Century* 10 (1995): 1-25.

Campbell, Lily Bess. *Scenes and Machines on the English Stage During the Renaissance*. New York: Barnes & Noble, 1960.

Chambers E. K. *The Elizabethan Stage*, 4 vols. Oxford: Clarendon, 1923.

Clark, Arthur M. *Thomas Heywood: Playwright and Miscellanist*. Oxford: Basil Blackwell, 1931.

Clode, Charles M. *The Early History of the Guild of Merchant Taylors of the Fraternity of St. John the Baptist*, 2 vols. London, 1888.

———. *Memorials of the Guild of Merchant Taylors*, 2 vols. London, 1875.

Cokayne, G. E. *The Lord Mayors and Sheriffs of London: 1601-1625*. London, 1897.

DeMolen, Richard. "Richard Mulcaster and Elizabethan Pageantry." *Studies in English Literature* 14 (1974): 209-21.

Dunlop, Ian. *Palaces and Progresses of Elizabeth I*. London: Cape, 1962.

Dutton, Richard. *Jacobean Civic Pageants*. Staffordshire: Keele University Press, 1995.

Fairholt, Frederick W. *Lord Mayors' Pageants: Being Collections towards a History of These Annual Celebrations*. Percy Society, 2 vols. London, 1843-4.

Fletcher, Ifan K. *Splendid Occasions in English History 1520-1947*. London: Cassell, 1951.

Freeman, Rosemary. *English Emblem Books*. London: Chatto & Windus, 1948.

Geertz, Clifford. "Centers, Kings, and Charisma: Reflections on the Symbolics of Power." In *Local Knowledge: Further Essays in Interpretive Anthropology*. New York: Basic Books, 1983. 121-46.

Gilbert, Allan H. *The Symbolic Persons in the Masques of Ben Jonson*. Durham: Duke University Press, 1948.

Girtin, Thomas. *The Golden Ram: A Narrative History of the Clothworkers' Company, 1528-1958*. London: n.p., 1958.

Gordon, D. J. "Poet and Architect: The Intellectual Setting of the Quarrel between Ben Jonson and Inigo Jones." *Journal of the Warburg and Courtauld Institutes* 12 (1949): 152-78.

———. "'Veritas Filia Temporis': Hadrianus Junius and Geoffrey Whitney." *Journal of the Warburg and Courtauld Institutes* 3 (1939-40): 228-40.

Grego, Joseph. "The Artistic Aspect of Lord Mayors' Shows." *The Magazine of Art* (London, 1890): 8-15.

Griffin, Alice Venezky. *Pageantry on the Shakespearean Stage*. New York: Twayne, 1951.

Grivelet, Michel. *Thomas Heywood et le Drame Domestique Élizabéthain*. Paris: Didier, 1957.

Gurr, Andrew. *The Shakespearean Stage: 1574-1642*. 3rd ed. Cambridge: Cambridge University Press, 1992.

Gutch, J. M. *Royal Progresses: Queen Elizabeth's Visit to Worcester, in 1575*. Worcester, 1848.

Heath, J. B. *Some Account of the Worshipful Company of Grocers of the City of London*. London, 1869.

Heckscher, William S. "Renaissance Emblems: Observations Suggested by Some Emblem-Books in the Princeton University Library." *Princeton University Library Chronicle* 15 (1953): 55-68.

Heninger, S. K. "The Tudor Myth of Troy-novant." *South Atlantic Quarterly* 61 (1962): 378-87.

Herbert, William. *The History of the Twelve Great Livery Companies of London*. 2 vols. London, 1837.

Hintz, Howard. "The Elizabethan Entertainment and *The Faerie Queene*." *Philological Quarterly* 14 (1935): 83-90.

Johnson, A. H. *The History of the Worshipful Company of the Drapers of London*. 5 vols. Oxford: Clarendon, 1914-22.

Kahl, William F. *The Development of London Livery Companies*. Boston: Baker Library, 1960.

Kelly, William. *Royal Progresses and Visits to Leicester*. Leicester, 1884.

Kernodle, George R. *From Art to Theatre: Form and Convention in the Renaissance*. Chicago: University of Chicago Press, 1944.

———. "Renaissance Artists in the Service of the People: Political Tableaux and Street Theaters in France, Flanders, and England." *The Art Bulletin* 25 (1943): 59-64.

Kimbrough, Robert, and Philip Murphy. "The Helmingham Hall Manuscript of Sidney's *The Lady of May*: A Commentary and Transcription." *Renaissance Drama* NS 1 (1968): 103-19.

Kipling, Gordon. *Enter the King: Theatre, Liturgy, and Ritual in the Medieval Civic Triumph*. Oxford: Clarendon Press, 1998.

———. *The Triumph of Honour: Burgundian Origins of the Elizabethan Renaissance*. Leiden: Sir Thomas Browne Institute, 1977.

Lambert, John J. *Records of the Skinners of London*. London: Allen & Unwin, 1933.

Leech, Clifford. "Sir Henry Lee's Entertainment of Elizabeth in 1592." *Modern Language Review* 30 (1935): 52-5.

Leinwand, Theodore. "London Triumphing: The Jacobean Lord Mayor's Show." *Clio* 11 (1982): 137-53.

Les Fêtes de la Renaissance, ed. Jean Jacquot. 3 vols. Paris: Editions du Centre national de la recherche scientifique, 1956-1975.

Lobanov-Rostovsky, Sergei. "*The Triumphes of Golde*: Economic Authority in the Jacobean Lord Mayor's Show." *ELH* 60 (1993): 879-98.

McGee, C. E., and John C. Meagher. "Preliminary Checklist of Tudor and Stuart Entertainments." *Research Opportunities in Renaissance Drama* 24-38 (1981-99).

Morse, H. K. *Elizabethan Pageantry*. London: Studio Publications, 1934.

Neale, J. E. *Queen Elizabeth I.* London: Jonathan Cape, 1954.

A New History of Early English Drama, ed. David Scott Kastan and John Cox. New York: Columbia University Press, 1997.

Nicoll, Allardyce. *The Development of the Theatre.* New York: Harcourt, Brace, 1927.

Nicholl, John. *Some Account of the Worshipful Company of Ironmongers.* London, 1851.

Ong, Walter J. "From Allegory to Diagram in the Renaissance Mind: A Study in the Significance of the Allegorical Tableau." *Journal of Aesthetics and Art Criticism* 17 (1959): 423-40.

Palmer, Daryl W. *Hospitable Performances: Dramatic Genre and Cultural Practices in Early Modern England.* West Lafayette: Purdue University Press, 1992.

Panofsky, Erwin. *Studies in Iconology.* New York: Oxford University Press, 1939.

Parry, Graham. *The Golden Age Restor'd: The Culture of the Stuart Court, 1603-42.* Manchester: Manchester University Press, 1981.

Parsloe, Guy. *Wardens' Accounts of the Worshipful Company of Founders of the City of London 1497-1681.* London: University of London/ Athlone Press, 1964.

Paster, Gail Kern. "The Idea of London in Masque and Pageant." In *Pageantry in the Shakespearean Theater.* 48-64.

Praz, Mario. *Studies in Seventeenth-Century Imagery,* 2nd edition. Rome: Edizioni di Storia e Letteratura, 1964.

Price, John E. *A Descriptive Account of the Guildhall of the City of London: Its History and Associations.* London, 1886.

Prideaux, Walter S. *Memorials of the Goldsmiths' Company.* 2 vols. London, 1896.

Renaissance Drama: Essays Principally on Masques and Entertainments NS 1 (1968).

Robertson, Jean. "Rapports du Poète et de l'Artiste dans la Préparation des Cortèges du Lord Maire (Londres 1553-1640)." In *Fêtes de la Renaissance.* I, 265-77.

Sayle, R. T. D. *Lord Mayors' Pageants of the Merchant Taylors' Company in the 15th, 16th and 17th Centuries.* London: privately printed, 1931.

Sharp, Thomas. *A Dissertation on the Pageants or Dramatic Mysteries Anciently Performed at Coventry.* Coventry, 1825.

Smith, Bruce R. "Pageants into Play: Shakespeare's Three Perspectives on Idea and Image." In *Pageantry in the Shakespearean Theater.* 220-46.

Smith, Hal H. "Some Principles of Elizabethan Stage Costume." *Journal of the Warburg and Courtauld Institutes* 25 (1962): 240-57.

Strong, Roy C., and J. A. Van Dorsten. *Leicester's Triumph.* London: Sir Thomas Browne Institute, 1964.

Strong, Roy C. *Art and Power: Renaissance Festivals 1450-1650.* Berkeley: University of California Press, 1984.

———. "The Popular Celebration of the Accession Day of Queen Elizabeth I." *Journal of the Warburg and Courtauld Institutes* 21 (1958): 86-103.

Tumbleson, Raymond D. "The Triumph of London: Lord Mayor's Day Pageants and the Rise of the City." In *The Witness of Times*, ed. Katherine Z. Keller and Gerald J. Schiffhorst. Pittsburgh: Duquesne University Press, 1993. 53-68.

Unwin, George. *The Gilds and Companies of London*, 4th edition. London: Frank Cass, 1963.

Wadmore, James F. *Some Account of the Worshipful Company of Skinners.* London: Blades, East, and Blades, 1902.

Watney, John. *An Account of the Mistery of Mercers of the City of London.* London: Blades, East, and Blades, 1914.

Welsford, Enid. *The Court Masque: A Study in the Relationship between Poetry and the Revels.* Cambridge: Cambridge University Press, 1927.

Wickham, Glynne. "Contribution de Ben Jonson et de Dekker aux Fêtes du Couronnement de Jacques Ier." In *Fêtes de la Renaissance.* I, 279-83.

———. *Early English Stages 1300 to 1660.* 3 vols. London: Routledge Kegan Paul; New York: Columbia University Press, 1959-81.

Williams, Sheila. "Les Ommegangs d'Anvers et les Cortèges du Lord-Maire de Londres." In *Fêtes de la Renaissance.* II, 349-57.

———. "A Lord Mayor's Show by John Taylor, the Water Poet." *Bulletin of the John Rylands Library* 41 (1959): 501-31.

———. "The Lord Mayors' Shows from Peele to Settle: A Study of Literary Content, Organization, and Methods of Production." Ph.D. thesis, University of London, 1957.

———. "The Lord Mayor's Show in Tudor and Stuart Times." *The Guildhall Miscellany* 1, no. 10 (1959): 3-18.

———. "Two Seventeenth Century Semi-Dramatic Allegories of Truth the Daughter of Time." *The Guildhall Miscellany* 2, no. 5 (1963): 207-20.

Wilson, Jean. *Entertainments for Elizabeth I.* Totowa, NJ: Rowman and Littlefield, 1980.

Wind, Edgar. *Pagan Mysteries in the Renaissance.* London: Barnes & Noble, 1968.

Withington, Robert. *English Pageantry: An Historical Outline.* 2 vols. Cambridge: Harvard University Press, 1918-20.

———. "The Lord Mayor's Show for 1590." *Modern Language Notes* 33 (1918): 8-13.

———. "The Lord Mayor's Show for 1623." *PMLA* 30 (1915): 110-15.

Wright, Celeste Turner. *Anthony Mundy: An Elizabethan Man of Letters.* Berkeley: University of California Publications in English, 1928.

Yates, Frances A. "Elizabethan Chivalry: The Romance of the Accession Day Tilts." *Journal of the Warburg and Courtauld Institutes* 22 (1957): 4-25.

Yoch, James J. "Subjecting the Landscape in Pageants and Shakespearean Pastorals." In *Pageantry in the Shakespearean Theater.* 194-219.

Young, Alan. *Tudor and Jacobean Tournaments.* London: George Philip, 1987.

Index

MRTS

MEDIEVAL AND RENAISSANCE TEXTS AND STUDIES
is the major publishing program of the
Arizona Center for Medieval and Renaissance Studies
at Arizona State University, Tempe, Arizona.

MRTS emphasizes books that are needed —
editions, translations, and major research tools —
but also welcomes monographs and
collections of essays on focused themes.

MRTS aims to publish the highest quality scholarship
in attractive and durable format at modest cost.